JUSTICE DENIED

The Law versus Donald Marshall

MICHAEL HARRIS

D1545499

A TOTEM BOOK
Toronto

First published 1986
by Macmillan of Canada
This edition published 1987
by TOTEM BOOKS
a division of Collins Publishers
100 Lesmill Road, Don Mills, Ontario

© 1986 by Michael Harris

All inquiries regarding the motion picture or other dramatic rights for
this book should be addressed to the author's representative, The
Colbert Agency, 303 Davenport Road, Toronto, Ontario M5R 1K5.
Representations as to the disposition of these rights are expressly
prohibited without the express written authorization of the author's
representative and will be vigorously pursued to the full extent of
the law.

Canadian Cataloguing in Publication Data
Harris, Michael, 1948-
   Justice denied: the law versus Donald Marshall

Includes index.
ISBN 0-00-217890-7

1. Marshall, Donald, 1953-   . 2. Murder – Nova Scotia
– Sydney. 3. Trials (Murder) – Nova Scotia –
Sydney. 4. Judicial error – Canada.
I. Title.

HV6535.C32N64 1987   364.1'523'0924   C87-093951-3

Design: William Fox/Associates

Printed and bound in Canada

Contents

To Junior, *a brave man dogged by old ghosts,
with every wish for deliverance.*

PRISONER B:	The longest you could do would be twenty years. More than likely you'll get half of that. Last man to finish up in the Bog, he done eleven.
LIFER:	Eleven. How do you live through it?
PRISONER B:	A minute at a time.

From *The Quare Fellow*
by Brendan Behan

On March 29, 1982, Donald Marshall, Jr., was released from Dorchester Penitentiary after serving eleven years in prison for a murder he did not commit. His case was reopened in 1982 when he learned the identity of the real killer of his boyhood companion, Sandy Seale, and passed the information along to the authorities. Imprisoned at seventeen, Marshall steadfastly professed his innocence throughout his lengthy incarceration and on May 10, 1983, he was formally acquitted of the crime by the Nova Scotia Supreme Court. This is his story.

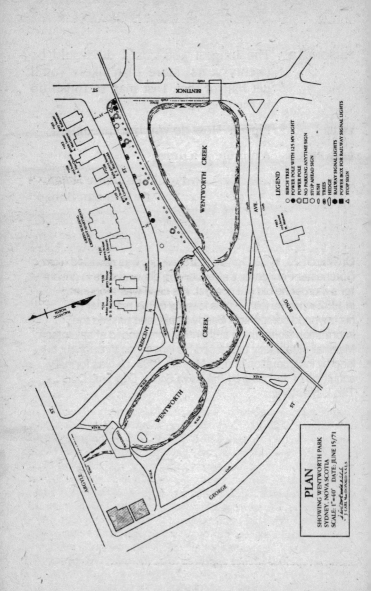

PLAN

SHOWING WENTWORTH PARK
SYDNEY, NOVA SCOTIA
SCALE: 1" = 40'   DATE: JUNE 15/71

J. CARL MacDONALD N.S.L.S.

LEGEND

○ BIRCH TREE
● POWER POLE WITH 125 MV LIGHT
◐ POWER POLE
▢ NO PARKING ANYTIME SIGN
◑ STOP AHEAD SIGN
◒ BUSH
◯ TREES
⌒ HEDGE
■ RAILWAY SIGNAL LIGHTS
■ POWER BOX FOR RAILWAY SIGNAL LIGHTS
△ STOP SIGN

WENTWORTH CREEK

CREEK

WENTWORTH

BENTINCK ST.

AVE.

WALK

MEMORIAL

MAGNETIC NORTH

ARGYLE ST.

GEORGE ST.

CRESCENT

Preface

I met Donald Marshall, Jr., for the first time in the spring of 1982. At the time, he was still the phantom figure at the heart of a tragic story of crime and punishment, and I used to meet his lawyer, Stephen Aronson, in a downtown Halifax restaurant to discuss his client's remarkable case over early-morning coffee. Unknown to me, the 28-year-old Micmac Indian was watching from another table, "sizing me up" as he would later call it. When he finally joined us one day, I was not prepared for the person I met: a soft-spoken young man who talked about his Kafkaesque ordeal in wispy generalities, as though it were the unfortunate experience of some distant acquaintance. It was inconceivable to me that he was just eight weeks out of Dorchester Penitentiary after having served a life sentence for a crime it would soon be established he had not committed.

At that time, I knew that Marshall and his lawyer had refused all interviews because Canada's justice minister of the day, Jean Chrétien, had yet to decide how to deal with the unprecedented case. Their reluctance to talk was understandable. If Ottawa chose not to pardon the parolee and the case became the subject of an appeal, anything Marshall might say would be evidence before that court. He would also be a crucial witness if new charges were laid in the bizarre, eleven-year-old murder case. Since the outcome of any of these potential court actions (all of which eventually proceeded) would have a profound impact on the compensation Marshall might be awarded for eleven years of wrongful imprisonment, scrupulous silence appeared to be in his best interests.

These legal reservations notwithstanding, I made a single point that morning which turned out to be true. Given the sensational nature of Marshall's dilemma, I argued that even if he remained incommunicado, his story would still be told, if not from his perspective, then from somebody else's. I said that if he ever decided to tell his story, I would record it to the best of my ability – a promise that would take the next three years to keep.

At the time, both Marshall and Aronson turned down my request for an interview, promising to reconsider if circumstances changed. A few weeks later they did. After reading several accounts of his story out of the mouths of others, including one of the witnesses at his original trial, whose perjured evidence had helped send the young Micmac to prison, Donald Marshall, Jr., agreed to his first public interview. It appeared in the *Globe and Mail* on Saturday, June 12, 1982, two and a half months after his release from prison on day parole. Four days later, Jean Chrétien sent his case to the Appeal Division of the Nova Scotia Supreme Court and one of Canada's most controversial criminal cases began a run on the front pages of the country's newspapers that would last for more than two years. It was the Wilbert Coffin case without the hanging, and Canadians were passionately interested in finding out how such a living nightmare could ever have happened.

It took the Nova Scotia Supreme Court almost a year from Jean Chrétien's call for a new hearing to acquit Donald Marshall, Jr., of murder. During that period, his story was closely followed by a number of talented journalists, including Alan Story and Martin Cohn of the *Toronto Star*, Kay Fulton of Southam News, Michael Clugston of *Maclean's*, Michael Vaughan of the CBC, and, not least of all, Roy Gould of the *Micmac News*. Though the court's decision was expected, all of us were shocked when the five Supreme Court justices went beyond their decision to acquit Marshall and blamed him for the course that justice had taken in 1971.

With that surprising and, as far as I was concerned, cruelly inadequate ruling, I waited for Premier John Buchanan to accede to Stephen Aronson's request and announce a full public inquiry into the Marshall affair. I assumed that any government would respect the public's right to know how an innocent man could be given a life sentence for a crime he did not commit.

I was wrong. With the government's inaction, the journalistic agenda was clear. If Canadians were ever to understand what happened to Donald Marshall, Jr., his story would have to be exhaustively re-created, from his life in Sydney, Nova Scotia, prior to the Sandy Seale murder in 1971, to his compensation award in the late summer of 1984, more than a year after his innocence had been established. Rather than trying to assign blame for what happened, I have tried to document the role that each participant played in this tangled affair, while supplying, I hope, some of the human resonance to a story that deeply affected many people's lives over a very long period of time.

The book that grew out of that approach is based on a combination of personal interviews and official documents, including court transcripts, police reports, prison records, and a variety of correspondence. All quotations and excerpts are taken directly either from taped interviews or from documents, and the book contains no author-reconstructed conversations. In particular, all conversations between members of the Sydney police and those they interviewed during their 1971 investigation of the Sandy Seale murder are verbatim records of those question-and-answer sessions, as are the accounts of the sessions held by the Royal Canadian Mounted Police during their reinvestigation of the crime in 1982.

Obviously, the hundreds of hours I spent with Donald Marshall, Jr., were central to the book, particularly when it came to illuminating those eleven years when he was buried alive in two federal prisons. These interviews, painful as they were for their subject, were guided by a simple principle: regardless of how brutal or unflattering the recollection, inmate 1997 related everything he could honestly remember about his odyssey of innocence. Close cross-checking of Marshall's version of prison life with the official records of those years reinforced an observation made during our interview sessions: the man who described himself as "just a toad in God's pocket" did not cast self-serving lights and shadows over the past, but spoke as freely about his faults as about his sufferings. This frankness was a great boon to a writer who believed that Marshall's story required a chronicler, not a champion.

If justice, as Benjamin Disraeli observed, is "truth in action", then Donald Marshall, Jr., got something very different in 1971 when he was falsely convicted of murder, and again in 1983 when he was blamed for that calamity. Just what that was will be for readers to decide as they follow the fateful path the teenaged Indian set his foot to so many years ago and which to this day still winds darkly ahead of him.

Michael Harris
Windsor, Nova Scotia
June 1985

ACKNOWLEDGMENTS

It is impossible to name all of the people who contributed to this book, but it would be graceless not to cite those who were especially helpful.

I would therefore like to thank Caroline and Donald Marshall, Sr., Oscar and Leotha Seale, Stephen Aronson, Felix Cacchione, Harry Wheaton, Jim Carroll, Maynard Chant, John Pratico, Ian MacNeil, Jack Stewart, Charlie Gould, Tom and Kevin Christmas, and, of course, Donald Marshall, Jr. All of them gave freely of their time and recollections to help unearth a long-buried story and to explain contemporary events that were at times equally impenetrable.

Thanks are also due to the Managing Editor of the *Globe and Mail*, Geoffrey Stevens, who generously allowed me time to work on the book and offered kind encouragement along the way. I would also like to thank Greg Stamp for his unstinting support of this project, and Anne Holloway of Macmillan, whose editorial work on *Justice Denied* added to whatever pleasure the reader may find in these pages.

I must add a special tribute to Leo Mroz, the Sydney police officer whose untimely death prevented me from publicly thanking him for the help he so kindly gave me with my research.

To those others whose names do not appear here, but who know how much I counted on their support while writing this book, my thanks and more.

1 / Escape

Moving as lazily as the flies that droned above the lemon meringue pie, the waitress pushed three Dixie cups across the counter and called to the dark-haired young man who was looking intently out the window of the roadside canteen. "You did say to go?"

Glancing over his shoulder, he crossed the room with cat-like suppleness. A smile flickered in his flat brown eyes as he handed her a two-dollar bill. "Yeah, to go."

As she made change, the waitress mistook that smile, slyly shared with his two companions, for a sign that the young man was somehow mocking her. She couldn't be blamed for missing their private joke. Had she known that all three were inmates of a federal penitentiary, that the man who'd just treated his friends to coffee was a convicted murderer about to escape, she might have appreciated the irony of his soft reply.

For the past five minutes, Donald Marshall, "Junior" to those who knew him, had been watching the man who was charged with returning him and his companions to the federal penitentiary at Springhill, Nova Scotia. A few minutes earlier, as their blue station wagon pulled off the Trans-Canada Highway at Alma, the guard had told them of the change in plans.

"Okay, I'm just gonna fill up the tank and then we'll make a straight run for the Hill. You guys get a coffee, wash up if you want to."

Now, watching the guard speaking to the gas station attendant, Junior knew he would have to make an unscheduled break for freedom. On their way back from a wilderness-survival course, the group had originally intended to stop in Truro, an itinerary that was critical to the young Micmac's plan of escape. Waiting there was a friend from the Shubenacadie Reserve who'd promised to pick him up when the prison party stopped for the night at the Abenacki Motel. The two were going to drive to British Columbia, where Junior planned to get a job in a lumber camp. He knew that, to the whites, "one Pow-Wow was the same as another," and no one would take particular notice of him. But if he made it to B.C. now, he thought discouragedly, it would be in a boxcar, not his friend's black Camaro. Riding the rails was hard on the hands and it was a good thing he'd taken those gloves from the prison welding shop after all.

Though he'd been mulling over his escape for months, he felt curiously numb now that the moment was at hand. Eight years in prison had made the prospect of sudden freedom terrifying. Sensing Junior's reluctance, his companions urged him to make a run for it.

"Look, man, they'll never let you out. You might as well go for it while you got the chance," urged Adrian P——, a fellow Micmac who had grown up with Junior on Membertou Reserve on Cape Breton Island.

For more than a year the two Indians had relieved the boredom of doing "long bits" by talking about breaking out of Springhill. Adrian P—— had already given his friend the address of a safe house in the United States. "You go to Boston, man, my sister and brother are down there. You'll be all right, they'll hide you."

With his rucksack over his shoulder, Junior Marshall abruptly left the canteen, halting in front of the door in a pretence of nonchalance. Squinting into the blinding afternoon sunlight, he saw that his keeper was still talking to the gas station attendant. His heart pounded: this was it.

Back inside, Adrian P—— and Brian S—— had moved quietly to the canteen window. The waitress, who was wiping down the counter, saw the two young men give a brief salute to the tall figure standing just outside the door. On the table behind them, steam rose from Junior's untouched coffee.

Junior sauntered behind the trailer towards the washroom, then struck out for the woods on the dead run. After a hundred yards he was breathing heavily and his legs felt like rubber. It was as if all those years of running the track behind the walls at Dorchester and Springhill, those thousands of miles of jogging that had left the 26-year-old with the physique of a professional athlete, had never taken place.

Exhausted and momentarily light-headed, he considered returning to the station wagon, where his two friends were awaiting the return of the guard. "To hell with it," he thought, slogging through a bog that sucked loudly at his sneakers with every stride. He had something to prove and it was a cinch he could never do it from behind bars, or so he thought. Besides, what did he have to lose?

Half a mile from the canteen, his mouth was sour and his lungs burned. Stopping to rest, he saw blood running down his bare legs, which were badly scratched from bulling his way through the underbrush. He changed into his long bluejeans and threw the cut-offs he'd been wearing into the bush. He would force his way through another half-mile of thicket before realizing that, along with the shorts, he had thrown away his address book, maps, and money. But there was no going back. He'd almost certainly been missed by now and a search party was probably already on his trail. That thought dispelled his momentary light-headedness. He began to think like a man with just one problem: how to keep ahead of the people who wanted to put him back in prison.

Back at the canteen, the guard was sitting behind the wheel of the gassed-up station wagon wondering why one of his charges was taking so long to clean up. As agreed before Junior had escaped, Adrian told the keeper that his friend had gone to the washroom to shave. Finally losing his patience, the guard got out of the car and banged on the washroom door. It opened obligingly to bluebottles buzzing in the pine-scented shadows.

"You fucking bastards," he shouted at the station wagon as he ran to a telephone.

"We got nuttin' to do with it. You're s'pose to be watching over us," Adrian yelled back.

The guard alerted prison officials and the Royal Canadian Mounted Police. Within minutes a news story hit the wires. Factually inaccurate, it advised that Donald Marshall, Jr., had escaped custody by overpowering his guards. Caution was advised: the escaped murderer was considered dangerous.

As police organized the search, Junior was gingerly emerging from the woods behind a white frame house. Satisfying himself there was no one around, he started for the highway, only to be stopped in his tracks by two large dogs. The animals terrified him. As a boy, he'd often been attacked by dogs when he sold Micmac baskets door to door in Sydney, the seaport steel town where he'd been raised. One day while he was walking to St. Rita Hospital to meet his mother after she finished work, some boys playing road hockey had unleashed a German shepherd on him. Even though he had beaten off the dog with a hockey stick hastily grabbed from one of his tormentors, the memory of its ferocious rage had stayed with him.

Luckily, one of the dogs was tied, but the other one, a black Labrador, bared its teeth and bounded towards him. The convict backed into the woods, wondering how he would defend himself if the dog followed. But after snarling into the underbrush where the intruder had retreated, the dog broke off its pursuit and trotted back to the house.

Junior slipped along behind the forest wall, putting two hundred yards between himself and the dogs before venturing into the open again. At Dorchester, where he'd begun his life sentence for murder eight years earlier, he remembered hearing inmates say that tracking dogs had trouble picking up a scent from pavement. He criss-crossed the highway four times before striking off into the woods.

Two hours had passed since he'd left the canteen and he was beginning to feel more relaxed. It was late September and everything stood out sharply in the crisp air. The trees were beginning to put on color and the smell of damp leaves rose from the forest floor. Junior stopped at a brook and watched a dark shape dart away through the mottled light along the bank. It was good seeing a trout again. He bent down to scoop up some water in his cupped hands. As he leaned over, his chain and the metal wafer that hung from it fell forward. Its words from Isaiah were distorted in the trembling water along with his own dark face. He thought of its powerful inscription: No Weapon Formed Against You Shall Prosper. On the other side, he had scraped his prison number, 1997. If ever he needed a good-luck charm, he thought, it was now.

As Junior left the cover of the woods and struck out across an open field dotted with dwarf Christmas trees, he became vaguely aware of a distant motor droning on the afternoon air. When he finally looked up and saw the blue-and-white aircraft, his heart sank. The RCMP.

Junior knew he'd been spotted when the plane passed overhead, then banked sharply and started back towards him. He scuttled under a three-foot Christmas tree, wrapping himself in a ball around its delicate trunk. He knew that if he were to have a chance of reaching the highway somewhere on the other side of these woods, where he planned to hitch a ride out of Nova Scotia, he would have to wait until dark. It was just three o'clock.

The sun seemed snagged on the horizon. As he waited for nightfall, Junior thought about Sylvester Paul, the ex-convict who had been one of the two people to sponsor him for the survival course. It had been out of respect for Sylvester that he had completed the eleven-day course before making his escape. He could have gotten away on that first night out of Springhill when the group had stopped at a campground just outside Truro. That was where he had met the Indian from Shubenacadie who offered to help him escape. They had shared liquor and marijuana, and his new friend had volunteered to drive him out west then and there.

Junior had declined. If he had gone, the other native inmates on the course would have been sent back to Springhill and Sylvester Paul would have been discredited. Instead, the two men had agreed to meet at the Abenacki Motel on Junior's way back to Springhill. "I guess I still screwed up on Sylvester," he thought, "but at least I finished the course." He wondered what his friend would think when he saw the news that night.

By eight o'clock the skies of Pictou County glowed a deep violet and Junior scrambled out of his hiding-spot and continued across the field. The plane had circled around for hours before finally flying off. But now he had other things to worry about. On the last day of the course, while reconnoitring a river for the main party, he had slipped down a steep embankment and hurt his leg. In the surprisingly frosty air, it was beginning to bother him. And he was ravenously hungry.

The sound of barking suddenly broke the stillness of the gathering dusk. It was difficult to tell the direction the sound was coming from. Figuring that tracking dogs had been sent in after the plane had failed to flush him out, Junior took a bottle of Brut 33 from his rucksack and doused a nearby tree. Then he threw the rucksack stuffed with dirty clothes into the bush. "Better they go after my clothes instead of me," he thought as he broke into a run across the field.

By eleven o'clock it was pitch dark and Junior Marshall was hopelessly lost. In the moonless night, he had spent the last hour and a half stumbling through swamps, tripping over roots and rocks, and starting at every unseen creature that broke the deep silence of the woods. His light summer clothing was soaked and he couldn't stop shivering. Worst of all, his wrists had begun to ache. Ever since he'd broken both of them in prison, cold weather brought on crippling pain that shot through his wrists and fingers like a knife.

Against his will, he began to think of the meal and the warm bed that would be his back at Springhill. The thought became an obsession as he stumbled around in the dark until a grimmer notion displaced it. What if a nervous policeman shot him before he had a chance to surrender? There was no such thing as getting wounded with a twelve-gauge fired at close range, and he was, after all, a convicted murderer. He decided that if the RCMP spotted him, he would give up peacefully. Rubbing his aching hands together, he suddenly heard traffic off to his right. Miraculously, he had found the highway.

His adrenalin flowing once more, the escaped convict ran towards the sound of the passing cars. A hundred yards dead ahead of him, across the highway, stood the Michelin tire plant, its yard lights visible through the undulating branches of a birch stand. That put him in Granton, not far from the town of Pictou, where he knew some people from prison. It was also where his girlfriend, Shelly Sarson, lived. If he could only get to Pictou, he could find food and shelter and some badly needed money for the road.

Between him and the highway stood a swamp that also served as an unofficial dump. He was halfway across it, picking his way through rusting appliances and rotting bags of garbage when he saw a dark shape loom up not ten feet in front of him. Backing up slowly, the young Micmac cast around for something to throw, coming up with a hardball-sized stone that he hefted in his left hand. Whatever animal it was, he could hear it fanning the air, trying to identify the intruder. Concluding he had surprised a wild dog digging in the dump, the star pitcher of the prison baseball team let the stone fly, hoping to scare it off. The creature bawled out in pain. A larger shape then ambled out of the bush, swaying menacingly. "Jesus Christ," he thought, "bears!"

Summoning all the strength from his six-foot-one-inch, 180-pound frame, he burst through the last fifty yards of the dump and dropped to his belly in a ditch just below the shoulder of the highway. He decided that if the bear attacked, he would run out on the highway, where he hoped the lights of the oncoming cars would frighten it away. His heart pounding, he listened with growing relief as the she-bear and her cub melted back into the woods.

Wriggling up the embankment, he surveyed the highway, ignoring the gravel that dug into his stomach through his soaked shirt. Plenty of cars were passing by and he considered trying to hitch a ride. But the headlights were too bright and he wouldn't be able to tell if a car was a police cruiser until it was too late. Still, he knew he couldn't just lie there on the shoulder of the highway waiting to be spotted.

A jeep passed, travelling more slowly than the rest of the traffic. A few moments later it returned, going the other way. Junior watched it travel down the road a few hundred yards, then pull off onto the shoulder. At right angles to the jeep, on a nearby side road, an RCMP cruiser was parked with its motor running, the plume of its exhaust rising on the frosty air. A half-mile away in the other direction, another patrol car was parked, waiting for the convict to come out of the woods.

"They got me down pretty pat," Junior thought, his heart sinking. Giving up once more crossed his mind.

But then, looking across at the Michelin plant, he had an idea. Judging from the number of cars that were coming into the parking lot, it looked as if the shifts were about to change. If he could mix in with the employees as they walked from the factory to the parking lot, he might just be able to hitch a ride to Pictou with a plant worker. There were no RCMP vehicles at the plant gate.

Waiting for a break in the traffic, Junior belly-crawled across the highway and waited for men to start leaving the plant before he scrambled out of the ditch and walked into the parking lot. The first car he stopped was occupied by an old man who asked him where he was going.

"Pictou," he replied, trying hard to sound matter-of-fact despite his bizarre appearance.

"I'm just going up the road a ways, but the fella behind me is going that way," the old man answered. He stuck his head out the window and shouted to the car behind him. The other driver, a younger man, motioned to Junior to get in. Covered with mud, his hair tangled with spruce twigs, Junior opened the car door and slid onto the seat. It still had the new-car smell, but if the driver objected to his unkempt rider, he wasn't saying so.

"What the hell happened to you?" he asked good-naturedly, offering Junior the makings.

A heavy smoker, the young man expertly rolled himself a cigarette, savoring the blast of warmth hitting his legs from the car's heater. Gratefully drawing in a lungful of smoke, he gave the only answer that occurred to him.

"I was on a course, a government course in wilderness survival. Didn't like it, so I packed my gear and decided to come home."

"You from Pictou?" the man asked, sliding the car out through the plant gate and swinging it onto the highway with a squeal of the tires.

"Yeah," Junior answered. He tried desperately to think of something to say to ward off having to answer the man's next question, fearing his reply might reveal that he had never been to Pictou in his life.

"I don't know many people from Pictou myself. I'm working all the time, so I don't get much chance to get out and around," the man added.

Junior breathed a sigh of relief until the driver tuned in a newscast reporting his escape. The man leaned forward and turned up the radio as the announcer said that the RCMP were combing the woods in the New Glasgow and Alma area for an escaped murderer. The voice warned motorists not to pick up any strangers. His nerves on fire, Junior drew heavily on his cigarette, hoping the driver wouldn't put two and two together but feeling in the pit of his stomach that he would. If that happened, he would simply jump out of the car and head back into the woods.

"Those yellow-striped bastards! They caught me enough times on this stretch of highway. I hope that fella gets away," the driver said.

"Me too," Junior answered quietly.

Just outside Pictou, the driver pulled into a service station and got out of the car to talk to the attendant. The two men kept looking over at the car and Junior was sure they had figured out who he was. He was just about to open the door and make a run for it when a county police cruiser rolled into the station. The officer glanced over at Junior, who glanced back. After its tank was filled, the cruiser slid away from the pumps and headed out onto the highway, its red tail-lights fading in the darkness.

Junior's driver walked back to the car and got in. "The brakes aren't just what they should be," he explained, slipping back into the driver's seat, "but Bob's got no time to fix 'em. That's what comes from being the best damn mechanic in the county." He turned the key and once again Junior Marshall was on his way to Pictou.

Trying to disguise the fact that he knew nothing about the town, he asked to get out in front of the Pictou post office. After he was dropped off, he thought of going to the local tavern, where a former inmate he'd known at Springhill worked the bar. But although Wayne McGrath would certainly have given him money and a place to stay, he decided it was too dangerous to walk into the tavern looking like he did. He had ducked into an alley to consider his next move when another inmate he'd known at Springhill passed by. Junior called his former acquaintance over and the man spoke to him in an excited whisper.

"Hey, man, every cop in the county is looking for you. So is your girlfriend."

"Shelly?" Junior asked.

"Yeah, it's all over the radio," the man said, looking over his shoulder.

"Go get her, bring her here," Junior told him.

In a few minutes the man returned with the small, dark-haired girl Junior had first met in prison three years before when she had been visiting her brother, John Sarson. Normally quiet, Shelly was furious with him.

"Are you crazy? Don't you know they might kill you? Turn

yourself in, now." Her voice had none of the softness he remembered from their talks in the visiting and correspondence room at Springhill. She was scared, scared to death.

"No way. Whether I go back now or when they catch me, I'll get the same punishment. Those fuckers never gave me a three-day pass in eight years, so I just took it on my own," he told her.

Unable to persuade him to surrender, Shelly Sarson took Junior back to her apartment, a third-storey walk-up in the heart of town. She phoned some friends and a few minutes later a young couple showed up with a case of beer. After a brief visit they left, and Shelly's younger sister arrived and offered Junior and Shelly the use of her bedroom.

Exhausted, Junior slept away the better part of the next day. He was still dozing when he heard the sound of heavy footsteps on the stairs. A gruff voice called out, "Where is he? We know he's in there."

Jumping out of bed, Junior cursed himself for not hitting the road sooner. Through the bedroom door he could make out a heavyset man standing in the hall in front of the open apartment door. "A goddam detective," he thought, just as the man caught sight of him.

"How you doin'?" he asked jovially.

Junior made no answer. Then a familiar face appeared over the shoulder of the stranger. It was Wayne McGrath holding up a bottle of wine. "Don't worry, this is my buddy, Earl Ray. How's it goin', Junior?"

As they sat at the kitchen table drinking wine, McGrath explained that he hadn't come earlier because the police were watching him. "You know the first place they looked was my house, eh? I told 'em 'I don't know where he's at, right, but if I find him, I'm gonna talk to him about going back.'"

There was an uncomfortable silence. "Look, man, I'm never goin' back, so just forget that shit," Junior told him. Two days of freedom wasn't much but it was enough to make the thought of returning to Springhill unbearable. "What I need is a place to lay low for a while."

Respecting his friend's wishes, McGrath promised to return the next night at nine o'clock to take Junior to a cabin he owned on a nearby island. "You can stay there and nobody'll ever find you if that's what you want," McGrath said. Junior readily agreed and the two men left.

As soon as the door closed behind them, Junior began looking for a place to hide in the event that his next visitors were less friendly. He settled on the refrigerator. With the food racks removed, maybe there would be just enough room for him to squeeze inside if the police raided the apartment. Even though he would only have enough air for fifteen minutes, he calculated that the police would quickly leave if they couldn't find him. And with Shelly doing her ironing in front of the fridge door, who would ever think to look inside? It was a desperate plan, but he had no other choice. "It'd be worth it just to see their faces, even if they do catch me," he playfully told her.

But his dark-haired hostess wasn't in the mood for jokes. She had fallen in love with the handsome young Micmac during her visits to Springhill, and the events of the last two days had done nothing to change that. Even though she believed he was innocent of the crime for which he had been sent to prison for life, she wanted Junior to go back and serve out his sentence while she waited for him on the outside. But if, as he now told her, he couldn't do any more time, she was prepared to join him on the run. But first, she would have to talk to her mother, who lived near by.

After she'd gone, Junior began to feel uneasy. He didn't like the idea of taking Shelly with him, a move that would only put her in danger as well as slow him down. He was beginning to get the feeling that he couldn't afford to stay in Pictou another night. He had a premonition that the police were closing in and decided not to wait for Wayne McGrath to take him to the cabin the next night.

After Shelly came back, he asked her to call Henry Morrison, another prison friend from Pictou. Henry had just bought a new Trans-Am and Junior was sure he would agree to drive him out west. When Morrison arrived, the two men discussed Junior's request over a bottle of rum and his friend agreed to help him get to the coast. They decided to hit the road later that night.

The two men were playing cribbage at the kitchen table when a horn beeped three times in the parking lot outside Shelly's apartment. Junior ran to the window and saw that it was Henry's girlfriend, who had gone out for cigarettes ten minutes before. He wondered what she was doing until he saw the two RCMP cruisers pull into the driveway, braking so hard that the cars rocked back and forth on their springs. Four officers jumped out and ran towards the building.

"It's the cops. Would your girlfriend rat on me, man?" he asked Morrison.

"No, no, no she wouldn't rat," the other man said as he headed for the door.

Morrison was telling the truth, but there was no time for Junior to worry about who had turned him in. He silently cursed himself for not having cleaned out the fridge. He thought about jumping out the back window, but it was a three-storey drop to the wooden verandah below. For the second time he heard heavy footfalls on the stairs. Wiping the sweat off his forehead, he ran into one of the bedrooms and braced himself inside the closet. Shelly joined him. He felt oddly calm. He had been offered a .38-calibre pistol since he'd arrived in Pictou and was glad now that he hadn't taken it. "If I had," he thought, "I'd use it, because there's no way I'm goin' back."

Shelly pleaded with him to give himself up. "They've got you now, Junior, you can't fight them any more."

Thinking of the agony of the last eight years, Junior Marshall shook his head and prepared to die. In the front room, Shelly's younger sister opened the door to the RCMP officers armed with pump-action shotguns.

"Anybody else in the house besides you?" one of them asked.

"Yeah, he's up there," the terrified thirteen-year-old blurted out. The police took a tighter grip on their guns and headed for the bedroom. Once there, one of the officers dropped to his knees five feet in front of the open closet, lowering the muzzle of his shotgun at the young man's chest.

"Donald Marshall, you are under arrest. Come out with your hands up."

"No fucking way," Junior answered, feeling Shelly trembling beside him.

"For your own good, come on out of there."

Junior could see that the man's hands were shaking as he tried to keep the 12-gauge levelled at the convict's chest. Still he refused to come out. The warning was repeated a third time. It was too much for Shelly Sarson. She walked out of the closet and began to cry. "Don't shoot him," she sobbed, "don't hurt him."

Junior's scalp prickled as the room fell silent. He had come to the razor's edge and clenched his fists tightly, just as he did in prison when trouble loomed. Then, in the crib behind the Mounties, a little girl stood up, rubbing her eyes and trying to figure out who all the strangers were. It was Shelly's niece, whom she'd been looking after. Junior had a sudden change of heart. "Why let her see them picking me off the walls?" he thought.

He walked out of the closet. It was as if someone had suddenly let the air out of a balloon that was about to burst. The Mounties lowered their guns. Junior noticed that the one who had been kneeling in front of him had dark circles of sweat on his shirt beneath both armpits. They handcuffed him and led him downstairs. From the windows of the other apartments, silent faces followed their progress to the cruisers below.

Shelly rode with Junior to the RCMP detachment in Pictou. There he asked her to phone his mother and let her know he was all right, unaware that it had been Caroline Marshall who had informed police as to his whereabouts.

The day after his escape, Junior had asked Shelly to call a friend's mother on Membertou with the message that he was all right, knowing the woman would pass word along to his mother. It was too dangerous to place the call directly, since there was a good chance the family phone would be tapped.

When Caroline Marshall got word of Shelly's call, she quickly figured out that her son must be staying in Pictou. Knowing that he was in grave danger as long as he was at large, she gave the RCMP Shelly's address and begged them not to hurt her boy. Now, with word that he was safe, she knew she had done the right thing.

The Mounties first took their prisoner to the New Glasgow county jail, where it was decided Junior would spend the night before returning to Springhill the next morning. This time Shelly wasn't allowed to ride with him. She looked very small waving to him from the sidewalk in front of the police station. Junior felt empty when she passed out of sight.

In a gesture of kindness, the county sheriff decided to take Junior back to prison that night. "I wouldn't keep a pig in here," he said. "At least in Springhill you'll have your bed and clean sheets. We'll take you up."

On the way, the sheriff asked the young man why he'd run.

Junior answered him calmly. "I never killed anybody. I'm innocent."

They arrived at the prison just after midnight. Before he handed Junior over, the old sheriff shook his hand and offered some advice. "If what you told me is true, kid, and I don't say it isn't, you just stick to your story."

"Don't worry," he answered, "I will."

The next day a small story appeared in the *Cape Breton Post*.

> ...police in the area were breathing easier after RCMP recaptured convicted murderer Donald Marshall Jr., 26, of Sydney, who escaped prison earlier this week. Marshall is serving a life term for the stabbing death of a young man in Wentworth Park several years ago. ...

2/Sydney

Hugging the banks of a broad river that runs down to the sea, Sydney, Nova Scotia, signals its presence from afar with pink clouds that rise from the stacks of its unseen steel mill into the vast Cape Breton sky.

The seaport city of thirty thousand is the old capital of Cape Breton, the rugged island on Canada's east coast that reminded early Scottish settlers so much of the Highlands from which they had emigrated. Sydney bills itself as the heart of "industrial" Cape Breton, more of a wistful invocation of the nineteenth-century dream of Boston tycoon Melville Whitney, who pioneered the city's steelworks, than a reflection of contemporary economic reality. Spewing red dust from the stacks of its steel mill and black dust from its coke ovens, the Sydney Steel Corporation dominates Sydney's economy, though not to the degree that its original predecessor, the Dominion Iron and Steel Company, once did.

The company's first general manager, Arthur Moxham, an American, was so bullish about the town's massive coal and lime deposits (and so anxious to impress prospective buyers of stock in the new enterprise) that he moved an authentic British castle from Lorain, Ohio, and reconstructed it, stone by stone, on Kings Road in Sydney. The three-storey architectural curiosity had fourteen fireplaces, and on a cold winter day a ton of coal was needed to heat its thirty-one rooms!

The castle's site had previously been part of "Rockaway", the estate of an English aristocrat who abandoned it after Indians allegedly murdered a clergyman there. Popularly believed to be cursed, the new headquarters for the manager of the Sydney steelworks soon lived up to its daunting reputation. Shortly after moving in, Moxham lost his son, who was killed by a locomotive in the yard of the Sydney steel plant. After standing for more than half a century, Moxham Castle was vandalized and destroyed by fire in 1966. The site of what was Sydney's most exotic landmark is now occupied by the utilitarian sprawl of a Holiday Inn.

In its heyday, between 1891 and 1921, Sydney increased its population tenfold to twenty-three thousand, affording a prosperous living to the wave of Scottish settlers who arrived in Cape Breton between 1802 and 1850, and became the island's undisputed establishment. Their magnificent houses, Victorian behemoths built when coal was king, still grace the tree-lined avenues of the city's older residential areas.

Nothing remains of the shanty town that was home to another of Sydney's main racial groups, Blacks from Alabama and the West Indies recruited at the turn of the century by managers at the Dominion Iron and Steel Company who believed they would be suited to work in the steel mill, accustomed as they were to sweltering climates. Their descendants, eight hundred strong, still live in Whitney Pier under the shadow of the steelworks. "The Pier", with its sooty but brightly painted frame houses standing shoulder to shoulder on streets that often end at the company fence, is one of Sydney's poorest but most distinctive neighborhoods.

For nearly seventy years, Sydney built its prosperity on coal and steel. At its peak, the steelworks employed six thousand workers, while another twelve thousand toiled in the coal mines. But by the middle of the century, the world began to change, for the worse as far as Sydney was concerned. In the early 1950s, coal accounted for fifty-two per cent of the energy market in Canada. By 1957 its share had declined to only twenty-five per cent. As coal mines closed, time also began running out on the city's badly outdated steelworks.

On "Black Friday", October 13, 1967, it finally ran out. Unable to compete with foreign steel producers and unwilling to reinvest in its now decrepit property, Hawker Siddeley announced plans to close the mill. With one job in four directly tied to the steelworks, and seventy per cent of all employment dependent on the steel company's twenty-million-dollar payroll, Sydney was suddenly confronted with a crisis of survival.

The Nova Scotia government came to the rescue, setting up a Crown corporation to run the outmoded steel mill. Ottawa stepped in and took over the coal operations under a separate agency, the Cape Breton Development Corporation, or DEVCO. But the city, and the island, never recovered their former economic prosperity. Ten years after the creation of the Sydney Steel Corporation, it was costing the Nova Scotia government a million dollars a week to subsidize the obsolete steelworks, while DEVCO's attempt to diversify Cape Breton's economy was nothing more than a well-subsidized failure covered over with a veneer of political rhetoric.

The tycoon's dream had become the bureaucrat's nightmare.

While Sydney agonized over its future, the four hundred Micmac Indians who lived on Membertou, a 66-acre urban reserve overlooking one of the city's elite residential areas, were unaffected by the change in the steelworks' fortunes.

Caught in a depressing cycle of odd jobs and welfare, they had simply never shared in the wealth created by the mill, as the reserve's collection of ramshackle houses and unpaved streets made clear. The men had never been employed at the steelworks, and although the reserve was a mere ten-minute walk from downtown Sydney, no Indian women worked in the shops along Charlotte Street. A number of them did hold jobs as scrubwomen in private households. Bleak and rundown, Membertou was a world apart, its poverty, alcoholism, and paralysing social isolation largely ignored by the city in whose midst it existed.

Sydney had never been preoccupied with the plight of its Micmac citizens. In the 1880s, the Indians came to town to sell baskets, axe handles, and other handcrafts, just as they had two hundred years before when their customers were Spanish fishermen and the place was called Cibou by the Micmacs, Spanish Bay by the whites. With the establishment of the steel industry in 1899, the Micmacs began building houses on the Kings Road reserve in Sydney, getting what work they could in town. Although there were a few tradesmen among them – carpenters, masons, and plasterers – most of the Indians were unskilled, unemployed, and unwanted.

Despite the eight-foot fence that surrounded the reserve's two acres (the perimeter facing Kings Road had a barbed-wire fence to prevent the inhabitants from straying onto privately owned property), Sydney's white residents drew up a petition to have the "troublesome" Micmacs removed. A hearing into the petition was held in 1915, and twenty-one witnesses, all of them white, successfully argued that the presence of the Indians was impeding Sydney's development and depressing property values. The 125 residents of the Kings Road reserve were forced to give up their homes and move to reserves at Eskasoni, Whycocomagh, and Caribou Marsh in rural Cape Breton.

Ten years later they began to re-establish in Sydney on land purchased for them by the Department of Indian Affairs. In 1925, six houses were built on Membertou complete with "outside closets". It would be thirty years before the reserve would have electricity or hook up to the city's water and sewer lines.

By 1970, the same cycle of despair that gripped Nova Scotia's other twelve reserves – joblessness, welfare, and alcoholism – had enmeshed Membertou's residents. A report issued by the Union of Nova Scotia Indians claimed that ninety-eight per cent of the violence on the reserves was linked to alcohol and drugs. Significant numbers of Indian children were found to be drinking vanilla and shaving lotion to temporarily escape the barren reality of reserve life. At that time, Dr. Mohan S. Virick of Sydney told the *Micmac News* that he was treating a growing number of Indian children for peptic ulcers, which he believed were being brought on by glue- and gasoline-sniffing. Dr. Virick said that the medical problems of the Micmacs rested on a mammoth social problem that could only be improved by an army of social workers.

The army never marched. But Indian students from the third to the eighth grade were given an alcoholism education program, partly to help them understand their parents' problems, partly to check the alarming growth of adolescent alcoholism. As one Micmac father of eleven told a Cape Breton newspaper during an interview about reserve conditions in 1970, "It's not exaggerating to say that people would be better off dead than living under this horrible system. If you've got a conscience at all, you've got to cry when you think of what these poor little kids have to look forward to."

It was into this troubled environment that Donald Marshall, Junior, was born on September 13, 1953.

③/ Little Rock

They called him "Little Rock". In the adolescent battlegrounds of Sydney, Junior Marshall was known as a kid who could "throw his hands" with the best of them. Although his parents were well aware of their good-looking son's growing reputation for wildness, they felt little need to put a stop to what seemed to them harmless enough behavior. He certainly wasn't the only teenager, on or off the reserve, who took a drink and raised a little hell with his friends on Friday night.

Donald Marshall, Sr., and his wife, Caroline, had one of the few households on Membertou where both parents worked; he as a plasterer and she as a cleaning lady at St. Rita Hospital in Sydney. Mr. Marshall was also Grand Chief of the Micmac Nation, the spiritual leader of five thousand Micmac Indians living in the Maritimes, primarily in Nova Scotia. Although his title was honorary, it carried real power on a day-to-day basis in the life of the Indian community. No major decision affecting the destiny of the Micmacs would be made without conferring with the Grand Chief, and his opinion was often sought when disputes arose between residents of the reserve.

The couple had a family of thirteen, four girls and seven boys of their own and two adopted children. As the eldest son, Junior would be the next Grand Chief, a position that was conferred for life. Devout Roman Catholics (the Micmacs were the first North American Indians to convert to Christianity), the Marshalls presided over an energetic clan, indulging their children as far as they were able. They worked hard and spent a lot of time away from the house, particularly Donald Marshall, Sr., whose duties as Grand Chief required his presence at a great many Micmac ceremonies around the Maritimes. "My mother and father tried to deal with us whenever they had the time but they worked a lot. In a way, we were brought up by baby-sitters," Junior recalled many years later.

Since the baby-sitters were often younger than he was (he dated several of them), Junior had no trouble slipping away from the reserve to join the gangs that were fast becoming the centre of his social life. Although he had enjoyed school on Membertou, things changed when he transferred to the white school off the reserve. Having failed twice by the time he reached the sixth grade, Junior was halfway through grade seven when he was expelled at fifteen for striking a teacher. "She tried to grab me by the ear–I was chewing gum–but she grabbed my hair too. It hurt like hell, so I hit her. I ended up in family court over that and they told me I had to leave school because I was taking up too much room."

The young Indian was given two choices: he could either go to work with his father or be sent to the Shelburne School for Boys. Junior was far from upset at the premature end to his formal education. The idea of working as an apprentice plasterer with his father was much more to his liking than going to a school where the white students were the spoiled darlings of the staff and the Indian kids were "treated like dirt".

After leaving school, his hero became Arty Paul, the rock-hard leader of the Shipyard Gang. With Junior at his side, Arty led a band of Micmac Indians from Membertou against the Mira Road Bunch, the East Broadway Gang, and the Whitney Pier Boys, all comers. With nothing on the reserve to occupy their time, the young Micmacs took their restless energy into Sydney, much to the consternation of city residents and the hard-pressed Sydney police.

Their jousting ground was Wentworth Park, a leafy oasis in the heart of Sydney with a band shell and a series of duck ponds bisected by railway tracks. By day it was the sedate preserve of families and old men who came to feed the ducks and doze in the afternoon sun. But at night fiercer custodians took over, young men in search of a proving ground for their budding machismo and garrulous "stemmers" looking for a place to drink their wine.

For the most part, the activities of the Shipyard Gang were the standard fare of teenage rowdies everywhere: petty vandalism, drinking, and fighting. When it came to the latter, it wasn't unusual for the fuse to be lit at the St. Joseph's Parish teen dance and the bang to take place later at Sydney's Chicken Coop restaurant or "down the park". It was also common to see a group of young Indians in Wentworth Park accosting passers-by for spare change. Depending on how desperate the group was for a drink, the panhandling could get quite aggressive.

"We used to drink what they call. . .bay rum and it's toilet cleaner I believe, and we would drink that. It cost a dollar eighty-nine for a bottle. We'd buy it at Sanitary Dairy, which was a block up from Wentworth Park. . .it would get you high–so we would drink the stuff, and it cost a dollar eighty-nine, and we had no real money at the time so we would bum to get enough money to get a bottle," a former member of the Shipyard Gang recalled.

Big for his age and considered more intimidating by his peers, Junior Marshall was often chief panhandler for the Shipyard Gang when money was needed for cigarettes or bay rum. One day, after asking several passersby in Wentworth Park for a much-needed dime, Junior made a young man "roll out" his pockets to prove that he didn't have any spare change. "I got the ten cents and a few sticks of gum, too. That's what we meant by 'rolling' someone in them days. You know, 'Roll out your pockets.' Most of the Indian guys down the park did the same and a lot of the white guys too."

Occasionally the gangs indulged in more boisterous pursuits. One night the North Enders appeared in Wentworth Park with stolen dynamite caps. The Shipyard Gang helped detonate some of them on the railway tracks that cut through the park. Someone proceeded to kick down the door of the band shell and carried off a cache of amplifiers and microphones, some of which were later sold to Membertou's unsuspecting reserve constable of the day, Roy Gould. After the equipment was cleaned out, more dynamite caps were blown up inside the band shell, touching off a flurry of complaints from local residents. "Come hell or high water, they wanted us out of that park," one Micmac, Kevin Christmas, recalled. "And there would be sporadic raids on the park by police. Like they would literally surround the park and converge on the park and they would arrest whoever was in the park, and there would never be any real criminal charges or anything but they would just take the people and arrest them for no reason. So we were getting a lot of this intimidation by the police constantly, constantly they were on to us."

Junior Marshall's brushes with the law weren't confined to his activities off the reserve. Late one night in May 1970, he and three friends showed up at the door of Uncle Joe McDonald, reputed to be one of Membertou's bootleggers. The young Indians had already been drinking and the last thing they were worried about was the hour. "Hey, Joe," Junior shouted, "give us a bottle!"

McDonald, a grouchy but likeable Newfoundlander, didn't take kindly to his noisy visitors. "Get the hell out of here. The store's closed."

His gruff reply riled Junior's companions.

"Hey, you're a bootlegger, you shouldn't be shuttin' your store down. A bootlegger's s'pose to be open all night!" one of them shouted.

Unmoved, Uncle Joe locked his front door, barred it from the inside with a two-by-four, and went back to bed. But the boys wouldn't take no for an answer. After waiting for a few minutes, one of them slipped around the back of the house and climbed in through an open basement window. He then opened the front door and let the others in. Uncle Joe was asleep on a cot by the refrigerator.

Junior sneaked past the cot and opened the fridge door. The light inside came on, awakening the old man, who blinked at the intruders in his living room.

"What the hell are you guys doin'?" he yelled, swinging his legs over the edge of the cot.

Junior grabbed a quart of wine from the fridge and ran to the front door. One of his companions wasn't as fast. Uncle Joe grabbed him and the two began to scuffle. Junior tried to break it up.

"Hey, Joe, here's the two bucks for your wine. We didn't mean nuttin'."

"You bunch of bastards," the old man roared, "you trying to fuckin' steal off me or what?"

Unable to placate Uncle Joe, Junior and two of his companions ran out the front door with the wine while the old man continued to grapple with the one intruder he had managed to collar. Outside in the bushes the three young Indians caught their breath and waited for their friend to join them. Five minutes later he still hadn't returned and Junior went back to get him.

The fridge door in Uncle Joe's shack was still open and what he saw by its single, bright bulb made him sick to his stomach. His companion was mercilessly pounding the old man, but Uncle Joe still wouldn't let him go. Junior grabbed the beleaguered bootlegger. "Here's your two bucks, man; now fuck off, let him go."

Uncle Joe released his assailant but the young Micmac, "crazy when he fought", kept swinging. Exasperated, Junior grabbed the teenager by the neck and threw him to the floor. While Junior tried to calm the young man down, Uncle Joe picked up the two-by-four he used to bar the door and hit the peacemaker a glancing blow over the head. A second blow, landing on his neck, took Junior off his feet. When he put his hand to his head, he felt blood. In a daze, Junior could hear dull thuds, as if off in the distance someone were beating a rug. As his head began to clear, he saw his companion kicking Uncle Joe, who was lying motionless on the floor.

"Christ, I'd better..." His thoughts still fuzzy, Junior staggered to his feet and grabbed his companion. "Get lost, get out of here," he hissed.

The boy ran out the front door and Junior picked up Uncle Joe and laid him on the chesterfield.

"Take it easy, ol' man," he said. But Uncle Joe wouldn't be consoled.

"I know you guys, I know you guys," he moaned, his face covered with blood.

Figuring the old man would bring charges against them, Junior tried to talk to him. The two were actually friends. On Fridays, when Uncle Joe got paid, he often shared a bottle with Junior on his front porch; when Junior had a bottle, he did the same.

"Hey, Joe, you know I didn't touch you, I backed you up, Joe," he said. Getting no response, Junior headed for the door. Two young girls who were passing by saw him leaving.

Word of the incident got back to Roy Gould, who went to visit Uncle Joe. The badly beaten old man told him what had happened and described how Junior had wrapped him in a blanket and put him to bed. Gould, who was fighting a losing battle trying to keep some of the reserve's young bloods under control, confronted Junior with the story.

"Listen, I didn't bodder the fuckin' guy," Junior insisted.

His story didn't convince Gould. He took Uncle Joe to the Sydney police station, where he swore out charges against the youths involved in the incident. Junior Marshall was the first to be charged. The Sydney police visited the small bungalow at 38 Micmac Street that was home to the Marshalls and their thirteen children. They checked the young man's shoes for scuff marks, hair, and blood but found nothing. The only sign of the encounter in Joe's house was a cut on his scalp which was still oozing blood. But the police never noticed the wound left by the two-by-four and Junior wasn't volunteering any information about what had happened. When it came to the Sydney police, the Shipyard Gang had a simple rule: the less said, the better.

In court, Junior insisted that he hadn't touched Uncle Joe McDonald. The judge believed him. Junior was convicted of stealing a quart of wine and received a day in jail. Time spent in court was deemed to have discharged the sentence. Fourteen days after the fight over a two-dollar bottle of wine, Uncle Joe McDonald died of uncertain causes.

His death brought an uneasy tension to Membertou. As Junior knelt down to pray at the old man's wake, a voice behind him said, "Dere's the bastard who killed the guy and he's got the nerve to come here and pray." Junior got up to leave. On his way out, someone punched him in the mouth.

While the whole community wanted to avenge Uncle Joe, no one carried a greater obligation than Noel Doucette, the future president of the Union of Nova Scotia Indians. For weeks after his stepfather's death, the soft-spoken Doucette had been besieged by family members to even the score with those they blamed for what had happened.

Despite the Micmac preference for solving their own problems, it wasn't Doucette's style to exact vigilante justice. Besides, he knew his stepfather had been seriously ill before the beating and there was some question about the precise cause of his death. A scrupulously fair man, Doucette worried about avenging himself on teenagers who might have done no more than what they had already been punished for. Still, he was troubled. Unable to eat or sleep, he left his house at three o'clock one morning to visit the one man he thought might be able to help him, Noel Morris.

On Membertou, they called him the Wizard. He lived alone,

spoke only Micmac, and was reputed to possess clairvoyant powers. He was believed to be in his nineties, though no one knew his exact age. Junior Marshall, for one, had always been "scared to death" of the strange old recluse, but amongst the older members of the band he commanded great respect. When Doucette showed up at his door, he was surprised to find that the Wizard was wide awake.

"Come in, I've been expecting you. The tea is nearly ready," he said.

For the next several hours, the old man listened as Doucette explained his dilemma. When he had finished, the Wizard spoke to him in the low, musical Micmac that was the trademark of the old people on Membertou.

"You don't have to worry. The ones who had a hand in Uncle Joe's death will be punished. There is nothing you have to do."

Afterwards, the two men sat silently in the cabin drinking tea. Just before first light, the supplicant noticed that the old man had fallen asleep, so he quietly slipped away. Walking the gravel roads of Membertou in the pre-dawn glow, the deep stillness over the reserve broken by the barking of a solitary dog, Noel Doucette felt at peace with himself for the first time in weeks. Comforted by the old man's advice, he could not know how accurate the Wizard's words would turn out to be. In less than a year, one of the boys who had broken into Uncle Joe's house would come close to drinking himself to death, another would commit suicide, and a third, Junior Marshall, would be sent to prison for life.

Shortly after the Uncle Joe McDonald incident, Junior and his cousin Tom Christmas paid a visit to a girl on the reserve who had "taken a fancy" to them several months before. One evening they were pursuing their relationship on her living-room floor when an unexpected knock came on the door. The boys had taken the precaution of locking the front and back doors and Junior was in favor of getting dressed and hiding under the bed until the intruder was gone. Working from sounder instincts, Christmas beat a hasty retreat out the back way as the knocking grew more insistent.

Unfortunately for Junior, his friend had left the back door ajar. The sixteen-year-old Marshall had just gotten his clothes on and was about to follow Tom when the girl's mother blocked his path.

"What the hell are you doing here?" she asked angrily, looking past Marshall to her daughter, who was fumbling to get dressed.

"Oh…g-good evening," the nonplussed youth stammered, vaulting over the back porch and disappearing into the woods where he soon caught up with Tom. The pair didn't go home that night. But early the next morning the police were waiting for them when they finally came out of the woods. Both were charged with rape.

When the matter went to court, the Crown's case quickly unravelled, to the humiliation of the Sydney police who had investigated the matter. The girl Marshall and Christmas were charged with raping testified that she had been having an affair with the two boys for six months. The presiding judge promptly dismissed the case. According to the recollection of the co-accused, Sgt./Det. John MacIntyre congratulated the two Micmacs on their acquittal and offered to shake hands. Tom Christmas gave him the Membertou salute. "I told him to fuck off. He just laughed and said he'd get us the next time."

Years later, with the court records of the case destroyed by fire, John MacIntyre would swear that the rape case had been investigated by another officer.

After the dynamite-caps incident, the Shipyard Gang moved its activities from Wentworth Park to St. Anthony Daniel Cemetery and a small island that they christened "The Jungle". During a drinking party one night, the gang went on a rampage, levelling $19,000 worth of headstones.

"There was a big, big MacIntyre headstone and the boys tore it down. They demolished it, right. MacIntyre was a kind of symbol to our group."

The symbol Junior Marshall referred to was the 260-pound head of Sydney's detective squad, John Fraser MacIntyre. A strapping six-footer who had once weighed close to three hundred pounds until he suffered a heart attack in 1964, Sgt./Det. MacIntyre was both feared and hated by the members of the Shipyard Gang, who felt that the policeman "had it in for Indians". Untroubled, he accepted their opprobrium as part of the job, the price a good policeman paid for "plucking" the four or five hotheads in every community who occasionally got out of hand.

After leaving high school, MacIntyre had worked as a car sales-man for three years before he answered a call for applications by the Sydney police. Out of sixty applicants, the force accepted three rookies, Peter and Bingo Morrison and John MacIntyre. Although he had no training in police work, he was intensely ambitious and quickly worked his way through the ranks of the force. In 1950 he was assigned to the investigation branch and five years later he made detective sergeant. He was promoted to sergeant of detectives in 1966.

Imbued with the work ethic, MacIntyre was as enterprising outside the force as he was within it. When a new church was built in his parish, the father of five was picked as campaign chairman to raise the necessary funds. He was also on the board of the Sydney Credit Union and made several astute real estate investments around the city–warehouse facilities on York Street and a number of private houses that he bought, renovated, and resold.

A self-made man with a rugged independent streak, John MacIntyre brought the same traits to his police work that he did to his private life. But if hard-driving self-reliance often makes a good businessman, it sometimes makes a bad investigator. As Sydney policeman Leo Mroz put it, "I don't think he thought there was a crime he couldn't solve all on his own."

After investigating the headstones incident, Sgt./Det. MacIntyre brought in Junior Marshall and some other Indian youths for questioning. Failing to get anywhere with Marshall when he asked who was responsible for vandalizing the cemetery, he tried a different approach.

"He asked me what would I do if he told me my buddies ratted on me. I asked who and he said Tom Christmas and Jimmy Gould. I told him I didn't knock no headstones down. I respect the dead."

Unconvinced, the detective went a step further. Marshall remembered being told that his two friends had in fact singled him out as the ringleader of the headstones rampage.

"I told him no way it was me. I told him I was there, I knew who knocked 'em down, but it was up to him to find out who. I wasn't giving him fuck all."

The ritual defiance had its roots in what the young Indians saw as a social and legal system that was stacked against them the moment they stepped off the reserve. If trouble broke out at Sydney's teen dances, for example, the Indians felt the treatment they got was very different from that given their white counterparts.

"We would never see them arresting non-Indian people. They would kick them out of the dance or send them home, but Indians they would arrest and take them down. And I mean we've seen, I mean I've talked to people who were arrested the night before and I'd see them the next day and they'd have black eyes and a tooth missing," said Kevin Christmas, recalling his youth in Sydney.

As soon as the three Micmacs were released by Sgt./Det. MacIntyre, Junior confronted his two friends.

"Hey, did you guys tell him I knocked down the headstones?"

"Fuck, no," Tom Christmas replied. "He told us you said *we* did it."

"Ah, that fucking guy, he's just fishing, man. Forget it," Junior told them.

Behind his bravado, Junior was worried. Too many members of the Shipyard Gang were being brought in lately for things they hadn't been caught in the act of doing. It could only mean one thing: someone in the gang was a police informant. Junior Marshall suspected it might be the gang's newest and only non-Indian member, John Pratico.

The sixteen-year-old Pratico had begun tagging along with the "Indian guys" in the summer of 1970, about the same time he had become a psychiatric patient of Dr. M. A. Mian of Sydney. An outcast of the white gangs and a heavy drinker, Pratico was diagnosed as a schizophrenic with a "rather childish desire to be in the limelight or centre of attention". From August 1970 he was placed on "continual medication" so that he could "function outside of a psychiatric institution", according to his doctor.

His father, an unemployed laborer, had long since left Margaret Pratico, John's mother, who now lived on social assistance in a small flat on Bentinck Street. According to his whim, young John would split his time between his mother's Bentinck Street flat and his father's apartment on Henry Street in Whitney Pier, often arriving at both doors courtesy of the Sydney city police. Although the pudgy youth with the jet-black hair was never a troublemaker, he was often picked up by police late at night roaming the city streets.

"When we saw this young fellow we would convey him to his

home generally and bring him to the attention of a parent. I found him unstable, I found him off-balance. I found he had a tendency to lie, I thought he was hallucinating sometimes. I know he often told me he was on medication," then-constable Leo Mroz of the city police remembered of Pratico.

To the normally clannish Shipyard Gang, John Pratico was an object of pity, a loner and drop-out who was as scorned on the streets of Sydney as they were themselves, and, if anything, even poorer. They fed him, gave him clothes and cigarettes, paid his way into dances, and included him in their drinking parties, despite the opinion of some gang members that Pratico "didn't look too trustful".

As for Pratico himself, the Shipyard Gang gave him an identity he couldn't have earned for himself. If anybody wanted to bully him, they would first have to deal with the likes of Junior Marshall or Tom Christmas. In the war zones of Sydney that was solid protection by anybody's standards.

Despite his sponsorship of John Pratico in the Shipyard Gang, Junior Marshall's suspicions about him sharpened when a police car pulled up in front of Membertou's carpentry school one afternoon and a policeman served him with a summons laying out a variety of charges, including destruction of the headstones in St. Anthony Daniel Cemetery.

Unconcerned about the headstones charge, he was dumbfounded when he saw that he was also being charged with giving alcohol to minors, one of them Joan Clements, his own girlfriend. Knowing the incident to be true, Junior immediately went to see her to find out why she had told the police about it. She told him that Sgt./Det. MacIntyre had been to her house talking to her father, who was dead against his daughter going out with "drunkards" and "hoodlums" from Membertou. She admitted to the policeman, who somehow knew about the Shipyard Gang's drinking parties, that she and some other girls had been given a drink of wine by Junior.

He got four months in jail on two counts of supplying liquor to minors. On November 17, 1970, two months after his seventeenth birthday, he entered county jail. His first stretch behind bars passed without incident.

"Arty [Paul] was in there and a lot of my cousins, so it wasn't bad.

Our keepers would let us out once a day and we'd put all the mattresses together and wrestle with each other until we were tired out. That way we got a good night's sleep out of it."

Two days after he was released from county jail on March 19, 1971, Junior was convicted of consuming liquor in a public place and fined ten dollars. Just over a month later, he was walking through Sydney's North End with some friends when he and Hubba Tobin decided to see if they could kick down a rickety front porch they passed. A light flashed on in the house, prompting the group's only sober member, Doc Tobin, to call it a night. Arty Paul and Hubba Tobin headed for the bus terminal to hide out, while Junior and Gomer Petrie made for the parking lot of the local IGA store, where the Sydney police picked them up five minutes later.

The police loaded Marshall and Petrie into the squad car and then picked up Arty Paul and Hubba Tobin at the Bentinck Street bus terminal. When asked what they were doing there, the two replied they were waiting for the bus. But the first bus didn't run until "steel plant time", 7 a.m., and it was only four in the morning. All four were placed under arrest.

By the time they appeared in court, Gomer Petrie had decided to take the rap for the group. He told the others he would confess to wrecking the porch if they would pony up the fine he expected to get. His friends readily agreed. But to Gomer Petrie's great surprise, instead of a fine, he was sentenced to a month in jail commencing on May 14, 1971.

There was high irony in Petrie's selflessness. Had Junior Marshall gone to jail for damaging private property, he wouldn't have been in Wentworth Park exactly two weeks later taking part in a bloody encounter that cost one youth his life and the young Micmac eleven years of freedom.

4/Prelude

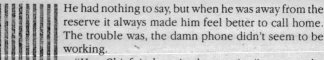 He had nothing to say, but when he was away from the reserve it always made him feel better to call home. The trouble was, the damn phone didn't seem to be working.

"Hey, Chief, it doesn't take pennies," a man at the gas pumps called out.

"Why don't you shut your goddamned mouth," the tall youth leaning inside the phone booth answered.

Not five minutes before, Junior Marshall, who looked older than his seventeen years, had been thrown out of a tavern in the Sunnyside Mall in Bedford, Nova Scotia. It seemed that every time he "put on a glow" somebody started treating him like a drunken Indian. He was in no mood for any more white man's shit, even if all he had for the telephone was a handful of pennies.

Although his temper had flared at the gas station attendant, it was really Roy Gould he was angry at. It was just like Roy, he thought, to go off and leave him alone in a strange place. Ten years older, Gould was one of Membertou's up-and-coming political activists, a man who fought for Indians with his head rather than his fists. Heavily involved in Micmac affairs and journalism, he was forever attending meetings of one kind or another and this time he'd invited Junior along. The teenager readily accepted, admiring the ease with which Gould moved in non-Indian circles and glad to get away from Membertou, and Cape Breton, for a while.

Their two-day trip had begun on the morning of Thursday, May 27, 1971. They had left Sydney in Roy's car and, after visiting the reserve at Shubenacadie, had spent the night in Bedford, just outside Halifax. It was fun being with Roy. Back on the reserve, money was scarce. While he was at school, Junior and his friends had collected bottles or sold their monthly allotment of government-supplied bus tickets to white students to pay their way into Sydney's teen dances. But Roy always had money and wine and, best of all, a car. Anyone on the reserve who had wheels was definitely "King Shit".

The next morning, Friday, May 28, Roy took a cab into Halifax for his meeting, telling Junior he would be back in a few hours. When he returned late that afternoon, the motel room was empty and his car was gone. He wasted no time in calling the RCMP. He suspected that Junior might have gone off for a joy-ride but he wasn't taking any chances. Cruising down the Bedford highway with the police, he spotted his young charge at a gas-station telephone booth. Junior was wearing Roy's yellow jacket and the missing car was parked near by.

Since the car had been reported stolen, the RCMP were ready to lay a charge, but Gould intervened. He told the officers that there had been a misunderstanding, that he would handle things. Although Gould concealed his anger from the police, he didn't hide it from Junior. "Don't you know you could be arrested for this?" he asked. "You just don't take off in someone else's car without asking."

"I was looking for you, man. You shouldn't have left me in that motel."

Roy could see that. Junior had been drinking and this was no time for a lecture. The younger man had spent four of the past five months in jail and Roy was trying to help him pull his life together. Getting into an argument wouldn't help. They got into the car and began the five-hour drive back to Sydney, unaware of the bloody events that would engulf the young Micmac before the night was through.

Gould and Marshall had just passed through New Glasgow on their way back to Cape Breton Island when Jimmy MacNeil and Roy Ebsary left the MacNeil house on Rear George Street, where they had been drinking wine with Jimmy's father. It was seven o'clock and they were headed for the State Tavern.

For the past six months, the 25-year-old MacNeil, an unemployed laborer who had never held a permanent job, had been a regular drinking companion of Ebsary's. Despite the difference in their ages – Roy was fifty-nine – a friendship had developed. Jimmy was a frequent visitor at the small house on Rear Argyle Street where Roy lived with his common-law wife, Mary, and their two teenage children, Greg and Donna. Uneasy at home, where his more vigorous brothers commanded the lion's share of attention and his docile manner had earned him more than one beating, Jimmy felt relaxed in his friend's house. There were flowers in the front porch, the kettle was always on, and the rest of the family seemed to genuinely like the tall young man with the prematurely receding hairline and the wide-set blue eyes.

But the real attraction was Roy. He was everything that Jimmy wasn't. Though only five foot two, the grey-haired war veteran filled any room with his presence. A great talker, he regaled his fellow drinkers with escapades from the war and made it easy to forget that the last job he'd held was as a vegetable-cutter at Sydney's Isle Royale Hotel.

When other people asked MacNeil what he saw in Roy Ebsary, Jimmy would say, "He's kind of like a father to me." His own father was more interested in cadging drinks at the State Tavern in return for playing the fiddle than in spending time with the son who was so different from his other children.

Ebsary completely won the young man over the day he bought a car for Donna and gave Jimmy the job of teaching her how to drive. He loved cars and didn't bother asking why Roy wanted his thirteen-year-old to learn to drive in the first place. Despite his enthusiasm for the project, bad luck dogged Jimmy's career as a driving instructor. During his very first lesson he fell asleep behind the wheel, jumped the curb, and ran the car into a tree. He was terrified of what Roy would say.

Strangely, the old man didn't seem to be bothered in the least.

Across the Sydney River in Westmount, far from the smoke-filled State Tavern where Jimmy MacNeil and Roy Ebsary had been drinking beer for almost an hour and a half, seventeen-year-old Sandy Seale was in the basement of the family home playing pool with friends. Just seven months earlier, the Seales had moved from Whitney Pier into the new ranch-style house at 985 Westmount

Road that Sandy, who enjoyed carpentry, had helped his father build.

Although Oscar Seale knew it was a sound move economically ("no matter how hard you worked on your place, resale value in the Pier was nil"), he had been anxious about how the Seales would fit in as one of the first black families in the all-white, middle-class neighborhood. He needn't have worried. The children had no problems, least of all the handsome teenager with the movie-star smile.

Sandy quickly made new friends in Westmount and his school work picked up dramatically. After failing grade nine the previous year, he became one of the best students in MacLennan Junior High School, much to the delight of his father, who had already purchased an insurance policy that would give his children four thousand dollars towards the cost of university if, as Oscar fervently hoped, they chose to go.

Although it was Friday night and there was a teen dance on at St. Joseph's Parish in Sydney, Sandy hadn't been planning to go. He had only been attending dances for a year, mostly in Whitney Pier, preferring to spend his weekly allowance of $1.50 "souping up" his bicycle to make it look like a motorcycle, or on his first love, sports.

A superb athlete, Sandy had travelled to Hamilton, Ontario, the previous Christmas with the Kinsmen Midgets, an all-star hockey team from Cape Breton, returning with a trophy as the tournament's Most Valuable Player. The other coaches at the tournament marked the 160-pound young defenceman as a kid who was going places.

Although Oscar Seale was close to all of his children, Sandy's athletic prowess forged a special bond between father and son. During the late forties and early fifties, Oscar had starred for the Whitney Pier Pirates in the Colliery Baseball League. The powerful clean-up hitter led the Pirates against the best local competition, as well as touring professionals, including the Colored Ghosts, an all-black professional team from the United States that he helped the local team to defeat.

Once invited to a trial with the farm team of the Detroit Tigers, Oscar was offered eighty-five dollars a week to play baseball in Sydney after the war. Uncomfortable in Toronto, where he had sought work after a strike had shut down the Sydney steel plant,

Oscar returned to his home town and settled down for good. Although he earned a good living from the steel plant, a small taxi business, and a tavern called The Goodwill Club, he always wondered whether he could have made the grade as a professional athlete. It was exciting to see that possibility resurrected in Sandy. He told people proudly, "My baseball talent was a gift from God and then when I seen one of my boys that was so versatile, it sure made me feel wonderful in my life."

Oscar Seale was upstairs in bed, listening to the crack of the snooker balls and enjoying the feeling of having his children around him, when Sandy's plans for the evening suddenly changed. Three black friends from Whitney Pier called on him to go to the St. Joseph's teen dance. The young man hollered upstairs to his mother, Leotha, asking for the three dollars she had put away for him, grabbed his brown corduroy jacket, and left with five friends to catch the bus into Sydney.

He didn't have to ask what time to be home. The rules of the Seale household were well known to all the children: curfew was nine o'clock during the school week, midnight on the one night, usually Friday, that they were allowed to go to the dance. It was 8:30 p.m. when Sandy Seale said goodbye to his parents and pulled the front door closed behind him. He would never return.

An hour after Sandy Seale left for the St. Joseph's dance, Roy Gould and Junior Marshall were driving along the bleak road into Membertou, having nearly completed the five-hour drive from Bedford. Once home, they headed for the reserve carpentry shop. Junior, who had been taking carpentry under a federal government job-training program, wanted to pick up his pay cheque, one hundred and six dollars, though at 9:30 p.m. it was too late to cash it. After borrowing twenty dollars from Gould, Junior and Arty Paul went to the liquor store, where they bought a forty-ounce bottle of rum. Stowing the bottle in a brown paper bag, Junior and Arty hitched a ride to town with Roy Gould and made their way to Doc Tobin's house on Intercolonial Street.

Doc Tobin, leader of a gang called the North Enders, was one of Wentworth Park's tougher customers. Reputation was the coin of gang mythology, and Doc Tobin swiftly answered all challenges to his supremacy as a scrapper. When a girl told him that she knew someone who could beat him, an Indian kid named Junior who hung around with Arty Paul, Doc immediately went looking for him.

It was one of the rare occasions when Junior Marshall wouldn't fight. But, unknown to Doc Tobin, his reluctance had nothing to do with the diminuitive Cape Bretoner with fists of stone. Junior's discretion was based on the fact that his own younger brother, Pius, a six-foot six-inch giant, was a friend of Doc's and would "back him up" if a fight started. It was an uninviting prospect. "I didn't want any part of Pius, nobody did, so I just offered Doc a drink. After that, we became the best of friends," Junior said years later.

An alliance flourished between the Shipyard Gang and the North Enders, much to the dismay of the Sydney city police. The North Enders began pilfering from the local Canadian National railway station, bringing their spoils back to the park to share with their new allies from Membertou. The Shipyard Gang, including Junior, were impressed. "Sometimes we'd go down in the park and the North Enders would have ten cases of wine stacked on top of the picnic tables. We wondered where the hell it came from but that didn't stop us from helping them drink it."

There were six other teenagers at Tobin's place when Junior and Arty arrived. Before heading over to the St. Joseph's teen dance on George Street, Junior suggested that they "put on a glow". Eight people, three girls and five boys, piled into Moose Tobin's broken-down 1963 Ford that was parked in the backyard of the house on Intercolonial Street and began passing around the bottle of rum Arty and Junior had brought along.

Impatient for another of the Tobin boys who was still in the house "to get in on the booze", Junior started blowing the car's horn. Furious at the noise the teenagers were making, which was disturbing the sleep of his seriously ill wife, Terrence Tobin stalked into the backyard carrying a bread-knife, demanding that the teenagers open the car door. "The girls were saying, 'Open the door for him,' and I said, 'No way he's getting near me with that knife,'" Junior recalled.

Frustrated at not being let into the car, Mr. Tobin headed back into the house, vowing to get the door open himself when he returned. As he slammed the back door behind him, Junior, Moose Tobin, and Frankie French decided it would be an expedient

moment to leave for the dance. During a brief stop at the Keltic
Tavern along the way, Junior got separated from his friends. Moose
Tobin and Frankie French proceeded to the dance alone. When
they arrived, they found it was sold out.

Standing in front of St. Joseph's Parish hall, the two teenagers
were challenged to a fight by a man who jumped out of his car
wielding a broken glass. Moose Tobin agreed to take him on if he
would drop the glass but the police shouted at the two from their
cruiser parked on the lot of St. Joseph's and the would-be assailant
jumped back in his car and drove off. Just another Friday-night
episode in Sydney.

The two friends joined the crowd that was milling around in
front of the red-brick parish hall, half expecting Junior to turn up.
When he didn't, they walked down George Street by Wentworth
Park, where just after midnight they unexpectedly ran into their
elusive friend. But he couldn't join them. Junior Marshall was
sitting in the back of a police cruiser. An ambulance was parked
beside the police car, flooding the surrounding grass with bursts of
red from its flashing lights. Something must have happened.

5/Murder

After becoming separated from Moose Tobin and Frankie French at the Keltic Tavern, Junior Marshall had started out for the dance by himself. He got as far as George Street by Wentworth Park when he decided to see if Tom Christmas or any of his friends from Membertou were down by the band shell with a bottle. He had only gotten one drink of his own rum in the back seat of Moose Tobin's car before the elder Tobin had run them off, and he wanted another before heading into the night's events. It was fifteen minutes before midnight.

On his way into the park, he passed two men, one a small, older man and the other younger and taller, who were trying to bum cigarettes from a couple sitting on a bench. Joseph MacDonald and his girlfriend, Linda Mann, had just come from the teen dance and wanted a few minutes by themselves before heading for Linda's house on Ankerville Street. Junior remembered MacDonald from Air Cadets (he and some other Micmacs had been kicked out of the organization for stealing Christmas-tree decorations for Arty Paul) but couldn't recall his name. MacDonald obliged the older man, whom he took to be a tramp.

Watching from a nearby path were two other youngsters returning home from the dance. George and Roderick McNeil noted the grey-haired man and his tall, younger companion asking the young couple on the park bench for a cigarette. They heard the old man say he had just lost a dollar. Thinking nothing of the incident, the teenagers went on their way. But the two boys didn't forget the two men they had seen, as events two days later would show.

For a moment Junior Marshall considered approaching the two men for a drink, but after watching them bumming cigarettes, he thought they weren't likely to have a bottle. He was on his way further into the park when he saw Sandy Seale coming down the path from Mac's Dairy. At last, someone he knew.

By the time Sandy Seale had arrived at St. Joseph's Parish after riding the bus from Westmount into Sydney, the dance was already sold out. Although there were two city policemen on special duty at St. Joseph's, Constable John Mullowney in the admittance area and Constable Freddy Lemoine in the dance proper, Sandy and his friends did their best to get into the crowded hall. Noticing that people who'd bought tickets had ink stamps on the backs of their hands, a companion drew a fake stamp on Sandy's hand. The police detected the forgery and turned him away. Twice more Sandy tried to slip into St. Joseph's, once by climbing through an open window, and on the last attempt Constable Mullowney threatened to charge him. "On the third occasion, I detected the smell of alcohol on his breath. The last time I told him if I saw him on the property again, he would be charged with consuming," the policeman would later report.

At around twenty to twelve, his curfew fast approaching, Sandy gave up trying to crash the dance and fell in behind three other teenagers, Alanna Dixon, Karen MacDonald, and Keith Beaver, who were walking down George Street towards Wentworth Park on their way home. When they reached the footbridge that led to the Crescent Street side of the park, Sandy left the group, explaining that he was going up town to catch a bus home. As he walked down the path that ran from Mac's Dairy along the George Street side of Wentworth Park, Junior Marshall called to him.

"Where you been?" he asked. Sandy replied that he'd been at the dance.

" I was just gonna head up there myself," Junior said.

"It's sold out," Sandy answered. The boys were acquaintances rather than friends. They had never attended the same school and, apart from running into each other at the occasional dance, had really only met on one other occasion – when Oscar Seale had been putting the finishing touches to his new house in Westmount. Sandy's father had hired Donald Marshall, Sr., to do the drywall work and he had brought along his eldest son, Junior, to do the closets and bathrooms. Junior and Sandy had played road hockey in front of the Seale home while Donald Marshall, Sr., finished the job.

Even though they didn't know each other very well, the two teenagers had one thing in common: both were known around Sydney as accomplished scrappers who wouldn't back down from a fight. Sandy was a powerful athlete who rarely started trouble but had a reputation for being able to finish it, whether on the ice or on the street. And Junior was feared in Sydney's gang circles as a tough customer who would back his friends to the limit, whatever the odds.

Walking through the park, the pair met Bobbie Patterson, a teenage friend who was so drunk that they decided to hide him in the bushes "so the cops wouldn't get him." Junior Marshall then put a fateful proposition to his companion.

"You wanna make a few bucks with me?"

"Well, how are we gonna make some money?" Sandy asked.

Sensing that Seale had no experience in "working the park", Junior had a ready answer.

"Well, man, like any other time, we'll bum it or something. If the guy wants to give us it, he'll give us it, we can take it off him if you want."

As the two teenagers talked on the footbridge in the middle of the park, Junior noticed two men up on Crescent Street, the same pair who had earlier bummed cigarettes from Joseph MacDonald and his girlfriend. The older men shouted down, asking for cigarettes. "There's a couple of guys up there, let's go see them," Junior said.

Seale agreed and the two teenagers ran up the hill toward Roy Ebsary and Jimmy MacNeil, who had left the State Tavern at around 11 p.m. and were on their way back to Roy's house via a shortcut through Wentworth Park. With seven beers apiece under their belts, as well as some wine imbibed earlier in the evening with Jimmy's father, the pair were feeling no pain.

For a few minutes, the foursome carried on a strange conversation. Roy Ebsary would later recall that Marshall and Seale said they were from Truro. Junior would remember that the old man dressed in the peculiar cloak claimed to be a priest from Manitoba who

wanted to know if there were any women or bootleggers in the
park. He would also remember Roy Ebsary inviting the boys back
to his house for a drink. The two boys hinted around for some
money, unaware that their words were unleashing a deadly rage in
Roy Ebsary. The unarmed teenagers had no way of knowing that
the former sea cook had been mugged on several previous jaunts
through the park and had sworn a terrible vengeance on the next
person who accosted him. Jimmy MacNeil heard Sandy Seale ask
Roy Ebsary for everything he had in his pockets. At the time, Seale
was standing directly in front of Ebsary, with his hands buried deep
in his jacket pockets.

"Dig, man, dig," MacNeil heard Seale say to Ebsary.

"Listen, you fucker, you're going to get everything I got in my
pocket," Roy replied.

Without warning, he drove a knife into Sandy and, with a powerful underhand thrust, hoisted the unsuspecting teenager on the
blade. The blow was struck with such force that the weapon passed
completely through Seale's abdomen. Marshall, who had been
scuffling with Jimmy MacNeil, turned when he heard Sandy
scream. He let go of the petrified MacNeil and had started for
Ebsary when the old man swung the blade again, this time slashing
the other teenager along his left arm. Slipping on the wet grass,
Marshall scrambled to his feet and ran for his life. Ebsary and
MacNeil hurried to the Ebsary home on nearby Rear Argyle Street,
where Roy proceeded to put on the barbecue and "break out a few
steaks".

Four years later, Ebsary related what happened in the park to a
relative visiting from Newfoundland. After acting out how he had
stabbed Sandy Seale, he turned to Robert McLean and said, "You
should have seen the look on the other fellow's face."

For Maynard Chant, it was to be an evening of missed appointments and gruesome destiny. Earlier in the evening, the fourteen-
year-old had driven with his parents the twenty miles from his
home in the fishing community of Louisbourg to attend church in
Sydney. Such piety was not unusual for the Chants. Walter Chant, an
undertaker, and his wife, Beudah, were well known as two of
Louisbourg's most devout Christians. Beudah Chant, whose own
father had been a famous evangelical preacher, and who, along
with her twin sister, Beulah, had been raised in the church, made a

point of instilling in her seven children a healthy fear of the Lord. Maynard particularly remembered one of her favorite admonitions, offered to him so frequently because he was rapidly becoming the black sheep of the family: "You can do anything you want with your life, son, but if you stray from the way, you'll have a troubled life; you can't toy with the Lord."

Although young Maynard seemed ready enough to embrace his parents' beliefs, he was having considerably more difficulty putting them into practice. After a series of minor scrapes with the law, he was convicted of stealing milk-bottle money in Louisbourg and put on probation as a juvenile offender in 1970.

As Maynard sat in the pews of the Pentecostal Church on Victoria Road, he simply couldn't keep his mind on the service. It was the first fine spring night of the year and partying, not religion, was on the young man's mind. Waiting for an appropriate moment, he slipped away and headed for Whitney Pier. A home-town friend was visiting there and he and Maynard planned to take the bus back to Louisbourg together.

After wandering around the Pier, Maynard finally called on the house where his friend was staying. The boy had already left. Having loitered around the smoky clubs of the Pier a little too long, Maynard was now in danger of missing the bus home. He hurried over to the terminal on Bentinck Street but the last Acadian Lines bus had pulled out ten minutes before. There was nothing to do but make his way over to George Street and hitchhike home. Maynard decided to take a shortcut that would lead him through Wentworth Park. He left the bus depot a little before twelve o'clock.

As he drew near the park, he was met by a youth in a yellow jacket coming towards him on the dead run.

"Look what they did to me," he said, showing Chant a four-and-a-half-inch gash on his left forearm.

"Who?" Maynard asked.

"Two fellows over the park," Marshall answered. "My buddy's over there with a knife in his stomach."

As the youths talked, two couples on their way home from the dance walked by. Once more the youth in the yellow jacket blurted out his story, exhibiting his now bleeding arm to back it up. One of the girls gave him a handkerchief to staunch the wound.

Although the two boys weren't aware of his presence, all of this commotion had Marvel Mattson worried. Shortly before midnight, the ex-RCMP officer had climbed the stairs of the red house at 103 Byng Avenue on his way to bed when he heard voices coming from his front lawn. As he stood at his bedroom window, it was too dark to see who was doing all the talking, but that didn't matter. What he overheard was enough to have him put in an urgent call to the Sydney city police.

Sergeant Len MacGillivary received the call at 12:10 a.m. and immediately dispatched three cars to Byng Avenue to check out a possible stabbing in Wentworth Park. The closest car, manned by Corporal Martin MacDonald and Constable Howard Dean, was less than a quarter-mile away on the parking lot of St. Joseph's Parish hall, where the teen dance was just breaking up.

After alerting police, Mattson returned to his bedroom window in time to see a youth flag down a brown Chevrolet Nova, show the driver his arm, and jump inside. He didn't notice that someone else also got into the car: Maynard Chant.

Convinced more than ever now that someone in the park needed help in a hurry, Mattson called police a second time. He told the dispatcher that a car carrying one of the youths he'd overheard on his lawn had driven off in the direction of George Street, the same direction Corporal MacDonald and Constable Dean were coming from.

At about the same time, on the opposite side of the park, Robert MacKay was running back to the figure he'd found lying motionless in the middle of Crescent Street a few moments before. MacKay and his girlfriend, Debbie MacPherson, had left the dance at St. Joseph's around 11:45 p.m. and walked to the park, where they sat on a bench for a few minutes before continuing up Crescent Street so that Debbie could catch a bus to her home in North Sydney.

It was Debbie MacPherson who first noticed the body curled up on the roadside. MacKay walked over and recognized the youth in the brown jacket and bib overalls as Sandy Seale.

"What's the matter?" MacKay asked. Seale's reply was a desperate mumble. "I've been stabbed...I need help."

Sending his girlfriend ahead to catch her bus, the dazed MacKay ran back through the park to Pollett's Drugstore on the corner of George and Argyle streets. It was closed. Not knowing what to do, he raced across the park again and was just getting to the spot where Sandy Seale lay in a pool of blood when a brown Nova slowed to a stop and two youths jumped out. One of them, Junior Marshall, stood quietly by Seale for a moment while the other one, Maynard Chant, feeling like the Good Samaritan he had heard about since childhood, took off his white shirt and placed it over the fallen youth's stomach.

"I'm gonna die," Seale gasped as Chant tried to comfort him. Behind them, Junior Marshall was showing his slashed arm to Robert MacKay. "I was with him," he said.

Watching Marshall, Maynard Chant thought he was behaving suspiciously. Why didn't he try to speak to Seale? Why did he keep showing off that cut?

MacKay then suggested to Marshall that they go for help. Inside 120 Crescent Street, the house nearest the scene of the stabbing, Brian Doucette was watching television when he heard voices on his front porch. Opening the door to see what was going on, he was met by Marshall, who showed him his injured arm and asked to use the telephone. He explained that his friend needed an ambulance. Doucette asked what had happened. After hearing the story, he agreed to call an ambulance. But his first call was to the Sydney police.

By this time, Corporal MacDonald and Constable Dean had received a second radio message from headquarters and were moving slowly up Crescent Street checking the park. The squad car's headlights suddenly picked up a man in the middle of the road waving them on. It was Junior Marshall.

Dean jumped out of the car and Marshall showed him his arm, telling the policeman that he and Seale had been the victims of a knife attack. After briefly checking the fallen youth, MacDonald and Dean radioed for an ambulance and gave headquarters the exact location of the incident.

Back at the Sydney city police station, Sergeant Len MacGillivary called T. W. Curry's ambulance service. Unluckily for Sandy Seale, there had been a major car accident at Big Pond that night, delaying the response time of the normally swift ambulance service. He then called Detective Michael R. MacDonald, a twenty-five-year veteran of the city police, who temporarily took over the investigation.

At 12:25 a.m. Oscar Seale was summoned to the phone by his wife, Leotha. The voice at the other end of the line advised him that it was the police department calling. "What's the matter?" he asked.

"Something's happened to your son, you better get down to the hospital right away."

The distraught father rushed out to the driveway, only to remember that his eldest son, John, had borrowed the family car. After a quick call to a neighbor, Oscar Seale was on the way to the Sydney City Hospital, wondering what on earth lay in store for him.

Back at the park, a second squad car carrying Constables Richard Walsh and Leo Mroz arrived at the scene, stopping beside Sandy Seale, who was lying near the right shoulder of Crescent Street. Constable Dean, who had been told by Marshall that "it was a tall fellow and a short fellow with white hair" that did the stabbing, passed the description along to Constable Walsh. He told Walsh that he was taking Junior to the Sydney hospital for treatment of his wound and asked the other two policemen to stand by until the ambulance came for Sandy Seale.

While they were waiting, Constables Walsh and Mroz decided to check Seale's condition. They noticed a bulge under his white T-shirt and thought he might be concealing something. Lifting his shirt, neither policeman was ready for what he saw: protruding through a long slash in his abdomen were the young man's intestines. Leo Mroz knew Sandy as well as his father and shuddered to think of the ghastly news the Seales were about to receive.

Meanwhile, having called the police, Brian Doucette came out of his house at 120 Crescent Street and walked over to the scene of the stabbing. He noticed that the Indian youth who had come to his door to use the phone was being whisked off in the back of a police cruiser. Doucette walked over to where Robert MacKay and Maynard Chant were hunkered down by Sandy Seale. The wounded youth kept trying to sit up and the two boys restrained him as best they could.

Leo Curry, ambulance operator and funeral director, received the call to proceed to Crescent Street at 12:15 a.m. When he got there, he found a group of people standing around a solitary figure sprawled on the pavement to one side of the road. With the help of Constable Walsh and Brian Doucette, he eased the victim up on one shoulder and slipped a canvas stretcher under him. Doucette helped Curry lift Seale into the ambulance. He then jumped in the back beside the stretcher and made the trip to the hospital.

Constables Walsh and Mroz escorted the ambulance to the Sydney City Hospital. Seale was taken to the out-patient department and placed on a table, where Constable Walsh heard him moan painfully that he couldn't breathe. His blood-soaked clothing was removed by Curry, Doucette, an orderly, and the attending physician, Dr. Mohamed Ali Naqvi. Shortly afterwards, a commissionaire asked Brian Doucette to leave.

Leo Curry remained at the hospital for another fifteen minutes, assisting Dr. Naqvi in setting up an emergency intravenous feed for Seale. Before the patient was removed to the operating room, he took two pints of blood and as many of saline. Curry, who had assisted with many grievously injured people, knew then that the youth had lost a tremendous amount of blood.

Sandy Seale's life now passed into the hands of Dr. Naqvi. The police tried to question Seale at this point, but the doctor wouldn't hear of it. For the moment, a great deal more was at stake than the identity of the person who had ravaged the young man's body with a single, brutal blow.

Oscar and Leotha Seale began their all-night vigil at the Sydney City Hospital with the incredible news that their son had been admitted "with a very bad stab wound". In a daze, they signed papers authorizing Dr. Naqvi to operate on Sandy, then were questioned briefly by police. They told Detective Michael MacDonald they had no idea how such a thing could have happened. Because of his serious condition, they weren't allowed to see Sandy, and for the next several hours, in a state alternating between shock and grief, the pair paced the hospital's lobby waiting for word of their son's condition.

Before Seale had arrived at the hospital, Dr. Mohan S. Virick had treated Junior Marshall for the cut on his left forearm. The wound was four inches long and even in depth throughout. Strangely, Dr. Virick hadn't observed any bleeding. Neither had Merle Davis, the registered nurse who had prepared Marshall for the surgeon. But Nurse Davis did notice something else: a tattoo on Marshall's left forearm bearing an inscription she would not soon forget.

After his arm was stitched, Junior Marshall was told he could go

home. Walking down the corridor, he saw a detective with Maynard Chant, the young man he'd met while fleeing from the scene
of the stabbing. Anxious to help in the apprehension of Seale's
assailant, he spoke to Chant and the detective.

"There were two of them, right?"

Chant, startled at Marshall's sudden appearance, nodded his
head and answered with a single word.

"Yeah."

Another policeman then asked Marshall to accompany him to
the lobby, where two suspects in the stabbing were being held.
Junior's heart pounded.

"All I had in my mind was that old man in that fucking hospital
lobby, where I could get at him. I ran over right away but when I got
there, they were two young guys and everything just died out. I
said, 'No, that's not them.'"

On the way out of the hospital, Junior saw what for him was to be
the night's enduring image: Sandy Seale lying on a table in the out-
patient department. "The guy had so much blood all over him, he
shined, his whole body was shiny. I only got a glimpse of him when
they were taking his pants off and I just seen the blood all over him
and I just looked and said to myself, 'Holy man, is that Sandy or
what?' But it was him. I knew he was the only one there, the only
black guy that was full of blood."

While Junior Marshall had been getting his arm stitched and
talking to police, Constables Richard Walsh and Leo Mroz had
already begun a desperate search for the two suspects he had
described. They checked all the restaurants that were open at that
hour and inquired at Sydney's three main hotels, the Wandlyn, the
Cape Bretoner, and the Isle Royale, for any parties that might have
registered during the night. They also checked with taxi-drivers to
see if two men fitting the description Marshall had given them had
been picked up in the vicinity of the park that night. Their inquiries
turned up nothing.

At 2:15 a.m. they picked up Constable Ambrose MacDonald, who
was patrolling the city's Esplanade area, and told him of the
stabbings in Wentworth Park. The three policemen then proceeded to Government Wharf, working on the theory that the men
they were after might be seamen. There were no ships at berth.

Constable MacDonald was then dropped off to complete his regular shift. He continued to check restaurants throughout the night while Constables Walsh and Mroz cruised the park.

Constables Frank McKenzie and John Johnstone were having almost as fruitless an evening. After attending at the hospital, they too took to the streets searching for the men who had attacked Seale and Marshall. Driving along George Street toward Route 22, the road to Louisbourg, they picked up a young hitchhiker with a bloody shirt whose head was full of impressive details of what had happened in Wentworth Park. It was Maynard Chant.

Chant had stayed at the park until the night's excitement had come to an abrupt end with the departure of the ambulance and the police cruiser carrying Seale and Marshall. After they had disappeared into the night, there was nothing left to do but make his way up Hardwood Hill and hitchhike home to Louisbourg. At least now he had a story to tell his parents that might make them forget that he had slipped out of church before the service was finished. He had been a Good Samaritan to Sandy Seale and hoped that might excuse his otherwise un-Christian behavior.

Not far along George Street Maynard got his first ride. The occupants of a pick-up truck, Tim Lynch and Wayne Nichols, were fascinated with the story he told them of what had happened in the park. But they weren't going far, and let Chant off just beyond St. Joseph's Parish, where the teen dance had been held. His next ride came courtesy of the Sydney city police.

After discovering that he had been at the park that night, Constables McKenzie and Johnstone decided to take Chant to the Sydney City Hospital, where he could be questioned by the officer in charge of the investigation, Michael MacDonald, or "Red Mike" as he was known to his fellow officers. MacDonald spoke to Chant for two or three minutes and was satisfied that the youth knew so little about the stabbing that he didn't think it necessary to take a statement from him. It was on the heels of that interview that Chant ran into Junior Marshall after he'd been treated for the knife wound to his left arm.

Maynard was then sent to the Sydney police station to await his father, who had been called to come in from Louisbourg to pick up his son. At 3:15 a.m. the police spoke to Chant for another ten minutes, then released him without taking a statement. At 3:30 a.m. his father arrived and the young man's involvement in the night's desperate events was at an end. But not for long.

When he finally left the hospital, Junior Marshall was driven back to Membertou by the Sydney police. The cruiser moved quickly along the deserted city streets, but not fast enough to outdistance news of the stabbing, which had already reached the reserve. A group of teenagers had gathered at the bridge leading into Membertou, bristling with the rumor that Junior himself had been murdered in Wentworth Park.

They swarmed around the police car, ready to vent their anger, until they caught sight of the deceased waving vigorously to them through the back-seat window. For the next half-hour, Junior explained what had happened in the park, removing the bandage from his wounded arm to show them his cut and describing the old man who had wielded the knife. His wrist was throbbing and one of his cousins obligingly slashed the elasticized cuff of his jacket with a knife to help relieve the pressure.

To Pius Marshall, Junior's brother, it was much ado about nothing, just another Friday night in Sydney that turned out badly. Advising Junior to forget it, he handed him a bottle of wine.

Around 2 a.m., the group began to break up and Junior headed for home, a partly finished bungalow at 138 Micmac Street in the heart of the reserve. Along the way, he ran into his cousins Tom and Kevin Christmas, who were sipping wine on Kevin's front porch. Once more he related what had happened to him. Tom noticed how excited Junior seemed.

"I got knifed down the park," he told them. "Two guys came up, man, they got my buddy, they got Sandy. I guess they got him in the gut. I seen him go down after this old fella stabbed him. I got stitched up down the City Hospital." For a moment he was quiet, gazing into the woods behind the row of identical box-like bungalows. "I wonder how my buddy's making out?"

After listening to Junior describe his and Sandy's assailant, Tom suggested that they go back to the park to take a look around. Tom and Junior were close friends as well as cousins. When Tom's father had died in Maine, Donald Marshall, Sr., acting in his capacity as

Grand Chief of the Micmac Nation, had brought the body home on a flat-bed truck. It was the kind of thing a person didn't forget.

"Maybe the guy dropped his knife and he'll come back to get it," Tom said. "Maybe we'll run into him."

Hopping on bicycles, the two youths pedalled down to the park, circling round and round the deserted ponds. Neither talked much, Tom because he didn't want any of the neighbors calling the police, and Junior because he was thinking of something his other cousin, Kevin, had said to him on the porch.

"You know, Junior, if they don't get the guy who did this, they're gonna blame you for it."

6/The Last Day

Dr. Naqvi wasn't saying so, but he had known that Sandy Seale was on the verge of death from the moment he first saw him. The youth had no pulse or blood pressure and was in a state of shock on arrival at the hospital. But for the next twenty hours the surgeon struggled to save his life. He performed resuscitation, supported Seale's respiration, and gave him a massive replacement of blood, twenty-seven pints in all.

The young man was operated on twice. In the first operation, Dr. Naqvi extended the slash in his abdomen and made an incision where the youth's blood vessels were torn. Seale was experiencing massive internal bleeding from the single insertion of a pointed object, roughly three inches in length, that had penetrated his abdomen clear through to his backbone. There was brisk bleeding through his entire gastro-intestinal tract, as well as a large amount of blood in the stomach. After repairing what damage he could, Dr. Naqvi closed Seale's abdominal cavity and hoped for a miracle.

After a few hours, the patient was continuing to experience massive internal bleeding. Assisted this time by Dr. David Gaum, the Seale family's physician, Dr. Naqvi operated again. This time he discovered a half-inch puncture in Seale's aorta, the body's major blood vessel, which he repaired with a silk suture. Dr. Gaum noted that a large section of Seale's bowel had been deprived of its blood supply and was becoming gangrenous. For the second time, Dr. Naqvi closed the young man's ravaged body. With his kidneys and respiration shut down, there was nothing to do but put him on an artificial respirator and wait.

At 4 a.m. on the morning of May 29, 1971, Oscar and Leotha Seale took the longest elevator ride of their lives. After waiting more than four hours for word of Sandy's condition, they were told by a nurse that the doctor was now ready to see them on the third floor, where their son was being kept. When Dr. Naqvi arrived, he sat down next to Leotha Seale wearing an expression that terrified the couple.

"What happened, Mr. Seale?" he asked in a gentle East Indian accent. After a night of unrelieved anguish waiting for information, Oscar Seale wasn't in the mood for answering other people's questions.

"I don't know. How is my son?"

"My, my, what happened?" the doctor persisted.

"Doctor, how is my son?" Oscar Seale's voice was arching toward hysteria and Dr. Naqvi knew he could hold back no longer.

"Bad knife wound, Mr. Seale, big knife, dirty knife," the doctor replied.

"Well, how is he now? Is he okay?"

"No, bad knife, dirty knife, Mr. Seale," the doctor replied.

Dr. Naqvi repeated his odd description three times, finally driving the normally retiring Leotha Seale to distraction.

"Look, doctor, my husband doesn't want to know what kind of knife it is. He wants to know how our son is."

The doctor's reply sent shivers down her spine.

"I can't do any more for him," he said, slowly shaking his head from side to side.

Leotha Seale felt the room tilt before she passed out. The next thing she heard was Dr. Naqvi saying, "Come on now, come on," as he slapped her on the hands. Numb with grief, Mrs. Seale watched as nurses ran towards her with needles. "They were jabbing me with needles, I could feel the pinches, you know, and then finally I was going, I could feel myself going down the elevator with two nurses." Everyone was crying.

Once in the lobby, the nurses tried to take her to a waiting wheelchair. One of them rubbed her hands while the Seales' eldest son, John, attempted the hopeless task of comforting his mother. "Come on, Ma, let's go home. There's nothing we can do here."

In the grip of an emotion that could not be sedated, Leotha Seale suddenly exploded. "The doctor said a lie. Sandy's not going to die. He can't die."

With those words, she swung free of the nurse who was assisting her and ran back to the elevator. A nurse in the lobby called up to Dr. Naqvi and by the time Leotha Seale arrived on the third floor, the doctor and her husband were waiting for her. She wanted to see her son and there was no one in the Sydney City Hospital who was going to stop her. Donning green hospital gowns, the desperate couple were led by Dr. Naqvi to Sandy's room.

Their hearts died a little at what they saw. Sandy was lying in bed with an array of tubes inserted into his body, including one in his mouth. He looked more frightened than they had ever seen him look in his life. As Oscar moved to the foot of the bed, Sandy sat up ramrod straight, then lay down again, repeating the action several times until he tired himself out.

Although he was unable to speak, he nodded his head in the affirmative when Dr. Naqvi asked him if he knew that the man at the foot of his bed was his father. The doctor then asked the wounded youth if his name was Sandy Seale. Once more Sandy nodded. Exhausted, he fell back on his bed, and what was to be the last visit between parents and son came to an end. Leotha Seale was taken home by John. Oscar followed them an hour later.

Before leaving the hospital Oscar Seale was given his son's belongings. Although he had worked hard to keep his composure while his wife was with him, he could not control the lump in his throat when he saw that even Sandy's boots and socks were full of blood. For the first time since the police had called him at just after midnight, he began to wonder with mounting rage who could have done such a thing to his boy. Surely, he thought, the other boy the police had told him was with Sandy would know. Oscar would call him.

At 8 p.m. on May 29, 1971, Sandy Seale died quietly in room 305 of the Sydney City Hospital. Oscar Seale knew that something terrible had happened when the doctors called him back to the hospital and met him wearing suits instead of their surgical gowns. Earlier in the day he had given them permission to perform a second operation on his son. "My God Almighty, look, what about my boy?" he asked. They had done everything possible to try and save him, the doctors said. "You can't tell me this, this can't be happening," he groaned.

Unable to look at Sandy's body, Oscar Seale returned home less than twenty minutes after he'd arrived at the hospital. The new house in Westmount was overflowing with friends, neighbors, and relatives. When the head of the Seale family walked through the front door, his massive shoulders shaking, no one needed to be told the news, least of all his wife Leotha. "Oscar," she cried, "he's dead, he's dead!"

Junior Marshall was on Membertou when he heard the gruesome news. He had spent the day in and around the police station and was on his way to the woods with two cousins and a bottle of wine when he met Clarence Gould and his wife heading for the reserve store. It was 9 p.m. "It's too bad about your friend," Gould said.

"Oh, he'll be all right, you know," Marshall answered.

Gould's terse reply fell on Marshall's disbelieving ears like a blow: "He just died."

To the surprise of his two cousins, Stuart Marshall and Margaret Matthews, Junior began to cry. With tears streaming down his face, he drained the bottle of wine they had just bought, all the while remembering the phone call he'd received that morning from Sandy's father.

At 7 a.m., Oscar Seale's tone had been harsh and accusatory. After spending the night watching the son he idolized slip ever closer to death, he wanted to know who had stabbed Sandy. Junior had been unable to tell him. Now the boy was dead and still he had no answers.

The previous night floated through Junior's mind like a dream. He remembered the conversation he and Sandy had had with the old man and his younger companion. The old man had worn a long blue cloak and Junior remembered telling him that he looked like a priest. The conversation had turned to women and liquor; then the old man had invited Sandy and Junior back to his house for a drink. They had declined and the two men had walked away.

Junior had called them back. The rest was a macabre vignette played out in a heartbeat: Sandy, with his hands buried deep in his pockets, hoisted suddenly on the old man's knife, the blade flashing towards Junior, a searing pain in his arm...then running, running, until he met Maynard Chant walking down Bentinck Street towards the park and the road home to Louisbourg.

A rage, sudden and violent, flared up in the sorrowing young

Micmac as he stood in the middle of the gravel road holding an
empty wine bottle. Taunted by the image of the old man's face, he
lashed out at a white teenager who happened by, "levelling" him
with a left hook that was famous in Sydney gang circles. A little later
he met another Micmac, Jerry Ginnish, who had heard the news
about Seale.

"So you finally killed someone, eh, Little Rock?" he said, using
Junior's Membertou nickname.

Ginnish, who had also been drinking, instantly regretted his
remark. Junior fell on him with a vengeance, but it wasn't Jerry he
was punishing beneath the fury of his fists: it was the old man in the
long blue coat who had so swiftly snuffed out the life of his
companion and just as swiftly vanished into the Sydney midnight.

7/The Investigation

On the night of the Sandy Seale murder, Detective Michael MacDonald had just returned home after working the four-to-twelve shift when he received a phone call from the station telling him that there had been a serious stabbing in Wentworth Park.

He immediately drove to the Sydney City Hospital to check on the condition of the victim, then called the home of his superior, John MacIntyre, to advise him of the night's dire events. "I thought we had a murder on our hands. I asked him if he would come out and he refused. I reported this to the chief of police, Gordon MacLeod," Detective MacDonald later told the RCMP.

If Chief MacLeod was upset about Detective MacDonald's report, he had his share of reasons. Not only was a possible murder in Sydney a sensational matter, "elephant shit stuff" measured against the usual fare on the police charge sheets of the day, but the city's last murder had gone unsolved.

A few years earlier, seventy-year-old Jimmy Seto had been found murdered in the basement of his Sydney restaurant. The side of his head had been caved in by a blunt object and the cash register upstairs had been rifled. John MacIntyre, who had been appointed sergeant of detectives in June 1966 after sixteen years in the investigation branch, took on the case, along with Detective Norman MacCaskill. No arrests were made. After the original investigation failed to find the killer of the elderly Chinese man, Sgt./Det. MacIntyre went to the RCMP, who assisted him in searching the restaurant for the object that had been used to crush Seto's skull.

Carpenters took down partitions in the basement, but the murder weapon was never found.

The Seto slaying, clouded by racial overtones and still on the books, had hurt the credibility of Sydney's detective squad. Now Sydney's first teenage slaying had been committed, involving seventeen-year-olds from the city's two major racial minorities. Chief MacLeod knew that the public wouldn't tolerate it if his men failed to apprehend the killer this time.

But on Saturday, May 29, when Sgt./Det. MacIntyre took over the case, he was faced with something more daunting than Chief MacLeod's impatience over the stumble start to an important investigation: no leads. The officers who responded to the call on the night of the murder hadn't come up with the two men Marshall had described to police as his and Seale's assailants, nor had they discovered any eyewitnesses to the crime other than Marshall himself.

To make matters worse, the murder weapon hadn't been recovered. The only physical evidence the police had retrieved was a blood-stained Kleenex that Constable John Mullowney picked up on a lawn when the sun rose brightly over Wentworth Park on Saturday morning. Along with the bloody clothing of Marshall and Seale, that Kleenex was the only exhibit entered in evidence at the Seale murder trial the following November.

Over the next twenty-four hours, the investigation picked up steam. Several youngsters who had been at the dance were interviewed but none had witnessed the stabbing. At five o'clock on Sunday morning, Sgt./Det. MacIntyre had the City Engineering Department drain the creeks in Wentworth Park in an effort to locate the murder weapon. The policeman already considered Junior Marshall a suspect and concentrated his search on the drained pond adjacent to the path the young Indian had taken as he fled the stabbing scene on the night of the murder. But while the police were conducting their search, someone had gone to the reservoir and cut the chain, letting the locks down and reflooding the area. The creeks had to be drained again, but the Sydney police never recovered the murder weapon.

Later that same morning, Junior Marshall, who had spent most of Saturday at the police station at the request of Sgt./Det. MacIntyre, was brought in to view a seven-man police line-up.

"They were all young men except one. I told police the killer wasn't there. MacIntyre asked me to look again at the old guy, a guy named Mickey Flynn, but I didn't even bother going back in because I knew it wasn't him."

As he had already done on Saturday, Sgt./Det. MacIntyre once more asked the young Micmac to stay around the police station in the event he was needed. More than a day after the knife attack, no one had as yet taken a formal statement from Junior Marshall, although he was their only witness to Seale's murder. The young Micmac talked to several policemen and chain-smoked, waiting to be called by John MacIntyre.

Sydney radio stations began broadcasting an appeal for anyone with information about the murder to report to the police. The investigation was going nowhere until Sgt./Det. John MacIntyre and Detective Michael MacDonald drove out to Louisbourg to call on Maynard Chant for what would be the first of two fateful interviews.

The Chant household was already buzzing over the part Maynard had played in the tragic events of Friday evening. On Saturday morning, as soon as he woke up, his mother had asked him what was going on. He assured her that he knew nothing about the stabbing and had only helped at the scene.

But when Walter and Beudah Chant got home from church that Sunday, they found two Sydney policemen sitting in their backyard. Even though Detective MacDonald had already talked to Maynard on the night of the murder and let him go without taking a statement, Sgt./Det. MacIntyre explained to the Chants that he believed their son had lied to police at the hospital. He didn't say why he believed that, but simply asked to question him again, alone. The boy's anxious parents agreed, advising their son, who was still on probation for stealing milk-bottle money, to "tell the truth".

The reason Sgt./Det. MacIntyre decided to question Maynard Chant had to do with a note one of his men had passed to him that same morning. Having heard about Seale's death on the radio, Tim Lynch, the man in the pick-up truck who had given Maynard a short ride on the night of the stabbing, went to the police station to make a report. The officer who spoke to Lynch seemed convinced that the boy from Louisbourg held the key to solving the murder, as the last line of his note made clear: "From what Lynch told me, it seems this Louisbourg man witnessed the stabbing."

The two detectives took the fourteen-year-old to the police car, where they talked to him briefly about the stabbing. Although Chant hadn't witnessed the murder, he remembered the story Junior Marshall had told him when they had met on Bentinck Street shortly after midnight, then later in the corridor of the Sydney City Hospital. He repeated it to the detectives, with one critical difference. Instead of merely attributing his information to Marshall, he told police he had actually seen the stabbing. Detective MacDonald, who had talked to Chant twice on the night of the murder, was stunned. Not once during interviews he had conducted at the hospital and then later at the police station had the youth even hinted he had seen who stabbed Sandy Seale.

After the informal chat in the police cruiser, Maynard was taken to Sydney, where he gave the police a written statement about his knowledge of the events of Friday, May 28.

"I walked down Bentinck Street, I came over Byng Avenue and started to cross the tracks. I got halfway across the tracks—first I seen two fellows who stabbed Donald Marshall and Sandy Seale—they talked for a few minutes over on Crescent Street. One fellow hauled a knife from his pocket and he stabbed one of the fellows—so I took off back across the tracks." When asked to describe the two men, Chant said they were both over six feet tall and wore dark pants and suit coats.

Despite telling them what he thought they wanted to hear, a skill Maynard had perfected in protecting his Christian parents from the realities of his "lustful" life, the boy was left with the distinct impression that the detectives were "very disappointed" in him. Lying came easily to Maynard in those days, but it was as if he had said the wrong thing. "It was almost a pressure-type thing," he recalled about that first interview. But the trouble was, the agreeable youth couldn't figure out just what the police were after.

For the second time in two days, Maynard Chant thought he had seen the last of the Sydney police; for the second time, he was wrong.

On the Saturday morning after Sandy Seale was stabbed, John Pratico awakened at 7:30 a.m., just in time to catch the end of a news report on the radio about the stabbing. He could be forgiven if his throbbing head wasn't quite ready to receive the alarums of a new day. The night before, he had been drinking heavily at the St. Joseph's teen dance, so heavily in fact that his Indian friends had taken him to a nearby lumberyard to sober up away from the watchful eyes of the two Sydney policemen who were patrolling the dance. "I was really out of it. I really didn't know where I was at, believe me," he later recalled of that night.

But his interest was piqued by the radio report about a stabbing. In a husky, sleep-thick voice he called out to his mother, "Who got hurt in the park?"–a strange question coming from the person who within a week would become the Crown's star eyewitness to the Seale murder.

Margaret Pratico told him what she had heard on the radio. John jumped out of bed and quickly pulled on his clothes. Without even combing his hair, he started out the door, telling his mother he was going to see some friends. She thought about trying to make him sit down to some bacon and eggs but when Johnny was in "one of his moods" there was no point in talking to him. Lately he had taken to throwing whatever food she put in front of him in the garbage, behavior she attributed to his medication. But whatever the cause of her son's tantrums, Margaret Pratico had herself and two children to look after on a welfare cheque that seemed to get smaller every month. Wasting food was a habit she simply couldn't afford; she let him go.

The next morning, Sunday, May 30, Junior Marshall was walking back to the reserve from the police station after viewing the police line-up when he saw John Pratico, Glen Lamson, and Rudy Poirier sitting on the Praticos' front porch at 201 Bentinck Street. One of the boys gave Junior a cigarette and asked what had happened on Friday night. Somewhat nervously, he recounted for what seemed like the hundredth time how he and Sandy had been stabbed by an old man with grey hair while a younger companion looked on. Junior pushed down his bandage and showed them the ten-stitch cut on his left forearm.

John Pratico was all sympathy. Just a week earlier, three local toughs were plaguing him in Wentworth Park when Junior Marshall arrived like a one-man cavalry charge and put an abrupt end to the fight. Now Marshall was in trouble and Pratico was determined to help. He offered to get together a gang to go looking for the old man who had wielded the knife.

"Don't bother, man," Marshall told him, "the cops are doing all that."

It was good advice, coming as it did from a would-be vigilante. The day before, the police had already stopped Junior and his cousin, Stuart Marshall, from going door to door in the park area looking for Seale's killer. During the conversation that preceded the stabbing, the old man had invited the two boys back to his house for a drink, raising his arm and pointing to a nearby street. Marshall couldn't remember exactly which way he had pointed, but he was prepared to knock on every door in the neighborhood to find out. But before they could begin, a Sydney police car picked him up and took him to the station. The officers told him it was for his own protection.

After spending the better part of two days at the Sydney police station, answering questions from Sgt./Det. MacIntyre that might help the policeman crack the case, Junior Marshall was finally called on to give a formal statement. At 4:50 p.m. on Sunday, May 30, he walked into the detectives' room, where John MacIntyre spoke to him for twenty-two minutes.

Junior told the detective that he and Seale had met in Wentworth Park around 12 p.m. on the previous Friday night. The two then met another teenager, Bobbie Patterson, who was drunk. After hiding him in the bushes so the police wouldn't catch him, they walked over to a footbridge, where they stood talking for a few moments. While they were standing on the footbridge in front of the band shell, two men called them up to Crescent Street. They wanted cigarettes. "I asked them where they were from and they said Manitoba. I asked if you guys are priests and the tall fellow said, 'We are.' One fellow had a long blue coat on. They told us, 'We don't like colored people and Indians.' The old guy turned to Sandy and said, 'There is one for you, black boy,' and he put the knife in his stomach. He then took the knife out of Sandy and swung at me and put it in my arm. He told me, 'There is one for you too, Indian.'"

As improbable as the story may have sounded, Junior was unwavering in his description of the two men. One was tall with black hair and wore a blue V-neck sweater, and the other, the one who had wielded the knife, was small with grey hair combed back, roughly fifty years old, and wore a long blue coat.

As he related what had happened to Sgt./Det. MacIntyre, Junior Marshall was unaware that the Sydney police had already informed the local RCMP that he was a suspect in the Seale slaying. In a routine unclassified telex to RCMP headquarters in Halifax concerning the murder, Sydney RCMP reported, "Circumstances presently being investigated by Sydney PD–investigation to date reveals Marshall possibly the person responsible...."

The telex was sent very early on the morning of Sunday, May 30, before Sgt./Det. MacIntyre had interviewed a single witness or even taken Junior Marshall's statement.

Sunday proved to be a good day for finding eyewitnesses. John Pratico, whom Marshall suspected of being a police informant and who had now been under psychiatric care for almost a year, was questioned by Sgt./Det. MacIntyre at 6 p.m. at the Sydney police station. He had sent for Pratico after receiving a tip from Rudy Poirier that the sixteen-year-old had been drinking in the park after the dance on Friday night and might know something about the stabbing. Poirier, who was painting a house for Sgt./Det. MacIntyre, also reported to police the conversation between Pratico and Marshall on Pratico's porch.

Practico was in bed trying to sober up from a bout of heavy drinking when his mother came in to tell him that the police were at the door. He had no idea why the detectives wanted to talk to him. "If you don't know nothing about it, don't get involved," his mother advised him as he hurriedly got dressed and went to the front door. "What do you guys want to talk to me for?" he asked. He was invited down to the police station to find out.

There, Sgt./Det. MacIntyre began the interview by asking where Pratico had been on Friday night. He told the policeman he had gone to the St. Joseph's dance and afterwards to the park. To drink? Pratico nodded. And did he see anything strange while he was drinking in the park? No. Was he sure about that, because some serious events had taken place there that night, a boy had been killed. Yes, Pratico agreed, he had heard about it on the radio. But wasn't it true he knew something about what happened in the park?

"No," he answered, "I'm afraid I don't."

That wasn't the way the police understood it, Sgt./Det. MacIntyre told him. And if John knew what happened and didn't tell, he could be in serious trouble. "He said if you don't tell us about it we're going to put you in jail until you do tell us," Pratico later recalled of that first interview.

Responding to what he took to be pressure from Sgt./Det. MacIntyre, pressure the detective would later swear had never been applied, John Pratico finally signed a statement in which he did little more than embroider on the facts of the stabbing as Junior Marshall had presented them to him on his porch the day before. "I was over by the courthouse when I heard a scream. I looked. I seen two fellows running from the direction of the screaming. They jumped into a white Volkswagen, blue licence and white numbers on it," Pratico lied.

He told police that one of the men was six feet tall and wore a grey suit. The other one, he said, was five feet, five inches tall and dressed in a brown corduroy jacket. When asked if he had seen these men at the teen dance, Pratico said he had.

"Yes. I seen them walking around. Bobbie, Robert Patterson, said they are from Toronto's Satan's Choice Bike Gang."

Suddenly Sgt./Det. MacIntyre had two witnesses who claimed to have seen the same stabbing. Unhappily for the man in charge of the Seale murder investigation, they were clearly identifying different assailants.

In less than a week, that problem would inexplicably resolve itself.

For two agonizing nights, Jimmy MacNeil couldn't get the events of Friday, May 28, out of his head. After learning of Seale's death on the radio, he lay on his bed, convulsed with loneliness and remorse, trying desperately to lose himself in sleep. But when he closed his eyes, it all came back to him as lucidly as a child's nightmare – the park, the two youths, Roy's sudden thrust, the wounded boy's cry.

There had actually been a time, immediately after Roy stabbed Sandy Seale and slashed Junior Marshall, when Jimmy had felt a dizzying hero-worship for his diminutive friend, who with his soiled cloak and white goatee looked more like an indigent Colonel Sanders than a swashbuckling savior. He had been terrified when the tall Indian had taken hold of him, and the terror had turned to soaring, irrational gratitude when Roy's knife cut down one youth and drove the other one off.

As the two men hurried from the scene of the stabbing to Roy's house just minutes away from the park at 126 Rear Argyle Street, Jimmy rattled on about Roy's bravery, totally convinced that the stories he used to tell in the tavern about his exploits in the Second World War were absolutely true. Feeling the effects of the seven beers he had downed earlier in the evening at the State Tavern, he was still praising his unlikely protector in the doorway of the Ebsary living room when Roy suddenly turned on him.

"Shut up, Jimmy."

"You saved my life, you did a good job," Jimmy continued rapturously, turning to Mary and Donna Ebsary as if he were going to explain his cryptic remarks.

"Don't say anything," Roy hissed, heading for the kitchen with Jimmy in tow. Mary Ebsary heard her husband tell his friend not to go through the park, to cut across the field on his way home and he wouldn't be caught.

If Mary had learned one thing after twenty-one years of common-law marriage to Roy Ebsary, it was that Roy was "a real Jekyll and Hyde" when drinking, and it was best under those circumstances to leave him alone. So, despite her curiosity about what was going on, she turned her attention back to the late-night TV news. Whatever it was that Roy and his friend had gotten themselves into, she didn't want to know about it.

But thirteen-year-old Donna Ebsary's curiosity was larger than her fear of her father, though she too knew how violent he could be. As a young child, she had watched in horror as an enraged Roy Ebsary had torn the head off her budgie bird when its chirping annoyed him. And just recently he had taken an axe to the family furniture, chopping it to bits before his rage was spent.

Spellbound, Donna watched as Roy and Jimmy walked down the hall to the kitchen. When she thought they were absorbed in what they were doing, she crept up behind them and saw Roy washing blood from a knife he was holding over the sink. After he had finished, Roy disappeared upstairs, brushing past his daughter as if she weren't there. When he returned, he wanted to have a barbecue, but he couldn't get the coals started. Minutes later, Jimmy left for home and the girl, who had seen what no one else in the family had seen that night, wondered what on earth her father and his friend had been up to.

Jimmy's euphoria about Roy's behavior in the park was already beginning to dissipate as he walked through the deserted city streets towards his parents' house at 1007 Rear George Street. With the draught beer wearing off in the bracing night air, he recalled that neither of the two youths had brandished a weapon, nor had they tried to hurt either Roy or himself. "All they wanted was cigarette money," he thought to himself; "maybe Roy should have just give it to them."

And where had he come up with that knife? Jimmy figured he must have been carrying it all along, and with that thought the gentle 25-year-old shuddered. Roy sure knew how to use it.

On Sunday morning, two days after the stabbing, a trembling Jimmy MacNeil showed up at the Ebsarys' door asking to see Roy. He was taken into the living room, where Roy was lying on the couch wrapped in a blanket.

"That young fella died, Roy," Jimmy said. "I heard it on the news."

"It was self-defence," Roy replied without looking at him.

"You should have give him the money, for cripes' sake, you didn't have to...he didn't put a gun in your face or any darn thing, for cripes' sake," MacNeil continued, close to tears.

"You've got to protect yourself today," Ebsary said. The old man turned his face to the wall and the conversation was over.

So was the friendship. Two days later, Roy's eighteen-year-old son, Greg, picked Jimmy up at his house and drove him to the Wandlyn Motel, where Mary Ebsary worked as a laundress. Greg went into the motel, returning in a few moments with his mother. "He got in and she said don't go to their house any more because of what Roy done. The young fellow told me if I mentioned what happened to the police, all your family will be in trouble. They will have to go to court."

Feeling more frightened and guilty than before, Jimmy MacNeil went on a binge to end all binges, only to discover that there were some memories that cheap wine and, when the money ran out, shaving lotion couldn't erase.

Throughout the week the pressure continued to build on the Sydney police to break the case. On Tuesday, June 1, Chief MacLeod received a letter from the Black United Front, a new lobby group, inspired by the example of America's Black Panthers, that spoke for Nova Scotia's thirty thousand blacks. The letter said that the black residents of Sydney were "deeply concerned" over the murder of Sandy Seale and were "watching the progress of this case with the greatest of interest". It ended with a call for a "quick and speedy apprehension of the assailant or assailants".

On Wednesday, June 2, Sandy Seale was buried. He was given a hero's funeral. Crossed hockey sticks adorned his coffin, and the children of Whitney Pier Elementary School lined the roadside and waved goodbye as the funeral procession made its way to Forest Haven Memorial Garden. The people of Sydney responded massively to the grief of the Seale family, inundating them with money and flowers. Overwhelmed by the community's reaction, Oscar Seale turned the money over to the Kinsmen Hockey Club and urged anyone who wanted to honor Sandy's memory to do the same. To commemorate his son's love of hockey, the grieving father donated a trophy in Sandy's name to the city hockey league.

At the graveside, Leotha Seale, who had been locked in a grief-stricken trance since Oscar had returned from Sydney City Hospital with his dread news four days before, tried to prevent the coffin from being lowered into the ground. Her broken-hearted sorrowing shook to their roots the hundreds of people who had travelled to the cemetery to see a young man, dead before his time, buried on a perfect spring day.

One person who wasn't at the cemetery was Junior Marshall, though he had wanted to be. A friend had warned Donald Marshall, Sr., that the killer was still on the loose and that until he was caught it would be better if Junior stayed out of sight. Unknown to everyone except the Sydney police, the head of the Marshall clan had other reasons for worrying about the safety of his son. On Sunday evening, an anonymous phone call had come into the Marshall home warning Caroline Marshall to get her family out of Sydney or they would be killed.

Although Junior wasn't allowed to attend the funeral, he had paid two visits to Curry's Downtown Chapel at 390 George Street where Sandy Seale had rested before being buried on Wednesday. The first time he went with Lawrence Paul, whose mother had driven the two boys to the chapel. The second time, Junior was accompanied by a group of Micmacs, who were there partly to honor Sandy Seale and partly to protect their friend from anyone who might want to harm him. During one of the two visits, Junior met the eldest of the three remaining Seale brothers, John. "I went over and I shook his hand and told him I was sorry about what happened. He told me he was glad one of us lived to tell about it. I said I hoped they find the guy."

Since he had learned of Sandy's death, Junior, like Jimmy Mac-Neil, hadn't been able to sleep, and there didn't seem to be enough wine in Sydney to make him forget what had happened. On Monday afternoon he had fainted, either from exhaustion or as a side-effect of the drugs he had been given to help dull the pain from his own stab wound. Everywhere he went, the only thing people wanted to know was the one thing he couldn't tell them: who killed Sandy Seale?

Standing over Sandy's open casket, Junior Marshall, a Catholic, didn't know how to pay his last respects. "I think he was a Protestant, because there was no cross around the casket or nothing, right, so I didn't know what to do. I just stood there because I didn't want to bless the guy, I didn't want to pray if that wasn't what they did. So I stood by the casket for about ten minutes and then walked out."

Outside, a fight had started just up the street from Curry's between whites and Indians. It was broken up by the police and Junior Marshall was put in a cruiser and whisked back to Member-tou.

The first threatening phone call to the Marshall home was followed by several more. On the advice of the Sydney police, the family decided to leave Membertou temporarily and move to a relative's house on Whycocomagh, a reserve seventy miles away—everyone, that is, but Junior. He was determined to stay behind and find out who was threatening his family and why.

Two days later, on the afternoon of Friday, June 4, he was at home alone when another call came in. "Nobody spoke for a second, I kept saying hello, and then a voice said, 'You better be out of the

Maritimes before tonight or we're gonna get you for what you did.' "

Frightened and confused, Junior went to Arty Paul, the best ally a person could have when the chips were down. The two friends rounded up a gang and plans were made to deal with anybody who might try to come after Junior. "I remember Arty telling me, 'Don't worry, if anybody comes in here after you, they'll never get off the reserve alive.' "

Tough words from a man Junior knew could back them up. Surrounded by his friends and the legendary leader of the Shipyard Gang, he felt safe. But his sense of security couldn't have been falser. In less than six hours he would be under arrest for murder, and neither Arty nor the assembled might of Membertou could help him.

With the letter from the Black United Front and the enormous public pressure generated by Sandy's funeral to find his killer, it hadn't been a banner week for Sgt./Det. John MacIntyre and the Sydney police. After statements had been taken from Maynard Chant, Donald Marshall, and John Pratico on Sunday, May 30, the investigation had ground to a halt. All day Monday the police were at a loss over what to do next. At just after 6:30 p.m. they took what would be their only statement of the day from George and Roderick McNeil, who appeared at the police station after hearing appeals for information about the Seale murder broadcast over the radio.

The pair told police that they had been on their way home from the St. Joseph's teen dance through Wentworth Park at around 11:40 p.m. when they had seen two men "hanging around". The boys described one man as "trampish-looking", with grey hair "flat on his head, straight back" and wearing a grey or white topcoat. The second man was six feet tall or better with dark hair and appeared to be much younger.

The description was close to the description Junior Marshall had given in his statement the day before of the two men he claimed called him and Seale up to Crescent Street moments before the stabbing. It was the first corroboration of the young Micmac's story, all the more significant because the McNeils had seen the two men in the vicinity of the murder scene just twenty minutes before

Seale was stabbed. But when the matter came to trial six months later, the two boys weren't asked to testify. John MacIntyre would later claim that their evidence was not followed up because it appeared to be "superseded in importance" by the evidence of Maynard Chant and John Pratico.

By Tuesday, the killer's trail was colder than ever. Sgt./Det. MacIntyre had his detectives at work compiling lists of teenagers who had been at the dance, and he himself had requested a haematology report on Sandy Seale's blood type. Because the Sydney police department didn't have an identification section, MacIntyre had also requested assistance from the RCMP in obtaining photographs of the murder scene. An offer by the Sydney detachment of the RCMP to assist in the investigation was turned down.

That afternoon, Sgt./Det. MacIntyre assigned the man who would work most closely with him on the Seale murder case, Detective William Urquhart, to find out more about Junior Marshall's movements in the hours leading up to the stabbing. The second detective took a statement from Frankie French, one of the teenagers who had been in the derelict car in Moose Tobin's backyard along with Marshall and several other teenagers on Friday night.

French told the detective that Moose Tobin, Arty Paul, and Junior split a pint of rum before everyone but Arty left for the St. Joseph's dance. Along the way, Tobin had stopped in the Keltic Tavern on Dorchester Street looking for his brother Blair while Junior and Frankie French waited outside. Five minutes passed and Junior grew impatient. Even though he was under age, he went into the crowded tavern to find his friends.

A moment after Junior disappeared into the bar, Moose Tobin came out. When Junior didn't come back, Tobin and French proceeded to the dance by themselves, where they got into an altercation outside the parish hall and were asked to leave by police. The next time they saw Junior, he was sitting in the back of a police car parked on Crescent Street near Wentworth Park, flanked by another cruiser and an ambulance. It wasn't until the next morning that Tobin and French had learned about the stabbing.

At 6:30 p.m., Sgt./Det. MacIntyre took a statement from sixteen-year-old Robert MacKay. The youth described how he and his girlfriend had found Sandy Seale lying on the road as they walked home from the dance along Crescent Street and how he had gone later to a nearby house with Junior Marshall to call an ambulance for Seale. MacIntyre asked MacKay if Marshall had said anything about the man who had stabbed them. "Yes, he said a man with glasses and a younger man with him. Junior said the man with the glasses stabbed Sandy and said, 'That is for you buddy,' and then Junior said he tried to get away and he stabbed him in the arm."

Without having learned anything new from Robert MacKay, Sgt./Det. MacIntyre tried again an hour later, this time with four-teen-year-old Lawrence Paul from Membertou. Paul knew nothing of what had happened in the park, but he had talked with Sandy Seale just before midnight outside St. Joseph's Parish hall. Sandy had told the Micmac teenager that he was "going down the street—taking a walk". As with the previous interview, there wasn't much in Paul's statement for an investigator to hang his hat on.

The last statement of the day was taken at 8 p.m. when Sgt./Det. MacIntyre interviewed Arty Paul. The twenty-year-old leader of the Shipyard Gang told the head of the Sydney detective squad that he had been with Junior at Moose Tobin's house on Intercolonial Street on Friday night but that the two had split up when Arty had decided to pass the evening with his girlfriend, Kay Tobin, instead of going to the dance. The next time he saw Junior was back on Membertou at 2:30 a.m.

"Did he tell you what happened?" MacIntyre asked.

"Yes. He told me him and Sandy met on the bridge in the park. There was two guys up on the hill. They were asking for a match and those two fellows were asking Junior if he was colored and Junior said, 'I am Indian,' and this fellow said, 'I hate niggers.' He said the short fellow with the white hair stabbed Sandy and then the short fellow stabbed him in the arm."

The next day, Thursday, June 3, Sgt./Det. MacIntyre took a statement from Gary Tobin which did little more than confirm the details he had already heard from Frankie French about Junior's whereabouts on the night of the murder. Once again the police-man asked if Junior had been drinking that night. "One drink of rum from me in my car," Tobin told him.

Since taking over the investigation six days before, Sgt./Det. MacIntyre had uncovered no physical evidence connecting anyone, including Junior Marshall, to the crime. As for the other eight people he had taken statements from, they had done little more than corroborate what the Micmac youth had told him the previous Sunday: that two men had asked him and Seale for cigarettes and that the shorter of the two, a grey-haired man of fifty, had stabbed them both.

Significantly, George and Roderick McNeil had given police a description of two men who were in the park shortly before midnight on Friday, May 28, that closely matched the two men Marshall had described to police. But Sgt./Det. MacIntyre had made no efforts to find those men, preferring to concentrate his investigative efforts in another direction.

The "big break" in the Sandy Seale murder case came on the morning of Friday, June 4, a week to the day after the stabbing. At 10 a.m., two Sydney detectives returned to 201 Bentinck Street, picked up John Pratico, and took him to the Sydney police station for a second round of questioning by Sgt./Det. MacIntyre. Still frightened by the threat of being jailed that had induced him to sign his first false statement, the sixteen-year-old was beside himself as he tried to figure out what the police wanted of him now as he rode to the station in the back of a cruiser.

From John Pratico's recollection, the interview began with the accusation that Pratico had lied to them in his earlier statement. Sgt./Det. MacIntyre had in fact returned the previous midnight to the scene of the crime to check out the lighting conditions that would have prevailed at the time of the murder. He concluded that neither Chant nor Pratico could have seen what they claimed to have seen from where they had told police they had been standing on the night of the murder. Pratico, who knew his first statement was false, tried again to say that he had seen nothing in the park. "They said, 'We know you're lying to us.' That's the words he used," Pratico later recalled of the interview.

Pratico, who was just two months away from a nervous break-down that would have him committed to a mental institution, listened to the police officer as he described what he, Pratico, must have seen. Slowly, the frightened youth slipped into the role that he thought was being created for him. As he had done the previous Sunday, John Pratico began to fantasize, only this time he was telling what would be the most terrible lie of his life. John MacIntyre, who was aware of Pratico's "nervous problem", carefully took down the boy's "statement".

"I went down Árgyle Street and over Crescent Street. I was walking on the park side. I seen Sandy and Donald on the other side of the bridge stopped. I did not pay much attention to them. I kept walking for the tracks. On the tracks, I stopped where I showed you. Then Donald Marshall and Sandy Seale were up where the incident happened. I heard Sandy say to Junior, 'You crazy Indian,' and then Junior called him a black bastard. They were standing at this time where the incident happened. They were still arguing. They were talking low. I could not make out what they were saying."

"Which way was Sandy Seale facing?" MacIntyre asked.

"Facing the tracks."

"Which way was Donald facing?"

"The street."

"How close?"

"Arm's length."

"What did you see or hear next?" the detective asked.

Although Detective William Urquhart was also in the room, he said nothing. It was Sgt./Det. MacIntyre's unwavering practice to ask all the questions in any interview he conducted, recording both question and answer as the conversation unfolded. If another policeman who was present wanted to interject a question of his own, the head of the detective squad insisted that he pass him a note. John MacIntyre liked to run his own show.

"I did not hear. I just seen Donald Marshall's hand going towards the left-hand side of Seale's stomach. He drove his hand in – turned it and pulled it back."

"What happened then?"

"I seen Sandy Seale fall to the ground and Donald Marshall running up Crescent Street towards Argyle Street."

"What did you do?"

"I run home up Bentinck Street."

Sgt./Det. MacIntyre now asked a crucial question. "Were you standing on the track at the time Sandy Seale fell to the ground?"

"Yes. I was," Pratico answered.

"Was there anybody else around the scene?"

"Nobody–not a soul."

"Why were you standing there?"

"I was drinking a pint of beer."

"Did Seale scream when Donald Marshall struck him in the stomach?"

"He screamed–aah."

"How long did you know Sandy Seale?"

"Four or five years."

"How long did you know Donald Marshall, Jr.?"

"Since last summer."

"Did you ever quarrel with either boy?"

"No."

"Were you talking to Sandy Seale at the dance?"

"Yes, outside about 10:30 p.m."

"How far away would you be from Sandy Seale and Donald Marshall when they were on Crescent Street?"

"Thirty to forty feet."

"How long were they standing there?"

"About ten minutes. They were arguing over something."

"How is it you did not come down where they were?"

"I was scared," Pratico answered. His ordeal was nearly at an end.

"Did they notice you on the tracks?"

"I don't know."

"Would there be any obstruction between you and Sandy Seale and Donald Marshall when you were on the tracks [to keep them] from seeing you?"

"Bushes between them and me–blocking the view on them. It was easier for me to see them."

"Did you see Donald Marshall since?" At last John Pratico had a chance to tell the truth.

"Yes. Saturday or Sunday."

Having given not just another version of his earlier statement, but a completely new and sensational account of the events of May 28, the boy who had awakened on the morning after the murder to ask his mother, "Who got hurt in the park?" was finally allowed to go home. He had now told police he had not been in front of the courthouse on the night of the murder and did not see two Satan's Choice bikers fleeing the scene in a white Volkswagen; rather, he had been in Wentworth Park on the railway tracks and had seen Donald Marshall stab Sandy Seale. Overcome with a deep sense of relief at being let go, he gave no thought to the momentous consequences of his devastating lie.

Sgt./Det. MacIntyre and Detective Urquhart then travelled to Louisbourg, where they met with Wayne McGee, the rugged fishing town's chief of police. The detectives told McGee that they wanted to re-question Maynard Chant about the fatal stabbing of Sandy Seale and asked him to bring the young man and his parents into the police station, which was in the basement of Louisbourg's town hall.

When Maynard and his mother were brought in, Sgt./Det. MacIntyre told Beudah Chant that they now had "evidence" that Maynard had lied to police in his previous statement. They wanted to question him again, and Mrs. Chant agreed. According to John MacIntyre, she and Maynard were joined by McGee and Lawrence Burke, Chant's probation officer. Several years later, two of the people whose signatures appeared as witnesses to Maynard's damning statement, his mother and his probation officer, would deny having signed the statement – Lawrence Burke because he hadn't been there, and Beudah Chant because she had been asked to leave the room so that the policemen could deal with Maynard on their own. Although John MacIntyre would insist that they had, in fact, been present, he would admit under oath that he had signed their names to the bottom of the statement the two were supposed to have witnessed.

Sgt./Det. MacIntyre began the interview by telling Maynard that the police had new evidence showing that his statement of Sunday, May 30, wasn't very accurate. The detective asked if Maynard might now tell them the truth. The boy answered that he hadn't seen anything. But, the detective continued, surely he must have seen something, just tell what he had seen, Maynard later recalled of the interview.

"Well, I tried to. I made a gesture to say, listen, I didn't see anything. And then after a couple of times they said, 'Did you know, that you, for the statement we already have, you've already perjured yourself by this statement and you could suffer very serious consequences. You could probably get two to five years?' I remember those exact words to be truthful with you. An ah, I didn't know what to do then, I just kept...I was basically mumbling to myself...like I was on a half-cry then, I was saying I didn't see anything."

Maynard remembers Sgt./Det. MacIntyre then asking his mother, Beudah, to step outside the room, telling her that if she were absent, the boy might talk a little more freely to the police. She complied with his request, as she later told the RCMP, and waited outside for her son. John MacIntyre would later swear in an affidavit that Mrs. Chant had been present throughout the interview with her son.

Maynard remembered Sgt./Det. MacIntyre getting straight to the point. "They said, 'Well, we got another fellow there who saw the murder. We got a witness there and he claims that he saw you there and you saw the exact thing that he saw. So I said, 'Oh, yeah, what did he say he saw?', so that basically they give me...they arranged it very easily for me."

John MacIntyre and William Urquhart would later swear in affidavits that they exerted no pressure on Chant to give false evidence, that his statement was voluntarily given. The third policeman present, Wayne McGee, backed up their version of events.

Sgt./Det. MacIntyre began writing as Maynard gave his latest rendition of the part he had played in the events of Friday, May 28.

"Last Friday night after 11:30 p.m., I left the Acadian Lines on Bentinck Street and walked down Bentinck Street to the tracks. Then I started down the tracks towards George Street. I noticed a dark-haired fellow sort of hiding in the bushes about opposite the second house on Crescent Street."

"Did you know him," MacIntyre asked.

"No. I did not know his name but I seen him before out at the dances in Louisbourg."

"Did you see him since?"

"Sunday afternoon at the Police Office in Sydney. I walked by this fellow on the track. I looked back to see what he was looking at. Then I saw two fellows standing about one and a half feet from each other on Crescent Street."

"Were they the same size?"

"One was taller than the other."

"Which one was facing you?"

"Short, dark fellow was facing the tracks."

"At this point did you recognize either of these two men?"

"The only man I recognized was Marshall."

"What was he wearing?"

"Dark pants and I think a yellow shirt with the sleeves up to the elbows. I wish to say that when he was arguing – I mean Donald Marshall with the other man – his sleeves were down to his wrist at that time."

"How long were you on the tracks watching them?"

"About five minutes."

"Could you hear what they were talking about?"

"No. I just heard a mumbling of swearing. I think Marshall was the one who was doing most of the swearing. Then I seen Marshall haul a knife from his pocket and jab the other fellow with it in the side of the stomach."

"What side?"

"The right side – I seen him jab it in and slit it down."

"How could you tell it was a knife?"

"By the figure of it – it was shiny and long."

"What happened then?"

"When Marshall drove the knife in, Seale, he bent over. Then I ran toward George Street down the tracks. I went into the park, through the park, then up to George Street, crossed the tracks and then on to Byng Avenue – about three houses over I met Donald Marshall and he said, 'Look at my arm.' It was his left arm, his sleeve was rolled up. The cut was on the inside of his arm – it was not a deep cut and it was not bleeding at that time – until we caught up to two boys and two girls who were walking. Donald said, 'Could you help us?' One of the fellows said, 'What is wrong?' Then he said, 'Look what they done to me.' Then the other guy said, 'Who?' and Donald Marshall said, 'The two fellows.' He said, 'My buddy is on the other side of the park with a knife in his stomach.' They said they would try and help us. At the time a car came along and Donald stopped it and we asked for help. They picked us up and drove to the other side of the park and we stopped about six feet away from Seale. At this time, Seale was lying on the opposite side of the street. Donald Marshall got out, came over near the body of Seale and stood there. There was another man came along and knelt by Seale and then went over to a house and called an ambulance. Then he came back and knelt along side of me about five minutes. I asked this dark-haired fellow to look after Seale while I went up and called again. I forgot to state that the minute I got to Seale, I put my white shirt on his stomach. I said, 'Hold it,' and he mumbled. Police and an ambulance arrived and he was taken to hospital."

"Did Donald Marshall call the police or ambulance at any time?"

"No," Maynard answered, directly contradicting what Robert MacKay had already told Sgt./Det. MacIntyre a few days earlier.

"Did you?"

"Yes, first at the house with railing coming down the centre of the steps."

"Who was with you?"

"Marshall stayed on the sidewalk."

"Was there any other conversation between you and Marshall at that time?"

"He said there were two men – tall one had brown hair – done the stabbing."

"This of course is not true."

"No."

"Did he know you were over the tracks?"

"No – he did not."

At 3:45 p.m. Maynard Chant signed his name to a statement that would solve the Sandy Seale murder case for the two Sydney detectives. Six days after he and John Pratico had told police substantively different and mutually contradictory stories, they were now saying the same thing. Elated by Chant's statement, MacIntyre and Urquhart raced back to Sydney to the office of Donald C. MacNeil, the Crown prosecutor of Cape Breton County, and showed him their new statements.

"You must be the two luckiest policemen in Canada. Go get him," Detective William Urquhart remembered MacNeil saying.

Had the Crown prosecutor carefully read the two statements that were the sole basis for arresting Junior Marshall, he would have noted some disturbing contradictions between the two purportedly corroborative eyewitness accounts of Sandy Seale's murder. In his statement to police, John Pratico said he had seen Junior Marshall stab Seale in the left side; Maynard Chant told police Marshall had knifed his victim in the right side. Pratico said Marshall ran down Crescent Street towards Argyle Street after the stabbing; Chant had him fleeing towards Bentinck Street, the opposite direction.

Most important of all, there was a crucial discrepancy in the vantage points from which the two boys were supposed to have observed the stabbing. Maynard Chant, who claimed to have seen Pratico hiding behind a bush, said in his statement that he had witnessed the murder from the railway tracks, the same tracks where John Pratico told police he was standing, "with nobody, not a soul" around, when Sandy Seale was stabbed.

If Pratico were telling the truth, Chant couldn't have been watching from the same stretch of railway tracks when the murder took place. And if Chant were right about Pratico hiding behind a bush, then Pratico was lying about where he was when the murder took place. Either way, the statements were mutually contradictory, except when it came to identifying the killer.

In spite of the wildly differing statements the two boys had given police on May 30, and the total lack of any other evidence against Junior Marshall, on Friday evening, Sgt./Det. MacIntyre, acting on the instructions of Crown prosecutor MacNeil, obtained a warrant from Judge John F. MacDonald for the arrest of Junior Marshall on a charge of second-degree murder.

On their way to Whycocomagh, the two detectives stopped at the Baddeck detachment of the RCMP. Fearing trouble if a Sydney police car showed up on the reserve to arrest the son of the Grand Chief of the Micmac Nation, Sgt./Det. MacIntyre travelled to Whycocomagh in an unmarked RCMP cruiser, along with RCMP Constable Stanley Clark, who was assigned to assist in the arrest. At 8:55 p.m., under a fiery Cape Breton sky, the party reached their destination.

Unaware of these developments, Junior Marshall had been passing time on Membertou, nervously waiting for nightfall to see if his unknown telephone caller would try to make good his threat. In the pale sunlight of the spring afternoon, he began watching a group of Indian children trying to catch ducklings in a brook. The birds were too fast for them and Junior tried to lend a hand. Reaching over to catch one, he lost his footing and fell into the still-chilly water, much to the amusement of his audience of five-year-olds.

He was standing in the water, dripping wet, when his father appeared. Donald Marshall, Sr., had heard the rumors about trouble that night and returned from Whycocomagh to pick up his son. "Come on, we're going to Whycocomagh," he said. Junior stubbornly insisted that he wanted to stay on Membertou. "No," his father said, "your life is on the line. Come on and get in."

The two drove to Whycocomagh, stopping for groceries along the way. When they arrived at the white frame house where Junior's grandfather had died just a month before, all was in darkness. As his father unpacked the car, Junior went inside to greet his mother. The fluorescent light had burned out in the kitchen and she asked him to put in a new one. He was standing on the chair trying to install it when he saw the police cruisers pulling into the driveway. The light, which had been flickering on and off in Junior's hands, went out as he got down from the chair to find out what was happening. Before he could get outside, his father met him at the front door.

"What's going on?" Junior asked. His father's reply was so soft he could barely hear it.

"They're blaming you for it."

As the seventeen-year-old stood there dumbfounded, Donald Marshall, Sr., placed his hands on his son's shoulders and put a single question to him in Micmac.

"Did you kill that guy?"

"No," Junior answered.

"Okay. Get in the car and don't give 'em no trouble." Junior Marshall kissed his sobbing mother and walked out the door.

The next voice he heard was that of Sgt./Det. John MacIntyre reading him his rights.

8/Interlude

The RCMP cruiser hadn't travelled very far down the highway before Junior Marshall, disregarding his father's parting advice, allowed his anger to boil over. There was something in Sgt./Det. MacIntyre's demeanor, a smug certainty that Junior was Seale's killer, that the seventeen-year-old prisoner couldn't abide. "You're not going to get away with this," he said.

Sydney's chief of detectives responded coolly with the standard police warning that anything Marshall said could be used against him.

"I don't give a fuck what you hold against me, I never did it."

Though he tried not to show it, the grim silence of the detectives sent a chill through the young Micmac. He had been in trouble before, but he knew this time it was different. Junior fell silent, looking out the car window on the pastel wash of approaching dusk mirrored on the stillness of the Bras d'Or Lakes. All the way back to Baddeck, he found himself remembering what his cousin, Kevin Christmas, had said to him on the night of the stabbing: "You know, Junior, if they don't get the guy who did this, they're gonna blame you for it."

Back at the Baddeck detachment of the RCMP, the prisoner was searched before being put into a Sydney police car for the drive back to town. When they arrived, he was taken to Sgt./Det. MacIntyre's office, where he again professed his innocence. "How can you blame me? I didn't do it," he said, a little more imploringly than he would have liked. He was then told for the first time of the two witnesses who had seen him stab Seale.

"Who?" he asked in bewilderment.

That, MacIntyre told him, he would find out in court.

"Ah, you're full of shit anyway," the exasperated teenager said, falling back on the argot he always resorted to when dealing with the police. They, after all, were the enemy, always had been for the boys on the reserve. MacIntyre was just up to the same game he had played in the gravestones affair, bluffing to see what he could get his prisoner to admit. This theory somehow lost its reassuring ring when two policemen arrived to take him to the city jail.

Going to the "city bucket", a place Junior Marshall knew well from previous liquor violations, was an unsavory prospect. "It was a dump. Your toilet was a piece of twelve-inch pipe, your room looked like a closet, had a steel bed, no light, the windows were beat out of it, and rats crawled out of that pipe." He refused to spend the weekend there awaiting a Monday-morning court appearance.

Adamant at first that Marshall was going to the city jail, the officers finally relented. Judge John F. MacDonald was brought to the station and Junior was remanded to the county jail until Monday morning. As victories go, it was less than epical. But with the desperate events of the last few hours, getting your choice of jails, even if you were innocent, was better than nothing.

Tom Christmas was on his way to a dance when his girlfriend broke the news to him of Junior's arrest. The girlfriend, who had been speaking to John Pratico, told Tom that Pratico himself had given police a statement saying he had seen Junior commit the murder.

Christmas couldn't believe it. For more than a year, John Pratico had enjoyed the friendship, protection, and limited largesse of the Micmacs. Tom knew Pratico as a quiet, pitiful figure, a boy who "never had no girls or nothing – nothing at all". More than once he had taken Pratico back to his house on Membertou, where Mrs. Christmas had fed him and, on one occasion, given him a shirt. Tom, like Junior Marshall, had stood up for Pratico, who not only wouldn't fight, but wouldn't even defend himself if trouble came his way – unless he was drunk.

As he listened to his girlfriend's story, Christmas recalled another, and not so innocuous, side of John Pratico. After one too many unexplained trips to the city lock-up, Tom too had reluctantly begun to suspect that Pratico might be "squealing" to the Sydney city police about the Shipyard Gang's activities. Although John had a reputation on the reserve as a kid who could "stretch a story", who would tell tales of daring deeds to impress the very people who knew he was utterly incapable of having performed them, Christmas still found it hard to accept that Pratico was "a rat". Now this.

Tom had another reason for being incredulous about what his girlfriend had told him. He knew that on the night of the murder Pratico had been taken out of the St. Joseph's dance by some of the boys from Membertou to "sober up" in a local lumberyard. John had had so much to drink that he'd actually gotten into a fight, and the Micmacs were worried that the police on duty at the dance would run him in for being drunk and disorderly.

They took him to Stephen's lumberyard, where he was monumentally sick, having imbibed, as he would later testify in court, half a bottle of wine, half a dozen quarts and two or three pints of beer, and an unspecified quantity of rum or gin–the ingredients for an unmemorable evening at the best of times, but, taken as they were on top of the Valium his doctor had prescribed for him, they had rendered him virtually oblivious to the events of that night. The group returned to the dance from the lumberyard around midnight, where Pratico promptly got into an argument with a boy named Ricky Riske, just about the time word was filtering up to St. Joseph's from the park that someone had been stabbed.

From what his friends on Membertou had told him, Tom Christmas knew John Pratico hadn't even been in Wentworth Park at the time of the murder, let alone witnessed it–a fact Pratico himself would confirm in a sworn affidavit eleven years later.

The next morning Tom paid Pratico a visit. Margaret Pratico answered the door and called John out on the front porch to talk to the Micmac youth, whom she knew as one of her son's friends. Tom asked Pratico what he had seen and heard in the park and the dark-haired youth, groggy from another night's drinking, repeated the story he had signed his name to on Friday morning in the Sydney police station.

Tom abruptly told him he was a liar. Frightened now, Pratico said that he was sorry for what had happened, that the police had pressured him into making a false statement.

"You're crazy," Tom said. "You can put Junior up for life doing that." Reminding the now trembling youth that both he and Junior had treated him well, Tom Christmas made no bones about telling John what he had to do. "You're lying, man, you got to go back and tell them that."

Alarmed by what she overheard, Margaret Pratico called the Sydney police. When Tom saw them coming, he ran away. The police immediately assigned a car to watch the Pratico house. The next morning Sgt./Det. John MacIntyre showed up at Tom's door on Membertou, where he arrested the youth for threatening a witness. Junior's only ally had suddenly become a fellow prisoner and, without knowing it, a powerful, though spurious, part of the Crown's case against his friend.

Not since the 1940s, when Sydney's mayor of the day, Jack MacLean, had used his car to kill Joe MacKinnon, the municipal Registrar of Voters, in an alley in the city's south end, had a criminal case commanded so much interest in the Maritime steel town. Charged with first-degree murder, MacLean was later convicted of manslaughter in MacKinnon's death, which took place after the two got in an argument at a local tavern during a bout of drinking.

Junior Marshall's arrest on June 4 exploded in the local media, and on Membertou, as the debate raged whether the teenager had in fact killed his companion. Public interest in the case was feverish, whipped up to an even higher pitch when it was learned that Membertou's Band Council had engaged the services of Moe Rosenblum and Simon Khattar to conduct the young Micmac's defence. Everyone knew that would mean yet another battle between Sydney's two best defence attorneys and the redoubtable Crown prosecutor of Cape Breton County, Donald C. MacNeil.

After accepting the case, Simon Khattar visited his client in county jail to get his version of events in Wentworth Park on the night of Friday, May 28. From the beginning, he realized it was going to be an uphill battle. "Marshall was not an impressive man to talk to at all. First of all, first of all, he had a sort of a defect, when talking he had difficulty in expressing himself, he mumbled at times, and he appeared to me to be a man who was suppressing information."

The veteran lawyer, who bore a remarkable physical resemblance to film star Anthony Quinn, fired a barrage of questions at his young client to see if he could lead him out of what he took to be a state of psychological withdrawal. But neither Khattar, nor, in subsequent interviews, Moe Rosenblum, could elicit anything from Junior Marshall that he hadn't already told police; he hadn't murdered Sandy Seale. And, far from suggesting a line of defence, Junior's story about an old man dressed like a priest doing the stabbing created doubt about their client's innocence in the minds of both lawyers. "I had my doubts about the story, particularly when he started to tell about meeting the man in the park, the priest. I was Christian myself and it just didn't seem to fit at all – but I didn't say, 'I don't believe you,'" Simon Khattar recalled.

He didn't have to. Not long into that first interview, Junior Marshall had the feeling his lawyer didn't believe the story he was telling him, increasing the anguish that was to characterize his first month in county jail. He had long since learned from his own experience and that of fellow Micmacs who had been in trouble that as far as the police and lawyers were concerned, the less an Indian said the better; you dealt with what you were arrested for and nothing else. He had been charged with murder and he had answered that charge truthfully: he was innocent. To admit to anything else would only make matters worse.

Although he knew several inmates from his previous four-month stint, he couldn't get used to "doing time". Luckily, his cousin, Al Monday, the eldest of the extended Marshall clan, was in jail on liquor charges. Monday could see that his younger cousin was distraught and asked guards to let him into Marshall's cell so the two could talk. The guards agreed.

It made Junior feel better simply to tell someone who would believe him that he'd been "railroaded some way". Monday advised him to take it easy, a tall order when Marshall had been hearing rumors that a gang of blacks was planning to rush the jail and burn him alive. But by the time the cell door clanged shut behind his cousin, the prisoner was feeling a little better.

"I kept saying to myself, 'I'll be out Monday or Friday or whenever it is the court will set me free.' I wasn't expecting to spend the rest of my life in a goddam prison."

On the Monday after Junior Marshall was arrested, Sgt./Det.

MacIntyre received a photostat copy of the haematology report he had requested from the pathologist at the Sydney City Hospital. The report confirmed that Sandy Seale's blood was group O Rh-positive. The day after the boy was buried, Detective MacDonald had collected the clothes Sandy had been wearing on the night of the murder from Leotha Seale: a brown corduroy coat and a pair of bluejeans with sixty-five cents in the pockets.

Detective Michael MacDonald then called Roy Gould on Membertou and asked him to bring the yellow jacket Marshall had been wearing on the night of the murder to the police station. Gould retrieved the coat from Donald Marshall, Sr., and turned it over to the detective. Sgt./Det. MacIntyre proceeded to take a statement from Gould, who told him that Junior had borrowed the jacket on the afternoon of May 28 when the two had been in Bedford. Gould confirmed that the jacket had been in good condition when he lent it to Junior, bloodstained and torn when he got it back.

The police now had four exhibits: Marshall's yellow jacket, Seale's brown jacket, his jeans, and the Kleenex Constable John Mullowney had found near the scene of the stabbing. Each exhibit was bloodstained and the implication for the investigation was obvious, as the detectives' notes made clear.

"Blood on kleenex. What type? Does it compare to exhibit on Jr. Marshall's jacket or deceased's coat? Blood on jacket sleeve or front of Donald Marshall's jacket, does it compare with Seale's jacket?"

If, in fact, the blood on Marshall's jacket matched the blood on the jacket of the deceased (*and* the young Micmac did not himself have group O blood), the prosecution's case would be greatly strengthened. Marshall would then have to explain how Seale's blood had gotten on his clothing in light of his statement to police that he had fled the scene without touching his friend after the grey-haired man had stabbed the two boys. But if there was no match, the four exhibits would become bloodstained irrelevancies.

Sgt./Det. MacIntyre turned the exhibits over to Detective Michael MacDonald, who delivered them to the RCMP crime laboratory in Sackville, New Brunswick. If police were looking for the results of that examination to supply damning physical evidence to support the "eyewitness" accounts they had obtained from John Pratico and Maynard Chant, they were to be sorely disappointed.

There was insufficient blood on the yellow jacket Marshall had been wearing to establish his blood type.

Despite that, the torn and bloodstained jacket continued to play a very important part in Sgt./Det. MacIntyre's unshaken theory that the young Micmac was in fact Sandy Seale's killer. From past experience with Marshall, he already believed that the "frisky" Indian was capable of murder. The lack of blood on the yellow jacket led him to doubt that someone else had inflicted the wound on Junior's left forearm. The policeman was also suspicious of what appeared to be fresh cuts on the jacket, particularly around the left cuff. Had Marshall made them trying to inflict a superficial stab wound to his own left forearm to back up his story that the two boys had been attacked by someone else?

Without ever asking the accused where the fresh cuts had come from, MacIntyre instead took his theory to the doctor who had stitched Marshall's arm on the night of the stabbing. He told Dr. Mohan S. Virick that he couldn't understand why Marshall's ten-stitch cut wasn't any deeper at one end, or in the middle, than at the other end. If the boy had in fact been stabbed by someone else, wasn't it more reasonable to assume that the cut would be deeper at the point of entry than at the exit point? Clearly disregarding the possibility of a slash rather than a stab wound, the detective asked Dr. Virick if the wound on Marshall's left forearm could have been self-inflicted. "He kind of agreed with that," the policeman later remembered of his visit to the Sydney doctor.

Before leaving, Sgt./Det. MacIntyre mentioned that there hadn't been enough blood on the accused's jacket to get a blood type and said that he was still very anxious to find out Marshall's blood group. He asked Dr. Virick if he could help. The doctor promised to try and get him a blood sample when he took out Marshall's stitches. But when the doctor appeared at the county jail, he discovered that the prisoner had already removed the stitches, which by that time had begun to dissolve on their own anyway. Marshall had also removed his bandage and flushed it down the toilet.

When John MacIntyre learned what had happened, he concluded that the young Micmac's actions were not those of an innocent man.

In the days and weeks following Marshall's arrest, the police investigation continued. Statements were taken from nine more people, beginning with Roy Gould on June 7 and ending with Rudy Poirier on July 2, just three days before Junior Marshall's preliminary trial. For the most part, the detectives added nothing to the case against the young Micmac.

Marvel Mattson, the ex-RCMP officer who had called Sydney police on the night of the murder, recounted how he had overheard two boys, Junior Marshall and Maynard Chant, talking about a stabbing on his front lawn. Brian Doucette described how two boys, Junior Marshall and Robert MacKay, had knocked on his door shortly after the stabbing asking to use his telephone to call an ambulance. He said one of the boys had shown him a cut on his arm, which Doucette remembered wasn't bleeding.

Sgt./Det. MacIntyre also interviewed the O'Reilley sisters, Catherine and Mary, who had been in the car in Moose Tobin's backyard on the night of the murder, along with several other teenagers including Junior Marshall.

Catherine O'Reilley told the detective that Junior had said that the killer was a grey-haired old man.

"Did you ever see Jr. Marshall with a knife?" Sgt./Det. MacIntyre asked the sixteen-year-old.

"Yes, last year down the park."

"Was it a large one?"

"About five-and-a-half-inch blade," she replied.

"What was he doing with it?"

"Sticking it in the trees," the girl answered.

Fourteen-year-old Mary O'Reilley added that on the day after the murder, Junior had called the sisters and told them that he and Seale had been stabbed by an old man with grey hair in Wentworth Park.

After a fruitless interview with Barbara Vigneau, a teenager who had been at the St. Joseph's dance but saw neither Seale nor Marshall that night, Sgt./Det. MacIntyre took a statement from Rudy Poirier. He had been one of the boys sitting on John Pratico's porch when Junior Marshall passed by on the morning of Sunday, May 30, returning home from the police station. Poirier, who had once been encouraged by MacIntyre to apply for a job with the Sydney police, now told the detective that Junior had told the boys on the steps of 201 Bentinck Street what was getting to be a very familiar story: that an old man with grey hair had stabbed him and Seale.

Unimpressed with Junior Marshall's story as he had told it to half a dozen different people, MacIntyre began to suspect that the young Indian was trying to make sure that everyone the police might interview would repeat the tale about the grey-haired old man stabbing the two boys. He became more convinced than ever that he had Sandy Seale's killer.

But after a two-and-a-half-week investigation, Sgt./Det. MacIntyre had been unable to find the murder weapon or any other physical evidence pointing to Marshall's guilt. In fact, the young Indian had been extremely consistent in his description of the killer, as the detective's interviews with a number of teenagers made clear. The police also had an independent description of two men from George and Roderick McNeil that closely matched the description of the killer that Marshall had given Sgt./Det. MacIntyre. The Crown's entire case continued to rest on the "eyewitness" accounts of the Seale murder that MacIntyre had obtained from John Pratico and Maynard Chant.

But early on the morning of June 18 the police managed to find a third witness whose false evidence would closely connect Junior Marshall to the crime.

When Patricia Harriss was taken to the Sydney police station on the evening of June 17, she wondered if the police would ever leave her alone. The fourteen-year-old had already talked to Detective Michael MacDonald on two occasions, both times telling him the same story.

On the night of the stabbing, Harriss said, she and her companion, Terry Gushue, had been at the St. Joseph's dance until Gushue had been thrown out for fighting. Afterwards, they had walked to Wentworth Park, where they met Bobbie Patterson. Harriss and Gushue smoked a cigarette on the park bench and watched Patterson, who was drunk, throw up on the grass. They then walked behind the band shell up to Crescent Street and started towards Kings Road, where Harriss lived. While on Crescent Street, they had met Junior Marshall and asked him for a light.

Junior and the twenty-year-old Gushue "didn't click". The two belonged to rival gangs and Junior had recently "flattened" Terry at a dance. One of Junior's cardinal rules was, "Don't ever be kissing your enemy's ass, 'cause you'll always be kissing it then." He didn't speak to Gushue. But he knew Patricia from the dances and held her hand briefly while Terry lit his cigarette.

While they chatted, Patricia Harriss noticed two men on Crescent Street whom she took to be companions of Junior's. The shorter of the two had grey hair and wore an unusual long coat. She asked him who they were and Junior told her they had asked him for cigarettes and were "crazy". One of them, the short man with greyish-white hair, made an impression on the young girl because of his bizarre appearance.

After the brief encounter, Harriss and Gushue continued up Crescent Street towards Kings Road. That was all she knew.

Now, at 8:15 p.m., she began for the third time to tell police what she knew of the events of Friday, May 28, only this time in statement form. Detective William Urquhart conducted what was to be the first of two interviews with Harriss before Sgt./Det. MacIntyre arrived and took over.

"On the night of the dance at St. Joseph's, May 28th, 1971, my boyfriend Terry Gushue, 2 Tulip Terrace, left the dance at 11:45 p.m. We sat on a bench near the bandstand. We sat on a bench. Robert Patterson was on the grass sick, throwing up. We smoked a cigarette. Terry and I left, walked back of the bandshell on to Crescent Street in front of the big green building. We saw and talked to Junior Marshall. With Marshall was two other men."

"Describe the other men to me," Detective Urquhart said.

"One man was short with a long coat. Grey or white hair, with a long coat. I was talking to Junior. Terry got a match from Junior and Junior said, 'They are crazy.' They were asking him, Junior, for a cigarette."

For the second time since George and Roderick McNeil had voluntarily come into the police station to give statements describing two men they had seen in Wentworth Park shortly before Sandy Seale was stabbed, a witness appeared to be describing the same men Marshall had told police had done the stabbing. The detective then asked a crucial question.

"Did you see Sandy Seale in the park?"

"No," Harriss answered.

"Was there anyone else in the park?"

"Yes, boys and girls walking through the park. Gussie Dobbin and Kenny Barrow, they left while we were still on the bench."

Detective Urquhart wrote up Harriss's statement, but before she could sign it, John MacIntyre arrived and the interrogation began afresh. Before the evening was through, the unaccompanied girl would sign her name to a very different version of events than she had related to Urquhart.

At 11:40 p.m. on the same night, with Patricia Harriss waiting in another room after giving her first statement, her companion on the night of Friday, May 28, was questioned by Sgt./Det. John MacIntyre. Terry Gushue, who admitted quaffing two quarts of beer and some wine on the night in question, told police that he and Harriss had run into Junior Marshall on Crescent Street.

"I remember seeing Donald Marshall, Jr., on Crescent Street with another man," Gushue said.

"Did you speak to Junior Marshall?" MacIntyre asked.

"Yes," Gushue answered, "I asked him for a match."

"Did you receive it?"

"Yes."

"Did you know the other man?" the detective asked.

"No."

"Did you know Sandy Seale, the deceased?"

"No," Gushue replied.

If the purpose of the detective's line of questioning was to establish that the other man Gushue had seen with Marshall was Sandy Seale, the next question was an obvious one: was the other youth black? But Sgt./Det. MacIntyre never asked it.

At 12:25 a.m., Patricia Harriss was questioned again by Sgt./Det. MacIntyre, because he was troubled by a contradiction between her first statement to Detective Urquhart and the statement Terry Gushue had just given him. "I couldn't have two different statements and be satisfied with it," John MacIntyre would later say of his decision to re-interview Harriss. If that was a statement of investigative principle, he had so far neglected to follow it in the conflicting statements of Pratico and Chant, which identified Junior Marshall as Sandy Seale's killer.

Harriss had claimed to have seen two men with Junior Marshall on Crescent Street, while Gushue, who was admittedly drunk, recalled seeing only one other person with him. Interestingly, Gushue was never confronted with this supposedly important discrepancy between the two statements, even though Harriss had given police a much more detailed statement and had not been drinking on the night in question.

During the interrogation, Harriss felt that the police were telling her what she should have seen, banging their fists on the table when they were unhappy with what she told them, and changing her statements repeatedly. Finally she, like John Pratico and Maynard Chant, signed a second, and false, statement. Both police officers would later swear that they at no time pressured Harriss into implicating Junior Marshall in the Seale murder.

"On May 28, 1971, I went to St. Joseph's Dance Hall. I met Terry Gushue there. We danced for a while and then a fight started. Terry got mixed up in it and he was asked to leave. So I went with him. I got mad at him for drinking and fighting. We went to the Park and sat on a bench and started arguing. Robert Patterson came to the Park with us. After a while, we crossed the park back of the bandshell. Then we went up to Crescent Street and by the green apartment building, we met Junior Marshall. Terry got a match of[f] him."

"Was there anybody with Junior Marshall?" Sgt./Det. MacIntyre asked.

"Yes."

"Who was it?"

A battle raged within Harriss as she remembered what the detectives had told her she should have seen and what she had actually observed. Wishing desperately that her mother were present, and wanting nothing more than to get out of the police station where she had been held for more than five hours, the young teenager changed her story dramatically. "He had a dark jacket on."

Instead of asking who the person was, MacIntyre supplied a name.

"Was it Sandy Seale? Do you know him?"

"Yes, I know Sandy and it looked like him."

"Did he speak to you?"

"No."

"Did Junior Marshall say anything else?"

"He was drinking," Harriss said.

"How was he dressed?"

"He had a light jacket on."

"Were they standing or walking when you met them?"

"Standing facing one another, but when we came closer, they sort of parted and Sandy Seale moved back. We talked to Junior, got a match, and left for home."

"Did you see anybody else in the area?" MacIntyre asked.

"No. Not on Crescent Street."

John MacIntyre couldn't have missed the importance of this statement to his case. He now had a witness who placed Marshall and Seale alone together at the scene of the murder, even though five hours earlier the same witness had flatly denied having seen Seale in the park and placed Marshall on Crescent Street with two other men, one of them grey-haired and wearing a long coat.

"Did you notice anybody on the railway tracks?"

"No."

"Where did you learn about the stabbing?"

"My mother told me."

"Did you see any weapons on either Junior Marshall or Sandy Seale?"

"No."

"How were they facing?"

"Sandy was facing the houses and Junior Marshall was facing the park."

"What time would this be?"

"I would say about 12 p.m.," the girl answered.

Patricia Harriss's second statement was promptly written up, and at 1:20 a.m., with no one in attendance but the two detectives, the fourteen-year-old girl signed it.

But unlike Pratico and Chant, Patricia Harriss couldn't live with the lies she felt had been put in her mouth by the detectives. She told her mother that she had been pressured into signing a statement that wasn't true. A week later Eunice Harriss and her daughter were in the offices of Alfred Gunn, one of Sydney's finest lawyers, asking what could be done about the situation.

Explaining to them that a police statement wasn't sworn testimony, he offered simple advice: go to court and tell the truth. Unfortunately for Junior Marshall, Patricia Harriss wasn't quite up to the task. Though she did repudiate major portions of her false statement from the witness-box, she never repeated the true story, the one she had tried to tell Detective Urquhart, about seeing the grey-haired old man in the long coat, a second man, and Junior Marshall on Crescent Street on the night of the murder.

As she would later tell the RCMP, "There were other men on Crescent Street in this area, two or three. I did not say this in court but I did say this at the police station. I felt that I was obligated to stick with the statement the police were happy with."

Despite the fact that Donald C. MacNeil planned to call twenty witnesses to testify on behalf of the Crown at Junior Marshall's preliminary hearing, John Pratico and Maynard Chant were the only ones who could directly link Junior to the murder of Sandy Seale. The serious discrepancies in their accounts of the crime left the case for the prosecution in a very precarious position.

In their June 4 statements, both Pratico and Chant claimed to have been standing on the same stretch of railway track when they saw Marshall stab Sandy Seale. But John Pratico also told police there wasn't a soul around as he stood there and witnessed the murder. Inexplicably, the police had gone on to arrest Marshall anyway. But since Maynard Chant was supposed to be standing on the tracks too, the Crown's case had a fatal flaw, unless one of the youths changed his June 4 statement with respect to the vantage point from which he had allegedly witnessed the murder.

The weeks following the arrest of Junior Marshall were tumultuous ones for John Pratico. After the Tom Christmas incident, the police had closely watched the house on 201 Bentinck Street, but Pratico never really felt safe from Micmacs like Donald Joe, who had taken him to Stephen's lumberyard on the night of May 28 and who knew he could not have witnessed the murder. When the pressure or the guilt became too great, Pratico would try to lose himself in his psychiatric medication or in solitary drinking bouts. Occasionally these furtive binges emboldened him to the point where he would show himself around town, as on the night he went to the circus and ran into Arty Paul.

Just as he had done when confronted by Tom Christmas, Pratico told the man who was generally regarded as the toughest member of the Shipyard Gang that he had been pressured by the police into identifying Junior Marshall as Seale's killer. Paul told Pratico to go back to the police and tell them the truth, that he hadn't seen anything. Pratico found it an attractive idea until he was on his own again and began to form the notion that the Indians were "after him". They had to be, or why would the police be watching his house? When these moods came over him, he would hide in his mother's house or report to police and ask to be locked up for his own protection. John Pratico had suddenly become a very impor-tant person.

Before the preliminary hearing, the police paid a crucial visit to Pratico, taking him to Wentworth Park. By the time he left, he had identified a new location as the place he had been standing while witnessing the stabbing, a location that was consistent with the June 4 statement of Maynard Chant, and would relieve the Crown prosecutor of having to explain why his star witnesses hadn't bumped into each other that night on the railway tracks.

Like John Pratico, Maynard Chant also received a tour of Went-worth Park before Marshall's preliminary hearing courtesy of the Sydney city police. The purpose of the jaunt was to pinpoint where he had been standing on the night of the murder. "I said, well, I was standing there, and they said, 'You couldn't have been standing there because you wouldn't have seen anything.' I don't know if they were trying to help me or they were just trying to make a story."

Chant could be excused for wondering the same thing about Donald C. MacNeil on the day before the preliminary hearing, when he and Pratico were put through their paces by the Crown prosecutor to make sure, as Chant put it, the witnesses "got it right".

"I remember Pratico didn't get it right, he had to go over it before and show him basically what arm it was and that. At that time what Pratico would guess, I'd guess different. That's the only way I knew what was happening, you know, really," Chant recalled.

John Pratico's recollections of the session with the Crown prose-cutor, whom he feared, mirrored Chant's. "Well, all he said to me was, 'You got your story straight?'. . . 'You watch you give 'em the same story in the courtroom, you give it to the jury and the judge, and the judge or whatever.' But he said, 'You know the story. Now tell the story the way it was told to us,' type thing."

The two boys got their chance on July 5, when for the first time in

just over a month they saw Junior Marshall again and he, in baffled
disbelief, finally met his accusers.

⑨/Dry Run

 Sydney's law courts are housed in a two-storey concrete building with imposing plate-glass windows in its central foyer that provide a view of Crescent Street and, beyond it, the largest of Wentworth Park's duck ponds.

To the knot of onlookers gathered on the courthouse steps on the morning of July 5, it must have seemed impossible that Sandy Seale had been killed on the same street, less than a block and a half away from where they were standing. In the brilliant sunshine of a perfect summer's morning, with ducks swimming on the pond in front of the courthouse and old men dozing on paint-cracked park benches by the water's edge, Wentworth Park seemed to be a neighborhood suited to killing nothing more than time.

Although it was unusual for preliminary hearings to attract much public attention, the courtroom had filled up early, partly because the sensational case, dealing with Sydney's first murder in five years, featured the city's best lawyers and keenest legal rivals: Donald C. MacNeil for the prosecution; Simon Khattar and Moe Rosenblum for the defence.

In 1971, Donald MacNeil was at the height of his considerable powers as a Crown prosecutor. Although the 41-year-old Sydney native started his career as a corporate lawyer in his father's law firm, he was bored by the work and sought out more exciting fields. Entering politics in the mid-fifties, he was elected to four consecutive terms as a Conservative Member of the Legislative Assembly from Sydney before accepting the Crown prosecutor's job in the late sixties.

A tall, portly man with a booming voice, MacNeil was a very effective prosecutor, though less for his knowledge of the criminal law, which he often augmented with scholarly blarney, than for his formidable courtroom manner. He had a habit of moving in on a witness and staring him or her straight in the eye when he wasn't satisfied with an answer. And if he got caught up in a cause or suspected someone was guilty of a wrongdoing, he could, as one relative put it, be "a dog with a bone".

His brother, Ian MacNeil, who covered the Sydney courts for thirty-five years as a journalist, was one person who knew how intimidating the Crown prosecutor could be. "I know most of the police who have worked with him here and they didn't like being questioned by Donny because he was so detailed and so adamant he struck fear in many of the witnesses."

Simon Khattar and Moe Rosenblum were both in their sixties and already had long, distinguished careers in the criminal law behind them when they faced Donald MacNeil in the Marshall murder case. A razor-thin five-foot-five, Moe Rosenblum didn't seem to possess the commanding presence normally associated with a successful courtroom performer. But the peppery Jewish lawyer with a taste for natty clothes possessed an arsenal of skills that his opponents, including Crown prosecutor MacNeil, had come to respect. Although he was known as a keen cross-examiner who could think on his feet, Rosenblum's strong suit was working with juries. His powerful summations had often kindled the spark of doubt that resulted in acquittal for his clients in cases that were otherwise in the balance.

Less colorful than Rosenblum, and even smaller at five-foot-four, Simon Khattar had built his reputation on an exhaustive knowledge of the law and a plodding attention to detail. He was known as a man who excelled at picking holes in the cases, and occasionally the personalities, of his adversaries. When he found a sore spot, the diminutive man with the cinnamon-brown eyes wasn't afraid to use it, as Donald MacNeil was soon to find out.

Aware of the enormous media interest in the case, and anxious to protect the rights of the accused, presiding provincial court judge John F. MacDonald, who had denied Junior Marshall bail on June 14, imposed a publication ban on the proceedings. But there was no banning the curiosity of the crowd that had come an hour before the hearing to catch a glimpse of the young Micmac as he was led into the law courts by three Sydney policemen. The crowd watched in silence as the tall youth with long black hair walked past them with his head down, passing through the large glass doors before finally disappearing from sight as the party climbed the stairs to the courtrooms on the second floor.

Junior Marshall's preliminary hearing began at 10 a.m. sharp. Crown prosecutor MacNeil called twenty witnesses, fourteen of them on the first day of the hearing, and the remaining six on July 28, when the exhibits that Detective Michael MacDonald had taken to the RCMP crime laboratory at Sackville, New Brunswick, had been returned by forensic specialists.

For the most part, Marshall's lawyers used the preliminary hearing to find out how MacNeil intended to prosecute their client. Of the fourteen witnesses called on July 5, they cross-examined only four: Carl MacDonald, Sydney's land surveyor, who provided the court with a detailed plan of Wentworth Park; Brian Doucette, whom Junior Marshall had asked to call an ambulance on the night of the murder; Terry Gushue; and Patricia Harriss.

Counsel for the defence called no witnesses on behalf of their client, who sat silently in the prisoner's box. Nor did they choose to cross-examine the Crown's star witnesses, John Pratico and Maynard Chant, after they had given their testimony. "Some lawyers take the view not to give too much indication at the preliminary as to what your defence may be. And there are others who go through an exhaustive cross-examination. We took a middle road on that one," Simon Khattar recalled. "We didn't know what we would have for the defence. We just pressed questions and clarified points. That's all we had to do there – that's all we did do."

As a harbinger of things to come at Marshall's Supreme Court trial in November, Patricia Harriss almost totally repudiated the statement she had given to Sgt./Det. MacIntyre on June 18. The part of it she maintained, though, was immensely harmful to the young Micmac's cause. "Now, as you walked along Crescent Street that night, did you and Mr. Gushue see anyone?" prosecutor MacNeil asked.

"Yes."

"Who?"

"Junior Marshall," the grade seven student replied.

"Donald Marshall, Junior, the accused in this case?" MacNeil continued.

"Yes."

"And where was he standing?"

"By the green apartment building on Crescent Street."

Seale had been stabbed on the other side of Crescent, directly in front of the apartments.

"Was there anybody with him?" the prosecutor asked.

"Yes, I think so," Harriss began, hastily adding an equivocation, "I am not sure."

Exasperated by the weak testimony of the same girl who just three weeks earlier had signed her name to a statement saying she had seen Marshall and Seale alone together at the murder scene, prosecutor MacNeil tried to salvage something that could back up what his eyewitnesses would later tell the court.

"Did you see another person there with Donald Marshall?"

"Well, there was somebody there," the fourteen-year-old answered, still trying hard to avoid a lie and the stint in the detention home that MacNeil had previously warned her perjurors received. "I didn't pay any attention."

The prosecutor pressed her relentlessly. "Was there more than one person with him?"

"No," she answered.

It would be the only part of her testimony in direct conflict with her unsigned June 17 statement to Detective Urquhart, in which she had described two other men with Marshall, one of them old with grey hair and wearing a long coat.

The impact of this small lie would be devastating. Instead of telling the court a story that would closely corroborate Junior Marshall's description of the two men he and Seale had met in the park that night, one of whom had stabbed Seale, Harriss told a story that seemingly backed up Pratico and Chant. Sensing the importance of Patricia Harriss to the prosecution's case, as well as her uneasiness with the story she was telling, Moe Rosenblum conducted his most effective cross-examination of the preliminary hearing.

"You can't be sure there was anyone with Donald Marshall at the time?" he began.

"There was somebody there but I didn't pay any attention,"

Harriss answered.

"You don't know if he was with Donald Marshall or not?"

"No, I don't know."

"You mean there was a person near?"

"Yes," the witness replied.

"And that other person, was that a man or a woman, a boy or a girl, or do you know?" Rosenblum continued.

"I don't know," Harriss answered.

"Whoever he was, whatever sex that person was, nobody had any conversation with that other person in your presence?"

"No."

With this line of questioning, the more flamboyant of Junior Marshall's lawyers had reduced the impact of Patricia Harriss's testimony considerably. Still sensing there was something amiss with the witness, he turned his attention to another matter: how the police had gotten her information from her. Without knowing it, Rosenblum came ever so close to finding out that Patricia Harriss had in fact told police another, and quite different, story before she ultimately signed the June 18 statement.

"The information you have given us here this morning, by questions from Mr. MacNeil, to whom did you first give it?" he asked.

"Three city detectives."

"To whom did you first tell that evidence about having met Donald Marshall, Junior?"

"I don't know his name," Harriss replied.

"Was it a police officer?"

"Detective."

Rosenblum turned with a flourish to the prisoner's box. "Sergeant MacIntyre here sitting beside Donald Marshall?"

"He wasn't the first," the witness said.

"He wasn't the first. Was it Sergeant MacDonald, sitting in the corner?"

"Yes."

"He was the first one you told it to?"

"Yes."

"Now, did you go to him or did he come to you?" Rosenblum continued.

"He called my mother up and told me to go down to the police station," Harriss answered, feeling as though she would never be allowed to leave the stand.

"How many times did you talk to him, Sergeant Michael R. MacDonald?"

"About two times."

"Who was the next person you talked to?" Patricia Harriss was thinking about the partial statement she had given to Detective Urquhart, but before she could decide whether to tell the court about that interview, Moe Rosenblum provided an answer to his own question. "...Sergeant MacIntyre?"

"Yes," she answered.

"How many times have you spoken to him about this evidence you are giving today?" The implication of Rosenblum's question was obvious: Harriss's version of events had in fact been the product of several sessions spent with the police rather than an independent recollection of the events of May 28.

"Twice," the girl answered.

"When was the last time?"

"Last Tuesday."

"And I suppose you signed a statement?"

"Yes."

"Was that on the first occasion you spoke to Sergeant MacDonald or the second occasion?"

"The second time with Mr. MacIntyre."

Moe Rosenblum let the impact of her answer, the fact that she had spoken to police on four different occasions before signing a statement, sink in before asking his next question. "The second interview with Sergeant MacIntyre you gave a written statement?"

"Yes."

The defence counsel proceeded to ask his most crucial question, designed to establish that Harriss's testimony had been colored during the process of several police interrogations. "Were you asked to give a written statement before that?"

"I don't think so," Harriss replied.

"Were you interviewed in the company of Terry Gushue or separate from him?"

"Separate."

"On all occasions?" Rosenblum continued.

"No, the second time we were together."

"The second time you were together in the presence of Sergeant MacDonald or Sergeant MacIntyre?"

"Both."

"They were both present on the second time?"

"Yes," the witness answered.

Moe Rosenblum should have been in a position to know that at this point Patricia Harriss was becoming confused. According to the statement she signed at 1:20 a.m. on the morning of June 18, Detective William Urquhart, not Detective MacDonald, witnessed what she told Sgt./Det. MacIntyre. But prosecutor MacNeil had not provided the defence with copies of statements taken by the police –a pattern that would be followed with dire consequences for Junior Marshall throughout his court appearances.

Although full disclosure of the Crown's case was not required by Nova Scotia law in 1971, it is considered to be one of the basic ethics of the legal profession. Years later, the assistant Crown prosecutor in the original Marshall trial, Louis Matheson, would say he couldn't imagine Donald MacNeil failing to make statements, including the first, crucial ones of Chant, Pratico, and Harriss, available to the defence. John MacIntyre would also swear that he had given all statements taken by the police during the course of the Seale murder investigation to the Crown prosecutor.

"How long after, do you know what date it was your mother got the telephone call and told you to go down to the police station?"

"I don't know."

"In the month of June?" Rosenblum asked.

"Yes."

"Was there any particular day in June you could attach that first interview with Sergeant MacDonald?"

"I think it was a Thursday."

"Have you any idea of the day or how far advanced in June it was?"

"No."

Rosenblum was now poised to ask what he hoped would be a telling question. "How do you know it was May 28 of this year that you saw Donald Marshall in the park?"

"They told me," the young girl answered. It was exactly the answer the defence lawyer had been looking for.

"Sergeant MacDonald, who is sitting in the courtroom and who has already given evidence today, told you it was on the night of May 28?"

"Yes."

Rosenblum drove the point all the way home. "If he had not told you that, would you have known what night it was?"

"I don't think so."

Without coming right out and saying it, Moe Rosenblum hoped he had demonstrated to the court that Patricia Harriss's testimony was the product of police coaching. After all, if the police had supplied the witness with a fact as obvious as the date of the meeting she had with Marshall, what else might they have suggested?

After implicitly criticizing the tactics of the police in obtaining a statement from Patricia Harriss, one member of the defence team flippantly raised a subject designed to get under the skin of Crown prosecutor Donald MacNeil.

"At the preliminary inquiry I set out to upset MacNeil," Simon Khattar remembered. "And something arose during the examination of one of the witnesses–MacNeil was opposing a submission I made to the court. I made the crack to him, 'Well, you don't care for Indians anyhow.' Well, that started almost a fight in the court."

In fact, as the Micmacs had told Khattar, the Nova Scotia Human Rights Commission had censured MacNeil on January 20, 1970, for remarks he made in open court about lawlessness among Indians and the need to teach them respect for the law. The complaint was lodged by Albert Julian, Band Manager of the Eskasoni reserve in Cape Breton, after MacNeil urged judges "to take drastic action against those persons from Eskasoni who are guilty of violations of the law." The Indian leader was outraged by the prosecutor's outburst.

"This is an outright declaration of discrimination by an officer of the court against a minority," he told a local newspaper reporter. "What hope does anyone have of getting justice when pre-trial prejudice has been openly announced in the news media? Is Eskasoni this man's magic word for guilty?"

The Human Rights Commission dry-cleaned the rhetoric but seconded the sentiment. In citing the Crown prosecutor, the Commission wrote, "MacNeil's statements were inappropriate and

tended to be prejudiced in suggesting discriminatory treatment of
Eskasoni residents before the courts and supporting such treatment in the general community."

Stung by the reference to his discrimination against Indians,
MacNeil refused to speak to Simon Khattar for the rest of the
preliminary hearing, directing his remarks instead to Moe Rosenblum when the necessity arose.

It was now the turn of another fourteen-year-old to take the stand,
but one of considerably more importance to the Crown's case than
Patricia Harriss. Maynard Chant had spent the month dreading the
arrival of this day, though prosecutor MacNeil had done his best to
prepare him for it. Both he and John Pratico had gone over the
details of their stories with MacNeil several times. According to
Chant, when he told MacNeil that he would have trouble getting to
court from Louisbourg,' the Crown prosecutor had arranged for
him to spend the night prior to the preliminary hearing at John
Pratico's house.

"He set the whole thing up for me to stay there. I remember
when we got in, it was coming on dark there and I watched a bit of
TV and just went straight to bed. Both of us slept in the same room
and everything and not a word was uttered. You know, I guess both
of us were ridden with guilt, you know, we were ridden with 'Hey,
man, like I'm really screwed up. I know what I'm doing is wrong.' "

But it was Maynard's fear rather than his conscience that dictated
what the young man did on the first day of Junior Marshall's
preliminary hearing. For the most part, he remembered his lines
quite well, beginning with his answer to MacNeil's question about
what he had seen that night in Wentworth Park as he was walking
along the railway tracks, railway tracks he had, in fact, never
reached on May 28.

"The first thing I noticed was a guy hunched over in the bushes
watching something."

"Did you recognize that man?"

"Not at first but after I did."

"Can you identify him today?"

"Yes."

"Do you know his name today?"

"I don't think I can remember."

"Would you point him out to the court, please." Maynard pointed at John Pratico, who was listening hard to what the other boy was saying and trying desperately to keep his own story straight in his head.

"Is that the man?" the prosecutor continued.

"Yes."

"That is the man you saw behind the bush watching something?"

"Yes."

Considering that Maynard had allegedly been looking at the back of a dark-haired man's head at midnight in a darkened park from a distance of at least thirty-five feet, it was a remarkable identification.

"In which direction was he looking?" MacNeil asked.

"He was looking down that way, he was looking towards the street."

"Do you know the name of the street?"

"I think it was Crescent Street," Maynard answered.

"What did you do?"

Maynard was finding that telling his story was easier than he thought it would be. With MacNeil asking the questions, one thing just followed on another.

"I looked back to see what he was looking at, then I saw two guys talking to one another."

"And do you know who these two guys were?" MacNeil asked.

It was to be Maynard's most awkward moment of the hearing, though it would scarcely compare to his near-disastrous performance on the stand in Marshall's November trial.

"I didn't know Sandy Seale at the time but I didn't recognize Donald Marshall either, until afterwards," he said.

"After what?" MacNeil asked.

"After what happened."

"Tell me, what did you see take place, if anything?"

Maynard had reached the heart of his perjury, the part of his story he knew best. "Well, first, the only thing I saw, I saw them talking and I guess they were using kind of profane language." It was a rather esoteric adjective for a grade six student who had already failed three times. "Donald said something to the other fellow and the other fellow said something back to Donald and I saw Donald haul a knife out of his pocket."

"That's Donald Marshall, Junior, who you see in court here today?" Maynard made no answer. "Would you point him out to the court, please."

It was one of the few occasions when Junior Marshall raised his eyes from the floor and looked squarely at Maynard Chant as the red-headed boy pointed in his direction. Surely, he thought, no one would believe Chant's lies.

"You saw him what?" prosecutor MacNeil continued.

"Haul a knife out of his pocket," Maynard answered.

"What, if anything, did he do with that knife?"

"Drove it into the stomach of the other fellow."

The Crown prosecutor wanted to make sure the judge heard that answer.

"What?" he asked.

"He drove it in the stomach of the other fellow," Maynard repeated, a little more emphatically.

"What did the other fellow do?" the prosecutor asked.

"Well, I just saw him keel over and I ran," Maynard replied. After offering a confusing account of where he ran immediately after the stabbing, Chant proceeded to tell the court that he and Marshall soon met up again on Bentinck Street, with Marshall presumably unaware that Chant had "witnessed" the murder.

"What took place there?" prosecutor MacNeil asked.

"He told me, he said, 'Look what they did to me.'"

"What did he show you?" MacNeil asked.

"He showed me his arm," Maynard replied.

"What did you observe about his arm, if anything?"

"It had a long cut from his wrist up his arm to his elbow."

"And was there any blood from this cut?"

"Not right at that moment, but after a few minutes it started to bleed," Maynard answered.

The implication of MacNeil's last question would become all too obvious before the day's proceedings were done. Without being questioned by counsel for the defence, Maynard Chant stepped down from the witness-box feeling as though he had done a good job, that prosecutor MacNeil was certain to be pleased with him.

Complying with the prosecutor's request, the Crown's other star witness, John Pratico, had listened intently to Maynard Chant's testimony. But he was still all butterflies when his turn came to take the stand. He didn't know if he could remember everything that had been so carefully rehearsed in the Crown prosecutor's office before coming to court and he had no idea what he would do if Marshall's lawyers challenged his story, even though MacNeil had told him to "stick to his guns". It all seemed a little unreal and the boy with the shock of unruly black hair tried to avoid looking at his former friend and one-time protector in the prisoner's dock, an effort that soon proved fruitless.

"Do you know Donald Marshall, Junior?" the prosecutor asked.

"Yes."

"How long have you known him?"

"About a year."

"Do you see him in court today?"

"Yes."

"Will you point him out to the court?"

As John Pratico pointed to Junior Marshall, the accused again had the feeling he was dreaming. Wasn't this the same John Pratico who had asked him who had stabbed Sandy Seale when, he, Junior, had been on his way home from the police station two days after the incident? Wasn't this the same John Pratico who suggested getting a gang together to go looking for Seale's killer, a plan Junior had scotched? He tried to put those questions in his eyes as he watched Pratico, but the boy in the witness-box quickly looked away after pointing unsteadily in Marshall's direction.

"Did you see him in the late hours of the 28 of May, 1971?" the Crown prosecutor asked.

"Yes," Pratico said.

"Where?"

"In Wentworth Park."

"Did you see him before you saw him in Wentworth Park?"

MacNeil was doing his best to steer Pratico back to the story he had told police about meeting Marshall and Seale on George Street and being invited to go down into the park, a story the young man knew to be false.

"I don't recall."

"Whereabouts did you meet him in Wentworth Park?"

"I went up around Crescent Street, I went down Argyle over to Crescent Street."

"Pardon me," the impatient prosecutor interjected, "before you did that, did you see Donald Marshall?"

"I don't remember."

"Did you have any conversation with him?"

"I don't remember," Pratico instinctively answered before the story he was supposed to tell suddenly came back to him. "I believe I seen him up on the street."

"What street?"

"George Street."

Prosecutor MacNeil proceeded to ask a question that betrayed his growing frustration with his witness. After being twice told by Pratico that he didn't remember having any conversation with Marshall, MacNeil prodded the boy's none-too-proficient memory for the third time.

"What was that conversation?" he asked. Pratico finally followed the prosecutor's lead.

"Just talking, then I left him, I had a little bit of talk and then I left him and I went down Argyle Street."

"Did he suggest anything to you?"

"I don't recall, I believe he did, coming down to the park or something like that," Pratico said half-heartedly, on the point of breaking down.

"Are you nervous, Mr. Pratico?" MacNeil asked, deftly assigning a cause to his witness's difficulties that the court might otherwise attribute to a lack of credibility.

"Yes," Pratico answered, relieved at last to be giving an honest answer.

"Would you tell us what happened and what took place?"

"I went down Argyle Street, eh. . ."

Once more prosecutor MacNeil cut off his witness and tried to steer him back to his police statement.

"No, you never got there yet, I am not finished where you met him up on George Street; whereabouts on George Street did you meet him?"

"By the store," Pratico answered.

"What store?"

"I don't know the name of the store."

"Do you know where Argyle Street is?"

"Yes."

"How far away were you from Argyle Street?"

"Five feet, a little more," Pratico said.

"What was that conversation?"

"I believe he said something about coming down to the park or something."

"What did you say?"

"I said no," Pratico replied.

"What did you do?"

"I left and went down Argyle Street, turned up Crescent Street, and I walked up the railway tracks. I went down and went into the bush and started to drink a pint of beer."

Prosecutor MacNeil produced the plan of Wentworth Park prepared by Carl MacDonald, Sydney's land surveyor, and asked the witness to show him the bush behind which he had gone to drink his beer. With a tap of his finger, the boy who had signed two police statements within a week of each other claiming to have seen different assailants from different vantage points stab Sandy Seale changed his location for the third and final time.

The same John Pratico who told police on June 4 that he had been standing on the railway tracks with "nobody–not a soul around" as Sandy Seale crumpled to the ground now pointed to a bush some thirty-five feet below the tracks as the spot from which he had witnessed the murder. The glaring contradiction between the Crown's two eyewitness accounts of the Seale stabbing was finally resolved without the defence knowing it had ever existed.

"...What did you see take place?" prosecutor MacNeil continued.

"I seen Marshall and Seale talking."

"Where were they talking?"

"First, Marshall was on the sidewalk, Donald Marshall was on the sidewalk, and Seale was facing him. They were talking for a while and I could hear mumbling, they were arguing there about something and I seen Marshall haul something from his pocket and stab Seale."

"What happened to Seale when he was stabbed?"

"He dropped."

Interestingly, prosecutor MacNeil neglected to ask two questions that the police had put to John Pratico: where had Marshall stabbed Seale, and in which direction had the Micmac run after the

attack? In his statement to police, Pratico said Marshall stabbed
Seale in the left side and then fled towards Argyle Street. Maynard
Chant, meanwhile, had him plunging the knife into the youth's
right side, and making off in the very opposite direction up
Bentinck Street.

Unfortunately for Junior Marshall, his lawyers weren't in a position to challenge these inconsistencies since they hadn't been
provided with copies of any statements given to police by Chant
and Pratico. Without a single question from counsel for the
defence, a much relieved John Pratico left the stand feeling as
though he had done his best to do what Donald C. MacNeil had
told him to: he'd stuck to his guns.

Junior Marshall's preliminary hearing was reconvened on July 28,
when the Crown called six more witnesses, two of whom left
prosecutor MacNeil relying more heavily than ever on his teenage
witnesses in his quest to have Junior Marshall committed to trial for
murder.

Adolphus Evers, a civilian hair and fibres expert with the RCMP
crime laboratory in Sackville, New Brunswick, testified that he had
examined the brown corduroy jacket worn by Sandy Seale and the
yellow jacket worn by Marshall on the night of the stabbing. He
found one fresh-appearing cut on the front lower left-hand side of
Seale's jacket approximately two and three-quarter inches in
length and another on the back which was roughly one inch long.
Despite the jargon of the crime lab, it was gruesome evidence:
whoever stabbed Sandy Seale had driven the blade in with such
force that the young man had been virtually run through.

When it came to Marshall's jacket, Evers's testimony was ambivalent, even confusing. He told the court that he'd found two separations on the left sleeve of the jacket, one of them a fresh-appearing
cut approximately eight inches in length and the other a fresh-
appearing tear, roughly an inch and a half long, running through
the elasticized cuff of the jacket.

"Tell me, sir, what is the significance in the cut in that sleeve and
the tear in that sleeve?" prosecutor MacNeil asked.

"The cut, the fibres appear straight, that is, like one would,
would see anything that is cut; the torn fibres are jagged and the
fibres are separated more than with a cut."

It was now becoming clear to Moe Rosenblum that the Crown was going to be arguing that the wound on his client's left forearm had been self-inflicted. That was why MacNeil had asked two witnesses on July 5 if they had observed any blood flowing from Marshall's wound and why he would ask two more people the same question on the second day of the preliminary hearing. Rosenblum decided to cross-examine Adolphus Evers.

"The cut that you speak of, would that be consistent with being cut by a knife?" he asked.

"It could be cut by a knife, it could have been cut by scissors, could have been cut by an axe, there is no way of determining what made the cut. The cut was quite irregular, that is, that there was not one straight, long cut."

"Would you say it was cut on two different occasions or could you tell?"

"Could you tell me what you mean by two separate occasions?"

"That the one cut you speak of, the length of it, that it wasn't done at the same time?"

"The cut is indicative of being not one straight, long cut in one continuous stroke, the cut was quite irregular, there were two cuts present, the one cut, which is quite distinct and separate from the longer cut, and because the bottom is torn it is not indicative of one separation at one time. And also there are several superficial cuts near the one long separation; all of these are indicative of being not cut in one continuous stroke," Evers replied.

If the findings of the hair and fibres expert added nothing of a definitive nature to the prosecution's case against Marshall, the testimony of serologist Sandra Mrazek was completely useless to MacNeil. Although the crime-lab specialist found three blood-stains on Marshall's jacket, two on the front left-hand side of the garment and a third on the cuff, she was unable to determine the grouping of the blood.

She did, however, find human blood of group O to be present on the other three exhibits she examined, Seale's jacket and jeans, and the Kleenex found by Constable John Mullowney on the lawn of the house at 130 Crescent Street. But without being able to match the blood on the victim's clothing with the blood on Marshall's jacket, as the Sydney detectives' notes showed they hoped would be possible, the only physical evidence the police had gathered on Junior Marshall was irrelevant to a determination of his guilt.

In his cross-examination of the serologist, Moe Rosenblum brought out another fact that further weakened the force of Miss Mrazek's testimony.

"Would you be able to tell on the date of your examination of these exhibits just approximately how long these bloodstains were on the exhibits in question?"

"No, sir, we are unable to tell the age of a stain."

"Was it a week old?"

"No, sir, we cannot determine that."

"So these bloodstains on all these exhibits that you are talking about could have been present for six months before you saw them?"

"I am sorry, I am unable to determine."

"They could have been?"

"It could be a day, a week, a month."

"A year?"

"Yes," Miss Mrazek answered.

Donald MacNeil's attempt to insinuate that Junior Marshall had slashed his own arm after stabbing Sandy Seale received a further setback from the testimony of Dr. Mohan S. Virick, who had treated the young Micmac at the Sydney City Hospital on the night of the stabbings. MacNeil's sole purpose in putting Dr. Virick on the stand was to get on record that the ten-stitch slash on Marshall's arm was superficial, thus setting the stage for the Crown's theory that he had scratched his own arm to divert suspicion from himself after stabbing Seale.

"And tell me," MacNeil asked, "would you describe that cut to me?"

"It was a laceration on the left arm approximately four and a half inches long."

"Was it an even cut, Doctor, or a jagged cut?"

"It was an even cut."

"Tell me, Doctor, was there any bleeding from this cut?"

"There was no bleeding."

"Now, Doctor..."

"There was no bleeding at the time I saw the patient," Dr. Virick continued; "he was prepared, already, in the Out-Patients to receive the treatment."

"And, Doctor, would you describe this cut by way of depth?"

"Well, it was not a very deep laceration and yet it was not a scratch, it was a superficial laceration."

"A superficial laceration; and what treatment did you administer?"

"I put ten stitches in it."

"Why did you put ten stitches in it?"

"Because of the length of the wound, and there is movement of that arm so much that there is a possibility of gaping of the edges. To be on the safe side we usually suture quite close by so that there is no cosmetic defect."

"But the cut was not deep enough to bring about blood from the arm?"

Prosecutor MacNeil's insinuation that the wound was too trifling to have caused bleeding brought a swift objection from Moe Rosenblum. MacNeil rephrased his question.

"Just what you saw from your own personal knowledge, what you observed, there was no blood coming from the cut?"

"That is right."

"Did you remove those stitches?"

"No, I didn't remove those stitches."

"Isn't it customary, Doctor, for a medical practitioner when he administers stitches to a patient to remove them at a later date?"

"Yes, I made an appointment for the removal of the sutures, I went to visit Donald in the jail; he had already removed the sutures himself."

Well aware that his adversary was trying to suggest that Junior's wound was self-inflicted, Moe Rosenblum decided to cross-examine Dr. Virick.

"Now, I think what you said, Doctor, was that Marshall had already been attended to by some nurse or some doctor in the Out-Patients department before you got him?"

"Yes, it is customary for the nurse to prepare the patient."

"The preparation, perhaps, would include the stopping of any blood that would have emanated from the wound?"

"Usually the only thing the nurse would do was to put pressure on the wound."

"Yes, and that would be to stop the flow of blood?"

"Yes, it is possible."

"And you can't say whether or not there had been blood coming from that wound before you saw it?"

"At the time I saw it, there was no bleeding."

"You can't say that prior to you seeing it there could have been blood emanating from the wound?" the defence counsel persisted.

"I can't say that."

"How long after you put these stitches in on this particular night was it that you called in to the jail to see him and to remove the stitches?"

"I would say it was between twelve to fifteen days."

"Between twelve and fifteen days later, you found that he had already removed them himself? Did the wound heal nicely?"

"Yes."

Moe Rosenblum decided to take a calculated risk. During Mac-Neil's examination of Dr. Virick, the Crown prosecutor had studiously avoided asking the obvious question: in his opinion, was the wound on Junior Marshall's left arm self-inflicted? Was that because MacNeil knew that the doctor's answer to such a direct question would be detrimental to the Crown's theory? There was only one way to find out.

"Doctor, was there anything at all about this wound that would interest you, that it would not be self-inflicted?"

"Yes. My only impression of that is a long wound like that, there would be an element of hesitation, a person couldn't just sit down and make a clean-cut wound, he would have hesitated a moment or two."

"Based on your knowledge at the time, your opinion is that the wound was not self-inflicted?"

"This point is against it," Dr. Virick answered.

"Your opinion is that it was not self-inflicted?"

"Yeah, I would say so."

Prosecutor MacNeil jumped to his feet.

"But it could be?" he asked.

"It could be," the witness allowed.

MacNeil then called Merle Davis, the nurse who had assisted Dr. Virick with Junior Marshall on the night of the stabbing. Once more, the purpose of her testimony was to establish the minor nature of the cut on the boy's arm in order to prepare the way for the Crown's theory that the wound had been self-inflicted.

"Did you examine Mr. Marshall at the time?"

"Yes."

"And what did you find?"

"A laceration on his left forearm."

"How long would it be?"

"Around three inches," she answered, shrinking the wound by an inch and a half from the doctor's testimony, a diminution that went unchallenged by the defence.

"Was it bleeding at the time he entered the hospital?"

"No."

"Did you see any blood coming from it at any time?"

"No."

"How would you describe the cut?"

"Well, it was a laceration, certainly not severe, not very deep."

After a brief cross-examination by Moe Rosenblum, during which Merle Davis made it clear she had not cleaned any blood from Marshall's arm before turning him over to Dr. Virick, the witness stepped down.

The last witness to take the stand was Sgt./Det. John MacIntyre, the chief investigating officer of the Seale slaying and the informant who laid the charge of second-degree murder against Junior Marshall.

After telling the court that he had taken a written statement from the accused on Sunday, May 30, with no one else present, the detective said, in accordance with standard police procedure in such matters, that he had neither threatened the young Micmac nor held out any promise or favor to him. Prosecutor MacNeil then marked Marshall's statement for identification and Sgt./Det. MacIntyre got ready to stand down. But Moe Rosenblum surprised him by launching into what was to be his most concerted, and caustic, cross-examination of the preliminary hearing.

"How did it happen that Marshall got there, Sergeant?" Rosenblum knew that his client had been asked by police to "hang around" the police station on the two days following the murder. He was trying to bring out that Marshall had voluntarily done so, not exactly the action of a guilty man.

"He had been around the station, Mr. Rosenblum, pretty well all day."

"At your request?"

"I mean, I was working on the case and I had him stay around."

"How was he brought to the station, did he come on his own?"

"He was asked to come."

"Did you send a police officer for him?"

"I believe, if my memory serves me right, he was in a car early that morning in the park area, which was Sunday morning. I couldn't say for sure if it was Saturday or Sunday but anyhow, he was asked to stay at the station."

"By who?"

"By me."

"What time would that be?"

"It was pretty well all day; I believe he had dinner at the station."

"So when you say all day, it would be the early morning?"

"Well yes, from the time I went out to work."

"Where was he at the station?"

"I believe he was just around the office. He could be at random as far as I was concerned."

"Was he guarded?"

"Oh no, he wasn't under arrest."

"No, no, I didn't say under arrest, was there a police officer near by him all the time?" Rosenblum asked, trying to emphasize the fact that his client had remained at the station of his own free will.

"Oh no."

"He was free to come and go, is that what you are saying?"

"Yes, just stay around in case that I needed him."

"You told him that?"

"Yes."

"Was that the first time you saw the accused in connection with this case?"

"At that time, yes. I believe I did talk to him on Saturday."

"What day of the week was May 30?"

"This was Sunday, this happened Friday night."

"And you saw him the day previous?"

"I believe."

"Where would that be?"

"At the station."

"How did he get there the day previous?"

"Well, I couldn't say. I likely sent for him."

"How long did he stay at the police station on Saturday, the 29th?"

"He could have been there considerable time, Mr. Rosenblum."

"Such as," the defence counsel continued.

"A matter of hours."

"Can you recall?"

"Well, I mean there was...I have an explanation for it, I can't recall how long he was there, no. I know I was there quite long myself."

"Would you say he was there four or five hours on Saturday?"

"He could have been."

"Where was he?"

"Just hanging around," the beleaguered detective answered.

"And you told him to wait until you were ready to see him?"

"Yes, just stay around, yes."

Sgt./Det. MacIntyre had helped the defence to depict their client in exactly the light that favored their case: a concerned young man anxious to help the police find Seale's killer in any way he could, even if that meant spending hours at the police station in the event the detectives might need him.

"And so when you had a discussion with him on Saturday, was it just the two of you or was there others present? Other police officers?"

"Could have been."

Rosenblum wasn't satisfied with the detective's off-hand reply. "I am asking you," he said.

"Well, I am not...the only time I could say that I was alone..."

"Was when you took the statement?"

"That's right, that's right."

"But I am asking you about the 29th, officer; who would be present when you were talking to him on the 29th, can you recall?"

"I can't just recall."

"And there could have been other police officers talking to him?"

"Oh yes, there could have been."

"Likely there were?"

"Likely."

"You yourself were talking to him on the 29th?"

"I talked to him on more than one occasion."

"For how long?"

"Well, it depended on what I wanted to know."

"How long did you talk to him on Saturday?"

"I couldn't tie that down for you, I couldn't, Mr. Rosenblum; could have been in the morning, could have been in the afternoon, could have been the evening."

"I know it could have been, but you don't remember?"

"No."

"You don't remember?"

"No, to tie the amount of time, I spent considerable time with the accused."

"On the 29th?"

"And on the 30th, talking to him."

"Did you talk to him in the morning of the 29th?"

"I can't recall too much about the 29th, but the 30th, he was at the station all day."

After hectoring Sgt./Det. MacIntyre at even greater length on his inability to remember what he had done with Junior Marshall on the day immediately after the stabbing, Rosenblum changed his tack.

"On the 30th we come to the day you feel you can remember; were you talking to him in the morning?"

"Yes."

"What time would that be in the morning, officer?"

"I would say in the vicinity of ten o'clock."

"Ten o'clock in the morning?"

"Somewhere in that vicinity, probably a little earlier than ten, somewhere between nine and ten."

"How long did you talk to him that morning?"

"Well, in fact, I had a line-up at the police station that morning."

"Well, just answer my question."

"I was talking to several people."

"I don't care about other people, how long were you talking to him in the morning of the 30th?"

"Just a few minutes at any time, but several times, Mr. Rosenblum."

"You say you spoke to him for just a few minutes?"

"Yes."

"How many times would you say you spoke to him in the morning?"

"Probably several."

"Well, what do you mean by several?"

"Well, more than once, more than twice, probably four or five or six times, it depended on what I wanted to know."

"Do you know?"

"No."

"How many times did you talk to him in the afternoon?"

"I couldn't say."

"Could it be five, six, seven, eight. . .?"

"Oh no, it wouldn't be that long, I was out questioning a few people."

"How many times did you talk to him?"

The badgering finally nettled the detective. "I said, Mr. Rosenblum, I couldn't tell you how many times, several, that is all I can tell you."

The defence counsel moved into the last phase of his cross-examination, the statement Sgt./Det. MacIntyre took from Junior Marshall on Sunday afternoon.

"You were alone with him in the room when you were taking the statement?"

"Yes."

"Who was in the other office, Sergeant?"

"There was nobody in the other office."

"Nobody?"

"No, I was alone."

"Nobody in the other office?"

"No."

Rosenblum pressed the detective on the point but to no avail. "How long did the questioning take place on Sunday afternoon when you took the statement?"

"Well, it started at 4:50–I have it here–5:12, twenty-two minutes."

"And that statement was written down by you?"

"That is right."

"And it was later typewritten?"

"Right."

"Did you know Marshall before the 29th of May, officer?"

"I knew him, yes."

"You knew him to see him?"

"Yes."

Counsel for the defence had no more questions and Sgt./Det. MacIntyre left the stand.

Judge MacDonald looked down at the accused in the dock and asked him if he wanted to say anything in answer to the charge. When Junior Marshall made no response, Moe Rosenblum answered on his behalf.

"Nothing to say at present, your Honor."

"Do you wish to call any witnesses?" the judge asked.

"Not at this time, your Honor."

"I will read the charge again: Donald Marshall Jr., you are charged at or near Sydney, in the county of Cape Breton, Nova Scotia, on or about the 28th day of May, 1971, 'that you did murder Sanford William (Sandy) Seale, contrary to Section 206(2) of the Criminal Code of Canada.' I commit you before the Supreme Court and jury for trial."

The proceedings in the hot, windowless courtroom had been incomprehensible to Junior Marshall – an avalanche of white words that had buried the truth, and, along with it, any sense of reality. He later recalled: "All through the preliminary, I kept thinking about a field up on the reserve where we used to play ball – big field, no trees. I thought I'd be up there when all the talking was done. Then the cops came to take me back to jail and I said to myself, 'I won't be playing ball this summer.' I just couldn't figure out why them guys lied."

10/Countdown

During that long, hot summer before his trial in November, Junior Marshall began having a recurring dream. In it, he was asleep in his cell at the county jail when a cascade of cold water suddenly drenched him from head to foot. Except that when he jumped out of bed, still dreaming, his clothes were soaked not with water, but with gasoline. And he wasn't alone. A crowd of black faces jeered at him from his cell door. Then a tall man struck a match, his eyes gleaming yellow by the light of its wavering flame. The prisoner scrambled to the far corner of his cell but to no avail; the gasoline glistened everywhere. The man flipped the match into the cell, instantly sending up a wall of fire that obscured Junior's fantastic tormentors as it roared towards him. He could hear their disembodied hoots of delight as the flames licked at him, engulfing his body in a white-hot shock of pain that jolted him from sleep and left him trembling in his empty cell.

On one occasion the terror didn't subside when he broke the surface of the dream. Sitting bolt upright on his cot, his clothes drenched with sweat, he heard people running down the corridor outside his cell, their muffled shouts echoing off the concrete walls. As the shouts grew louder, he was convinced the Blacks were coming for him, as he had heard that they would through the prison grapevine. He fumbled in his mattress for the paring knife he'd taken from the kitchen, preparing to make what he thought would be his last stand.

"I was sure they were coming in to get me until I heard someone say, 'Open that goddam door, we want out of this place,'" he recalled.

It was a jail-break, and the people doing the shouting were the Warren brothers, convicted murderers who had once been suspects in the Seto slaying, though there had never been enough evidence to lay a charge against them. The pair had taken a hostage and were trying to negotiate their way to freedom, but from what Junior Marshall could hear, the authorities weren't in a mood to make deals. "You know where the door is," someone shouted, "why don't you go for it!"

"They probably got guns out there just waiting for us," Junior heard one of the convicts say, a theory that received gruff confirmation from a taunting voice on the other side of the door.

"Yeah, that's what we got all right. Gonna blow you right the fuck off this earth."

Dismayed by the prospect of such unlovely celestial deliverance, the Warrens thought better of their escape plans. They released their hostage and surrendered. Junior Marshall stretched out on his cot, savoring the wave of relief that washed over him as the convicts and the phantoms alike vacated the corridors outside his cell and the jail fell silent.

As the weeks dragged on, Junior found himself adjusting to the deadening routine of life behind bars. He got up, slopped out his cell, ate his meals, and went to bed according to an unvarying schedule that at first stretched out, and then blotted out, time. The medication that he'd been given for his frayed nerves during the preliminary hearing, and that he was still receiving, also helped.

But there was one thing he couldn't get used to: the incessant questions from other inmates about what had landed him in jail. At first he simply refused to answer them. A macabre joke began to circulate. The young Micmac was in for "killing seals out of season". Sick of trying to explain what had happened, he went along with his inquisitors as the handiest way of dropping the subject. "I joked along with them. I'd say I was in for killing seals out of season, like they said. It come to a point where I got so fucking tired of being questioned about it I said, 'Yeah, okay, I did it, so shut up, fuck off, leave me alone.' "

If the tactic bought Junior Marshall momentary peace of mind, it was purchased at a heavy, and unforeseen, price. While visiting a friend in the county jail, Maynard Chant was told that Junior had admitted to other inmates that he'd stabbed Sandy Seale. Even though he hadn't seen Junior murder Seale, this piece of news assuaged Maynard's conscience and made it easier to live with the lies he had told.

The monotony of life inside was broken by a variety of visits, including two from Sgt./Det. John MacIntyre. "MacIntyre kept saying, 'You plead manslaughter if you did it in self-defence,' that's what he told me. I just kept walking out on him, twice, and he never came back."

The visits from family and friends were more welcome, though sometimes just as depressing. For one thing, he learned that his father's plastering business had collapsed. There had been so many crank phone calls since Junior's arrest that Donald Marshall, Sr., got an unlisted telephone number. Since most of his jobs were con-tracted over the telephone, and he had no office, his work began to dry up.

Although his father didn't come out and say it, Junior knew that the family was suffering terribly on his account. Donald Marshall, Sr., was first and foremost the Grand Chief of the Micmac Nation and Junior's situation made it more difficult for him to go about his official duties. Caroline Marshall faced a different kind of pain. One day after Junior's arrest, a neighbor appeared at the Marshall home and silently removed her five-year-old daughter who had been playing with the Marshall children.

There was little Junior could do about his family's pain until the case came to court. So for the time being he told his parents the only thing he could to ease their suffering: he wasn't Sandy Seale's killer. Intended to give comfort, his words always seemed to make his father look strangely older and his mother cry.

For the most part, the time in county jail passed without inci-dent. Junior received his share of privileges, including regular food baskets from a girlfriend, Barbara Vigneau, and his keepers often let him out of his cell to join in whatever recreation his fellow prisoners, many of them from Membertou, could improvise. He wrestled with his cousins, as he had while doing time on the liquor offences, and took part in floor-hockey games played with mops and a tied-up roll of toilet paper.

He liked to be tired when he hit his mattress at night. If he wasn't, he would lie awake for hours wondering about what was happening up on the reserve or thinking about his girlfriend, Barbara. She looked so pretty in her summer dress.

One day he and some other inmates were rough-housing while they mopped the jail floor and someone complained to a guard. Caught throwing a bucket of water at another inmate, Junior was taken to "the bird-cage", a six-by-six steel cell whose occupant had to sleep propped in a corner, since there wasn't a bed. After spending a few days there, he was allowed to return to the general population, but not before he cleaned the bird-cage. Before he finished, he saw the inmate he suspected had informed to the guards about the water fight. No one hated a rat more than Junior Marshall.

"You're next," he said to the man from the window of the bird-cage, then returned to his own cell. Shortly afterwards, three guards showed up, one of them carrying a truncheon. Two other inmates, Jimmy McDonald and Sylvester Paul, were with Junior. The guards told them to leave. "Why?" Sylvester Paul asked, certain his young friend was in for a beating.

"Because this wise-ass is going back in the bird-cage until he learns not to threaten people. Now you two get downstairs," one of the guards said.

"I'm not movin' nowhere unless he comes with me," Paul said. McDonald, too, stood his ground. The guard with the truncheon walked over to Junior and tapped him gently on the bridge of the nose.

"Next time you step out of line, you're gonna get it."

Junior read the look in the man's eyes and decided against replying with the ritual surliness he and his friends reserved for white authority figures who tried to win their respect by force. After the guards left, the two older inmates congratulated him for his prudence.

"Never let no idiot beat on you," they told him.

They took him back to his cell and told him to sleep under his bed, explaining that the guards sometimes came back in the middle of the night to settle old scores, one of them always carrying a flashlight. "With that flashlight in your face, man, you can't recognize nobody. But the beds are bolted to the wall, so just get under it and if they do come for you, they can't kick you or swing nothing at you."

Junior would not soon forget this lesson in prisoner solidarity.

Like his falsely accused cousin, Tom Christmas was having more trouble than he could handle. After his arrest in June following the incident at John Pratico's house, he was taken to the police station and questioned by Sgt./Det. John MacIntyre. Christmas was asked where the knife was that he'd used to threaten Pratico. Tom told police there was no knife and that he hadn't gone after the Crown witness. The police searched him, found nothing, then charged him with obstruction of justice.

"They locked me up and they told me that Marshall was charged with that fellow's stabbing in the park that night," Christmas recalled. "I told them that they were wrong. I told them all I done was I asked this guy Pratico not to do what he was doing, that he was lying and that he shouldn't do that, because we treated him good and Junior didn't stab nobody."

On June 23, Tom Christmas was released from jail with the proviso that he appear in court that October to face the charge of obstructing justice. While out on bail, he was arrested a second time by Sydney detectives, this time for break and enter. At his October trial on that charge, he pleaded guilty to breaking into a house on Membertou, expecting to get a few months in county jail. He was sentenced to three years in federal prison. On October 6, prosecutor Donald MacNeil offered no evidence to support the Crown's allegation that Tom Christmas had threatened John Pratico. The charge of obstructing justice was dismissed.

A very different interpretation would be put on these events when Junior Marshall had his day in court a month later. Nor would Tom Christmas be testifying at his friend's trial, as he had planned to, about John Pratico's story that he'd been pressured into giving false testimony by the police. By the time Junior Marshall's trial began, his teenage friend would already be in federal penitentiary in another province.

For John Pratico it was a summer of Valium and dark fantasy. Alternately excited and depressed over the central role he was playing in the important affairs swirling around Junior Marshall, Pratico felt that for once in his life people were taking notice of

him. During the investigation, the police had driven him around
Sydney in their cruisers, and after the Tom Christmas incident they
had even let him sleep in the jail once or twice. They called it
"police protection" and they didn't give that to just anybody.

The funny thing was, though, John knew that the Indians weren't
really after him. If they had been, it would have been an easy matter
for Arty Paul, whom he'd met down at the circus, to give him a
beating. All the Indians wanted to know was what he had seen that
night. And John had no qualms about telling them the truth, as he
did to Tom Christmas and Theresa Paul when they asked him what
had really happened: he hadn't witnessed the stabbing and was
only saying he had because of pressure from the police.

But somehow he couldn't do what Arty Paul and Tom Christmas
wanted him to: go to the police and tell them he hadn't seen a
thing. He'd tried to do that once before and they'd come up with
another fellow who'd seen him in the park. Besides, the detectives
and the Crown prosecutor had spent a lot of time with him and he
knew they wouldn't like it very much if he decided to take back
what he had agreed he'd seen. "You see, my nerves was all but
addled," John recalled years later.

But, try as he might, Pratico couldn't feel good about what he
was doing. If there were moments when he almost believed he had
seen Junior Marshall stab Sandy Seale, there were many more
when he knew he had not. Torn by guilt and fear, Pratico couldn't
sleep and became increasingly truculent around his mother and
sister. A trip to the family doctor ended with a stronger prescription
of Valium, but the drug couldn't arrest the young man's deteriorating mental condition. At five o'clock in the morning on August 25,
1971, Margaret Pratico and her son left Sydney by car and drove to
Halifax, where John was admitted to a mental institution suffering
from a nervous breakdown. A detective of the Sydney city police
provided them with the ride.

On October 25, John Pratico was discharged from the Nova
Scotia hospital and a week after that perjured himself at Junior
Marshall's trial.

On Sunday, November 1, the night before his trial, Junior Marshall
received a visit from Membertou's court worker of the day, Bernie
Francis. As Junior remembered it, "Bernie mentioned a knife,

saying that they got my knife with my fingerprints, right. I told him he was crazy, right. There was no knife. I tell him I'll see him in court tomorrow because I was going to court next morning. Bernie Francis, he wanted me to plead guilty to manslaughter; he said, 'I'll get you ten years,' right. I told him no." Years later, Francis denied he had ever tried to induce Marshall to enter a guilty plea on a reduced charge.

Junior Marshall, who had turned eighteen in jail, spent the rest of a sleepless night wondering what would become of him after the trial. Whatever happened, he knew one thing: however terrible the consequences, no one was going to make him admit to something he hadn't done.

The decade to follow would show him to be as good as his word.

11/On Trial

Junior Marshall went on trial for murder on November 2, 1971, in an atmosphere supercharged by Sydney's pent-up desire to see Sandy Seale's killer brought to justice.

Feeling freakish in handcuffs and looking pale from a summer spent behind bars, Junior avoided the silent stare of the crowd as he was taken by police escort into the law courts. The throng had lined up on the steps several hours before in hopes of getting one of the hundred seats in the second-storey courtroom where the case would be tried. Sydney's two main minority groups were well represented in the queue, and there was a palpable tension between the normally cordial Blacks and Indians.

Over the five months since the murder, details of the police investigation had filtered back to both communities. Micmac leaders were convinced that Sydney's Blacks had shown up with one thing in mind: to see Junior Marshall punished for Sandy Seale's death. "They wouldn't look at us. You could see it on their faces, they were blaming Junior for it," Donald Marshall, Sr., later recalled. "I tried to talk to Oscar Seale but he ignored me."

Several Micmacs believed that the white community, too, had rushed to judgment in the Marshall case, a suspicion fed by a comment that appeared in the *Cape Breton Post* more than a month before the trial. A small item in a gossip column urged the public to "give credit" to John MacIntyre and three other Sydney detectives "for their work in the Seale murder case". Already upset by the fact that Donald MacNeil, who had been censured for discrimination against Indians, was conducting the prosecution, the Micmacs were livid. "What made us so upset was that the paper was asking the public to praise the police before the court had a chance to see if they had come up with the right man," Noel Doucette later remembered. "It was the same old story: the Indian was guilty before the trial even began."

J. Louis Dubinsky was the presiding judge, a veteran justice of the Nova Scotia Supreme Court whose brother-in-law, Moe Rosenblum, was representing Junior Marshall. The fact that Dubinsky and Rosenblum were related, an obvious conflict in other jurisdictions, was of no concern to Crown prosecutor Donald MacNeil. In the tightly knit, and at times casual, legal community of Cape Breton, it was well known that the two were related and just as accepted that Justice Dubinsky was impartial to a fault. As Simon Khattar later said of any potential conflict of interest, "You would say normally he would be inclined to bend over towards us, but it [the relationship with Rosenblum] had no effect on him at all."

The presence of Louis Dubinsky in so high-profile a case guaranteed spectators what he was best known for as a judge: stirring charges to juries that featured all of the Thespian verve of the avid amateur actor that the judge in fact was. If all the world was a stage, a courtroom was a particularly good one, as Louis Dubinsky well knew. "Here you had a man on the bench who had been in a number of theatrical productions, a consummate actor. He loved to orate, to perform, and his charges sometimes came very close to straight direction, he was so persuasive," remembered Harry Wheaton, an RCMP officer who had watched Dubinsky in court many times during his police work in Sydney.

At 3:30 in the afternoon, after examining more than fifty prospective jurors, Crown and defence counsel agreed on the peers before whom Junior Marshall would be tried: twelve white males. With the jury finally empanelled, Donald MacNeil moved for the arraignment of Donald Marshall, Jr. The clerk of the court read the charge, then turned to the accused. "How say you? Are you guilty of this crime whereof you stand indicted or not guilty?" His voice sounded as indifferent as an auctioneer's.

Junior Marshall answered forcefully. "Not guilty!"

Although Donald MacNeil spoke for more than thirty minutes in his opening remarks, telling jurors what they could expect to hear from the twenty witnesses he would call, the Crown's case still boiled down to three people: Maynard Chant and John Pratico, who claimed to have witnessed the murder, and Patricia Harriss, who placed Junior Marshall and another man alone on Crescent Street by Wentworth Park on the night of Friday, May 28. The rest of the Crown's case was thin, as the list of exhibits showed: Sandy Seale's blood-soaked bluejeans and coat, Marshall's bloodstained yellow jacket, a bloodstained Kleenex, and an engineer's plan of Wentworth Park. Five months after the stabbing, the Sydney police still hadn't found the murder weapon or any other piece of physical evidence connecting the accused to the crime.

In fact, the Crown prosecutor entered the Supreme Court trial with no more evidence than he had produced at the preliminary hearing, an oddity in itself. Normally, just enough evidence is introduced at the preliminary to send the case to trial, where the burden of the Crown's case is presented.

The Crown's first two witnesses were members of the RCMP crime laboratory in Sackville, New Brunswick. Serologist Sandra Mrazek repeated the testimony she had given at Marshall's preliminary hearing: blood of group O was found on Sandy Seale's clothing and the stains on Marshall's jacket could not be typed. Her evidence added nothing to the Crown's case against the accused. The defence waived its right to cross-examine.

Adolphus Evers, the hair and fibres expert, again testified that he had found two cuts on the left sleeve of the yellow jacket that the accused was wearing on the night of the murder. One cut was approximately an inch long, the other eight inches long. Six and a half inches of the longer separation were "indicative of being cut". The remaining one and a half inches resembled a tear, Evers told the court. The second RCMP expert also left the stand without a question from the defence.

Court adjourned at five o'clock.

On day two of the trial, fifteen witnesses took the stand, starting with Dr. Mohamed Ali Naqvi when court was reconvened at 10:20 a.m. Dr. Naqvi described how Sandy Seale was rushed to the operating room after arriving at the hospital with neither pulse nor blood pressure. The doctor told the court how the victim had been placed on an artificial respirator after the operation but without success. Seventeen hours and two operations later, the teenager had died from massive trauma to his bowel caused by the insertion of a pointed instrument.

Whether it was to correct an omission in his notes, or to help the jury through the medical jargon, Justice Dubinsky interceded to ask some questions of his own.

"Doctor, I didn't get the width of the incision of the wound; I thought you said..."

"I said approximately, approximately three inches."

"That was, you said the cuts..."

The witness completed the judge's sentence. "Made by the object."

"And through which cut the intestine extended?"

"The cut into the intestine extended right from the front of the vessels supplying the large intestine, the vessels, the small intestine, the large intestine itself, then right to the aorta."

"And what was extending outside the man's body, as a result of the cut? What organs were visible?"

The jury shuddered and Oscar Seale, who was sitting with other members of his family, lowered his head as the doctor answered.

"All the intestine was outside, all the intestine was outside. I wouldn't say all, but most of the intestine was outside."

Dr. Naqvi was followed to the stand by his colleague at the Sydney City Hospital, Dr. Mohan S. Virick, the doctor who had stitched Junior Marshall's left forearm on the night of the stabbing. If the Crown had any chance of convincing the jury that Junior Marshall had murdered Sandy Seale, it would have to account for his own wound in a way that was consistent with his guilt. If MacNeil could convince the jury that the wound was so superficial that it hadn't even bled, he would have an easier time suggesting that Marshall had slashed his own arm after stabbing Seale to divert suspicion from himself.

Dr. Virick was instrumental in setting up that argument. At the preliminary hearing, his evidence would have led a jury to the opposite conclusion, but this time out his opinion inexplicably changed. After getting the doctor to describe the cut on the accused's arm, the Crown prosecutor returned to a favorite subject: the lack of blood from the four-and-a-half-inch slash.

"Tell me, Doctor, was there any bleeding from this cut?"

"No, at the time I went there, there was no bleeding. The patient had already been prepared by the nurse. I just went and stitched it."

"Yes, well, we'll have that nurse later on, but as far as you observed personally, did you observe any blood at any time?"

"No," Dr. Virick answered.

"All right, how would you describe this cut?"

"This is a superficial laceration, even in depth throughout, approximately four inches long."

"Now, you say a superficial laceration. Would you break that down into other language, Doctor."

"It isn't a bruise, but on the other hand the deeper tissues, the muscles and deeper tissues are not involved in a laceration."

"I see," the Crown prosecutor said, "and what did you do for this man?"

"I administered stitches under local anesthetic."

"Yes, and how many stitches did you insert?"

"Ten," the doctor replied.

It was an impressive number for a cut the prosecutor wanted the jury to believe was no more than a subterfuge. MacNeil had somehow to weaken the seeming impressiveness of those ten stitches. "All right now, Doctor, why did you insert ten stitches in a superficial wound?" he asked. With any luck, Dr. Virick might repeat the phrase he'd used at the preliminary: "for cosmetic purposes".

"This wasn't a bruise exactly. It is a laceration which needs to be sutured. If I wouldn't have done it, he would have had a scar and probably infection."

This was not the answer MacNeil had been looking for; he tried another tack. "Did you remove the stitches in due course, Doctor?"

"No, I didn't."

"Did you make an attempt to remove them?" the prosecutor continued.

"Yes, I did. I had an appointment to see Donald and to remove his sutures, but when I went to the jail – that's the Cape Breton County Jail – the sutures were already removed."

"Already removed? Did Mr. Marshall say by whom?"

"He said he had done it himself," Dr. Virick answered.

"Now, Doctor, considering your medical experience, I would

like to ask you for your opinion. In your opinion, could this, or did this, cut have the appearance of being self-inflicted?"

Moe Rosenblum sat forward in his seat as Dr. Virick pondered his reply. If he testified as he had at the preliminary hearing, an important prop would be knocked from under the Crown's case. For if the wound was not self-inflicted in the opinion of the very man who stitched it, Junior's story that another man had stabbed both teenagers on Crescent Street that night would receive a measure of corroboration. More important, the Crown would be left with a major hole in its case: if Junior Marshall hadn't slashed his own arm, who had?

"It's possible," Dr. Virick answered, sending Moe Rosenblum racing through the transcript of his testimony at the preliminary. If left unchallenged, Dr. Virick's changed testimony would have serious consequences for his client.

"Was it deeper at one end than it was at the other, or anything like that?" MacNeil asked.

"No, superficial throughout."

MacNeil made sure the doctor's choice of words wasn't lost on the jury. "Superficial cut down the arm, same depth all the way down," he repeated. Donald MacNeil, like Sgt./Det. MacIntyre before him, placed great significance on that fact.

"Yes."

"And caused no bleeding?"

"Mr. MacNeil, don't lead the witness," Justice Dubinsky interjected.

"But you saw no blood at any time?" he said, rephrasing the question.

"I didn't see any, no."

After establishing that Dr. Virick had treated Marshall for approximately half an hour, the prosecution turned the witness over to Moe Rosenblum, who wasted no time in going on the attack.

"Dr. Virick, you will recall that you gave evidence in this case at the preliminary hearing in the Provincial Magistrates' Court?"

"I did."

"And I ask you, Doctor, to recall your testimony at that hearing, when I cross-examined you as to whether or not you formed an opinion as to [whether] this wound on the left arm of Mr. Marshall was self-inflicted. Now, based on your knowledge, your observations of the accused's arm, at that time and the type of wound that it was, did you not say, Doctor, at that time, that you were of the opinion that it wasn't self-inflicted, although possibly it could have been?"

"If you remember, Mr. Rosenblum, I was trying to clarify the evidence at that time."

"But did you not say that your opinion was that it wasn't self-inflicted, but that it could have been?"

"Yes. I don't know, it's just a laceration I sutured which is even, it is possible, it could be self-inflicted or it may not be. It is very hard for me to say."

It hadn't been so difficult at Marshall's preliminary hearing, and Moe Rosenblum brandished the transcript of those proceedings to prove his point. "Now, on page fifty-four of the transcript of evidence taken from the Magistrates' Court, this question was asked by me of you: 'Based on your knowledge at the time, your opinion is that the wound was not self-inflicted?' And your answer, 'This point is against it.' Do you recall saying that?"

"Yes, I remember it, but this is..."

"I am doing the questioning," Rosenblum snapped. "Now, my next question to you, on page fifty-four, line twenty-five, 'Your opinion is that it was not self-inflicted,' and your answer is: 'Yes, yes I would say so.' Do you remember making those answers to those questions?"

"Yes, right."

Once he'd established that Dr. Virick had testified under oath as having said that in his opinion the wound had not been self-inflicted, Moe Rosenblum addressed the issue of the severity of the wound. He asked Junior Marshall to approach the stand and roll up his sleeve so the doctor could inspect his wound. All eyes followed the tall youth's progress towards the witness-box as he complied with his lawyer's request.

"Now, from its appearance today, Doctor, from your inspection of it today, would you not say that it did more than just scrape the skin –this wound? Isn't that so?"

"Yes, that's true."

"Otherwise it wouldn't bear a scar, such as there is now, today, on November 3, following an incident on May 28. And, Doctor, I realize that there was a nurse who attended Donnie Marshall before you saw him and that she would be in a better position to say what his condition was before you saw him, but nevertheless, would you not give an opinion that there had been bleeding from that wound before you saw it, that blood had flowed from this wound? Would you not say that was in all likelihood the case?"

"It's possible," the doctor replied.

"Well, I know anything is possible, Doctor. But in all likelihood?"

"It is likely, yes. It's possible."

"Not only possible, but likely?" the defence attorney persisted.

"Yes."

After eliciting that single, unequivocal word, Moe Rosenblum had done all he could to repair the damage of Dr. Virick's earlier answer to the Crown prosecutor. He hoped the jury had followed him through the thicket of words to the doctor's original opinion: that the wound on Junior Marshall's arm had not been self-inflicted.

The next Crown witness was Carl MacDonald, Sydney's land surveyor. His testimony consisted of explaining the plan of Wentworth Park which he'd prepared as an exhibit for the trial. He told the court that there were two power poles bearing streetlights in the vicinity of the murder scene. He also explained that there were six bushes, in full bloom, a couple of feet from the curb on Crescent Street. A leafy bush, a few feet from the murder scene, close to power poles with streetlights on them: the scene that Donald MacNeil wanted in the jury's mind when it came time for John Pratico to take the stand.

The last witness called before court adjourned for lunch was Dr. David Gaum, who had assisted Dr. Naqvi with the second operation on Sandy Seale. His testimony was a simple reiteration of his colleague's, right down to the opinion that "some sharp instrument" had inflicted the mortal wound on the deceased. Moe Rosenblum waived his right to cross-examination, but Justice Dubinsky once more exhibited interest in some of the more grisly medical testimony.

"Doctor, would you please stand up and indicate to the jury just where on your own person, where the stab wound was."

"Up in the upper region—upper region of the abdomen as I recall it."

"Where does the aorta run?" the judge asked.

"The aorta runs from up around this region of the chest, curves right down to the. . ."

"The aorta is the. . ."

"The major blood vessel that originates from the heart to supply the rest of the body."

"You say that was punctured?" the judge said.

"Yes, a sharp puncture about, as I recall, maybe half an inch."

"When you were there, was any of the intestines exposed or. . ."

Dr. Gaum acknowledged that they had been and went on to volunteer that Sandy Seale had also been suffering from gangrene. If the jury had been inclined to forget just how gruesome Seale's death had been, Justice Dubinsky's interventions made that very difficult to do.

Leo Curry, ambulance operator and funeral director, was the next to take the stand. He told the court that he'd received the call to proceed to Crescent Street by Wentworth Park at approximately 12:15 a.m. early on Saturday, May 29. On arriving, he found Sandy Seale lying almost in the middle of the street, apparently in critical condition. He took the wounded youth to the Sydney City Hospital and helped Dr. Naqvi set up an intravenous feed.

Curry's evidence had no bearing on the issue of Junior Marshall's guilt, but Moe Rosenblum saw a chance to lay the groundwork for a question he wanted to raise about Maynard Chant's credibility. If Chant had indeed seen Marshall stab Seale, then why hadn't he turned the Indian youth in when police arrived on the scene?

Rosenblum knew that Chant had been there with Marshall, but it would be useful to have Leo Curry place Marshall, Chant, and the police together on Crescent Street shortly after the stabbing. Once that was done, he hoped to get the jury wondering why Chant hadn't told police about the stabbing right away.

"Mr. Curry, were there any police there when you got there?"

"There were two policemen, I believe."

"Could one of them have been Richard Walsh?"

"Yes, I think."

"Are you not familiar with the City of Sydney policemen?"

"I'm familiar with them but this was a split second. . ."

"Oh yes, yes, but there were. . ."

". . .and my memory is not that good," the funeral director interjected.

"That's quite all right. But there were one or two of the City of Sydney police force there?"

"Yes."

"Now tell me, who else was there when you got there, Mr. Curry?"

"The only other one, other than the young man in question who was injured, was Brian Doucette."

"He helped you?"

"Yes."

"Any other people there?"

"Might have been but I don't remember."

"Was Donnie Marshall there?"

"I didn't see him."

"Well, were there a number of people there whom you can't tell us who they were except that there were several policemen there and the man who helped you, were there a number of other people there?"

At the very least, defence counsel wanted to get the unobservant Mr. Curry to admit that other people had been at the scene that later witnesses might be able to identify, but it was no use.

"But you'd be aware if there was a group of people around or not, you know," Rosenblum suggested.

"Funny thing, this question has been put several times before by different people, they'll ask you how bad the car was and how bad this was and that..."

"No, no," Rosenblum said, trying to cut off Curry's rambling reply.

"...and I didn't look. I know Brian Doucette was there. I know there were two policemen and the injured man in question and I don't remember seeing anybody else."

Moe Rosenblum gave it a last try. "To the best of your recollection would you say there were a number of other people there? As far as you can remember, although you can't tell us who they were: can you answer that?"

"I sound like the town nut here, I guess. I don't remember really."

"You don't remember: all right, I'll take that. That's all I wish to ask him, my Lord," an exasperated Moe Rosenblum said. Figuring out another way of raising his reservation about Maynard Chant's strangely retroactive eyewitness account would prove to be a much harder task than the defence counsel realized.

Donald MacNeil proceeded to call Merle Faye Davis, a witness who would allow him to talk once more about Junior Marshall's supposedly bloodless wound. Davis, the registered nurse who'd prepared Marshall for Dr. Virick on the night he stitched the young man's arm, was asked to describe the accused's condition on the night in question.

"He had a laceration on his left forearm about three inches long."

"And can you describe this laceration?"

"Well, it was just a plain laceration. There was no blood."

"There was no blood?" the Crown prosecutor said.

"No."

"Did you observe any blood coming from the laceration at any time when you were administering to Mr. Marshall?"

"No," the nurse answered.

The Crown prosecutor proceeded to slip in a deadly line of questioning that caught the defence off guard.

"Did you also have occasion to see Mr. Marshall's arm here today in court when he displayed it to the jury?"

"Yes."

"Did you notice anything else about his arm?"

"I noticed a tattoo on his arm."

"What part of the arm was that on?" MacNeil asked.

"On the outer aspect of his arm."

"Can you tell us what that tattoo is?"

" 'I hate cops'," the witness replied.

A chill went through Junior Marshall when he saw the look on the faces of the jurors who turned their collective gaze his way. No objection was raised by the defence, even though the twelve men who controlled their client's fate had just been provided with a very damaging, and irrelevant, insight into Junior Marshall's character. Several years later, the blunt declaration of that tattoo would be the only thing some jurors recalled of the trial.

Moe Rosenblum knew that the Crown prosecutor's preoccupation with Marshall's bloodless wound was no more than a provocative red herring. Even if the wound had never bled, that neither proved that his client had stabbed himself, nor was inconsistent with another person's having slashed his arm. And with no match between the blood on Seale's clothing and the blood on Junior Marshall's jacket, MacNeil could never prove what he was so anxious to have the jury believe: that the blood on Marshall's jacket had to be Sandy Seale's. But there was no telling what effect MacNeil's innuendo was having on the jury. The peppery defence counsel jumped to his feet to cross-examine the witness.

"Mrs. Davis, Dr. Virick has told us that there were ten stitches put in this wound of Mr. Marshall's. You wouldn't feel that Dr. Virick made any unnecessary stitches, would you?"

"No, I..."

"And would you think that was necessary, the services provided by Dr. Virick for that type of wound that you saw?"

"Yes."

"You would. That it would require ten stitches?"

"Well, I guess if he felt it necessary."

"You would feel that he was competent to judge that?"

"Right," the nurse said.

After establishing exactly what Davis had done on the night in question, Rosenblum closed on the question of Marshall's wound.

"Mrs. Davis, with your experience, which I am quite sure is lengthy as a nurse, would you not expect that there had been bleeding from that wound before you saw Mr. Marshall? Would you not ordinarily expect that from the type of wound that...."

"Yes, I guess."

"But that it had congealed or dried up by the time you saw it: that's what you would expect?"

"Well, yes," nurse Davis answered.

Prosecutor MacNeil asked a single question on redirect examination. "Did you see any congealed blood in this wound?"

"No," the witness answered.

Roy Gould, the first of three Micmacs who would give evidence at Junior Marshall's trial, was now called by the prosecution. Gould told the court that he and the accused had returned from Bedford on the night of the murder and that Junior had borrowed Roy's yellow jacket, which was now one of the exhibits in the trial.

"What is the difference in its appearance today and when you loaned it to him?" MacNeil asked.

"It wasn't in that condition."

"What?"

"The tear."

"The tear on the sleeve of the jacket."

"There was no tear on the sleeve, in other words."

"What about the front of the jacket?" MacNeil continued.

"There was no bloodstains on it either," Gould said.

After establishing that Gould had retrieved the jacket from Junior's father at the request of the Sydney city police, prosecutor MacNeil turned the witness over to Moe Rosenblum. But the defence had no questions, for the very good reason that nothing in Roy Gould's testimony had the slightest bearing on the guilt or innocence of their client.

It would be the same with the accused's father, Donald Marshall, Sr. He told the court that the jacket Roy Gould had lent his son had been placed in a closet in the family home for a week after the incident. It had been returned to Gould when he asked for it.

"Did you notice the condition of the jacket when you gave it to Mr. Gould?"

"Yes."

"Would you look at Exhibit 3 and tell me if that is the jacket and if that is the condition in which it was when you turned it over to Mr. Gould?"

"Yes," Marshall answered, and his testimony was over. Moe Rosenblum had no questions. Father and son exchanged a silent glance as the Grand Chief of the Micmac Nation rejoined his wife in the gallery.

Ironically, when it came time for a representative of the Sydney city police to take the stand, the Crown didn't call the chief investigator of the Seale murder and the informant in the case, Sgt./Det. John MacIntyre. Perhaps Donald MacNeil remembered the grilling Moe Rosenblum had given MacIntyre at the preliminary hearing, a hectoring cross-examination that revealed how little the detective could remember about his own investigation. It was also possible that MacNeil wanted to avoid getting into the subject of how the police found their eyewitnesses to the murder or how their statements were obtained, something that could be nicely achieved if the man who had interviewed all the witnesses didn't take the stand.

The Crown's only purpose in calling Detective Michael Mac-Donald was to prove continuity of possession of the various items that were exhibits in the trial. MacDonald told the court that he'd picked up the clothes both boys had been wearing on the night of the murder, as well as the bloody Kleenex found by police near the murder scene, and delivered them to Adolphus Evers of the RCMP crime laboratory in Sackville, New Brunswick.

Moe Rosenblum had another, and from the defence's point of view much more important, line of questioning for MacDonald. Knowing that he had talked to Maynard Chant at the Sydney City Hospital on the night Sandy Seale was admitted, Rosenblum intended to use the detective to show that, although Chant had had the opportunity that night to tell police what he was now claiming to have seen on Crescent Street, he hadn't mentioned a word about Marshall stabbing Seale. Since he had failed to raise this paradoxical fact in his cross-examination of Leo Curry, it was imperative that Rosenblum bring it out in his questioning of MacDonald.

"Now, was there a young fellow there by the name of Chant?"

"Not at that time, sir."

"All right, when did you see him? Maynard V. Chant, I'm speaking about."

"2 a.m. in the morning," the nervous officer answered. Moe Rosenblum had a reputation with the police as a tough questioner who was quick on his feet. He could make a fellow look pretty bad if a fellow wasn't careful.

"2 a.m. – where did you see him?"

"At the City Hospital."

MacDonald had been the first investigator at the hospital on the night Seale was brought in and conducted the initial investigation until John MacIntyre took over the case the next day.

"So you stayed there from ten after twelve until what time?"

"I left there five minutes to three in the morning," the detective answered.

"So you saw Maynard Chant there about two o'clock in the morning. Now, who was there when you saw him there?"

"Constable Jackie Johnstone and Constable Howard Dean."

"Both of the City of Sydney Police Force?"

"Yes, sir."

"All right, were you talking to Chant?" Rosenblum asked.

"For a moment," MacDonald said.

"How long did he stay there in your company?"

"Two or three minutes."

"So you just had a short conversation with him?"

"Very short. I sent him down to the police station."

"Quite all right," Rosenblum said, beginning the factual descent to the point he was trying to make. "You never wear a uniform, do you, Sergeant?" he asked.

"No sir."

"Did you make yourself known to Mr. Chant, as to your position?"

"The police officers brought him right in to me where I was and identified..."

"The police officers were in uniform, that is, Walsh and who else?" Moe Rosenblum wanted to be sure the jury realized that Maynard Chant knew he was surrounded by police when he was brought in to the hospital after being picked up by Constable Jackie Johnstone as he hitchhiked back to Louisbourg on the night of the murder.

"No, Howard Dean and Constable Jackie Johnstone."

"And you notified Mr. Chant that you were a sergeant with the City of Sydney Police Force?"

"That's right."

"And then, did you see him later that day, Chant?"

"Again that morning," the detective answered.

"Where at?"

"At the police station."

The detective's answer couldn't have been better from Rosenblum's point of view. For if Maynard Chant had witnessed the murder, what better, or safer, place could he choose to tell the authorities what he knew than the police station?

"What time would that be?"

"Quarter after three, twenty to three."

"Who was present on that occasion?"

"Sergeant Len MacGillivary, myself, Corporal Martin MacDonald, and Mr. Chant's father."

After establishing that police had spoken to Chant a third time on Sunday, May 30, Rosenblum backtracked and came to the point.

"Now, going back to midnight, ten after twelve, at the City of Sydney Hospital when you saw Mr. Chant and you had a brief conversation, was Donald Marshall present?"

"No sir. He was in the building."

"Did Chant tell you anything?"

Donald MacNeil was on his feet raising an objection before Rosenblum could finish his question. "Conversation that took place between the officer and Mr. Chant is inadmissible unless the accused is present," he told Justice Dubinsky.

The judge sent out the jury and the first of the trial's three voir dire sessions took place. Moe Rosenblum argued passionately for his right to put the question to the detective.

"Cross-examination of the witness, my Lord."

"And you're asking him about. . ." the judge began.

". . .whether any statement was made to him by Chant on that occasion in the hospital and I will lead him down to the other contacts that he had with Chant concerning Donald Marshall. My Lord, this is of such great importance to the case that I ask your usual serious consideration."

"Every piece of evidence is important," the judge told him.

"This goes to the nub of the case, my Lord."

Rosenblum was convinced that if the jury could be shown that there were three occasions when Maynard Chant could have told the police about witnessing the murder-but hadn't, then they would have to consider another possibility: that the police, in fact, had told Chant that Junior Marshall had stabbed Seale.

"Actually, you are asking him in your question, you are of course asking the witness what the other man had said," Justice Dubinsky told him.

"No. I'm asking what he didn't say. I'm asking what he didn't say, my Lord, not what he said."

Crown prosecutor MacNeil proceeded to interject a neat bit of obfuscation that raised Rosenblum's ire. Knowing full well that Rosenblum intended to show that Chant hadn't mentioned a thing about witnessing the murder to MacDonald, an obvious benefit to the accused's case, MacNeil claimed that the question under consideration was objectionable because it abridged the rights of Junior Marshall. "I know of no rule that would allow a conversation to go in that may work to the detriment of the accused when he wasn't present. Now, take for example – I don't know what my learned friend expects to get from this answer – but let us suppose the answer came back like this, 'Yes, he said that Donald Marshall, Jr., stabbed Sandy Seale on Crescent Street.' Then, my Lord, I suggest that it wouldn't take two minutes for the Appellate Division of the Supreme Court to rule on that."

"I will be responsible for my questions," Moe Rosenblum bristled.

"I'm saying it is inadmissible regardless of who asks it," MacNeil continued.

Rosenblum exploded.

"If I was foolish enough to ask a question like that, I would be bound by the answer. I wouldn't ask a question unless I know what it's going to be, what he has to tell me. I don't ask a foolish question. I got to know the answer before I ask the question. If your Lordship would like time to deliberate on it, we're going to the heart of the case."

"You are asking him, Mr. Rosenblum, to give you a conversation which he had with Mr. Chant with respect to an accusation. You're asking him about conversation which he had with Mr. Chant, and however you may phrase it, it gets to what Chant said to him."

The exasperated defence counsel tried to make his point as forcefully as possible. "Or didn't say – or didn't say! This is the point. Silence!" he said.

"And isn't that also applicable, the matter of silence?" Justice Dubinsky asked.

"The only way I can bring it out, my Lord, is to ask him whether Chant told him anything. That's how you prove silence."

"It is now near recess and I will take the time to look into it. But I would say, Mr. Rosenblum, that my inclination is that you cannot ask this witness anything about conversation."

"Or the lack of it," the defence counsel persisted.

"Anything that has to do with the conversation, inasmuch as the accused man was not there."

Instead of retiring to consider the matter, Justice Dubinsky instructed Rosenblum to proceed with the precise question he wanted to ask the witness.

"Was Mr. Marshall there or not?"

"Not in person, no. He was in the building," the detective answered.

"He wasn't present when you were talking to Maynard Chant?"

"That's right."

"And Maynard Chant was aware of the fact that you were a sergeant of the Sydney police force?"

"Yes, sir."

"And he had been escorted into your presence by two other police officers?"

"Yes, sir."

"Did Maynard Chant on that occasion say anything to you to implicate Donald Marshall, Jr., the accused in this case, in connection with the injuries which had been sustained by the late Sandy Seale?"

On the brink of bringing out the evidence he felt was vital to his client's defence, Moe Rosenblum was stymied by Justice Dubinsky.

"Don't answer that question!" the judge told the detective.

The jury was brought back in and Justice Dubinsky recessed court until he made a ruling on the point of law raised by Rosenblum's line of questioning. When court resumed at 2:15 p.m., nearly two hours later, the judge sustained the Crown's objection.

"Now, Mr. Rosenblum, you said it was a very material point in the case. I say I appreciate very much your position. Nonetheless, Crown counsel in his opening remarks made it quite clear that the person [Chant] was going to be called and undoubtedly will be called. Indeed, it would be unthinkable that he wouldn't be. Therefore, that witness will be available and will be subject to cross-examination as to things he said at the time, and any point you may very well have in regard to his testimony can be established and brought out at that time."

Although he was apparently trying to be fair to the accused, there was a problem with the judge's decision. If he was ruling that the detective's conversation with Chant was inadmissible on the grounds that the accused wasn't present, then how could Chant's conversation with the detective, which was also held in the absence of the accused, be admissible? Moe Rosenblum was left to ponder that legal mystery as he continued his cross-examination of Detective MacDonald.

With his sights set on the argument he would later make, that the police had told Maynard Chant what to say, Rosenblum proceeded to bring out how many times the detectives had been with the youth before he finally gave them the statement incriminating Junior Marshall. MacDonald admitted seeing Chant twice on the night of the murder and a third time in Louisbourg, in a two-hour session in the back of a police car that ended in a trip to the Sydney police station and Maynard's first statement to Sgt./Det. MacIntyre.

But the detective did not tell Rosenblum about that trip or about Chant's first statement in which the fourteen-year-old claimed to have witnessed two men attack Seale and Marshall. It would not be the first time in the trial that the failure to fully disclose the Crown's case would work against the interests of the teenager in the prisoner's box.

There was another important matter Moe Rosenblum wanted to elicit from Detective MacDonald: the treatment of his client by police in the days immediately following the stabbing. Although he wasn't charged with the murder until June 4, exactly a week after the stabbing, Sgt./Det. MacIntyre had him brought to the station, where he languished for several hours on successive days waiting to be of assistance. Rosenblum asked the detective when he had first seen the accused at the police station.

"On May 29 he was at the police station," MacDonald said.

"That was a Saturday morning?"

"Saturday morning."

"How long was he there?"

"Four or five hours."

"And who was talking with him?"

"Nobody in particular," was the detective's vague reply.

The answer nettled Rosenblum. "What was he doing, just sitting there looking at the walls for four or five hours?"

"He was there."

"He was there, I know, but what was he doing there? What was he doing there? Who was talking to him? Were you?"

"No sir."

"You didn't speak to him the whole time he was there?"

"No, I didn't have any conversation," MacDonald answered.

"Well, did you see anybody having a conversation with him?"

"No sir."

"Well, where was he? Was he standing for four hours or five hours?"

"He was sitting around."

"Where at? Sitting around where?"

"In the detectives' office, outside the front office and out in the alleyway, the driveway where the police cars are, he was smoking out there, back and forth."

"What was he doing there? For four or five hours, what was he doing there?"

"He was asked to be there by Sergeant MacIntyre," MacDonald said, adding that he saw the accused again on the following day.

"Where did you see him?" Rosenblum asked.

"At the police station."

"How long was he there then?"

"Four or five hours."

"Was anybody talking to him?"

"Ah..."

"...or was he all alone for four or five hours and speaking to nobody as he was the day before, in your opinion? On Sunday, what happened when he was there for four or five hours?"

"On Sunday, we had him for a line-up, Sunday morning."

"Who was talking to him was my question," Rosenblum said icily.

"Sergeant MacIntyre might have spoke to him."

"Well, did you see anybody talking to Marshall?"

"No, sir."

"On Sunday when he was there for four or five hours?"

"That's right."

"Nor on Saturday, when he was there for four or five hours?"

"That's right," the detective repeated.

As the Sydney detective left the stand, Moe Rosenblum hoped that the jury had understood the point of his lengthy cross-examination. From the outset of the investigation, the police had treated Marshall as their prime suspect even though they had no evidence against him. More importantly, Junior had co-operated fully with their request that he remain around the station. He wanted the jurors to see that Marshall's actions were hardly those of a guilty man.

Although the next two witnesses had nothing to tell the court about the guilt or innocence of Junior Marshall, their mere presence galvanized the large and sympathetic gallery. Crushed by the loss of their son, Oscar and Leotha Seale made a brief appearance, the father to tell how he'd picked up Sandy's bloody clothes and boots from the hospital on the night of the stabbing, and the grieving mother to report how she had turned them over to Detective MacDonald a few days later. It was grief's last absurdity, the reduction of their son to the mundane list of articles that were now exhibits in the trial. Moe Rosenblum saw that Oscar Seale was having trouble giving his testimony. "You may lead him, Mr. MacNeil," he said gently.

After a few painful moments on the stand, the distraught couple resumed their places in the gallery. The next person to take the stand was the first Crown witness whose testimony would have a bearing, however slight, on the issue of Junior Marshall's guilt or innocence. Donald MacNeil was finally ready to bring forward the evidence he hoped would convict the accused.

Because Patricia Harriss was only fourteen years old, Justice Dubinsky asked some preliminary questions to ensure she understood the oath she had sworn, the common test in Nova Scotia before allowing a juvenile to give evidence. Did she know what it meant to tell the truth? Yes, she replied.

"Before whom did you take the oath?" the judge asked.

"The court, jury," she said softly. The judge had been thinking of a considerably more exalted entity.

"Do you remember the words 'So help you God' ?"

"To tell the truth and nothing but the truth," the youngster replied hopefully.

"So help you God?" Justice Dubinsky gently prodded.

"Yes."

"Would you venture to say what happens to anyone who tells a lie."

"It's perjury," Harriss answered.

"It is perjury. What is perjury? What is your idea of perjury?"

"Well, if you don't tell the truth, you go to jail, or school for girls," the witness replied.

Satisfied that the petite dark-haired girl understood the nature of an oath, Justice Dubinsky turned her over to prosecutor MacNeil. After establishing that she had attended the St. Joseph's dance on the night of the murder, MacNeil asked her how long she had been there. Her answer supplied him with the first shock of an afternoon that was to be filled with unpleasant surprises.

"Oh, until about 10:30."

"And what did you do at 10:30?"

"Well, my boyfriend was asked to leave the dance, so I went with him down to Wentworth Park, in front of the band shell, and we stayed there for a while. First we got a package of cigarettes. We went down and sat on the bench. A friend walked by and we asked him for a match and lit the cigarette. After that, we left and come on to Crescent Street."

"All right now, what time would this be?"

"Oh, about a quarter to eleven," Harriss answered.

"Quarter to eleven!" MacNeil exclaimed. He had good reason to be upset. The primary value of Harriss's testimony was that it placed Junior Marshall on Crescent Street with one other person just before the murder, an event that occurred around midnight. Now the witness was testifying that the meeting had taken place more than an hour before the stabbing.

"Are you sure of that, Miss Harriss?" MacNeil asked.

"Left the dance about 10:30, we were there for a while; we walked back of the band shell and came up on Crescent."

"How long did you remain in the park, the band shell?" MacNeil asked.

"Just long enough to smoke the cigarette."

"All right, you say it was what time when you decided to leave Wentworth Park and the band shell?"

"I'm not sure – twenty to eleven, around there."

Her testimony was a serious blow to the Crown's case. If she had met Marshall around 11 p.m., a full hour before the stabbing, and not around midnight, as was recorded in her police statement, the company the accused was keeping was almost useless in connecting him to the stabbing.

Harriss described how she and her boyfriend walked along Crescent Street and got a light from Junior Marshall in front of the green apartment building, not far from where Seale was later stabbed.

"Was there anyone with Mr. Marshall, the accused?" MacNeil asked.

"I think so, yes," Harriss said.

"Did you have any conversation with Donald Marshall yourself?"

"Not long – like I said – he asked, 'Were you at the dance?' and I said, 'Yes.'"

"Then what did you do?"

"Well, Terry lit the cigarette and then we just said 'Bye'. and went home."

MacNeil now asked the only question that could remotely help his case: was there more than one person with Junior Marshall when the couple met him on Crescent Street?

"I don't know really, but there wasn't many there."

The prosecutor was aghast. Not only had Patricia Harriss changed the time of her chance meeting with Marshall from what she had told police, she was now backing away from that part of her statement where she claimed there had only been one other person with the accused, a person the Crown prosecutor wanted the jury to believe had been Sandy Seale.

"I beg your pardon?" the boisterous Crown prosecutor said to the grade eight student.

"There wasn't many there," Harriss answered timidly.

"What?"

"There wasn't many there," she repeated.

"Now, what do you mean by that?"

"Well, there wasn't a crowd of people there."

Having asked the same question four times, MacNeil tried another approach. "I may have confused you. Miss Harriss, you saw Donald Marshall and did you see anyone else there?"

"Yes."

"Who was it, do you know?"

If Patricia Harriss didn't answer for a long moment, it may have been because she was remembering the two men she had actually seen with Junior Marshall on Crescent Street, one of them short, with grey hair. But she also remembered how upset the police had been with that story, how they banged their fists on the table and supplied her with another version of events that they had wanted to hear about. She couldn't decide which story to give: the one that had satisfied the police, or the truth. In the quiet law office of Alfred Gunn, telling the truth had seemed easy enough. But in court, confronted by the overbearing presence of Donald MacNeil, it was another matter. Harriss remained silent.

"Answer me, please," MacNeil said sternly.

"No," Harriss told him, she didn't know who they were.

"And how many people did you see there with Donald Marshall?"

"One," Patricia Harriss lied. It was the only part of the false statement she gave to Sgt./Det. John MacIntyre that she would repeat under oath.

"The one person."

"Yes."

"Tell me, did you have any physical contact with Junior Marshall at that time?"

"Yes," Harriss said.

"What was that?"

"He held my hand."

"And did you notice anything about his condition in so far as liquor is concerned?" the prosecutor asked.

"No, not really," Harriss said. "You couldn't tell."

After pointing out Junior Marshall at the request of the Crown prosecutor, Patricia Harriss prepared to face questions from a very different kind of lawyer. Unlike Donald MacNeil, Moe Rosenblum believed that you caught more flies with honey than with vinegar.

On cross-examination, the defence lawyer amiably brought out how pitifully thin Harriss's testimony had been. She agreed, as she had at the preliminary hearing, that she couldn't tell if that other person with Marshall was a man, woman, or child and confirmed that the meeting with the accused had been pleasant. Rosenblum had no way of knowing that her testimony on this point was false, as well as irrelevant, since he had never been shown her June 17 statement to Detective William Urquhart describing two men with Marshall. If he had been, he would have seen a description of the two men Harriss had actually seen with Marshall on Crescent Street that night that closely matched his client's description of the man who had stabbed Sandy Seale.

"And so the sum, net result is that you and Terry Gushue went to a dance, you left the dance, you went to the band shell for a cigarette, a smoke, whatever it was; then you started to walk towards your home over there on Kings Road, and on the way you met Junior Marshall, who gave Terry Gushue a match: is that right?"

"Yes."

"And that's all. Isn't that it?"

"Yes."

"Anything else?"

"No."

Patricia Harriss was followed to the stand by her companion, Terry Gushue, who had been thrown out of the St. Joseph's dance on the night of the murder for drinking and fighting. Gushue told Simon Khattar that he and Harriss left the dance around 10:30 and then walked to the park. A short while later, at approximately 10:50 p.m., they had walked over to Crescent Street, where they met Junior Marshall, who gave Terry a match to light his cigarette. Gushue said there had been someone else with Marshall, but, like his girlfriend, he didn't know if it was a man or a woman.

Despite the fact that Harriss and Gushue both placed the time of their meeting with Marshall at around 11 p.m., MacNeil would persist in presenting the meeting as having taken place moments before the stabbing, when he came to cross-examine Junior Marshall. The result would be devastating to the accused.

Gushue was excused. Counsel for the defence were beginning to feel guardedly optimistic. Fifteen of the prosecution's twenty witnesses had taken the stand and there still wasn't a shred of evidence against their client. But both men knew eyewitnesses could turn a trial around in a hurry, as Donald C. MacNeil fondly hoped Maynard Chant and John Pratico, the heart of the Crown's case, were about to do.

Maynard Chant was the first to take the stand. But the red-haired teenager had no sooner been sworn in than the legal duelling between the Crown and the defence began in earnest. Both sides knew that the trial would be won or lost by the testimony of the next two witnesses.

Moe Rosenblum asked that the rest of the Crown witnesses be excluded while Chant gave his evidence. Although there were four more Crown witnesses under subpoena, Rosenblum was interested in making sure that one of them in particular—John Pratico—didn't hear what Chant had to say. Suspecting from information supplied by several Micmac youths that both boys had been given their stories by the police, defence counsel didn't want Pratico taking his cue from the evidence Chant was about to give. Donald

MacNeil complained to Justice Dubinsky that the defence motion was inappropriate, coming as it did so late in the trial. But he couldn't give the court an authority for his objection. The motion was granted and the remaining Crown witnesses left the courtroom, including an already overwrought John Pratico. Nettled by this turn of events, the Crown prosecutor immediately asked for the exclusion of all witnesses for the defence. Justice Dubinsky agreed. But there was only one such witness, and he remained in the courtroom: the accused, Junior Marshall.

Chant told the court he'd been in Sydney attending church with his parents on the night of May 28 (he neglected to add that he'd left before the service was over to "do a little partying") and that later he missed the last bus home to Louisbourg. He decided to hitchhike home and took a shortcut along the railway tracks through Wentworth Park to George Street, when his involvement in the night's grisly events allegedly began.

"You started to walk along the railway tracks?"

"Yes."

"Did you notice anything as you walked along the railway tracks?"

"I noticed a fellow hunched over into a bush," Maynard answered.

"Good and loud now," prosecutor MacNeil advised the witness.

"I noticed a fellow hunched over into a bush."

"You're pointing to a bush that is opposite a light," MacNeil said, wanting to be sure the jury understood that whatever happened on Crescent Street was clearly visible from behind that bush. Maynard marked an X on the plan of Wentworth Park where he claimed he saw someone squatting down. He told the court that he didn't recognize the person who had caught his attention.

"What did you do?" MacNeil asked.

"Oh, I kept walking down a little farther. I walked down a little farther and looked back to see what he was looking at. He was looking over towards the street. So I looked over and saw two people over there."

"Did you recognize either of these people?"

"No," Maynard answered. Without further prompting, he continued with the story MacNeil had gone over with him so many times in the Crown prosecutor's office before the trial. "And I guess they were having a bit of an argument."

"Why do you say that?" the prosecutor asked.

"I don't have no reason why."

"Could you hear what they were saying?"

"No," Maynard answered, though he had testified at the preliminary hearing that the boys had been using "profane" language.

"What took place?"

Had Donald MacNeil known that Maynard Chant had already decided he wasn't going to be the one to "put the finger" on Junior Marshall for Seale's murder, that he intended to change his testimony back to the story that the police had rejected in the Louisbourg town hall when he told them he hadn't seen anything, the Crown prosecutor might have thought twice about asking that question. Maynard hadn't got very far into his answer when MacNeil realized that he had a very big problem on his hands.

"Well, one fellow, I don't know, hauled something out of his pocket – anyway – maybe – I don't know what it was. He drove it towards the left side of the other fellow's stomach."

This new testimony amounted to a gaping discrepancy with his testimony at the preliminary trial, when he had told the court he had seen Donald Marshall "take a knife out of his pocket" and stab Sandy Seale. It was an abyss quite capable of swallowing up the Crown's entire case against Marshall and MacNeil asked more questions as he contemplated the unpleasant prospect of having to ask Justice Dubinsky to declare his own witness hostile.

"What took place, what then?"

"Fellow keeled over and that's when I ran."

"You ran from the scene?"

"Yes, sir."

"Can you describe these two men, what they were wearing?"

"The fellow what keeled over, he had a dark jacket and pants and that on. The other fellow had, I thought it was a yellow shirt at first, but after a while he caught up to me and it was a yellow jacket."

"Tell me, sir, before you ran from the scene did you recognize either of these two gentlemen?" MacNeil asked, hoping to get Chant to identify Marshall as the person who had stabbed the victim, as he had testified at the preliminary hearing.

"No, sir."

"Then what did you do?"

"I ran down the tracks and cut across the path right onto – I don't know the name of the street – the street up from George Street – I started to walk up towards the bus terminal and I saw a fellow running towards me. I turned around and started to walk up the other way. He caught up to me and by that time I recognized him and it was a Marshall – Marshall fellow."

From this point on, Maynard Chant's testimony recounted events as he had actually participated in them on the night in question. He told the court that he and Junior Marshall flagged down a car and returned to the scene of the stabbing, that while he helped Sandy Seale, Junior and another boy went to call for an ambulance. He also mentioned a fact that Donald MacNeil would conveniently omit from his bombastic charge to the jury two days later. "He showed his arm and it was bleeding," Maynard said.

Chant told the court he was picked up by police on Hardwood Hill as he was hitchhiking home to Louisbourg after Seale and Marshall were taken to the hospital. He described how the police then took him to the hospital after he told them what he knew about the stabbing in the park. After talking to Detective Mac-Donald (who correctly gathered that Chant's knowledge of events was restricted to what had happened after the stabbing), he was then driven to the police station, where he waited for his father to come in from Louisbourg to take him home.

Despite having told a number of lies that were very damaging to the cause of the accused, Maynard Chant had stopped short of repeating his deadly testimony of the preliminary trial: that he had seen Donald Marshall, Jr., take a knife out of his pocket and stab Sandy Seale. But before prosecutor MacNeil could solve that problem, he would have to deal with another and very much more serious one that had suddenly developed outside the courtroom.

What happened in the ensuing half-hour recess made clear that Maynard Chant wasn't the only Crown witness who was having second thoughts about what he had seen that night on Crescent Street.

For Donald Marshall, Sr., his son's trial was the sorrow of his life. Ever since that spring night on the reserve at Whycocomagh when the police had arrested Junior, the Grand Chief of the Micmac Nation had been living in unrelieved misery. First, there was the terrible loss of the Seale family, which nothing could set right. Then there was his own son, the future Grand Chief of his people, turning eighteen in jail for a crime his father was convinced he hadn't committed. And now this trial, with all its terrible possibilities. He had no words to explain to his children why their brother didn't come home any more, no words to stop his wife's weeping.

Listening to Maynard Chant telling the story that could very well send his son to prison for life had somehow been too much for the troubled father. Halfway through the boy's testimony he walked out of the courtroom and began to pace the corridor. He was so preoccupied that he didn't at first notice the young man with the shock of black hair falling across his forehead watching him intently from across the hall. When he finally did, it took him a moment to recognize John Pratico. The boy seemed to want something.

"I got to talk to you," Pratico said anxiously.

"If you want to talk, talk," Marshall replied.

"Look, boy, that fellow in there didn't do it," Pratico said excitedly.

Donald Marshall, Sr., was astounded, but he realized at once what had to be done. "Hold it," he said to Pratico. He then called over one of the court attendants, telling him to get Simon Khattar as fast as he could. When Khattar emerged from the courtroom, another court attendant told him that John Pratico wanted to talk to him. Khattar joined Pratico, who was still standing beside Donald Marshall, Sr.

"What do you want, Mr. Pratico?"

"Donald Marshall didn't do it, didn't do the stabbing. I want to tell you about the evidence I gave before," the sixteen-year-old said.

Simon Khattar stopped the youth and immediately sent for Sheriff James MacKillop. Only after the sheriff joined the rapidly expanding group outside the courtroom did Khattar allow Pratico to continue. "Jim, this fellow wants to talk to me. I don't want to talk to him alone," Khattar explained, then turned to Pratico. "Tell me what you have on your mind, Mr. Pratico."

"That statement that I gave in the court before..."

For the third time, Pratico was stopped before he could say what was on his mind and his conscience. This time it was Sheriff

MacKillop who interrupted. "Hold it a minute," he said, sending for the Crown prosecutor. A moment later Donald C. MacNeil "came flying out of court," as John Pratico recalled, with Sgt./Det. John MacIntyre, Detective Michael MacDonald, and assistant Crown prosecutor Louis Matheson close behind.

Pratico was whisked into the barristers' room and in the presence of five people tried to change his evidence. "The statement I gave in court before wasn't true," he told them.

"What do you mean? What is not true?" Simon Khattar asked.

"Donald Marshall didn't do it, didn't stab Seale."

"Why did you say it, if it wasn't true?" Khattar asked the young man.

"I was afraid," Pratico said, bringing prosecutor MacNeil to his feet.

"You weren't afraid of me were you?" MacNeil said.

"No, no, no, I wasn't afraid of you," Pratico blurted.

But from where Simon Khattar sat, it was "obvious" that the young man was terrified of the Crown prosecutor. Then Sgt./Det. MacIntyre broke into the conversation. "I didn't say anything to you," Simon Khattar recalled the detective saying to Pratico. The defence counsel had a final word for Pratico before the bizarre meeting ended. "Look, my friend, you tell the truth. Don't you be afraid, you tell the truth."

As John Pratico left the barristers' room, Crown prosecutor Donald MacNeil also had some parting advice – on the subject of the penalty for perjury. It would be the next day before it became clear whose advice Pratico would take.

When court was reconvened at five minutes to four that afternoon, prosecutor MacNeil began his questioning of Maynard Chant as if he hadn't asked his witness a single question prior to the thirty-minute recess. After listening to half a dozen questions he had already heard, Moe Rosenblum objected that MacNeil was exercising a privilege he didn't have: subjecting the witness to a second examination-in-chief.

"If your Lordship pleases, I refer you to page thirty-four of the transcript of the evidence of the preliminary hearing. This is what I am laying the groundwork for," the Crown prosecutor explained.

"Are you asking that this witness be declared hostile?" Justice

Dubinsky asked incredulously. After all, Maynard Chant was a Crown witness.

"Yes, my Lord."

For the second time in the trial, the jury was sent out. To demonstrate why he wanted to impeach his own witness, MacNeil read a portion of Maynard Chant's testimony from the transcript of the preliminary hearing. It contained two inconsistencies with his trial testimony which the Crown viewed to be critical. At the preliminary hearing, Chant claimed to have witnessed Junior Marshall plunge a knife into Sandy Seale's stomach; at the trial, he would only say that a man he couldn't identify at the time hauled an unidentified object out of his pocket and "drove it" into the other man's side. In his earlier testimony, Chant said he recognized the man crouching behind the bush as John Pratico; at the trial, he said he didn't, at the time, recognize whoever had been hiding there.

While Donald MacNeil was reading Chant's previous evidence, Chant himself, the very witness whose testimony he was trying to impugn, was sitting on the stand taking it all in!–a less than ideal state of affairs that Moe Rosenblum brought to the attention of Justice Dubinsky. Ignoring Rosenblum, the judge told the Crown prosecutor to continue with the line of questioning that had been interrupted by an objection from the defence.

"You started to walk down the railway tracks and you noticed this man behind the bush?" MacNeil asked.

"Yes," Chant replied.

"Did you recognize that man?"

"No," Chant replied.

"Did you know him by sight?" MacNeil pressed.

"The only time I knew him by sight was when he was up the police station that Sunday, that following Sunday."

"All right now, as you stood there and watched these two men on Crescent Street, what did you see take place?"

"Saw two men arguing and one fellow hauled an object from his pocket," Chant answered.

"What was that object?"

"I'm not sure."

Maynard Chant was beginning to feel as though he might soon be in trouble for contradicting what he'd said in the other court. He remembered the police saying he could get from two to five years in prison for perjury, and there was still the matter of his being on probation for stealing milk-bottle money in Louisbourg. His resolve not to "put the finger" on Junior Marshall was almost gone.

"And what did he do?" MacNeil asked.

"He drove it into the other fellow's stomach."

After eliciting that answer, prosecutor MacNeil received some unsolicited assistance from Justice Dubinsky, something that would happen more than once before the trial was over, to the consternation of counsel for the defence.

"Who was that man?" the judge interjected.

"Pardon?"

"Who was the man that hauled out the object and drove it—"

"Donald Marshall," Chant answered.

"Pardon?" the Crown prosecutor asked.

"Donald Marshall," Chant calmly replied.

"Did he say that before?" Justice Dubinsky asked.

"No, my Lord. He did not say that before. In his evidence he did not recognize him. I think in his evidence at the preliminary hearing of this inquiry he named Donald Marshall, the accused, and pointed him out to the court as the man who hauled a knife from his pocket and plunged it into the [victim's] abdomen," MacNeil answered.

"I didn't recognize him at that time but after I recognized him," Chant explained.

"After when?" Justice Dubinsky demanded.

"After, when he met me on the other side of the street, after I ran."

"You recognized him?"

"When he came up to me," Chant replied.

"...as being Donald Marshall?" the judge asked.

"Yes."

"But more, what do you say about the man that you recognized as Donald Marshall and the person who you saw doing something, hauling out something and putting it into the stomach of the other person: what do you say about that?" the judge asked. He was confident that the ghosts of Abbott and Costello, who had been haunting his courtroom for the past twenty minutes in a legalistic version of "Who's on first", were about to be exorcised.

"The only thing I know is..."

"Never mind," Justice Dubinsky said impatiently, "tell me, do you or don't you – what do you say as to who that person was?"

"I don't know who that person was," Chant answered, to the exasperation of the judge.

"You say you don't know who the person was who pulled out the knife and stuck it in Seale's body?"

"No, I didn't."

"And you don't even know now if it was a knife or not?" a distraught prosecutor MacNeil added.

Over Moe Rosenblum's objection that what was happening amounted to cross-examination, Justice Dubinsky got the Crown prosecutor to read over the part of Chant's evidence from the preliminary hearing in which he named Donald Marshall as the man who had stabbed Seale in the stomach with a knife. When MacNeil finished reading, the judge turned to Chant once more.

"Did you say that in the court below?"

"Yes, I did."

"You said that?"

"Yes."

"What are saying today?" the judge asked.

"The only reason I knew his name, I mentioned his name because I knew his name – well, I knew who it was after, but up the police station there –" Maynard Chant ended in an incoherent verbal tangle, snared in a lie from which he could not seem to free himself. "I don't know how to put it," he finished weakly.

The judge offered some help. "The man you saw afterwards you recognized as Donald Marshall?"

"Yes," a relieved Maynard Chant answered.

"Did you see him do anything to the other man?"

"Yes," the youth answered.

"You did?"

"Yes."

"What did you see him do?"

"I saw him haul an object out of his pocket and drive it into the stomach of the other man," Chant lied. Moe Rosenblum had heard enough.

"May it please your Lordship, I must protect the rights of the accused by placing my objection on the record. We are now, my Lord, going through a proceeding in the absence of the jury

whereby, with all deference, my Lord, and as respectfully as I can
say it, you yourself have interrogated the witness; my learned
friend has interrogated and cross-examined the witness; my
learned friend has read out aloud in the presence of the witness the
testimony in the court below and I say, my Lord, that my learned
friend's conduct at any rate is now attempting to condition the
witness for his testimony when the jury is brought back into this
room."

Justice Dubinsky was unmoved by Moe Rosenblum's passionate
objections. The jury was brought back in and prosecutor MacNeil
read Maynard Chant's testimony from the preliminary hearing,
asking him answer by answer if what he had previously said was
true. It was an invitation to perjury that Chant couldn't accept. By
the time Rosenblum rose to cross-examine him, the youth was
once more on record as having witnessed Donald Marshall, Jr., stab
Sandy Seale. But not for long.

"Now, Mr. Chant, you're fifteen years of age. And you're in grade
seven?"

"Yes."

"Did you miss any grades in school or have to repeat any
grades?"

"I repeated grade six and grade two and I think grade five," the
witness answered.

"So out of the seven grades that you're in, you repeated three
grades, two, five, and six?"

"Yes."

Hoping that Chant's educational setbacks would incline the jury
to reassess his evidence, Rosenblum took the witness through the
meeting he and Junior Marshall had on the night of May 28. After
getting Chant to tell the court that Junior Marshall's arm had in fact
been bleeding at some point that evening, he asked his biggest
question of the cross-examination. "Now, this question, and you
know you're under oath and I know you're not enjoying this. Under
oath as you are, can you swear before God that Donald Marshall,
whom you met on Byng Avenue, is the man you saw previous; are
you sure of that, under oath before God?"

"Uh, you mean, like, uh – Donald Marshall, when I seen him on
that there street that you were talking about, is the same fellow over
on Crescent Street?"

"Yes."

"No, I'm not sure," Chant answered.

Moe Rosenblum wanted to make sure that the jury didn't think it was hearing things. "When you were talking about the fact that you saw two men over there on Crescent Street arguing, you can't swear that one of those men was Donald Marshall, can you?"

"No, sir," the witness said.

"No!" Rosenblum exclaimed. "All right, and as a a matter of fact you can't swear under oath that the man, whoever he was, that he pulled out a knife; you didn't see a knife or anything like that, did you?"

"Well...."

"You didn't see a knife."

"Listen..."

"Go ahead," Rosenblum told the wavering witness.

"I saw a long, shiny object."

"Yes, but you can't say it was a knife, can you?" Rosenblum said, keeping up the pressure.

"It appeared to myself that it was a knife," Chant answered.

"You thought it was."

"Like the statement I gave here today."

"I don't care what you said today. I'm asking you," Rosenblum began, only to be interrupted by the Crown prosecutor.

"Let him answer the question, my Lord," MacNeil complained.

"I'll let him. I'll let him. I won't be unfair to him, my Lord. He is young and I was young once myself," Rosenblum intoned before returning to the witness. "You thought it was a knife?"

"Yes," Chant replied.

From the defence point of view, the cross-examination was going quite well. Chant had admitted he couldn't positively identify Junior Marshall as the person he had seen stab Sandy Seale, despite his previous testimony during MacNeil's direct examination. Chant also confirmed that he now only thought he had seen a knife. Rosenblum proceeded to turn his attention to Chant's peculiar failure to tell police what he'd seen until a week after the murder — a point Justice Dubinsky hadn't allowed the defence counsel to bring out in his cross-examination of Detective Michael MacDonald.

Picking up Chant's story at the point where he and the accused

returned to the spot where Sandy Seale lay dying on the night of
May 28, Rosenblum had Chant confirm that Junior Marshall flagged
down a passing police car.

"And he was telling them about these two men who had stabbed
Seale and stabbed him, wasn't he?"

"Yes."

"And not only that, not only that, how many police were there?"

"At that time?"

"At that time," said Rosenblum.

"I think there was only two," Chant told him.

"Now, how many police arrived after that?"

"Two more."

"Two more police. And the ambulance–were you there when
the ambulance came?"

"Yes."

"And the police were there then?"

"Yes."

"Now, Maynard, at no time that evening, at no time that evening
in the company of at least four policemen in which you were–
weren't you–"

"Yes," the witness said.

"–did you say to any of those policemen that this boy here
stabbed the man on the ground, did you?" Rosenblum asked.

"No, I didn't," Chant answered.

Rosenblum tried to fortify his point by bringing out that Chant
was picked up by police later that same night and taken back to the
Sydney City Hospital, where he spoke to the detective who was
temporarily in charge of the investigation.

"And at no time did you tell any of those officers on that occasion
that this boy, Donald Marshall, Jr., was the one who stabbed the
fellow who was laying on the ground, Sandy Seale."

"Objection, if your Lordship pleases, register it for the record,"
prosecutor MacNeil interjected. The Crown prosecutor was object-
ing to the admission of a conversation that had taken place without
the accused being present, just as he had successfully done when
the other participant in that conversation, Detective MacDonald,
had been on the stand. This time, he did not bother to present his
objection as a concern for the rights of the accused. He was
overruled by the judge and Rosenblum was allowed to put his
question to Chant again.

"No," the witness replied.

The defence counsel now brought up the third occasion when Maynard Chant had been with police and hadn't told them about seeing Marshall stab Seale: the Sunday morning in Louisbourg when Sgt./Det. MacIntyre and Detective MacDonald had paid him a visit.

"And at no time did·you tell Sergeant Michael MacDonald on Sunday or the other officer or anybody else that it was Donald Marshall who stabbed this fellow who fell down on the street."

Over the objection of the Crown prosecutor, the witness repeated his previous answer.

"No."

Moe Rosenblum was now ready to come to the point he hoped his line of questioning had adequately set up. Was the reason Maynard Chant didn't tell police he'd seen the murder because in fact he hadn't? Had someone else put that story in his head?

"Now, just to clear up something and to help the court and the jury and everybody concerned with this case, the only reason, I'm suggesting to you, that you mentioned in the court below, in the magistrates' court, from which my learned friend read to you, that it was Donald Marshall who pulled out this object that looked to be a knife was because the police told you it was Donald Marshall who did it."

"No, I never," Chant replied.

"They're the ones who told you the name Donald Marshall."

Chant looked desperately at the police officers sitting in the courtroom.

"Don't look at them! Look at me!" Rosenblum thundered.

"No," he said weakly, but Rosenblum didn't hear any conviction behind the words.

"What?" he asked.

"Uh–" Maynard's emotions were coming into play, the same way as they had that day in Louisbourg when he remembered trying to tell police he hadn't seen a thing. And when he became emotional, he was the first to tell you that the truth "just flowed right out".

"Is that the only reason you said that in your evidence in the magistrates' court, was because it was the police told you it was Donald Marshall who did that?"

"Police didn't tell me Donald Marshall did it at all," Maynard replied, trying to hold on to his false story as best he could.

"No, and you didn't tell the police that he did it?" Rosenblum continued.

"No," Chant replied.

"No?"

"Not until afterwards," Maynard said.

"Oh?"

"See, I told them a story that wasn't true."

Maynard Chant was referring to his first false statement to police in which he claimed to have seen two men, six feet tall and wearing overcoats, stab Seale and Marshall – a statement that had never been provided to the defence. But rather than asking the witness what false story Chant had told police, Moe Rosenblum took his cross-examination in another direction.

"When did you tell that untrue story to the police, Maynard?"

"Sunday afternoon," the beleaguered witness answered.

"That was in Louisbourg?"

"That was in Sydney," Chant replied.

"Oh," the surprised defence counsel answered, "I thought you met them in Louisbourg Sunday."

"I did, but they took me in."

"Oh, they took you in to Sydney. How long did you stay at the police station in Sydney on Sunday afternoon?"

"Six o'clock," the witness answered.

"How long a period of time – a half-hour, an hour, two hours?" Rosenblum asked.

"Oh, approximately two hours," Chant said.

"Two hours. And who was questioning you at the police station on Sunday afternoon after you had been speaking to the police in Louisbourg in the earlier afternoon? Who were the police then?"

"I'm not too sure but I think it was that one there." Chant pointed out Sgt./Det. John MacIntyre.

"He was questioning you?" Rosenblum asked, within an ace of stumbling over the fact that Chant had initially given police a first, and equally false, statement.

"Yes."

"And another police officer was questioning you. There was two of them?"

"Yes."

"And for several hours?"

"Yes," Chant replied.

"That's all, my Lord," Moe Rosenblum said, unaware of how close he had come to making Maynard Chant admit that he hadn't seen a thing.

As Chant himself would later say of Rosenblum's cross-examination, "If they had asked me any further questions, I think I would have started to tell the truth, because it was just coming that way. I was brought up to be very emotional with my feelings. And whenever that emotional side would come to me, I would definitely come forward with the truth. That's what happened to me out there at the town hall that day in Louisbourg. The emotional side come through and I said, 'no, I didn't see anything'...but the police rejected that."

Before Maynard Chant left the stand, prosecutor MacNeil asked a single question on redirect examination, a complete answer to which might have broken the case wide open.

"You told my learned friend in your evidence that you told the police an untrue story. Why did you tell them an untrue story?"

"Because I was scared," the fifteen-year-old said, but Moe Rosenblum, with no way of realizing what he was doing, intervened.

"Excuse me, just a moment. Now, my Lord, we're going into the recesses of a man's mind. There's an old saying that even the Devil doesn't know what's going on in a man's mind, it's not triable."

Justice Dubinsky agreed. "Any further questions?" he asked MacNeil.

"No, no further questions but do I understand that your Lordship won't allow the question?" MacNeil asked.

"That's right," the judge answered.

Eleven years later, Maynard Chant would say in an affidavit that he had given his false statement because he had been afraid of the police. He tried to tell the court the same thing in 1971, but he didn't get the chance.

If Maynard Chant's testimony had ended there, Moe Rosenblum's cross-examination might have gone a long way towards discrediting him as a witness. But before Chant left the stand, Justice Dubinsky asked a series of questions whose effect was to reinforce the impression that Chant had indeed seen Donald Marshall, Jr., murder Sandy Seale.

"When was it that you told them the untrue story?" the judge asked.

"On Sunday afternoon," Chant answered.

"On Sunday afternoon in Sydney?"

"Yes."

"Did you at any time tell them the true story?"

"Yes," Chant lied.

"When was that?"

"I don't know what day it was," Chant replied.

"Was it after you had told them first the untrue story?"

"Yes."

"Now, witness, will you look at that – when you saw those two people, you saw one man do something to the other."

"Yes."

"Do you recall anything about the clothing that was worn by the man who did that something to the other person?"

"Yes," Chant answered.

"What do you recall?"

"That he had a yellow jacket on and a dark pair of pants."

"What, if anything, do you say as between the clothing that was worn by this man whom you saw do something and the clothing that was worn by the accused, Donald Marshall?" the judge asked.

"I don't understand," Chant replied.

"What do you say about the clothing that was worn by this man whom you saw do something as regards the clothing that was worn by Donald Marshall whom you saw a few minutes later?"

"They had the same clothing," Chant answered.

With that reply, Maynard Chant was excused from the stand. Donald Marshall, Jr., turned to look at his mother, slowly shaking his head.

Nine days after his release from the mental institution where he had spent the last two months, John Louis Pratico, who had been dead drunk on the night of the murder, took the stand as the second person to claim he had seen Junior Marshall stab Sandy Seale.

In the interval between Pratico's sensational claim in the barristers' room that Junior Marshall hadn't in fact stabbed Seale and his taking the stand, Donald C. MacNeil had decided to begin the examination of his second star witness with an explanation of his extraordinary claim that would leave the Crown's case more or less intact. Pratico, the Crown prosecutor would argue, had repudiated his earlier testimony because he had been afraid of reprisals from the Indians.

"Until you were excluded as a witness in this case a few minutes ago, when you left this courtroom did you discuss this case with anyone?"

"Yes."

"With whom?"

"Mr. Khattar."

"Anyone else?"

"Mr. Marshall."

"Mr. Marshall?"

"Didn't discuss the case with him. I was talking to him," Pratico explained.

"With Mr. Donald Marshall, Sr.?"

"Yes."

"The father of the accused?" MacNeil asked.

"Yes, sir," Pratico told him.

"And as a result of this conversation that you had with Donald Marshall, Sr., what did you do?"

"Went and asked Mr. Khattar–"

"Simon Khattar, Q.C., solicitor for the defence?" MacNeil interposed.

"Lawyer," Pratico answered.

"Yes, lawyer. And with anyone else?"

"No, besides Mr. MacNeil, you and Mr. MacIntyre and Mr. MacDonald."

Unaware of what was going on, Justice Dubinsky interrupted the Crown prosecutor's line of questioning and ordered him to proceed with the evidence. "I have nothing before me that would warrant my listening to what has been up to now your questioning. So proceed with the questioning of the events of that night," he said.

Under questioning from the Crown prosecutor, John Pratico told the court he had met Junior Marshall and Sandy Seale outside the

St. Joseph's Parish hall and walked down by Wentworth Park with them. The witness said the two boys went down into the park and he went in another direction.

"I went down Crescent, down Crescent Street, as far as the railway tracks, there on the railway tracks, and went up behind a bush and I stayed there and I went and sat down in a squat position, kind of behind the bushes where I was sitting."

"What time of the day or night would this be?" MacNeil asked.

"I wouldn't know what time it was. What I'm thinking, it would be 11:30, quarter to twelve. I wouldn't know for sure."

"What were you doing behind the bush?"

"Drinking," Pratico said.

"Tell me, sir, what did you observe, if anything?"

"Well, soon as I observed Donald Marshall and Seale talking, it seemed like they were arguing," Pratico said, offering an observation that wasn't invited by MacNeil's question, the same unsolicited detail with which Maynard Chant had begun his eyewitness account.

"Did you recognize them at the time?"

"Yes," Pratico answered.

"Were there any streetlights in the area?"

"Yes, sir."

"And could you recognize them at that time?"

"Yes," Pratico answered.

"What, if anything, did you see them do?"

"Well, they stood there for a while talking and arguing and then Marshall's hand come out, his right hand come out like this—" Despite John Pratico's gallant attempt at mimicry, he forgot to take into account a significant fact: Junior Marshall was left-handed.

"What do you mean, this way?" MacNeil asked.

"Come out like that, you know, and plunged something into Seale's—like it was shiny and I—"

Having had so much difficulty with Maynard Chant, the Crown prosecutor wanted to be sure the jury wouldn't miss the implication of what Pratico was saying. "Pardon me. You're confusing me. The hand came out of his pocket and you said something about shiny. Now, how does this connect in there?"

"Well, it looked like a shiny object. Come out this way, you know," Pratico said.

"What did he do with the shiny object?"

"Plunged it towards Seale's stomach."

"Into whose stomach?" the Crown asked.

"Seale's," Pratico lied.

"What did Seale do?"

"He fell. And that's the last I seen."

The Crown prosecutor showed John Pratico exhibit three, which the witness proceeded to identify as the coat Donald Marshall, Jr., had been wearing in the park when he stabbed Seale.

It was ten minutes to five when Simon Khattar requested an adjournment. Justice Dubinsky granted it, but not before he gave some blunt instructions to the witness. "I'm not going to have you locked up tonight, but I want you to remember that if anyone apart from your family – your own family – talks to you tonight, between tonight and tomorrow, about this case, you are tomorrow morning to give me the name of every person who says anything to you about the case."

"Yes, sir," John Pratico answered, feeling as though he had solid protection against all of his enemies, real and imagined.

The following day, John Pratico's cross-examination by Simon Khattar began with the admission that he had been dead drunk on the night of the murder.

"Were you sick at the dance on May 28?" Khattar asked.

"Sick?"

"Sick, rum-sick."

"Liquor-sick, yes," Pratico said.

"Were you taken into the washroom and given some help by some of your friends?" Khattar asked, knowing that a number of Indians had helped Pratico into the washroom so he wouldn't be arrested by the police who were on duty at the dance.

"Yes," the witness admitted.

Pratico, who had spent a restless night prowling his mother's darkened house at 201 Bentinck Street, terrified by what the next day might bring, felt surprisingly comfortable. He liked the way Simon Khattar had asked if it was all right to call him by his first name, the way his friends did. And he was glad the defence lawyer didn't have a harsh voice like the Crown prosecutor, who was even "rougher" than Sgt./Det. MacIntyre. The nervous teenager decided he had nothing to fear from the small man who asked his questions slowly and gave him plenty of time to remember the story Crown prosecutor MacNeil had led him and Maynard Chant through so many times in preparation for court.

Speaking in a measured voice, Simon Khattar began to question Pratico on his alleged meeting with Junior Marshall and Sandy Seale on George Street by Wentworth Park, asking the witness if he had spoken to the boys.

"Oh, yes, I said 'Hi' to them," Pratico answered.

In the lower court, Pratico had testified that Marshall and Seale had invited him down to Wentworth Park in a threatening way. Khattar noted the discrepancy and gave the witness a second chance to describe the conversation.

"And you said 'Hi' to them?" he repeated.

"Yes," Pratico answered. "I think it was them two. I'm not sure."

The witness had just looked over at the accused, who was watching him intently as Pratico spun out an event that had never occurred. It was the first time Pratico had ever seen Junior Marshall look frightened.

"You're not sure it was them?" Khattar asked.

"No," Pratico replied.

Khattar quickly established that the section of George Street where the alleged meeting took place was well lit. He then read Pratico a lengthy portion of his evidence from the preliminary hearing in which he claimed a longer conversation had taken place. Pratico, sensing a change in Khattar's friendly demeanor, stuck to his new evidence that no more conversation had taken place than saying hello.

Although Simon Khattar and Moe Rosenblum conducted no independent investigation of their client's story, they did receive some very valuable information on John Pratico from a number of Micmac teenagers with whom the sixteen-year-old loner was friends, information that Khattar now brought out in an attempt to discredit John Pratico's credibility.

"Where did you see Mary Theresa Paul?" Khattar asked. The defence lawyer knew that the Indian girl had been told by Pratico that Junior Marshall hadn't stabbed Sandy Seale.

"Oh, the day I seen her she was at my place," Pratico answered, identifying his residence as 201 Bentinck Street.

"While there, did you make a statement to her that Marshall, that is, Donald Junior Marshall, the accused in this case, didn't do the stabbing?"

"I don't remember that," Pratico said.

"Are you prepared to say you did not make the statement?"

"I'm not saying I didn't make it. I'm just saying I can't remember," Pratico replied.

His nerves were beginning to bother him as Khattar subtly increased the pressure of the cross-examination.

"Do you know Tom Christmas?" the defence counsel asked.

"Yes," Pratico answered, explaining that the two teenagers had met in Wentworth Park the day after the stabbing and the day before he would tell police that he had seen two Hell's Angels from Toronto stab Seale and Marshall and escape in a white Volkswagen. As had been the case with Maynard Chant's first statement to police, the defence was never made aware of Pratico's first statement.

"Were you sober on that occasion?" Khattar asked.

"Yes."

"Was Mr. Christmas sober on that occasion?"

"I believe so."

"Did you talk to him?"

"Yes."

"Did you tell him that Donald Marshall, Jr., did not stab Sandy Seale?"

"Yes," Pratico admitted.

Simon Khattar's strategy was to bring out that Pratico had told a number of people that Junior Marshall had not stabbed Sandy Seale before he gave his June 4 statement to the contrary. Khattar then planned to bring up Pratico's repudiation of his own testimony the day before in the barristers' room. But, before doing that, he wanted to leave the jury with a picture of just how drunk John Pratico had been on the night he claimed to have seen the accused murder Sandy Seale.

"Did I understand you earlier in your evidence to say that you had been drinking on that day, that is, May 28 of this year?"

"Yes, sir," Pratico answered, telling the court that he began his binge at seven or eight o'clock on the night of the murder. He later testified that all of his drinking was done between the hours of seven and ten o'clock.

"What did you first drink on that evening?"

"I think it was wine," Pratico said, identifying a brand called "74". He told the court he drank half the bottle of wine before switching to beer.

"Beer – how much beer did you drink?"

"Maybe half a dozen quarts I drank and pints," Pratico replied.

"Half a dozen quarts and how many pints?" Khattar asked, hoping the jury shared the astonishment he tried to put into his voice.

"Two or three," the witness replied, unable to remember when he had had the beer.

"Did you drink anything else besides beer and wine?" Khattar asked.

"I think so," the witness answered, though he couldn't recall if it had been rum, vodka, or gin. "Well, I would've drank rum if I had it," he told the court. He then recalled leaving the dance, unable to remember if he had been alone.

"Do you remember the time you left the dance?"

"No."

"You have no idea of the time at all?" Khattar asked him.

"No," Pratico replied.

"Were you wearing a wristwatch or a watch of any kind, time-piece of any kind?" Khattar asked.

"No," Pratico answered.

Khattar's last questions presented an interesting point for the jury's consideration. How could John Pratico, drunk, oblivious to the time, and without a watch, know that he had been hiding behind the bush in Wentworth Park between 11:30 and 11:45 p.m., as he had earlier testified?

Simon Khattar now prepared to get down to what John Pratico claimed to have seen that night on Crescent Street. He asked the witness if he noticed anybody else in the vicinity as he made his way down Crescent Street towards his eventual destination, a bush beside the Canadian National Railways tracks behind which he claimed to have witnessed Seale's murder.

"I can't remember seeing anybody," Pratico said.

"Are you prepared to say there was nobody around?" Khattar asked.

"No."

"Was the fact that you couldn't see them because you were so intoxicated?" Khattar asked.

"Might have been," Pratico agreed.

"Were you carrying some liquor on your person?"

"One pint of beer," the witness said.

He went on to say that after parting company with Marshall and Seale, whom he in fact had never seen together that night, he had walked down Crescent Street and then cut into the park, where he proceeded down the railway tracks until he came to a bush. It was from that vantage point, while quaffing his beer, that he claimed to have witnessed the murder.

"When I seen them on Crescent Street they were talking to one—more or less arguing," he said.

"They were arguing. What were they arguing about?" Khattar asked.

"I wouldn't know what they were arguing about. Then I seen Mr. Marshall's hand come out like this here and go towards Mr. Seale's stomach and that's all I seen."

"Give us the details of that now," Khattar told him.

Pratico proceeded to describe the imaginary stabbing. He claimed that Junior Marshall had knifed his victim using his right hand while Sandy Seale stood in front of him with both fists up, an odd position for someone who was about to be stabbed in the abdomen, especially since Pratico was portraying Seale as obviously expecting trouble.

Feeling sick to his stomach, Junior Marshall lowered his head in the prisoner's box. Pratico's lies had conjured up an image of Sandy Seale he would never forget: the young Black standing in front of his killer with both hands tucked deeply into his pockets, never dreaming what was about to happen.

"Now, let me get that clearly. You say your first observation was that Mr. Seale had his fists up?" Simon Khattar asked.

"Yes."

"And then the next, both fists? Right and left?"

"Yes," the witness replied.

"And the next move that you observed was that Mr. Marshall raised his right hand—you know the difference between right and left?" Khattar asked.

"Yes," Pratico answered.

"And it is right you say?" Khattar asked, knowing that the accused was left-handed.

"Yes," Pratico lied.

Sitting in the courtroom, where he had been every day since the trial began, Rudy Poirier couldn't believe his ears. On the morning of Sunday, May 30, he had been sitting on the front porch of John Pratico's house when Junior Marshall passed by on his way home from the police station. Pratico had asked Junior who had done the stabbing, and the young Indian had told them about the grey-haired old man wearing the long coat, and his taller companion. Pratico had even suggested getting together a gang to seek out his friend's assailants. If Pratico had really witnessed the murder, why hadn't he said that day on his porch after Marshall left?

Simon Khattar now returned to an event he hoped would totally discredit Pratico's testimony: his disavowal the previous day in the barristers' room of his evidence at the preliminary hearing.

"Now, Mr. Pratico, were you here yesterday?" Khattar began.

"Yes."

"And do you recall talking with me yesterday afternoon?"

"Yes," the witness answered, unable to remember the time of the conversation.

"Was there anyone else present?"

"Yes."

"Who was present?" Khattar asked.

"The sheriff," Pratico answered.

"The sheriff? What did you say to me in the presence of the sheriff?"

Pratico brushed the shock of black hair from his brow and cocked his head to one side as he answered, a nervous habit he would display several times before the day was through.

"I said that Mr. Marshall didn't stab Mr. Seale."

"That Mr. Marshall didn't stab Mr. Seale – now just to qualify that: before you started to talk, you were introduced to the sheriff?" Khattar asked, wanting the jury to know other people had been privy to the conversation.

"Yes," Pratico agreed.

"By me?"

"Yes."

"And didn't I indicate to you that I didn't wish to talk with you without the sheriff being present?" Khattar asked.

"Yes," the witness said.

The defence counsel then asked what else Pratico had said in the presence of the sheriff. He specifically wanted to bring out that the witness had also told them that his testimony in the court below had been untrue. When Pratico said he couldn't remember saying anything else, Khattar asked him to relate the rest of the conversation in the corridor as it pertained to his testimony in the court below.

"Now, you tell his Lordship and the jury about that conversation, every part."

"I—"

"—concerning the evidence that you had given on June 5 [the preliminary hearing had actually been held on July 5] of 1971," Khattar went on.

Unfortunately for the defence, Justice Dubinsky took that question to be an invitation to conduct a rehearing of the preliminary, something he wasn't prepared to permit. After a lengthy voir dire, he made clear he wanted the cross-examination to deal only with specific inconsistencies in John Pratico's previous testimony.

"Mr. Khattar," the judge said, "you will confine yourself only to that one statement in the evidence in the court below if you wish to do so. Then you go on to matters which are relevant, namely, what took place on the night of May 28, if you want to do so."

Rightly or wrongly, Simon Khattar took the judge's ruling to mean that the only statement he could bring out when his cross-examination resumed was Pratico's assertion that Junior Marshall hadn't stabbed Sandy Seale. The question he had been asking when Justice Dubinsky sent the jury out and ordered the voir dire—what John Pratico had told Khattar and the sheriff about his lower-court testimony being untruthful—was never raised again. John Pratico's eleventh-hour attempt to "get the trial stopped before it went overboard" foundered on a technicality.

"Mr. Pratico, immediately after you made the statement in my presence and the presence of the sheriff, 'Donald Marshall didn't do it, didn't do the stabbing', did you make the same statement to my learned friend, Mr. Donald C. MacNeil, the learned Crown prosecutor?" Khattar asked after the jury was recalled.

"Yes."

"And to whom else did you make the same statement?"

"No, no, no," Justice Dubinsky interrupted, upset by the defence counsel's unfocussed question.

"I'm sorry," Simon Khattar said to the judge, quickly reformulating his question.

"Did you make the same statement to the sheriff again?" he asked.

"The sheriff was there when you were there," the witness answered.

"And wasn't the sheriff present at the time you made the statement to Mr. MacNeil?"

"I think he was."

"And was Sgt./Det. MacIntyre present?"

"Yes."

"Did you make the statement to him?" Khattar asked.

"Made it there when he was there," Pratico said.

"How many times did you make the statement?"

"Just the one statement?"

"These statements to which I have been referring, that is with the sheriff in my presence, with Mr. Donald C. MacNeil, learned Crown prosecutor, Sgt./Det. MacIntyre, were they made in this courthouse?"

"Yes."

"Yesterday afternoon?"

"Yes."

"Thank you. That's the cross-examination."

There was one piece of information that Simon Khattar could have raised with devastating effect had he only been aware of it: the fact that for the last two months John Pratico had been in a mental institution receiving treatment for a nervous breakdown. Not everyone was as oblivious to that as Simon Khattar. The troubled boy had been driven from a psychiatric institution in Cape Breton to another psychiatric institution in Halifax by a detective of the Sydney city police. No one informed Marshall's lawyers about Pratico's condition and they never independently learned about his hospital stay.

When Donald C. MacNeil rose to put questions to Pratico on redirect examination, he knew he had a formidable task ahead of him. Only the day before, he had been forced to ask the judge to declare his first star witness hostile before he could get him to admit by a bald invitation to perjure himself that he had seen Junior Marshall stab Sandy Seale. Now he was faced with John Pratico's extra-courtroom pronouncement that the accused had not stabbed the deceased. It was a secret to no one, least of all the Crown prosecutor, that the case was very much on the table.

The behavior of Chant and Pratico had even stirred doubts in the mind of assistant Crown prosecutor Louis Matheson. Although he had had little day-to-day involvement in the case, which was handled almost exclusively by Donald MacNeil and John MacIntyre, he felt uneasy as the two boys gave their evidence.

"My concern about these two witnesses was they were not very mature, they were erratic, they weren't stable people. I really wondered if the jury would give credit to their testimony. At the time, I myself attributed their erratic behavior to fear of reprisals from the Indians," he recalled many years later.

MacNeil began his reexamination by trying to point out that at the preliminary Pratico had given a very different account of his encounter with Marshall and Seale than he had given to Simon Khattar. But when he started to read to Pratico from his testimony, the same tactic that had brought an unruly Maynard Chant back in line, Justice Dubinsky upheld a defence objection that repeating previous testiomy wasn't, in fact, reexamination. MacNeil promptly turned to Pratico's sensational corridor declaration of the day before.

"Now, with reference to the statement by my learned friend referred to, that you made to the sheriff, to myself, and to Johnnie MacIntyre that took place yesterday afternoon."

"Yes."

"And that took place after his Lordship excluded the witnesses from this courtroom, is that not true?"

"Yes."

"All right. Did you discuss this case with anyone from the time that you left this courtroom on his Lordship's order—"

Simon Khattar rose to object that MacNeil was cross-examining the witness, but Justice Dubinsky overruled him.

"Maybe his voice is a little bit—he naturally has a brusque manner. Not everybody is like Cassius, lean and hungry. But he is directing his questioning to the cross-examination that you brought out," the judge said.

MacNeil was allowed to continue. Once more he asked Pratico if he had discussed the case with anyone after being excluded from the courtroom.

"Yes," Pratico answered.

"With whom did you speak?" MacNeil asked, looking for the name of the accused's father, Donald Marshall, Sr. If he could get Pratico to admit that he had talked to him, he could plant the notion in the jury's mind that his witness's otherwise devastating reversal had been prompted by a fear of reprisals from the Indians.

But Pratico never mentioned the person MacNeil so desperately needed him to identify. There was more to this omission than forgetfulness. Although Pratico had in fact talked to the accused's father outside the courtroom, Donald Marshall, Sr., had not let him talk about the case without first getting a witness–Simon Khattar. The Crown prosecutor himself finally provided the name he had been unable to elicit from Pratico.

"Do you know Donald Marshall, Sr.?" he asked.

The defence immediately objected but Justice Dubinsky allowed MacNeil to continue, telling the accused's lawyers that the question was admissible because Donald Marshall, Sr.,'s name had come up in testimony the previous day.

"All right now, who was that person?" MacNeil continued.

"I spoke to Mr. Marshall," Pratico answered.

"Which Mr. Marshall?" MacNeil asked.

"Senior."

"That is, the father of the accused?"

"Yes."

"You knew him?"

"I knew him to see him," Pratico replied.

"Where did the conversation take place?"

"Just spoke out in the hall for a couple of minutes."

"And as a result of that conversation –"

The defence once more interrupted the Crown prosecutor, prompting Justice Dubinsky to begin his own interrogation of the witness.

"You spoke to Mr. Marshall, Sr., in the hall, you say?" he asked.

"Yes."

"How long did you speak?"

"Just a couple of minutes," Pratico answered.

"What?"

"Just for a couple of minutes."

"Spoke for a few minutes?" the judge repeated.

"Yes."

Prosecutor MacNeil moved in to reclaim his witness. "After you had this conversation with Donald Marshall, Sr., what did Donald Marshall, Sr., do?"

"He got Mr. Khattar," Pratico said.

"Did you talk to Donald Marshall, Sr., after the conversation between my learned friend, Mr. Khattar, myself and Sgt. MacIntyre?" After a confused pause, Pratico said that he had.

"Just for a minute or so. He told me to—"

John Pratico was interrupted before he could say that Donald Marshall, Sr., had told him that if what he was saying was the truth, he had to go on the stand and say that. But Simon Khattar objected that Justice Dubinsky had already ruled that conversations made in the absence of the accused were inadmissible. Ignoring him, the judge began once more to interrogate the witness.

"You talked with Donald Marshall, Sr., afterwards again?"

"Yes," Pratico told him.

"Did you talk with him last night?"

At best, it was a rather wild speculation. Nothing had arisen in evidence to suggest that Donald Marshall, Sr., and Pratico had been talking about the case after the previous day's court session, as Pratico's answer made clear.

"No."

"You didn't?"

"No."

"With anyone?" the judge asked, apparently rising to the prosecutor's suggestion, so far only implicit, that Pratico had changed his story because he'd been pressured.

"No."

"Did anyone come near you?" Justice Dubinsky asked for the fourth time.

"No," the witness answered.

With the subject of possible intimidation of a Crown witness so clearly in the judge's mind, prosecutor MacNeil decided to raise the question of Tom Christmas. If he could suggest that Christmas, the Indian who'd been charged with obstructing justice when he'd paid a visit to Pratico the previous June after learning of Junior Marshall's arrest, had in fact threatened the witness, two things would be accomplished. The Crown could claim that Pratico's sudden reversal of testimony on the previous day, right after talking to the accused's father, had been caused by fear. The Crown could also claim that Pratico's telling Tom Christmas that Junior Marshall hadn't stabbed Sandy Seale, which Simon Khattar had brought out in cross-examination, was attributable to the same thing: fear.

"Now, my learned friend asked you about a conversation that you had with Thomas Christmas. Do you recall a conversation that you had with Thomas Christmas on Bentinck Street in the City of Sydney?"

MacNeil had no sooner finished his question than Moe Rosenblum was on his feet making an objection, advising the judge that the question might be prejudicial to the accused. He did not want something that Tom Christmas might have said to John Pratico helping the jury to the conclusion that his client had something to hide. For the second time in John Pratico's testimony, the jury was sent out.

"If your Lordship pleases, my questions [relate] to a conversation that took place with Thomas Christmas on Bentinck Street in the City of Sydney, at which time Mr. Christmas threatened the witness," MacNeil began to argue.

"Just ask him," Justice Dubinsky said, irritated at the number of interruptions in the trial caused by having to send the jury out.

"What was the nature of that conversation?" MacNeil asked Pratico.

"He come to my house and he asked for me and I was coming out the door at the time he knocked on the door. So Mr. Marshall— I mean Mr. Christmas—said, 'Come on down the park, I want you.' I said, 'No.' He said, 'Why?' I never told him. He said, 'I know why' and he told me, he said, 'You're going to get it now.' He said, 'You squealed on Junior,' which is Donald Marshall."

Pratico went on to say that another Indian, Arty Paul, had directly threatened his life.

"Now, my Lord, I say that this is extremely material as to this witness, that this witness's life has been threatened."

"Is Thomas Christmas here?" Justice Dubinsky asked.

"No, he is a resident of another province for a period of time, my Lord," the Crown prosecutor replied, stressing once again how crucial the threats were to the matter at hand.

"Mr. MacNeil, I would agree with you that it is vitally disturbing and may very well be the subject of another proceeding. I would think it amazing if a witness' life was threatened or his well-being, and the Crown did not take steps against the person who made these threats," Justice Dubinsky said.

"An information was laid, my Lord," MacNeil replied. Strictly speaking, the Crown prosecutor was telling the truth, or at least a part of it. An information had been laid against Tom Christmas the previous June 8. But the charge of obstructing justice by threatening a witness had been dismissed a month earlier when MacNeil himself failed to lead any evidence at Christmas's trial—something the Crown prosecutor must have momentarily forgotten when he began the voir dire by telling Justice Dubinsky that Tom Christmas had threatened John Pratico.

The rest of the voir dire was devoted to a single question: how much of what John Pratico had just said about his conversation with Tom Christmas could be brought out in front of the jury? Because Christmas's side of the conversation was being related by Pratico as hearsay, Justice Dubinsky ruled that MacNeil had to restrict himself to asking the witness why he told Sheriff MacKillop and others that Junior Marshall hadn't stabbed Sandy Seale.

"I can only make my ruling as I see it, which may certainly not be in accord with people—as we call it—'upstairs'," Justice Dubinsky observed.

Simon Khattar then asked if the defence would be permitted to ask a similar question: Why had Pratico recanted his evidence to Khattar and then made a different statement in court? The defence too, expected that the answer would be fear, but not of Indians.

"Would you like to know—do you really want to know the answer why he did?" Justice Dubinsky asked.

"Yes, I do!" a somewhat surprised Simon Khattar replied.

"You don't want that answer, Mr. Khattar," the judge somewhat cryptically pronounced, implying that Pratico's answer would be detrimental to the accused.

Before the jury was recalled, Donald MacNeil told Justice Dubinsky that he also wanted to ask the witness about a conversation he had had with the accused the day after the murder, a conversation he claimed would shed light on why Pratico had changed his story.

"The accused said something to him, leading to his making this statement?" Justice Dubinsky asked, faced with another allegation that Pratico had been threatened by Indians.

"Right," MacNeil answered. "Making the inconsistent statement, yes."

Over the objections of the defence, the judge ruled that MacNeil could ask Pratico about his conversation with Junior Marshall, but he had an admonishment for the Crown prosecutor.

"Now, you understand, Mr. MacNeil, and I rely upon you, that you are not going for any fishing expedition."

"I know what answer I expect, my Lord. I'm not going on a fishing expedition. I am instructed..." he said.

Before asking for the jury, Justice Dubinsky addressed a remark to Moe Rosenblum and Simon Khattar that would later seem highly ironic.

"Like yourselves, we are all endeavoring to do what is justice in this case and we may make mistakes. No judge is known not to have made mistakes."

When court resumed, prosecutor MacNeil got right to the point.

"Now, why did you make that statement yesterday that Mr. Khattar referred to as being made–why did you make that statement which is inconsistent with your evidence as given before these gentlemen and his Lordship in this trial?"

"Scared," Pratico answered, his voice barely above a whisper.

"What's that?" Justice Dubinsky asked.

"I was scared," Pratico answered, repeating verbatim the answer he had already heard the Crown prosecutor give Justice Dubinsky in the voir dire. But the judge wanted more detail.

"Scared of what?"

"Of my life being taken," Pratico replied.

MacNeil began to ask about the conversation between the accused and Pratico that had taken place the day after the murder. The defence objected but Justice Dubinsky allowed the Crown prosecutor to continue. When MacNeil had trouble bringing out the information he was looking for, that Junior Marshall had threatened Pratico the day after the stabbing, the judge took over.

"Mr. Pratico, Mr. MacNeil asked you why you made the statement outside yesterday to Mr. Khattar, to the sheriff. You now say you made it because you were scared of your life."

"Yes," Pratico said.

"Now, being scared of your life, is that because of anything the accused said to you at any time?"

"No," Pratico replied.

"I take it that concludes that line of questioning on the meeting on Saturday," the Crown prosecutor sardonically observed.

"I'm sorry that I had to take over but I had to put an end to this," Justice Dubinsky explained.

"That's all right," the Crown prosecutor said.

Prosecutor MacNeil tried to ask a final question of the witness that would determine whether or not his fear had been justified, but the judge wouldn't permit it. But he did want to know the name of the Indian who prosecutor MacNeil had told him was the cause of John Pratico's fear.

"That man's name was Tom Christmas, was it?" the judge asked, writing down his name without knowing that the Micmac teenager was already in Dorchester Penitentiary.

Vastly relieved that the judge was more interested in Tom Christmas than in him and that his evidence was now over, Pratico left the stand. Twenty-five days later he was readmitted to the same psychiatric institution in Halifax where he had been a patient for the two months preceding Junior Marshall's trial. It would be March 29 of the following year before he would be released.

The Crown called three more witnesses after the lengthy testimony of John Pratico. Pearl McMillan, a laboratory technician at the Sydney City Hospital, told the court that Sandy Seale had type O-positive blood. On cross-examination, Moe Rosenblum emphasized two facts: that the largest segment of the population had type O blood, and that no one at the Sydney City Hospital had typed Junior Marshall's blood on the night his arm had been stitched.

Constable John Hugh Mullowney then testified that he had found a Kleenex on a lawn near the murder scene, also stained with type O blood. Although it had never been linked to the events of May 28, Justice Dubinsky had the policeman mark on the plan of Wentworth Park exactly where the Kleenex had been found. He was then instructed to show the Crown exhibit to the jury. This solemn irrelevancy performed, Constable Mullowney admitted on cross-examination that he'd found the Kleenex the morning after the murder. Whether it had been stained by the mortally wounded boy or someone's bloody nose would never be established.

The last Crown witness was ex-policeman Marvel Mattson, the man who called police after overhearing people talking on his front lawn about a stabbing in Wentworth Park. He testified that he hadn't known that those people were Junior Marshall and Maynard Chant. Mattson said he called police a second time when he saw a man flag down a car and jump in.

On cross-examination, Mattson told Moe Rosenblum that he hadn't noticed a second man get into the car. The second man, who had voluntarily followed Junior Marshall into the brown Chevy Nova, had been Maynard Chant, who, if his story was to be believed, had just witnessed the Indian youth plunge a knife into Sandy Seale's stomach.

At 12:15 p.m., after just under two days of testimony, much of it irrelevant to the question of Junior Marshall's innocence or guilt in the murder of Sandy Seale, the prosecution rested its case.

Over the lunch break, Moe Rosenblum and Simon Khattar finalized the decision to put the accused on the stand. From the interviews both men had conducted with him in county jail, they knew he was not likely to be an impressive witness, largely because he had what Khattar described as "a sort of defect" in his speech. But with Chant and Pratico ultimately sticking with their stories, the defence thought it was a necessary risk to have Junior Marshall testify on his own behalf.

It was the longest afternoon of Junior Marshall's life, though he would in fact spend only an hour and a half in the witness-box. Baffled by the false testimony of Chant and Pratico and unnerved by the packed gallery, he felt his scalp tingle when his name was called, feeling oddly embarrassed by the schoolchildren in the crowd as he walked to the witness-box to be sworn in. "I felt like something in a zoo," he later said of his court ordeal. "I still remember all the kids brought to the courtroom every day by their teachers. They would line up their lunch buckets outside the door, and I remember thinking, 'What am I, some kind of animal on display?'"

He walked to the witness-box with his head down, so nervous

about the prospect of what was to come that his voice would be no more than a whisper when he tried to answer the questions put to him by the lawyers and, on more than one occasion, the judge. Several people who attended his trial would later remember that Junior's extreme shyness and often inaudible answers created an impression of guilt.

After establishing that Marshall had been wearing Roy Gould's yellow jacket on the night of the murder, Moe Rosenblum asked where he'd been before he went to Wentworth Park.

"Home of Tobin's," the witness replied. He would never relax on the stand, answering many questions with a single word as he tried not to make a mistake, tried to figure out what his inquisitors seemed to want him to say.

Rosenblum asked if he had been in Sydney on the days leading up to Friday, May 28.

"No."

"Where were you?"

"Trying to think of the name–"

"Take your hand down, Donnie," Rosenblum said, a request for Junior to take his hand away from his mouth that would be repeated twenty-one times by both lawyers and Justice Dubinsky before Marshall left the stand.

"Bedford," he replied.

Rosenblum asked if he'd been drinking at the Tobin house before going to the park.

"No," Junior replied, though in fact he had had one drink of rum.

This small lie had causes other than Junior's desire to give the "right" answer. Every night after court, alone in his cell in the county jail, he had agonized over whether to admit that he and Seale had been after money from the strangers they had met in the park before the older of the two had done his deadly work with the knife. After watching Chant and Pratico testify, he decided against it. If he said that he and Sandy were out to panhandle from, or roll, the two strangers, the admission would just be grafted onto the lies that had already been told by the Crown's two eyewitnesses. He was already in enough trouble without admitting to anything that could put him in a worse light, even something as trivial as having an illegal drink. Besides, he hadn't murdered Sandy, and that was the charge he was here to answer.

Rosenblum established that the accused had gone to Wentworth Park after he left the Tobin house. "Did you meet anybody in the park?" he asked.

"Sandy Seale," the witness answered.

Oscar Seale leaned forward in his seat. Junior Marshall could feel his eyes on him as Rosenblum asked his next question.

"Sandy Seale. Did you have any argument with him?"

"Will you kindly ask the witness to tell the story. Don't lead him," Justice Dubinsky interjected.

"What happened when you met Sandy Seale?"

"Talking for –" the witness said softly, bringing another interruption from the judge.

"Speak up, Mr. Marshall, please."

"Unfortunately it is very difficult for him to do," Rosenblum interjected. "I have instructed him to do it and I am standing back for him to do that very thing. Take your hand down, Donnie, and speak loud. Now, when you met Sandy Seale, what happened when you met him in the park?"

"We were talking for a couple of minutes and Patterson come down..." Marshall described how he and Sandy Seale put the drunken teenager on the ground and walked over to the bridge in the middle of Wentworth Park.

"Who walked up to the bridge?"

"Me and Seale," he replied.

"Will you put that hand down, Donnie. We want to see and hear you. Yes, you and Seale walked up to the bridge. Go ahead."

Upset by Rosenblum's constant badgering about his hand, Junior began to feel that his own lawyer was against him. It was just like Tom Christmas used to say, "The white guys always stick together in court and don't ever forget it."

"Two men called us up Crescent Street," he replied.

"Two men what?" he asked, becoming concerned that Marshall's mumbled replies might be taken by the jury as a sign of guilt.

"Crescent Street."

"Crescent Street, yes. What happened when you met these two men up there?"

Justice Dubinsky intervened before Marshall could reply. "I appreciate your problem, Mr. Rosenblum, but you must try, to whatever extent you can, not to lead. You're doing it all right now."

"Thank you, my Lord," Rosenblum replied, then returned to the witness. "Yes, you met two men. You'll have to take that hand down, Donnie. I will tell you repeatedly. You met two men and you walked up towards Crescent Street. Go ahead."

"Bummed us for a cigarette," Marshall replied.

"Umm?"

"A cigarette."

"What?"

"Smoke," the witness said, trying to find a word the lawyer would accept.

"What about them?"

"Asked for cigarette," Marshall said again.

"What?"

"And a light."

"When they asked you for the cigarettes and the light, what did you do?"

"I gave it to them," Marshall answered.

"Go ahead," Rosenblum urged.

"I asked them where they were from. Said Manitoba. Told them they looked like priests," the witness said.

"Told them what?" Rosenblum asked.

"Looked like priests."

A murmur went through the crowded courtroom at this strange reply, the part of Junior's story that raised doubts even in Simon Khattar's mind about his client's story. Although the defence counsel had resolved those doubts in Marshall's favor, he wasn't so sure the jury would. Where, after all, would you find the priest who would go around stabbing teenage boys in the park?

"Why did you make that remark to them? Take your hand down, Donnie," said Rosenblum.

"Looked like it."

"In what way?"

"Dress."

"Umm?"

"Dress," the witness repeated.

"What kind of dress? How were they dressed?"

"Long coat," Marshall said, thinking of what the man who had stabbed Sandy was wearing.

"What color?" Rosenblum asked.

"Blue," Marshall replied.

Had Simon Khattar seen the first statement of Patricia Harriss, or the statements of George and Roderick MacNeil, he might not have found his client's answer quite so bizarre. All three had described two men in the area of the park that night, one of them dressed in a long coat. Unfortunately for the accused, defence counsel were never made aware of those statements.

"What religion are you yourself?"

"Catholic," the witness answered.

"So when you asked them if they were priests, did you get an answer?"

Prosecutor MacNeil objected that Rosenblum was misquoting the testimony of the witness, nettling the defence lawyer, who knew that his examination of Marshall wasn't going well.

"I'm very grateful for your interruption," he said acidly, "but please, it is difficult enough without having this."

"Just one minute, if your Lordship pleases, I take an objection to my learned friend leading the witness. I am suggesting that he is putting words into the mouth of this witness that he never uttered."

"Now, gentlemen," Justice Dubinsky said, before Moe Rosenblum made a complaint of his own.

"It is very harsh language, my Lord, with the accused on the witness stand. I resent that."

Watching the three white men, Junior Marshall wondered what on earth they were arguing about. Throughout the trial, he was often bewildered by being forced to listen to endless arguments in his second language.

"What did you say to these men?" Rosenblum asked, rephrasing his question.

"They looked like priests."

"Yes, go ahead. Did you get an answer to that?"

"Yeah."

"Tell us."

"The other guy, the younger one, said, 'We are.' "

"Go ahead."

"They asked me if there were any women down the park. Told them there were lots of them down the park. And any bootleggers. I told them I didn't know."

"Take your hand down, Donnie, please. Go ahead."

"Told us, don't like niggers or Indians," Marshall said.

"Can't hear the witness," prosecutor MacNeil interjected.

"We don't like niggers or Indians," the witness repeated. "Took the knife out of his pocket–"

"Who did?" Rosenblum interrupted.

"The older fellow," came the reply.

Oddly, Moe Rosenblum never asked the witness to describe the man whom Marshall claimed had wielded the knife.

"What did he do?"

"Took the knife out of his pocket."

"Yes?"

"Drove it into Seale." The witness indicated the knife had gone into his friend's stomach.

"Yes. And then?"

"Swung around me, moved my left arm and hit my left arm," Marshall replied.

"Hit your left arm? Just roll back your sleeve, please. Is there a scar now visible from the slash of the knife?"

"Yes," Marshall answered, complying with a request to show the scar to the judge and jury.

"Yes, after that happened what did you do?"

"Ran for help."

"Where did you run?"

"Byng Avenue."

"Take your hand down, Donnie. Did you meet anybody on Byng Avenue?"

"Yeah."

"Who did you meet?"

"I don't know his name," the witness answered.

"Take your hand down," Rosenblum told him.

"Don't know his name."

"Take your hand down, please. Did you see him on the witness stand here?"

The accused identified Maynard Chant and described how they flagged down a car and returned to the scene of the stabbing together. Marshall testified he then went to a house and asked a nearby resident to call an ambulance and the police.

Moe Rosenblum then brought out that Junior spent most of the week following the stabbing at the police station, behavior he hoped the jury would see as being inconsistent with a guilty person's actions, particularly given his client's lack of sophistication. The hesitant, awkward young man on the stand was hardly the sort of person who could devise that kind of ploy to divert suspicion from himself, or so Moe Rosenblum hoped the jury would believe.

"Now, did you stab Sandy Seale?"

"No."

"Or lay hands on him of any kind?"

"No," the accused softly replied.

Moe Rosenblum had asked his last question of Junior Marshall. It was now time for him to face the less friendly fire of Donald C. MacNeil.

The Crown prosecutor wasted no time trying to discredit Marshall's testimony. Quickly establishing that the murder had taken place on Crescent Street, with four participants involved in the incident, according to the accused's account, he confronted the witness with the testimony of Patricia Harriss and Terry Gushue.

"My question is this, didn't Miss Harriss – you know – you know Miss Harriss, the lady who gave evidence in court and Mr. Gushue –"

"Yeah."

"Did you hear him say they were walking along Crescent Street and they saw you?"

"Well, I might have meet them there."

"Are you telling me now that you were called up to these two men from the footbridge?"

"Yes."

"And that is where the incident took place?" MacNeil asked.

"Yeah," Marshall replied, groping for the trap in the prosecutor's question.

"Well, all right, how could you have met Miss Harriss –"

"I don't know where I met –" Junior Marshall began, unable to find the right words. "My mind blacked out on me."

It was a fatal turn of phrase. MacNeil pounced on the opportunity to portray Marshall's answer as a flimsy attempt to get around what he would present as a damning inconsistency in his story: if there really had been four people involved in the incident that led to Sandy Seale's death, why had both Harriss and Gushue testified that they had seen only one other person with the accused on Crescent Street near the murder scene?

"Oh, now there is a blackout in your mind, is there?" he said sarcastically. "When did this blackout take place?"

"After he stabbed me," Junior replied, making yet another blunder. If the blackout had occurred after the stabbing, why would it impair his recollection of meeting Harriss and Gushue, an event that had happened before the murder?

"All right, then, when did Miss Harriss and Mr. Gushue talk to you on Crescent Street? Can you explain that? Take your hand down from your mouth and explain that."

The truth was, as Junior Marshall had initially answered, he had no precise recollection of where or when the meeting had taken place. As he would recall years later, "The guy kept contradicting me every time I opened my mouth, so I just started agreeing with him to get it over with."

MacNeil allowed the witness a few more floundering attempts to explain himself before beginning a series of questions designed to illuminate what he wanted the jury to see as a glaring inconsistency in Marshall's story.

"Well, all right now, what I'm trying to drive at – take your hand down from your mouth, please – what I'm trying to drive at is this, you and Sandy Seale took a walk to the creek and got to the footbridge which separates the creek that is down in the middle of the park – you know where that is?"

"Yeah."

"And that is where you were when these two men called you up onto Crescent Street?"

"Yeah."

"Now, had you been up on Crescent Street before that with Sandy Seale?"

"No," Junior answered, although the truth was he wasn't sure. But as Marshall remembered years later, "The guy just didn't give me time to think. Half the time I didn't know what I was saying."

"All right, then. As you walked up to these two men that called you, when did Miss Harriss see you?"

In his zeal to set a logical trap for the accused, prosecutor MacNeil introduced a critical inconsistency of his own. His question rested on the premise that Marshall had met Harriss and Gushue at the same time as he and Seale were on their way up from the footbridge in Wentworth Park to talk to the two strangers Marshall claimed had called to them from Crescent Street. But that assumption was in direct conflict with the testimony of both Harriss and Gushue, who said that they had left the St. Joseph's dance at 10:30 p.m. and were up on Crescent Street, where they had their brief meeting with Marshall, just before 11 p.m. In other words, Harriss and Gushue had met Marshall an hour *before* Sandy Seale was stabbed. The inconsistency the Crown prosecutor was trying to bring out dwelt in his own question, not in Junior Marshall's admittedly befuddled attempt to answer it.

"Well, there were four of us there, I guess," Marshall answered weakly.

"Did you hear Miss Harriss say that there was one other person?" MacNeil asked, reducing the witness to silence with the single lie in Patricia Harriss's testimony.

"You heard her giving evidence in court yesterday?"

"Pardon," the confused witness answered.

"Did you hear her giving evidence in court yesterday?"

"Yeah."

"Did you hear her say that you were alone except for one other person and didn't know whether it was a man or a woman, because they were standing back away from you?"

"Did she say one?" Marshall asked.

"Yes. My recollection is that she said there was one other person there. Take your hand down from your mouth and answer my question."

But Junior Marshall had no explanation for the erroneous set of facts he was presented with by the Crown prosecutor. Years later he would remember that he had been up on Crescent Street well before he had met Sandy Seale on the footbridge and that Roy Ebsary had asked him for a cigarette. "That must have been when Patricia Harriss saw them two guys with me, like she first told police. But back at my trial, my mind was just a blank, like I told MacNeil. I didn't remember nothing about when I met Harriss and Gushue but he wouldn't listen."

Marshall was then confronted with his version of the conversation he and Seale had with the two strangers just before the stabbing.

"And they asked you for a match, cigarettes, something, and then they said, 'Is there any women around,' and you said, 'Yes, there's lots of them in the park,' and this is when the knife came out and the action took place?" MacNeil asked.

"Yeah," Marshall answered.

"You didn't mention anything about Miss Harriss, meeting Miss Harriss on the road or Mr. Gushue!" MacNeil said, referring to the fact that Marshall's police statement contained no reference to the meeting. "You can't explain that away, can you?" the Crown prosecutor declared triumphantly.

Having painted the young Micmac as a liar, Donald MacNeil now tried to portray him as a hoodlum. "Let me see that arm again. Pull your sleeve up," he said. "Just let the jury have a look at that, please." Marshall complied and the Crown prosecutor then made a strange request.

"Would you turn your arm around and see if there is any other wound on your arm?"

There was no other wound and the prosecutor knew it. But there was the tattoo that read 'I hate cops', a declaration the Crown prosecutor wanted the jury to remember when they began their deliberations. Moe Rosenblum jumped to his feet.

"I object to that, my Lord. The witness is being asked to show a specific part of his body and I don't think he has to expose any other part of his body except that which has relevance to this case."

"That's an arm that has been put into exhibit, if your Lordship pleases," MacNeil blustered.

"No, it hasn't – " Rosenblum answered.

"It has been referred to and on exhibit. It has been referred to by my learned friend. If he is entitled to refer to one portion or a particular part of the arm, surely it is within the right of cross-examination to look at the whole arm to see whether there are any other cuts or bruises or marks of any kind," MacNeil argued.

"There's been no suggestion, my Lord, of any other bruises or marks. We've had medical testimony from two nurses, from three doctors, and from other witnesses and the accused himself, and he has shown the part that he says was wounded and which has been referred to by the medical people. He doesn't have to expose any other part of his body at all," Rosenblum said.

Justice Dubinsky upheld his objection but MacNeil wasn't yet finished with the wound on Junior Marshall's arm. Despite the evidence of his own witness, Maynard Chant, to the contrary, he tried to maintain that the slash on the accused's left forearm had not bled.

"Is it true that when you got down to Brookland Street or Byng Avenue, after running that distance, that you showed your arm to the people down there and there was no blood?"

It wasn't true, either in fact or according to the record of the trial proceedings, and the witness said so. "There was blood on my arm."

"There was blood in it. Did you hear Mr. Chant say there was not blood in it, when you showed it to him?" MacNeil asked, prompting another objection from the defence.

"That's not borne out by the evidence, my Lord. Mr. Chant–and I challenge a reference to the court reporter–that Chant said very shortly after he first looked at the wound, blood was seeping from the wound. That's what Chant said."

Undeterred, Donald MacNeil pushed on. "I asked the witness if when he first showed his arm to Mr. Chant–I forget my wording now–no blood in the wound at all. Did you hear Mr. Chant say that in his evidence?" he once more asked the accused.

"He said a couple of minutes later," Marshall replied.

"Now, did you hear the nurse, Mrs. Harris, I believe–Mrs. Davis–the nurse who admitted you to the hospital, say there were no signs of blood in the wound?" MacNeil continued irrelevantly.

"Yes," the witness answered.

"Pardon," MacNeil said, wanting to make sure the jury heard this answer at least.

"Yeah."

"Did you hear the doctor say there was no sign of blood in the wound?"

"Yes."

"That it didn't bleed," the prosecutor emphasized.

"Yeah. It bled," Marshall replied.

"Pardon?"

"But when I got to the hospital it wasn't bleeding."

"Well, wouldn't the doctor be able to see–was there any reason why the doctor couldn't see where it had bled if there was any blood there?" MacNeil insisted.

Moe Rosenblum objected that the Crown's line of questioning was argumentative, but he was overruled.

"Will you answer my question?" MacNeil boomed.

"A girl gave me a handkerchief," Marshall replied.

"A girl gave you a handkerchief?" MacNeil said mockingly.

"Yes."

"Where did this girl give you the handkerchief?"

"On Byng Avenue."

"What did you do with the handkerchief?" MacNeil asked.

If the Crown prosecutor doubted what the witness was saying, he had only to check with the court reporter. Maynard Chant had previously testified that a passing girl gave Marshall a handkerchief while the two boys were talking on Marvel Mattson's front lawn.

"I don't know," Marshall replied.

MacNeil then suggested to the witness that after he returned to the murder scene on the night of May 28, he had deliberately kept to the back of the wounded youth.

"You stood there where he couldn't see you, when you went back to the scene," he said.

"He was all curled up," the accused answered.

"Yes, that's right, and you stood in such a position that he could not see you, isn't that correct?" MacNeil persisted.

If he was implying that Marshall had done this out of guilt, the Crown prosecutor made no attempt to answer the obvious question: why hadn't Sandy Seale identified Junior Marshall as his assailant to any of three other people who attended him that night while he was still conscious, or later at the hospital during his parents' brief visit?

When Marshall explained that he hadn't lingered around his wounded companion because he'd run for help, MacNeil changed the subject to his flight from the murder scene immediately after he and Seale were stabbed.

"Did these men attempt to follow you?" he asked.

"I started running."

"You started running?"

"Yes."

"Did they attempt to follow you?" he repeated.

"Well, I looked back. They ran behind the house," Marshall answered.

"They ran behind the houses. Why did you not go to a house to seek aid, assistance?" MacNeil asked.

"Well, I wasn't going to take a chance going back," Marshall answered, remembering how his heart had pounded in those terrifying moments after the stabbing. When MacNeil pointed out that there were nine houses on Crescent Street where the accused could have gone for help, Marshall's answer reflected the fear he had felt on the night of the murder.

"By the time somebody comes up, I'm liable to be dead."

"What was that answer, please? I didn't hear the answer, my Lord," Moe Rosenblum said.

"What did you say?" Justice Dubinsky asked. "Take your hand down and keep it down," he added before MacNeil resumed his questioning.

"And tell me, these stitches that the doctor put in your arm, who removed them?"

"I did," the accused answered.

"Why?"

"They were on there too long."

"They were on there too long," the Crown prosecutor said mockingly.

"Yeah," Marshall answered.

"And whose opinion was that, your opinion they were on too long?" MacNeil asked.

"Yeah."

"What?"

"Yeah."

"I can't hear."

"Yes."

"How long did you leave them in there?"

"Fifteen days," Marshall answered. (Normally, doctors allow one day per stitch for proper healing, which in Marshall's case would have meant the stitches were left in five days longer than they should have been.)

"Did you ask to see a doctor in that time in order to get the stitches removed?" MacNeil asked.

"He said he was coming up but he didn't come up," Marshall replied, explaining that the stitches had been falling out by the time Dr. Virick eventually showed up.

"When he got there you had already removed them?" MacNeil asked.

"Yeah."

"Tell me – no, I won't ask that question," the Crown prosecutor said. Had he continued, he would likely have advanced a theory that the investigating officers held: that Marshall had taken out his own stitches and flushed his bandage down the toilet so that authorities couldn't get any material from which they could ascertain his blood type. Without that connection, MacNeil's line of questioning about the stitches was completely irrelevant.

The Crown prosecutor then turned to the fact that the accused had been at John Pratico's house on the two days immediately following the stabbing, visits he would later imply Marshall had made to intimidate the Crown witness.

"I saw him Saturday afternoon," Marshall told him.

"You saw him Saturday afternoon?"

"Yeah."

"Did you see anyone on the railway tracks that evening [Friday night]?" MacNeil asked, eliciting a negative response from the witness.

Justice Dubinsky chose this moment to ask some questions of his own. "Did you say you went to see Pratico on Saturday?" he asked, putting the question as if the accused had set out to visit Pratico.

"I went by his house. I met him on the step," Marshall replied truthfully.

If Justice Dubinsky didn't know that, Donald MacNeil did. On July 2, Rudy Poirier had told police that Marshall "came along walking", and "stopped and talked to us", while the boys were sitting on John Pratico's front porch. It was not a planned visit. He went on to say that Marshall told them that a fifty-year-old man with grey hair had stabbed Seale and that he'd just been at the police station talking to the authorities. Poirier, however, was never called as a witness. Was that because the prosecutor knew that during that Saturday, May 29, conversation, John Pratico had exhibited absolutely no knowledge of the stabbing?

"On Saturday?" the judge continued.

"Yeah, and Saturday," the witness mistakenly answered.

"And Sunday?" the judge corrected him.

"Yeah."

"You say, 'I went by Pratico's house Saturday afternoon'?"

"Yeah."

"And Sunday?"

"And Sunday evening," Marshall replied, unaware of what the Crown prosecutor would make of those meetings in his summation to the jury.

"And you say, 'I met him'–where?"

"Over his house. His place."

"On Saturday where did you meet him?" the judge asked.

"His place," Marshall answered.

"Were you inside?"

"No."

"And on Sunday where did you meet him?"

"His house," Marshall answered.

"Inside?" Justice Dubinsky asked again.

"No."

"Outside?" the judge asked.

"Yes," the witness replied.

After Justice Dubinsky was finished with the witness, Donald MacNeil embarked on his last series of questions dealing with the inconsequential testimony of Adolphus Evers, the RCMP hair and fibres expert. After reiterating the expert witness's opinion that there were a number of superficial separations on the cuff of the jacket Marshall had been wearing on the night of the murder, MacNeil reminded the accused that in the opinion of the RCMP expert the separations had not been caused by a cut.

"Tell me, did you hear the RCMP officer saying that that bottom portion of the sleeve was not cut but that it was torn?" he asked.

"It was cut," Marshall calmly replied, explaining that his cousin had cut it on the night of the stabbing because the pressure of the elasticized cuff was hurting his wrist.

"I know there was a cut there. I realize that, but getting down to the last inch of it, it was torn," MacNeil replied.

The Crown prosecutor's irrelevant observation drew a casual reply from the witness.

"He might have torn it. It was hurting my wrist."

MacNeil quickly changed the subject. "Tell me, was there blood on the front of this jacket?" he asked.

"Yeah."

"Were you near Sandy Seale after he was stabbed—"

"Pardon?"

"Were you near Sandy Seale after he was stabbed?" MacNeil repeated.

"I was near him."

"Were you near enough to him to get blood on your clothing?"

"No."

"Of course, you have never seen these gentlemen before or since?" MacNeil asked facetiously.

"Who?" the witness asked.

"These two gentlemen you talked about that looked like priests."

"No," Junior Marshall replied, answering the last question that he would face from the Crown prosecutor. But not from the judge.

"Mr. Marshall," Justice Dubinsky began, "I didn't get what you said. You saw two men. Two men, and one asked for a cigarette?"

"Yeah."

"Speak up," the judge told him.

"Yes."

"'I gave them a cigarette and a light,'" the judge continued, quoting Marshall's testimony.

"Yeah."

"Now, they were from Manitoba," the judge continued.

"Yeah."

"Who said that? How did you know?"

"I asked them where they were from," Marshall said, repeating his earlier testimony.

"And they said one or two of them was from Manitoba?"

"Yes. The older fellow."

"The old fellow said they were from Manitoba. Then I have here, 'I said, you look like priests.'"

"Yeah."

"Is that correct?" the judge asked.

"Yeah."

"Then what did the younger man say?"

"'We are,'" Marshall answered.

"'We are.' Now then, then what?"

"I don't understand."

"The younger said, 'We are,' and who spoke then, the same one?" Justice Dubinsky asked.

"Pardon?"

"Who went on to say that they didn't like –"

"Colored –"

"The younger or the older?" the judge asked.

"The older," the witness said.

"The older man said what?" the judge repeated.

"We don't like niggers."

"'We don't like niggers or Indians.' That's the older man said that?"

"Yeah."

"And then what happened?"

"He took out a knife and he drove it into Seale's stomach."

"He took a knife from where?"

"His pocket," Marshall answered.

"Out of his pocket and drove it into Seale's stomach."

"And turned on me," the witness answered.

"'Turned around to me,'" the judge repeated.

"Swung the knife at me," Marshall replied.

"'Swung the knife at me,'" the judge echoed.

"I moved my left arm. He cut me in the left arm."

Justice Dubinsky ordered a fifteen-minute recess, and when he returned he had some final questions for the accused.

"Did you know on Saturday that Pratico had been in the park the night before? The night, May 28, did you know when you were over at Pratico's home that Pratico had been in the park the night before, did you know that?" The judge's question was a clear attempt to supply a motive to what in fact had been a chance encounter.

"You mean on Friday night?" Marshall asked.

"Yes," the judge replied.

"No," Junior told him.

"On Saturday, when you were over at his home, at that time did you know that this man had been in the park on Friday night?"

"No."

"You didn't?" the judge asked again.

"No."

"You didn't know on Saturday, nor did you know Sunday, that he had been there?" the judge asked for the third time.

"No," the witness repeated.

"But you were over to his place on Saturday and Sunday," he said, inviting the accused to repeat what he had already told the Crown prosecutor and the judge himself.

"Yeah," Marshall answered.

"And you were talking to him on each occasion?"

"Yeah."

The white men had at last run out of questions and Junior Marshall left the stand uncertain whether he had helped or hurt his cause. On the way back to his seat, he noticed that some of the jurors were looking at his left arm, the arm Justice Dubinsky had ruled they could not see. Judging from their faces, he had a good idea what they were thinking.

12/Life

At 3:18 p.m. on the afternoon of November 4, the defence rested its case. Twelve minutes later Moe Rosenblum was on his feet giving his summation to the jury.

It was the perfect forum for the talents of the feisty attorney who had often crossed swords with Donald MacNeil. Speaking forcefully, without notes, he paraded up and down in front of the jury box, ridiculing the prosecution's case, a case he argued depended entirely on two witnesses and two witnesses alone – John Pratico and Maynard Chant. For the next forty-three minutes, Rosenblum worked with the fervor of an experienced counsel who knew his client's only chance of acquittal depended on discrediting the testimony of the two teenagers. He began with an assault on Maynard Chant.

"Maynard Chant, fifteen years old. He's in grade seven. He has failed in grade two, five, and six. He says that he's walking along and saw a man behind a bush and he looked to see what he was looking at. You remember, gentlemen, what he said in response to questions by me? When I asked him, in the presence of God, under oath as he was, could he say that he saw Marshall stab Seale?, and he said, 'No, I couldn't. I couldn't say that.'"

From Chant's indecisiveness on the stand, Rosenblum moved on to his peculiar behavior on the night of the murder, after returning to the scene of the stabbing with Junior Marshall.

"Chant was there. Now, gentlemen, did Chant say to the ambulance driver, to any of the police, to anybody at all – the man was laying there stabbed – 'There's the fellow who did it, he's standing alongside of me, arrest him'? Did he say that? No." Pausing theatrically to allow his words to kindle doubt in the minds of the jurors, Rosenblum then drove the point home. "Nothing! Nothing! Not only did he not accuse Marshall, he did not tell the police that he saw anything involving Marshall at all, either that night or later. He said, 'I lied to police.' This is what Chant says, this fifteen-year-old boy who failed three grades and is in grade seven."

Rosenblum took a sip of water, then turned his attention to John Pratico.

"He told you what he was drinking – beer, quarts and pints. And he drank a half a bottle of wine. Now, gentlemen, if you don't think that combination wouldn't make a young man drunk, why I don't know what would. He was drunk. Now, we're going to be asked here today – you're going to be asked here today – to take the word of a drunken man, take his word."

Rosenblum paused, walked closer to the jury box, poised to strike what he hoped would be a deadly blow to Pratico's credibility. He began by reading back a portion of the sixteen-year-old's testimony from his notes. "'I was so drunk that I don't know if there was anybody in the park. I don't know if there was any people in the park at all. I don't know.'"

Rosenblum paused to look at the jurors, then continued, "But I will tell you a very significant thing he said, he said Marshall whipped out a knife or a sharp object with his right hand. That's what he said!"

There was no telling if the contradiction had registered with the jury, but the point was a good one. How could a man as oblivious to his surroundings as Pratico was that night observe from behind a bush, while drinking yet another pint of beer, which hand Marshall had allegedly used to pull a knife from his pocket – an action that would have had to be carried out swiftly? While the jurors were considering this oddity, Rosenblum hit them with the delayed punch-line. "Little did he know – little did he know Marshall is left-handed! Marshall is left-handed and he swore it on the witness stand!"

Rosenblum hoped to accomplish two things with this thrust: to discredit Pratico and to lay bare a serious flaw in the Crown's theory that the wound on Marshall's left forearm had been self-inflicted. It was one thing to credit the accused with the kind of surgical control to self-inflict a four-and-a-half-inch cut, uniform in depth throughout, in the instant after murdering his companion, and to do it quickly enough to be able to catch up to Maynard Chant, who ran from the scene with a fifty-foot lead after the stabbing. But to have done it with his right hand when he was left-handed strained credibility to the breaking point.

And then there was Pratico's dramatic denial outside the court-room that Marshall had in fact stabbed Seale. "What did he tell Mr. Khattar in the presence of the sheriff? 'Marshall didn't do the stabbing'; what did he say a few minutes later in the presence of my learned friend, Mr. MacNeil, in the presence of Sergeant MacIn-tyre, in the presence of Sergeant Michael MacDonald? 'Marshall didn't do the stabbing.' And then, ten minutes later, he comes in here on the witness stand and says, 'Marshall did the stabbing.' "

Reminding the jury of Pratico's own explanation of his peculiar behavior–that he was afraid for his life–Rosenblum asked an interesting question, his subtlest of the trial: "Well, why would he be afraid in the barristers' room yesterday? I don't think that there were any gunmen there." Rosenblum hoped the jury would draw the conclusion that Pratico had been afraid not of the Indians, but of the police who had pressured him into signing a false statement.

It was now time to deal with the question of the police.

"They arrested Marshall. On what evidence? On the evidence, on statements which were highly contradictory by Chant because he told them different stories. Chant says so. And Pratico, the drunken man–the drunken man. Well, the question is, gentlemen, as I have asked you before, would you convict a human being, any human being, on the evidence of Pratico or Chant or both of them? I'm suggesting that you shouldn't, that the evidence is unreliable, that it's untruthful, that it's not believable, that it shouldn't con-vince you beyond a reasonable doubt that they're telling the truth, either of them."

Moe Rosenblum turned finally to his own client, the young Micmac sitting with his head down in the prisoner's box. Unsure of whether racial prejudice was playing a part in the proceedings, he prefaced his remarks by cautioning the jury not to have their deliberations influenced by "any intolerance, and discrimination by reason of colour, race, creed or anything of that kind".

Describing Marshall as "a seventeen-year-old boy: uneducated;

untutored," Rosenblum asked the jury to consider whether his actions on the night of the murder were those of a guilty man. "As soon as he gets on Byng Avenue, he says to Chant, 'Look what they did to my arm! C'mon, let's get up there!' Flagged the first car down! This is what Marshall does! They get up to the scene and he runs into the house and gets the police; he's looking for an ambulance, and he stays there. He doesn't run away. He stays there. Would this man act that way? Is Marshall such an actor? Does he look the part? Is he so clever that he could conduct himself in that way? I doubt it! I doubt it!" Rosenblum told the jury.

Rosenblum hoped his doubt would be catching. Before returning to his chair at the defence table, he reminded the jurors that the entire case for the Crown depended on two witnesses, witnesses he mauled a final time before surrendering the floor to prosecutor MacNeil, who had been frantically scribbling notes while Rosenblum spoke. "Chant I told you about. He lied; he's of an inferior mentality. He lied to the police. He never accused Marshall, never. Pratico was drunk, and who said he was in the park except himself and he contradicted himself all over the place. And he told people before he came to court, 'Marshall didn't do the stabbing.' He told that to people, he told it yesterday, as recently as yesterday, in the presence of the sheriff, in the presence of the Crown prosecutor, in the presence of sergeants of the police force: when are you going to believe him? Now? Five minutes later? Ten minutes later? Whenever he changes his mind?"

Moe Rosenblum drew a much-needed breath, looked steadily at the jury box, and offered his final words on the Crown witnesses: "Would you trust them in your everyday life? Would you? Would you? On less important matters than the future of the accused? Would you? I leave you with that."

The experienced Rosenblum knew he had given a stirring speech, but as he took his seat and watched the huge bulk of Donald C. MacNeil rising to speak, he had the strange feeling that the jury had been unmoved by his words. It had been like speaking into a pillow.

Faced with Moe Rosenblum's forceful attack on John Pratico and Maynard Chant, Donald MacNeil decided to give the jurors something else to think about besides the foibles of his star witnesses. Reversing the order in which evidence had been given in court, he began his summation by reviewing the testimony of the last person to take the stand, Donald Marshall, Jr.

Although he told the jurors that it was difficult speaking after the eloquent defence attorney, MacNeil well knew the great advantage involved in speaking last: he would have a chance to refute what had been said by Moe Rosenblum while no one would have the same opportunity with his summation – a very lucky thing, riddled as it turned out to be with half-truths, misinformation, and unsupported innuendo.

MacNeil began by reiterating the bare bones of the accused's story: that he and Seale were standing on the footbridge in Wentworth Park when they were called up to Crescent Street by two men; how the two men, who looked like priests, asked for cigarettes, then inquired if there were any women or bootleggers around, until one of them said, "I don't like niggers and I don't like Indians," and knifed the two boys.

It was "a pretty good story", MacNeil admitted, except for the fact that it didn't account for that meeting with Patricia Harriss and Terry Gushue on Crescent Street. Just as he had in his cross-examination of the accused, he posed what he wanted the jury to believe was a critical contradiction in Marshall's account, a contradiction MacNeil hoped would make the young Indian out as a liar and, by implication, a killer. If the accused and Seale had gone directly from the footbridge in Wentworth Park to join the two men who had called to them from Crescent Street, why had Patricia Harriss seen only one other person with Marshall?

"Now, gentlemen, that's where the key comes in testing the credibility of his story. His story was trimmed unquestionably by the fact that he cannot account for the encounter with Miss Harriss. . . .Gentlemen, there's a very important witness that just took the legs out from under the story and the alibis that's given to you by the accused."

It was a curious use of the word "alibis", since Marshall had never suggested he was somewhere else when the stabbing took place. Even stranger, MacNeil was using an apparent inconsistency – one that was based on a false police statement and the prosecutor's own misconstruction of when the murder and the meeting took place – to dismiss Marshall's entire account of the knife attack. The implication for the jury was that the only conclusion consistent with the story Marshall told was that he had stabbed Sandy Seale. In fact, it meant no more than what the accused had told the court: he couldn't remember exactly when and where he'd met Harriss and Gushue that night.

MacNeil then flatly denied Moe Rosenblum's statement that Junior Marshall called an ambulance for Seale – a fact that was important to the defence argument that Marshall's actions on the night of the murder were not those of a guilty man. "There is no evidence as to him calling an ambulance, [that he] went to a house or something to get them to call an ambulance," he told the jury.

Junior Marshall had, of course, testified that he had run to a house to get an ambulance for Seale. And at the preliminary hearing, which the Crown prosecutor was so fond of quoting from to bring recalcitrant witnesses back into line, two people had also testified that Junior Marshall and Robert MacKay had knocked on Brian Doucette's door and asked him to call an ambulance on the night of the murder. MacNeil knew that, because the witnesses in question had been called by him. Interestingly, the Crown prosecutor called neither man to give testimony at Marshall's Supreme Court trial.

MacNeil now brought up two matters that he had previously raised during the trial, attempting to connect them in a way that would indicate Junior Marshall's guilt. It was to be his most flagrant abuse of the facts during his forty-five-minute summation. The first was the wound on the accused's left arm, a wound which, despite direct trial evidence to the contrary from his own star witness, MacNeil tried once more to say had never bled.

"Gentlemen, you heard evidence here from the admitting nurse at the Sydney City Hospital. You heard her say that she examined the wound of Sandy Seale – I'm sorry, the arm of Marshall. It was a superficial laceration, which means in everyday language a very mere cut, a mere slice. I asked her, and she is a professional, this is her business, was there any blood on that cut and her answer is, 'No, there was not.' I put the same question to Dr. Virick, who came and stitched up the arm, and the reasons why he put the stitches in it. He said to make it a more equal healing so that there would be no scar left and to prevent fraying at the edges or something. But he said, and it's his job to examine it closely, he said that there was no blood or bleeding in the arm!"

Without mentioning that Maynard Chant had testified not only that he'd seen blood flowing from Marshall's arm, but that a girl had given the accused a handkerchief which Marshall testified he had used to clean the wound while the two boys had been talking on Marvel Mattson's front lawn, MacNeil revealed why he was so anxious to make the cut on Marshall's arm bloodless.

"Well, gentlemen, if that is so, where did the blood come from that's on this exhibit, the yellow jacket? If there was no blood coming from the arm of the accused, where did the blood come from that is on his jacket that was identified by Mrs. Mrazek of the RCMP Crime Laboratory as being human blood–where did that blood come from?" Without having entered anything into evidence to establish the blood type found on Marshall's yellow jacket, the Crown prosecutor invited the jury to assume that the blood had been Sandy Seale's.

"Now, gentlemen, we also had in the area found another exhibit, a piece of Kleenex with blood on it, what appeared to the officer who was searching the area, what appeared to be blood. That blood was type O. The same type of blood that Sandy Seale had. Do you know what blood type the accused has? Do you know?"

The jury did not know, and neither did the Crown prosecutor. But the effect of his question was to suggest that he did, which became obvious from another statement he made on the subject of Junior Marshall's blood type. "If, if, Mr. Donald Marshall was blood type O, what do you think the first question the defence lawyer would ask him?" Apart from the logical absurdity of that statement (had the accused's blood group in fact been type O, that would have been equally consistent with his guilt or his innocence), MacNeil's question violated the presumption of innocence in which all accused persons are clothed. He was, in fact, suggesting that Marshall had to prove his innocence by introducing his own blood type to disprove something the Crown had been unable to establish.

Having dispensed with Marshall, Donald MacNeil took off his prosecutor's robes to become counsel for the defence for Maynard Chant and John Pratico. He couldn't be sure what impact his attempt to discredit the accused's testimony would have on the jury, but one thing was certain: if he didn't rehabilitate the two boys, whose credibility had been skilfully eroded by Moe Rosenblum, the case could still be lost, eyewitnesses notwithstanding.

"Now, my learned friend tries to discredit Chant by saying that he failed grade two, three, and six – whatever it was. Well, I'm sorry gentlemen, I'm sorry for that but there were no Ph.D.s that we know of in the park that night."

There were no Ph.D.s on the jury either, and MacNeil pressed his small advantage forcefully. Glancing at his notes on Maynard Chant, where he had indicated the words "Boy had a good set of honest eyes", he went on to talk about his second star witness.

"There's nothing wrong with Chant's eyes. There's nothing wrong with what he said. You don't have to be a doctor, you don't have to be a lawyer, you don't have to be an engineer, to see a man on the street getting stabbed and plunged in the abdomen. Whether he passed grade six or not is unimportant."

He then pointed out to the jury that Chant had come into Sydney that night to go to church, an observation he tried to use to buttress his witness's credibility. "Mr. Chant came in here to go to church! He [Rosenblum] didn't say very much about that when he was talking about Mr. Chant! And any man that would go to church on Friday evening can't be all that bad! He was in here to go to church on Friday evening and he did go to church. That's where he spent the evening."

The Crown prosecutor went on to defend John Pratico against the defence charge that he was an unreliable witness because he had temporarily repudiated his own evidence. Agreeing that Pratico had indeed changed his story on the first day of the trial, MacNeil went on to supply a reason, unencumbered by any proof. "But, gentlemen, my learned friend Mr. Rosenblum forgot to mention to you a little conference that Pratico had with Donald Marshall, Sr. Now, what was that conference? What was that conference?"

Although he never ventured to answer the question, MacNeil's innuendo was obvious: the Grand Chief of the Micmac Nation had somehow pressured Pratico into changing his story. He proceeded to mention the names of other Indians who had "talked" to Pratico before his appearance in court. "And he [Pratico] also said to you the names of the people whom he spoke to or spoke to him before this trial and before the preliminary hearing. I believe their names to be, if my notes serve me correctly, a Mr. Thomas Christmas, Miss

Paul, and another man whose name escapes me at the present time."

Something else escaped the Crown prosecutor. For the second time in the trial, he had neglected to inform the court that Tom Christmas had been acquitted a month earlier of the charge of obstructing justice by threatening a witness in a case that MacNeil himself had handled. "Gentlemen, these two young youths were scared to death," he continued, implying that both of his witnesses had been threatened by the Indians, although no one, including MacNeil, had ever made that claim during the trial with respect to Maynard Chant. "He [Pratico] admitted he was scared. He admitted that is why he told the statement. But, gentlemen, he was in here. He was not under oath when he made those other statements. He came in here and after a very close examination by his Lordship that he knew what an oath was and the consequences of taking an oath, the penalty for lying under an oath, that he could be convicted of perjury and sent to jail, and he went on that stand and he gave his evidence. The evidence is exactly the same as he gave at the preliminary hearing."

Arguing in a similar vein, the Crown prosecutor brought up the subject of the accused's encounters with John Pratico on the Saturday and Sunday following the stabbing–outdoor meetings that took place on Pratico's front porch as Marshall walked along Bentinck Street from the police station on his way back to the reserve.

"Now, gentlemen! Do you wonder why of the thirty-three thousand citizens in the city of Sydney that the accused, Mr. Marshall, goes visiting Mr. Pratico if he didn't know he was in the vicinity of the park that night? Why would he pick Mr. Pratico to go to? I'll tell you why! Because Mr. Pratico saw he and Sandy Seale up on George Street and going into the park! He knew that he was seen by Mr. Pratico going into Wentworth Park with Sandy Seale and that when they found Sandy Seale dead or wounded, and eventually dead in the hospital, Mr. Marshall knew that one of the witnesses was Mr. Pratico, who could place him in the presence of Mr. Seale. Why was there this display of brotherly love and going back on Sunday if it wasn't to get some kind of message across to Mr. Pratico?"

As useful as it was to the prosecution's case to paint Junior

Marshall as an intimidating felon out to silence a potential witness, there was a fundamental problem with MacNeil's theory: it simply wasn't true, as John Pratico had already testified. During MacNeil's redirect examination of Pratico, Justice Dubinsky had interrupted with this question: "Now, your being scared of your life, is that because of anything the accused said to you at any time?" Pratico had denied this suggestion.

MacNeil now spoke to the problem of Pratico's drinking, a subject not so easily talked away. He began by making a virtue of the fact that his witness had been honest about how much he had to drink on the night of the murder. "Now, my learned friend makes a great deal, in fact he exaggerates it in saying the man was drinking. He admits that! If he was a liar, wouldn't it be the easiest thing in the world for him to say, 'No, I had a pint of beer. I had a pint of beer and that's all.' He told you to the best of his recollection and honestly – if he was going to lie, he could have cut down on his consumption of liquor to any degree that he wanted to because there was no way to dispute him. He could have said, 'No, I had nothing to drink,' or 'The pint of beer that I was having behind this bush over here at the park was the first pint I had that night.' He didn't say that! He gave you an honest recollection of what he had to drink."

Before the jurors had a chance to reflect on the particulars of Pratico's liquid honesty – half a bottle of wine, six quarts and two or three pints of beer, and an unremembered quantity of rum – MacNeil forged ahead with his defence of Pratico. "He then said that he came down to – from the dance – he left the dance. He apparently got sick at the dance. This, I suppose, isn't unusual for a – how old is Pratico? sixteen? – fifteen or sixteen – isn't unusual for a man who is indulging in the finer spirits. But, in any event, he did get sick. But he [Rosenblum] worked him into a drunk. If he was drunk, he wouldn't have remembered leaving the dance."

MacNeil then turned to the third problem with Pratico's credibility that he couldn't afford to ignore, partly because the same shortcoming also applied to the testimony of Chant. If the two boys had in fact witnessed the murder, why hadn't they come forward on the night of the attack? Why did it take them both a week to tell police what they had seen?

"My answer to that is quite simple and I am submitting it to you:

fear. And secondly, not wanting – which is a great menace to our society today in the United States of America and in Canada, of not wanting to get involved. That is why they did not tell the police for a week until what I would say brilliant police work brought the whole matter out in the open."

In his final words to the jury the Crown prosecutor praised the quality of evidence he had presented against Junior Marshall. "I am submitting to you gentlemen that the Crown has in the only possible way except if they had a movie camera set up on Crescent Street that night, they have given you the best evidence that you could possibly get and that's an eyewitness. Not one eyewitness, but two eyewitnesses, and I suggest to you that the Crown has discharged its obligation and it is your duty – bound under the oath that you took for office – to find the accused guilty as charged."

The next morning at 10 a.m. sharp, Justice Louis Dubinsky began his charge to the jury. If Moe Rosenblum and Simon Khattar were hoping for a tacit boost to their cause, they must have found his opening remarks as ominous as they were discouraging.

"So long as jurymen and jurywomen approach their task without weakness, without misplaced sympathy, so long as they comply with the oath that they have taken before God, so long will the jury system endure."

The judge then addressed the standard legal principles involved in a murder trial – the types of culpable homicide, presumption of innocence, reasonable doubt, credibility of witnesses, motive, and intent. He told the jurors that when deciding upon the credibility of a witness, they should consider "what chance the witness had to observe the facts" they testified to, and whether the witness was "biased or prejudiced".

On the subject of motive, Justice Dubinsky offered faint assistance to the hopeful defence team. Rosenblum and Khattar believed the prosecution's case was seriously flawed because the Crown hadn't offered any explanation of why Donald Marshall, Jr., would have wanted to slay Sandy Seale. While the judge allowed that proof of a motive in a crime was "permissible and often valuable", he stressed that if all the evidence proved that a person committed a crime, "the presence or absence of motive becomes unimportant."

After speaking for just over an hour, Justice Dubinsky ordered a short recess. When court resumed at 11:30 a.m., the atmosphere had suddenly become tense. The legal generalities had been dispensed with and the lawyers knew that the judge would now turn his attention to the facts of the case – and an implicit assessment of their respective arguments.

Justice Dubinsky got straight to the point, starting with his assessment of the prosecution's case. "I think it is clear that the Crown's case is based principally upon the evidence of two witnesses, Maynard Chant and John Pratico."

Beginning with Chant, he proceeded to review the evidence of the Crown's star witnesses. The first problem he dealt with was the inconsistency in Chant's trial testimony with evidence he had given in the lower court, an inconsistency that led to his being declared a hostile witness on the first day of the trial. "Once a witness is declared hostile and cross-examined upon a previous statement, the jury should be instructed – which I am doing to you – that they are only to consider the previous statement in relation to the witness's credibility and not as relevant to the proof of any fact in the case – unless adopted."

It was a perplexing charge for laymen. What the judge appeared to be saying was that because Chant had said one thing at Marshall's preliminary hearing and another at his trial, the jury were obliged to view his previous and inconsistent testimony as a guide to his overall credibility – and no more than that.

"You do not accept the statement that he made previously as being the truth. You look at it for the purpose of deciding whether or not such a fellow can be believed, a fellow who says something one day and something else the next day."

Left at that, Chant's overall credibility would have been seriously damaged. But the judge added a proviso: "But the law is too that you can accept what he said before if it is adopted by him....My recollection is that he adopted here before you the previous statements that he had made in the court below."

With those words, Justice Dubinsky diverted the jury's attention from Chant's dramatic repudiation of his previous eyewitness testimony – the statement that he couldn't identify Marshall as the man who stabbed Sandy Seale with a knife – and directed it to his grudging reversion as a hostile witness to his testimony in the lower court. The inconsistencies in Chant's evidence, along with the impact they might have had on his overall credibility, slipped behind a cloud of legal smoke.

That left the judge to deal with what he called the two-pronged "main attack" by the defence on Chant's credibility: first, that he had failed to identify Marshall as Seale's assailant on the night of the murder, though he had several opportunities to do so, and second, that he'd lied to police in an earlier account of what he'd seen. Although the judge agreed that the defence criticisms of Chant's testimony were justified "strictly speaking", he urged the jury to be very careful in assessing the young man's evidence.

"In discussing his testimony, you will ask yourselves, did Maynard Chant exhibit the tendency that as reasonable people you might feel many people would have of desperately not wishing to become involved in a very serious matter? You will keep in mind the age of this boy. You will ask yourselves what possible motive would Maynard Chant have in telling the story implicating the accused, Donald Marshall?"

Justice Dubinsky reinforced his point by referring to John Pratico, whose evidence he would shortly consider. "In my opinion there is not the slightest suggestion in this case that Maynard Chant was in collusion with John Pratico, that they acted in cahoots together to concoct a story. There's not the slightest suggestion that these two people were anywheres near one another prior to the events of that night or around that time up to the time when Chant saw Pratico, and that afterwards they got together to tell a story implicating the accused, Donald Marshall, Jr. He [Chant] says that he saw Marshall and this other man arguing. Pratico said that they were arguing. He said – what he said here first – that he saw him haul out something. Later he acknowledged it was a knife, or, as he put it, 'he hauled out something which I thought was a knife, something shiny.' Pratico said the same thing. Is he [Chant] a liar?" the judge asked rhetorically.

Since Justice Dubinsky had linked the corroborating evidence of Chant and Pratico before asking if Chant was a liar, the effect of his rhetorical question was to present the jury with a dilemma. If they decided Chant was a liar, they would have to come to the same conclusion about John Pratico, who was telling the same story. They believed either both witnesses or neither. And since Justice

Dubinsky had already ruled out the possibility of collusion between the two boys, any juror who wanted to discount Chant's testimony was faced with a very unlikely proposition: namely, that two unrelated witnesses were independently falsifying evidence in a murder trial to frame the same innocent man for no discernible reason. As the judge himself put it, "what possible motive, what motive, would Maynard Chant have in telling the story implicating the accused, Donald Marshall?"

Although the case for the defence had not fared very well with Justice Dubinsky's account of Maynard Chant's testimony, they had reason to believe their fortunes would improve when it came time to assess John Pratico's evidence. After all, by Pratico's own admission he had been extremely drunk on the night he claimed to have witnessed the murder. And then there was his sensational declaration outside the courtroom that Donald Marshall, Jr., hadn't stabbed the deceased.

From the defence point of view, Justice Dubinsky's review of Pratico's evidence began auspiciously enough. "He drank that night, disgracefully—drank disgracefully. It certainly is a sad commentary on the authorities in this community that a young man of that age would be able to arrange to have liquor from the liquor store or wherever he got it. He drank wine and beer and whatever else he could get his hands on," the judge said.

But having raised the issue of Pratico's drunkenness, Justice Dubinsky didn't relate it to his credibility as a witness. Instead, he returned to the same question he'd asked about Maynard Chant's testimony: motive.

"What motive would lead this young man to concoct a story, a dreadful story if untrue, to place the blame of a heinous crime on the shoulders of an innocent man? What possible motive would Pratico have to say that Donald Marshall stabbed Sandy Seale? He had been drinking. In assessing his evidence you will have to ask yourselves, is this a drunken recital or is it a recital of two eyewitnesses as to whom there is no evidence by the Crown that they got together, were in collusion, to concoct the story?"

It was becoming clear to the defence team that the strange behavior of Chant and Pratico during the trial had made less of an impression on Justice Dubinsky than the fact that they ended up telling the same story on the stand. Moe Rosenblum began jotting down points that might be used in any future appeal, should the verdict go against his client. One of them was that the learned trial judge erred by his charge to the jury in that he gave his own opinion on certain aspects of the evidence, an opinion that was highly prejudicial to the accused.

In conclusion, Louis Dubinsky turned his attention to the testimony of Donald Marshall, Jr. He reminded the jury that the accused didn't have to convince them of his innocence – something Donald MacNeil's summation might have led them to forget. But, having taken the stand, Marshall was a witness like the twenty people who had testified before him; the jurors would have to assess his credibility along with the others'.

The judge said there were two ways of looking at Marshall's testimony. In his favor, he had stood up to "a very rigorous cross-examination by a very capable Crown prosecutor". On the night of the murder, he had returned to the scene of the stabbing and flagged down a passing police car. Later, he had willingly accompanied police to the hospital. "I think you have to ask yourselves, on the one hand, is that the action of a man who has just committed a crime, who will flag down a police car, who will go with the police, who will do the things he did and who maintains the consistency of his story? Keep in mind, as I said, that he does not have to prove his innocence."

The judge then came to Marshall's story that two men in priest-like clothing made a racially inspired attack on the young Black and the young Indian after having a conversation about women and liquor – a story that he understandably questioned. Neither the judge nor any of the lawyers knew about the true nature of the confrontation in the park on the night of the murder between the two teenage boys out for some money and Ebsary and MacNeil.

"Why, without the slightest gesture, without the slightest verbal attack or physical gesture, without the slightest provocation, would one of these so-called priests take out a knife and make a murderous attack on Sandy Seale and on the accused himself?"

For the third time since he had begun talking nearly two and a half hours earlier, Louis Dubinsky had raised the issue of motive, or rather the lack of one, to implicitly lend weight to the prosecution's case. Nor did he ask the question that Donald MacNeil had carefully ignored: why would Junior Marshall want to kill Sandy Seale?

At 12:35 p.m. Justice Dubinsky sent the jury out with the reminder that an accused person was entitled to "a fair and impartial trial without any sympathy, without any misguided sentimental feeling. . . ."

After the twelve men left, the Crown prosecutor raised a few points he wanted to have expressed to the jury. In rejecting Donald MacNeil's request, Justice Dubinsky made a prophetic remark: "I am satisfied that, based upon my experience on the Bench and the cases I have read, that the matter has been properly decided. I may of course some day find to my great surprise that it wasn't so."

Just under four hours after the judge finished his charge, the jury returned.

"Gentlemen, have you agreed upon your verdict?" the Clerk of the Court asked.

"Yes," replied its foreman, J. T. Townsend.

"Do you find the Accused, Donald Marshall, Jr., guilty or not guilty?"

"Guilty," the foreman replied. A murmur went round the courtroom, and Donald Marshall, Sr., buried his face in his hands.

"Gentlemen of the Jury, hearken to your verdict as the court hath recorded it: you say you find the Accused, Donald Marshall, Jr., guilty; as one says, so you all say?"

The rest of the jurors indicated their assent.

Justice Dubinsky thanked them, congratulated Moe Rosenblum and Simon Khattar for putting up the best defence effort he'd seen in his years on the bench, and praised the Crown prosecutor for displaying an attitude that was "in the best tradition of the profession of law".

In his pre-sentence remarks, the judge said there was no sentence he could pass that could "equal the personal anguish that he [Marshall] must carry throughout his life that he had taken the life of a fellow human being." He hoped that the case would provide "a lesson to others" about the heartache caused by people who resort to violence.

Turning to the teenager in the prisoner's box, Justice Dubinsky said, "What the future will be for the Accused is not for me to speculate at this time. The institution to which I will send him will be one where his conduct in the future will be looked upon and much will depend upon himself in the years ahead."

The judge asked the accused to stand up, and at a quarter to five on the afternoon of November 5 he pronounced sentence. "The sentence of the Court is that you, Donald Marshall, Jr., shall be imprisoned in Dorchester Penitentiary in Dorchester, New Brunswick, subject to the rules and regulations of that institution for life."

"I heard his words but they seemed to come apart, they made no sense. I felt like I did sometimes when I got lost in the woods. I didn't know where I was. Then it hit me: I was going away for life." With that realization, Junior Marshall hung his head and wept.

Maynard Chant was outside on the courthouse steps talking to John Seale, Sandy's older brother, when he got word of the verdict. Years later he recalled: "I know I didn't see him do it and that was playin' on me. But I'd been told he was braggin' that he did it down at the jail. So basically I didn't feel no remorse because, uh, there was a chance that I thought maybe he was guilty and I wasn't doing such a terrible thing after all."

John Pratico was at home when he found out about Marshall's conviction. Fittingly, he got the news over the radio – the same way he had first learned about the stabbing in Wentworth Park. "I was feeling bad for Marshall, yet I was scared of the police. I felt sorry for the poor bugger."

13/The Truth

All of Sydney may have known about the Seale murder and Junior Marshall's life sentence for the crime, but one native son who was oblivious to the sensational events of the past few weeks was thirty-year-old John Joseph MacNeil, Jimmy MacNeil's older brother. A rambler, John MacNeil had left Sydney several years before, settling in Toronto, where he found work with an office supply company. It was John's job to ride the endless canyons of the city's business district, picking up broken filing cabinets and bringing them back to the shop for repair. Although the work was steady and the money was good, Toronto still didn't feel like home. So every two years or so he left the apartment he shared with his common-law wife and headed down East for a visit.

On the 14th of November, 1971, the six-foot-three red-head boarded a train at Union Station bound for Sydney, Nova Scotia. He had purposely chosen not to call ahead so he could surprise his mother. It was just as well. By the time he swung down from the train into a bone-chilling Maritime blow, it was 2:30 in the morning. Feeling glad to be back, he turned up his collar and walked the few blocks to the family home at 1007 Rear George Street.

John MacNeil was the kind of person you heard before you saw. From the moment one of his brothers opened the living-room curtains a crack to see who was making all the noise, the homecoming was a big success. John's mother put the kettle on and his brothers and sister gathered round for a talk that went on far into the night. It was like old times. At five in the morning, when John finally went to bed, he found himself wondering why he'd ever left Sydney in the first place.

But the train-ride and the tea had left him restless as a cat. He was up again at seven, wide awake and hungry. When he went down to the kitchen to get something to eat, he was surprised to find his younger brother, Jimmy, red-eyed and intense, huddled over a cup of coffee.

Jimmy and John were close, despite John's penchant for practical jokes that often featured his meek younger brother as their butt. Once Jimmy had visited John in Toronto and the husky red-head promised to set him up with a girl, provided he could match him drink for drink in a local bar beforehand. It was a hopeless task ("John was a big man, I could go inside him twice"), but Jimmy did his best. Next morning when he woke up on the chesterfield in John's apartment, he could feel heavy breathing against his cheek, proof that his brother had kept his word. "John must have got me a big one," Jimmy thought until he rolled over and found himself face to face with a wheezing St. Bernard!

But whatever was bothering his younger brother on this particular morning, John MacNeil knew it was no joking matter. "What's wrong with you? There's something wrong with you, Jim," he said.

"There's something on my mind," Jimmy admitted.

After a little prodding, Jimmy said he hadn't been sleeping lately on account of the recent murder and trial. John pricked up his ears.

"There's an innocent fellow in jail for something he never done," Jimmy said, explaining that he'd been with the real killer on the night of the murder, had in fact seen everything. But his buddy, Roy Ebsary, had told him to forget the whole thing. It was self-defence, Ebsary told him, and besides, he had two kids. Nervous of the police and afraid of Roy, Jimmy had kept the story to himself.

"Truth is," he told his brother, "I never thought they'd convict that Indian fella. He had nothing to do with it."

"Go down to the police, for Christ sake, don't—go down to the police!" was John's immediate and decisive reply.

All that day, the MacNeil brothers, sister Florence, and their mother talked over what should be done. In the end everyone agreed: they had to go to the police. Even if it caused him trouble, Jimmy himself had nothing to fear; he had done nothing wrong. Though still nervous, Jimmy agreed to go, provided his brothers John and David accompanied him.

At 6 p.m. they showed up at the Sydney city police station and asked to see a detective. The officer on the desk returned with Detective William Urquhart, one of the investigators of the Seale murder case. After listening to their remarkable story, Urquhart and Detective Michael J. MacDonald took a statement from John MacNeil at 6:25 p.m.

"He said he was there and a fellow got life for it and he had nothing to do with it," John told the two detectives. "So I asked him how he didn't go to the police. He said he was scared. He said the guy said for him to forget about it. He said he saw the fellow stab the fellow in the park. He said the Indian guy had his hand behind his back."

"Did he tell you the name of the man that stabbed the man in the park?" Detective Urquhart asked.

"Yes, but I can't remember the name. It sounded French," MacNeil replied.

Before taking a statement from nineteen-year-old David Mac-Neil, who had heard Jimmy's story two weeks before his brother John had, a call was put in to Sgt./Det. MacIntyre, advising him of the situation. At 7:10, the youngest of the MacNeil boys gave police a much more detailed account of what Jimmy had told him happened in the park on the night of May 28, including the crucial fact his older brother hadn't been able to remember: the name of the man who stabbed Sandy Seale.

"About two weeks ago, my brother James told me that himself and Roy Ebsary were walking through the Wentworth Park. He said Donald Marshall and Sandy Seale were on Crescent Street. Donald Marshall grabbed my brother. He put his arm up behind his back. Marshall and Seale asked for money. Marshall asked Seale to search James' father [Roy Ebsary]. Seale went to search him and Roy Ebsary said, 'Wait, I have something,' and he pulled out a knife and stabbed Seale in the stomach. Then he stabbed Marshall in the arm. My brother went to Roy's house on Argyle Street and he [Ebsary] washed the knife under the tap."

An hour after the MacNeils showed up at the station, a very nervous Jimmy MacNeil took his turn in the detectives' room. By this time, Sgt./Det. John MacIntyre, the chief investigator of the Seale murder case, had arrived to take over the questioning.

"Shaking" with fear, the tall young man with the wide-set blue eyes proceeded to give his eyewitness account of the Seale murder.

"Myself and Roy Ebsary were at the State Tavern, George Street, Sydney, late in the evening in May of this year. We were there about an hour or so. We left. We walked down George Street and took the short cut through the Park [Wentworth]. We came up to Crescent Street, we were approached by an Indian and a colored fellow from behind. The Indian put my right hand up behind my back. The colored fellow said, 'Dig, man, dig.' Then Roy Ebsary said, 'I got something for you.' He put his hand in his right pocket and took out a knife and drove it into the colored fellow's side."

An experienced detective, MacIntyre had been listening hard for a detail that would give MacNeil's story away as false.

"What side?" he asked, knowing that Seale's wound had been to the left side.

"The left side of the colored fellow. I seen Roy's hand and knife full of blood," Jimmy said, adding that he had not seen Roy stab Marshall.

"What happened next?"

"Roy went home and I was with him. He washed the knife under the tap and washed his hands off. Then he told me not to say anything about it."

"Did you ask him why he done it?"

"Yes. He said it was self-defence."

MacIntyre, who was astonished by MacNeil's story, tried once more to trip him up on a point of fact. Knowing that the murder had taken place a little before midnight, he asked the nervous 25-year-old what time he had arrived at Ebsary's house.

"About 12 p.m." MacNeil had passed the test again. Rear Argyle Street, where Roy Ebsary lived, was a five-minute walk from the scene of the murder. At the very least, Jimmy MacNeil's story remained plausible.

"When did you see Roy again?" the detective asked.

"The next day I went to his house. He was laying in bed. I told him, 'That fella died,'" Jimmy answered without hesitation.

"What did he say?"

"He said it was self-defence. I told him he did not have to kill him. He told me he had two children – a girl and a boy – and not to say anything to the police. I left then."

Still thinking of ways to test the credibility of MacNeil's increasingly detailed story, MacIntyre tried another tack.

"Who seen you at the house besides Roy?"

"His wife, daughter, and son," Jimmy promptly answered.

"Did they say anything to you?"

"No. Not that day," MacNeil said. "About two days after that his son, about eighteen or nineteen years old, came to my house with his car. He drove me out to the Wandlyn Motel and his mother came out to the car. She got in the back seat. He got in and she said don't go coming to their house no more because of what Roy done. The young fellow told me if I mentioned what happened to the police all your family will be in trouble. They will have to go to court."

"Was his mother present when he said that?" the detective asked.

"No."

Knowing that Marshall had said in court that his assailant had been dressed in a long cloak, like a priest's soutane, the detective now asked a crucial question.

"What was Roy wearing?"

"A black shawl over his shoulders, something like a priest wears over his shoulders," MacNeil answered. It was exactly the same word Junior Marshall had used at his trial to describe the singular coat worn by Sandy Seale's killer.

"When did you tell somebody about this?"

"The first one I told was my mother. She noticed I was not sleeping. And walking around since the trial. She asked me and I told her about the stabbing. And the Indian man who was in jail for something he didn't do. It isn't fair. Then I told my brother Johnnie last night. He told me to go to the police," MacNeil replied.

"Did you know Marshall or Seale that night?" the detective asked.

"No," Jimmy replied.

The interview ended with a remarkable omission. Sgt./Det. MacIntyre never asked Jimmy MacNeil for a description of Roy Ebsary.

Before he was permitted to leave, Jimmy MacNeil had to retell his explosive story to one more person, the assistant Crown prosecutor, Louis Matheson. Matheson had just finished his supper when he got a call from Detective Norman MacCaskill asking him to get down to the police station right away. When he arrived, he listened in astonishment to what Jimmy MacNeil had to say, wishing that Crown prosecutor MacNeil were not out of the country in Virginia.

"My impression of him [Jimmy MacNeil] was he seemed to be very nervous, upset, and I didn't know whether to believe him or not," Matheson later said.

Matheson ordered the police to pick up the other people Mac-Neil had mentioned in his statement, keep them separated, and question them. After that was done, they would see what they had on their hands and, if necessary, work out further plans.

Just before 8 p.m., a vastly relieved Jimmy MacNeil joined his brothers and left the police station. Outside, he felt good for the first time in two weeks. Although he hadn't come forward during the trial, the minimum of harm had been done by his silence. Marshall had served only ten days of his life sentence for a murder he didn't commit and now, surely, he would be freed.

The atmosphere in the Sydney city police station had suddenly become electric. Faced with devastating eyewitness evidence that possibly meant that the wrong man had been convicted of murder, the Sydney city police dispatched separate cars to the Ebsary home at 126 Rear Argyle Street and picked up Roy, his wife, Mary, and their teenage son, Greg, for questioning.

Inexplicably, the detectives decided not to interview thirteen-year-old Donna Ebsary, despite being told by Jimmy MacNeil that she was one of the family members present when he and Roy Ebsary returned from Wentworth Park around midnight on May 28. It was a critical oversight. Donna had followed her father and Jimmy MacNeil into the kitchen that night, overheard their conversation, and watched Roy wash off a bloody, brown-handled knife in the sink before taking it upstairs. But the girl who knew where the murder weapon had been taken was left in a car with the family dog for three hours while her father, mother, and brother were questioned.

Mary Ebsary was the first to be interviewed by Sgt./Det. John MacIntyre at 8:45 p.m. Mrs. Ebsary was a bundle of nerves. Although she wanted to believe that Roy wasn't mixed up in the Seale murder, she was well aware of his violent side. When the children were small, she often had to get them out of the house to

protect them from Roy. The detective asked her about the meeting
Jimmy MacNeil claimed took place in a car outside Sydney's
Wandlyn Motel. Mrs. Ebsary readily confirmed it, admitting that
she had been the one who'd sent for her husband's former
acquaintance. "The conversation was about this boy Jim and my
husband being attacked that night coming home by the park," she
said. "Jim thought that it may be the same two–the Marshall boy
and Seale boy. I told him making statements like that–I would
prefer he stay away from my house."

She told Sgt./Det. MacIntyre that her son Greg had been in the
car at the time. He asked if she had seen Jimmy MacNeil prior to the
night of the murder.

"Quite frequently," she told him.

"Where?"

"At my house."

"What was he doing there?"

"Drinking with my husband," she replied.

"Was Jimmy back and forth to your house at that time?" Sgt./Det.
MacIntyre asked.

"Not after. He came about fifteen times over a period of a couple
of months."

Sgt./Det. MacIntyre ended his interview with Mary Ebsary without asking if her husband carried a knife. Had they inquired, she
could have told them quite a story: that Roy had knives of all shapes
and sizes, that he habitually carried them, and that he was almost
certain to have been carrying one on the night of the murder in
either of his two favorite places, stuck in his belt or concealed
inside the hollowed-out handle of a cane. She could also have told
them about his peculiar hobby of honing his collection of daggers
to stiletto sharpness on a grindstone in the basement.

But Sgt./Det. John MacIntyre didn't ask and Mary Ebsary wasn't
about to volunteer any information about her common-law husband of twenty-one years. She had spent most of her adult life
indulging Roy Ebsary in what she regarded as his quirks and
infirmities, and even though she was embittered by the succession
of young men that had passed through their house over the years,
she wasn't about to change that now.

At 9:15 p.m., Sgt./Det. MacIntyre turned his attention to Roy
Newman Ebsary. A native of St. John's, Newfoundland, and a

former merchant mariner, Ebsary was something of a local character in Sydney, as the police would later explain to Louis Matheson. At fifty-nine, he was a well-known "stemmer" – what in other places would be less elegantly known as a wino. He had a taste for flamboyant clothes and never tired of talking about his glory-studded war record. More than once the small man with the whitish hair and the goatee had told his half-impressed, half-incredulous cronies that he'd been present at the sinking of the *Bismarck* and that he had been decorated by Winston Churchill and Charles de Gaulle. Although none of them dared to say so (Roy was known for his explosive temper), many of his acquaintances thought Roy's small stature was behind his need for self-glorification. At five foot two, the vegetable-cutter at Sydney's Isle Royale Hotel was a most unlikely protagonist for the swashbuckling tales he could so easily invent.

The story he told to detectives that night closely paralleled Jimmy MacNeil's. After drinking with the young man at the State Tavern – six or seven beers apiece – Ebsary confirmed that the two men were on the way back to his house through Wentworth Park when they were accosted by two youths. "When we were almost over to the corner of South Bentinck Street, two chaps who were behind us came around the sides of us and asked us if we had cigarettes and if we had any money. We told them we didn't. They asked us to turn out our pockets, so we turned out our pockets."

So far MacNeil and Ebsary appeared to be describing the same event, something between high-pressure panhandling and a low-grade mugging. But while MacNeil said the confrontation had turned into a brutal murder, Ebsary claimed it had ended in an abortive robbery, thwarted by his own heroics. "The short fellow tried to take my ring off my finger while the tall fellow had his arm around the other fellow's throat and had him on the ground," Ebsary told detectives. "I tried to wrestle him. He slung me onto the ground. I made a kick at him and he got up and ran off. I went over to see how Jim was getting along with the other fellow and he dropped Jim and ran off with the other fellow."

Jimmy MacNeil had mentioned nothing of this kind of altercation, saying only that Marshall had held his arm behind his back.

"Did you stab the man you were wrestling with?" Sgt./Det. MacIntyre asked.

"Hell no. Why would I stab him?" Ebsary said. Even though he was lying, his answer made one thing clear: he certainly hadn't felt in fear of his life during the encounter in the park.

"How old were these fellas?"

"Young men – one fella was tall. I had to look up at him."

"What were they wearing?"

"I would not be able to say," Ebsary replied.

"What nationality were they?"

"I believe Canadian. I asked them where they were from when they asked us for the money and they said Truro."

"Were they white or colored?"

"Well, the tall fellow, I seen his face, I thought he was white."

"What about the short fellow?"

"I would say he was white too." Ebsary's answer was not as contradictory as it might have seemed, especially to Sgt./Det. John MacIntyre, who would later describe Sandy as "more of the mulatto type" and "very light for a black person".

"Where did you go then?" Sgt./Det. MacIntyre asked.

"I went home."

"Where did Jimmy go?"

"He went to my place for a few minutes and then he went home to Hardwood Hill."

As critical as those few minutes were, Sgt./Det. MacIntyre never asked Ebsary if he had washed off a bloody knife in his kitchen sink that night, as Jimmy MacNeil claimed.

"When did you next see Jimmy?" he asked instead.

"The next day – him and his father."

"Did he tell you the Seale boy died?"

"No. I don't recall."

"Do you carry a knife?"

"No," Ebsary lied.

"Does Jimmy still come to your house?"

"No. I have not seen him for a long time. He was not a regular caller at my house."

Sgt./Det. MacIntyre could not have missed the discrepancy with Mary Ebsary's statement that MacNeil had been to their house fifteen times over the last two months.

Although the policeman would later swear that as an investigator he "couldn't have two different statements and be satisfied with it," he made no attempt to confront Roy Ebsary with this contradiction. His treatment of Ebsary was very different from his handling of Patricia Harriss, who was grilled for several hours until a discrepancy between her recollection of a meeting with Junior Marshall on the night of the murder and that of her boyfriend, Terry Gushue, had been resolved.

"Have you been to his house?"

"Once," Ebsary answered.

"Can you tell me when this disturbance took place on Crescent Street?" the detective asked.

"After 11 p.m."

"What month?"

"In May," Ebsary told them, "the same night this boy was stabbed."

"What were you wearing that night?" Sgt./Det. MacIntyre asked.

"A reversible top coat – blue," Ebsary replied.

The interview ended with an unmistakable echo from Junior Marshall's trial. The accused had described Seale's killer as an "older fella", wearing "a long, blue coat". He had also given the same description to the chief of detectives during the investigation.

According to Sgt./Det. MacIntyre's style of taking statements, he would move from one interrogation room to another if there were more than one person involved in the police matter in question, and tonight was no exception. Coincident with his interrogation of Roy Ebsary he also interviewed his seventeen-year-old son, Greg, as the overlapping times marked on their signed statements indicated. The session with Roy began at 9:15 p.m. and ended at 10:10 p.m. and the one with Greg commenced at 9:55 p.m. and finished at 10:20 p.m.

The teenager confirmed that a meeting between his mother and Jimmy MacNeil took place at the Wandlyn Motel, where Jimmy was told to stay away from the Ebsary home. At first Greg told Sgt./Det. MacIntyre he couldn't remember warning MacNeil that he would end up in court if he went to the police over what happened in the park. But when pressed, he backed up that part of MacNeil's story, too. "I said there would be trouble, court. I meant if he, Jimmy, would go back to our house any more."

The detective didn't ask what kind of trouble or why the MacNeils would have to go to court.

"Did you see Jimmy at your house the following day after the Seale stabbing?" MacIntyre asked.

"Yes."

"Did he talk to your father?"

"Yes."

"Did he tell him Seale was dead?"

"I don't know what they talked about," the teenager said.

"Did you know your father and Jimmy were attacked that night on Crescent Street—the same night as the Seale stabbing?"

"I found out about a week later," Greg answered.

"Who told you?"

"My mother said they were attacked."

"By whom?"

"Two fellas were going to beat them up for cigarettes or something."

"Did you ask your father?"

"No," the teenager said, "I never said anything about it."

After the teenager left, Sgt./Det. MacIntyre reported what he'd learned from the Ebsarys to Louis Matheson and recommended that the matter be turned over to the RCMP for reinvestigation. Matheson, who wasn't present for the interviews with the Ebsarys, "was at a loss to know where to go next." But influenced by Sgt./Det. MacIntyre's briefing, he tended not to believe MacNeil's story. "I was satisfied that all of the Ebsarys had given an account of their father's actions inconsistent with MacNeil's story," Matheson would later recall.

That was a strange assessment, since Mary and Greg Ebsary had confirmed everything that Jimmy MacNeil had said about their involvement in the night's events—except for the one thing they in fact didn't know: that Roy had been involved in the murder of Sandy Seale.

Despite his own feelings that everything was in order, Louis Matheson decided to call the Attorney General's Office, rightly concluding that there was no ignoring the possibly explosive situation he had on his hands. A man fitting the description of the person that Junior Marshall testifed had murdered Sandy Seale had now been identified by a new witness. And Jimmy MacNeil not only claimed to have seen the stabbing, but also said he'd returned to the killer's house and watched him wash off the murder weapon in the sink—a murder weapon the Sydney city police had never found.

Apart from this striking corroboration of Marshall's courtroom testimony, MacNeil's account of events must have disturbed the detectives, particularly Sgt./Det. MacIntyre, for a number of other reasons. During the original investigation of the case, three other people had also described a man closely resembling the one both Junior Marshall and now Jimmy MacNeil had identified as the one who stabbed Sandy Seale—something Louis Matheson could not have known.

George and Roderick McNeil had told police that they had seen two men "hanging around" Wentworth Park at 11:40 p.m. on the night of the murder. They described one man as tall, six feet or better, which Jimmy MacNeil was, and the other as "grey-haired", with his "hair flat on his head, no wave—straight back". In Marshall's statement to Sgt./Det. MacIntyre two days after the murder, he also described the two men—one tall, around five feet eleven, and the other small, with grey hair "combed back". And then there was Patricia Harriss's first statement to police on June 17, in which she described to Detective William Urquhart two men she had seen with Junior Marshall on the night of the murder. Harriss had said that one of them had "grey or white hair, with a long coat".

Neither the police nor the assistant Crown prosecutor did either of the two things that would have quickly tested the veracity of Jimmy MacNeil's story: getting Donald Marshall from the nearby county jail to see if he identified Roy Ebsary as Seale's killer, or searching the Ebsary residence for the murder weapon that MacNeil told police had been taken there and washed off in the sink.

Instead, anticipating an appeal of Junior Marshall's murder conviction, Louis Matheson called Robert Anderson, Director of Criminal Prosecutions in the Nova Scotia Attorney-General's Department, to inform him of developments in the case and to seek assistance. As a result of that call, in which the possible use of another police force was mentioned, Matheson was authorized to invite the RCMP to conduct a reinvestigation of the Seale murder case, including a polygraph test for both Jimmy MacNeil and Roy Ebsary.

With that decision, Sgt./Det. John MacIntyre, the man who knew the Seale file better than anyone – including the evidence that backed up Marshall's story from those people who had given statements to police but who had never been called to court – was formally off the case.

Thirteen years later, the former Sgt./Det. John MacIntyre, who became Sydney's chief of police in 1976, would claim that if Junior Marshall had told the truth about the attempted mugging, he would have investigated that matter back in 1971. But although he already had that information from an even better source, Jimmy MacNeil, the man who claimed to be with the killer on the night in question, the Sydney policeman adopted quite another course; as he himself put it, he "bailed out".

14/Rubber Stamp

The next day, November 16, 1971, Sergeant G. M. McKinley from Sydney and Inspector E. A. Marshall of the Royal Canadian Mounted Police in Halifax began what they would later describe as "a thorough review" of the Seale murder case.

After being briefed by the Sydney city police, they ordered polygraph examinations of Roy Ebsary and Jimmy MacNeil. They immediately requested the equipment and an operator and were granted the authority to have Corporal Eugene Smith from the polygraph section of the Criminal Investigation Branch, Regina, Saskatchewan, proceed to Sydney to assist them. Corporal Smith had begun his training as a polygraph operator five months before, and the tests he would administer to Ebsary and MacNeil would be among the first of his new career.

Despite his extreme nervousness, Jimmy MacNeil gave the RCMP his written consent to undergo the polygraph and also agreed to speak to the investigators before taking the test. Inspector Marshall's impressions of that conversation left little doubt about how he viewed the credibility of the man who was responsible for bringing the RCMP officers to Sydney in the first place. Years later he recalled: "We interviewed MacNeil and it was obvious by his demeanor and speech that he has subnormal intelligence and is slightly mental. He was, nonetheless, convinced that Ebsary stuck a knife into the deceased and that later they went to Ebsary's home, where he, Ebsary, washed off the knife. Because we were certain that MacNeil's account of the altercation, in so far as it concerned Ebsary allegedly stabbing Marshall, was a figment of his imagination, we did not immediately question him or take any further action with respect to MacNeil at this time."

Or, indeed, at any future time. After concluding that Jimmy MacNeil had imagined his account of the events of May 28 – a conclusion based on amateur psycho-analysis rather than professional investigation – the RCMP officers were given a tour of the murder scene by Sgt./Det. MacIntyre, who would claim many years later that he had nothing to do with the Seale reinvestigation after the RCMP took over. The RCMP investigators then decided their time would be best spent going over statements of various witnesses at Marshall's trial and preliminary hearing while awaiting the arrival of Corporal Smith from Regina. In so doing, they apparently didn't give the matter the attention to detail that doubtless characterized their other police work.

In recounting what he presented as Maynard Chant's "testimony", Inspector Marshall said in his report that Maynard was walking down the railway tracks in Wentworth Park when he saw a person he later identified as "John Lawrence Pratico" (Pratico's middle name, as recorded on the 1971 police statements he signed as well as on court documents of the day, was Louis) hiding behind a bush. Inspector Marshall then had Chant seeing two men on Crescent Street, one of whom he recognized as Donald Marshall – something the witness directly denied under cross-examination in his testimony at the Supreme Court trial. Chant, the report continued, then witnessed Marshall take a "knife" from his pocket and stab Seale. In fact, when Chant gave his testimony at Marshall's trial, he neither identified Donald Marshall as the person he'd seen stab Sandy Seale, nor described the object the victim had been attacked with as a knife. Lastly, according to Inspector Marshall, Chant testified that the wound on the accused's left forearm that had been shown to him on the night of the murder hadn't bled. Chant had in fact testified that the wound had bled – a point Donald C. MacNeil had misstated in his summation to the jury.

When it came to John Pratico, Inspector Marshall wrote that on the night of the murder, Seale and the accused had invited Pratico to come down to the park with the intention, apparently, of rolling him – a claim that Pratico himself had never made in his court testimony or in either of his two statements to police. According to Inspector Marshall, Pratico also saw Donald Marshall run up Crescent Street towards Argyle Street after the stabbing. If that were true, the RCMP officer might well have puzzled over how, after the stabbing, Junior Marshall could have "walked over to Byng Avenue", as he had claimed on the previous page of his report, citing Maynard Chant's testimony. The two streets were in entirely different directions.

Inspector Marshall's most blatant factual error pertained to the alleged evidence of Terry Gushue, who had been on Crescent Street on the night of the murder with Patricia Harriss. "They were in the Park for some time," Marshall wrote, "and in fact saw and had conversation with Marshall and Seale, although they did not know Seale at the time."

Neither Harriss nor Gushue had ever made such a claim in court or in any statements to police. They had testified to seeing one other person on Crescent Street with Marshall on the night of the murder without knowing if that other person was a man or a woman. There was never the slightest suggestion of a conversation with anyone other than Marshall himself – except in Inspector Marshall's report and in the mind of the person who so informed him.

Interestingly, the RCMP were told by the Sydney police that neither Chant nor Pratico had told the truth when first interviewed by Sgt./Det. MacIntyre, raising the possibility that, unlike Marshall's lawyers, they had been shown the first statements of Pratico and Chant. Despite the obvious contradictions involved, the RCMP, like the Sydney city police before them, had an explanation for these inconsistencies. "However, this can be put down to the fact they were both scared and that Pratico is not too bright," Inspector Marshall wrote.

It is puzzling how he arrived at that conclusion, particularly the assessment of Pratico's intelligence, since the RCMP officer never interviewed either Maynard Chant or John Pratico. Inspector Marshall also concluded in his report that there had been "no collaboration" between the two eyewitnesses, another opinion that was reached without talking to the parties in question.

Inspector Marshall's report of his reinvestigation also contained a very interesting theory based on the fact that the accused had removed his own stitches while in the county jail awaiting his trial. "While in gaol, Marshall removed the bandage from his arm and flushed it down the toilet and even removed the sutures himself, suggesting that he did not want to have anything around with his blood on that could be picked up by the police from which his blood type might be determined."

The merits of that theory to one side, it was a notion that did not come from either the court proceedings of Junior Marshall's preliminary hearing or his Supreme Court trial, and had never been mentioned by anyone in a statement to the Sydney police. But thirteen years later, Sgt./Det. MacIntyre, the man who had nothing to do with the Seale case once the RCMP became involved, would cite the incident of Marshall removing his own stitches and pose this question: "I ask you, is that the, you know, is that the actions of an innocent person?"

There was, however, one thing that the RCMP did do which hadn't been done by the Sydney police: they requested a search of RCMP files in both Halifax and Ottawa to see if Roy Ebsary or Jimmy MacNeil had criminal records. In MacNeil's case, the search came up empty. It was different with Roy Ebsary.

Around midnight on the night of April 9, 1970 – less than a year before Sandy Seale's murder – Mary Ebsary had called the Sydney city police to say that Roy was on his way to the Isle Royale Hotel to stab someone. After her phone call to the station, Roy was picked up by Constables Edward MacNeil and Frederick Lemoine half a block from the Isle Royale with a twelve-inch butcher knife stuck in his belt. Accompanying him was a seventeen-year-old boy, Michael LeBlanc. Ebsary was arrested and subsequently convicted of carrying a concealed weapon and violating the Liquor Control Act.

After a week of "reinvestigating" the Seale murder, the two officers turned matters over to the polygraph specialist from Regina. Once briefed on the particulars of the crime by Inspector Marshall, Corporal Eugene Smith proceeded to give the test to Ebsary and MacNeil on November 23 in a room at the Wandlyn Motel.

Roy Ebsary was asked four questions: (1) "Around the end of May this year, do you know for sure who stabbed Sandy Seale?"; (2) "Around the end of May this year, did you stab Sandy Seale?"; (3) Around the end of May this year, were you right there when Sandy Seale was stabbed?"; (4) Around the end of May this year, did you wash blood off a knife?". Jimmy MacNeil was also asked four questions: (1) "Around the end of May this year, did Roy really stab Sandy?"; (2) "Around the end of May this year, did you see Roy stab Sandy?"; (3) "Were you right there when Roy stabbed Sandy?"; (4) Around the end of May this year, did you see Roy washing blood off his knife?"

Corporal Smith reported that there were indications of truthfulness in Ebsary's polygraph recordings when he answered no to all four questions. He concluded, "It is my opinion, based on Ebsary's polygraph examination, that he was telling the truth to his questions." Jimmy MacNeil didn't fare as well. Corporal Smith reported that he could "render no opinion as to whether or not MacNeil was telling the truth when he answered yes to all four questions." But Smith went on to say that he didn't think MacNeil was "mentally capable of responding to a polygraph examination and for that reason, no other tests were administered."

Summing up the RCMP reinvestigation less than a month later—a report of which was informally given to Crown prosecutor Donald MacNeil and his assistant, Louis Matheson, before being officially dispatched to the Attorney-General's Office, Inspector E. A. Marshall offered the following account of the Seale murder:

> Seale and Marshall entered Wentworth Park shortly before midnight intent on "rolling" someone. Ebsary and MacNeil, somewhat intoxicated, happened to walk through the park and were accosted by Seale and Marshall. Their attacks were not successful and following the altercation a violent argument ensued between the two attackers culminating with Marshall stabbing Seale and then inflicting a superficial wound on his own forearm to divert suspicion from himself before he made the pretense of summoning aid for Seale. Later MacNeil, because he had been drinking and because of his sub-normal intelligence, formed the idea that Ebsary had in fact stabbed Seale when they were set upon. This became a fixation in his mind which surfaced in the form of positive action after Marshall had been sentenced to life imprisonment.

With this flight of armchair psychology, the "thorough review" of the Sandy Seale murder case ended. Not a single witness at Junior Marshall's trial had been re-interviewed. Without talking to either

John Pratico or Maynard Chant, the two eyewitnesses who had falsely accused the young Indian of stabbing Seale on the night of May 28, 1971, the RCMP officers concluded that their account of events was "factual", presumably on the basis of statements already taken by the Sydney city police and a factually incorrect recitation of selected court documents. Among other things, the RCMP report of 1971 was eloquent confirmation of Junior Marshall's fear that if he told the truth about what was going on in Wentworth Park that night before Roy Ebsary had murdered Sandy Seale, it would somehow be incorporated into the lies Maynard Chant and John Pratico had told the court.

Despite the fact that Jimmy MacNeil's polygraph test proved inconclusive, which at the very least left unresolved his claim that Roy Ebsary had stabbed Sandy Seale, his remarkable allegations were never further investigated. Like the Sydney city police before them, the RCMP never searched Roy Ebsary's house on Rear Argyle for the knife that MacNeil said had been used to slay the teenager and then washed off in the sink on the night of the murder – even though they knew that on at least one occasion Roy Ebsary had in fact carried a knife.

Strangest of all, Donald Marshall was never given the chance either to comment on MacNeil's story or to identify Roy Ebsary as the man who had wielded the knife that night by Wentworth Park, even though he, Jimmy MacNeil, and three other people who had given statements to police appeared to be pointing the finger at the same man.

Eleven years later, on February 2, 1982, the man who conducted the polygraph examination of Ebsary and MacNeil wrote a telling letter to John MacIntyre, who by then had been Sydney's chief of police for more than six years. In part the letter read: "The results of Ebsary's polygraph examination were given to Mr. Donald MacNeil, and it is my understanding that he so advised Donald Marshall's lawyer and gave him the opportunity to submit his client to the examination. It is also my understanding that Marshall, through his lawyers, declined the examination."

In fact, neither Marshall nor his lawyers were advised by the Crown prosecutor, the police, or Mr. Anderson in the Attorney-General's Office that a reinvestigation had ever been conducted, despite the fact that Moe Rosenblum lodged an appeal of his client's conviction, an appeal the lawyer would later claim would "certainly" have succeeded had he been apprised of Jimmy MacNeil's remarkable new evidence. Nor had Marshall or his lawyers ever been asked if the newly convicted youth wanted to undergo a polygraph examination. Whoever gave that "understanding" to Eugene Smith had been sorely mistaken.

Without knowing how close he had come to regaining his lost freedom, Junior Marshall prepared for his first Christmas behind bars. Ten more would pass before the truth would be known.

15/Dorchester

Viewed from the bottom of the hill which it commands, Dorchester Penitentiary is almost far enough away for its grimly utilitarian purpose to escape notice. From the first guard-post at the bottom of the long driveway leading to the summit, the blackened three-feet-thick walls appear reassuringly institutional, vaguely reminiscent of an ancient university or an old fortress. Even the coils of barbed wire atop the walls surrounding the yard look delicate and insubstantial from a distance. Nor can the naked eye pick out the armed guards in the watch-towers who constantly survey the prison's 470 inmates, as well as every prison-bound vehicle from the moment it turns off the main road into Dorchester's very private driveway.

But the maximum-security prison, the oldest in the Canadian penal system, quickly announces its true nature as you draw near its impenetrable walls. The barbed wire, strung in looping hoops wider than the reach of any man, bristles with razor-sharp metal teeth. Armed guards, sometimes travelling with dogs, patrol the perimeter outside the walls. If an unidentified vehicle strays beyond the first guard-post and approaches the main entrance of the prison unannounced, it can expect to be greeted by a gun truck carrying a detail of uniformed correctional officers armed with automatic weapons.

Inside the cell blocks of the seventeen-acre institution, Dorchester lives up to its S-6 security rating, the highest in the Canadian prison system with the exception of so-called "special handling units" which segregate extremely dangerous prisoners from the general population. Prisoners spend from ten to fifteen hours a day in their sixty-square-foot cells, where they eat, sleep, and, during recreational periods, visit each other's "houses". Their five-hour work day accounts for most of the time they spend out of their cells. Five times a day, beginning with the 6:30 a.m. public-address-system announcement inmates jokingly refer to as their "wake-up call" and ending at 11 p.m. when the prison is locked down, the population is scrupulously counted. No one moves from one location to another without a pass, and the three "feedings" per day take place in shifts to reduce the number of prisoners moving through the institution at any given time. Each day passes like a record stuck on the the same groove: shower, breakfast, work, lunch, work, supper, recreation, and lockdown, a hypnotic pattern that both dulls and drags out the tedium of doing time.

Junior Marshall was sent to Dorchester on June 20, 1972. The arrival of the convicted murderer from Sydney, accompanied by a single guard, had been carefully, if belatedly, arranged by an exchange of documents and phone calls. When he walked through the prison's enormous front doors to begin serving his life sentence, the young Indian was met by his induction officer. Dorchester's newest inmate, number 1997, was eighteen.

Through no fault of his own, Marshall's arrival at the federal prison was delayed far beyond the regulations pertaining to prisoners serving life sentences. An oversight by officials in Sydney left him in county jail for nearly eight months longer than he should have stayed. That overstay made possible a chance encounter with one of the boys whose perjured testimony had clinched the young Indian's conviction. On the anniversary of Junior's first year behind bars, he found himself face to face with Maynard Chant. "I was coming from the basement when I opened the door and he was standing right there. We looked eye to eye and I never seen a guy look so scared in my life. He thought I was long gone," Junior later remembered.

Ironically, Maynard was at the jail visiting the same friend who had related Marshall's grisly pun about killing "seals" out of season. For a terrifying moment he found himself five feet away from the man his lie had put away for life. Chant ran to the front desk, called a cab, and quickly disappeared. Shortly after that incident, the order was given for the young prisoner to be transferred to Dorchester.

"I remember that last day at the county jail. We had to wash the walls down and wash the floors because there was a big inspection going on, people from Halifax coming, correctional officers. So they came in and we had to stand at our cell doors to be called off, to be named. When this guy gets to me he says, 'What's your name?' I told him who I was and he said, 'Aren't you doing life?' I said, 'Yeah.' He said, 'When did you get that life sentence?' I said, 'Oh Christ, about six or seven months ago.' He said, 'You shouldn't be here at all.' He called the warden down and told him, 'I want this boy transferred, tomorrow morning.' Then he turned to me and said, 'How long you been here altogether?' I said, 'Fourteen months.' 'Well, son,' he said, 'you'll be going to Dorchester tomorrow.'"

The news was less than welcome. It was the first time since his conviction that Junior Marshall wondered if he should have pleaded guilty to the lesser charge of manslaughter in exchange for a reduced sentence – a thought that would torment him over the slow roll of the years ahead. After all, he thought, sticking to the truth, or as much of it as he dared tell, had won him a life sentence in one of the country's toughest prisons, a place he might never get out of if the stories he'd heard about Dorchester were even half true.

On his last night in county jail, Marshall was given the whole visiting room so that his family and friends could pay a final call before the youth departed for the federal penitentiary and another province. It was a sombre affair, despite the universal effort to cheer up the despondent, and frightened, prisoner. "My father told me Rosenblum had an appeal going and that maybe, with what Pratico said about his story not being true, I would be out before too long. He asked me again if I killed Sandy and I told him no. He said never to forget that, not to worry about anything, that he and my mother were behind me all the way."

Even though everyone assured him they would visit, the young prisoner knew better. None of them, least of all his parents, had the money to travel regularly to New Brunswick. There would be no more daily visits to break the monotony of doing time, no more food baskets, no more wrestling matches with cousins thrown in jail on liquor charges. It was, he knew, a kind of goodbye.

Before Marshall left Sydney for Dorchester, a guard asked him if he thought he could survive "in there". Filled with braggadocio, the eighteen-year-old vowed he would be back one day to shake the man's hand.

After his first half-hour in Dorchester, he wasn't so sure.

"They told me to undress. The windows were open right in front of the parking lot where they wanted me to strip off and I could see all these cars out there. I said, 'You mean right here?' He said, 'Yeah, greenhorn, right here.'" Marshall was fingerprinted, photographed, and given the regulation prison haircut. "I thought I was going to lose my goddam ears. They give a real haircut up there," he recalled.

By the time his initial interviews were complete, his induction papers gave a shadowy outline of the innocent man who now passed into the care of the warden of Dorchester Penitentiary: "Donald Marshall Jr, a Micmac Indian and Roman Catholic, six ft. one inch, one hundred and eighty-eight pounds, brown eyes, dark brown hair. A deer's head tattoo with the name 'Barb' on left upper arm; grass, scroll and flowers on forearm. Skull and cross bones, right upper arm; 'Junior', 'heart', 'Mom', right forearm."

The other tattoo, amateurishly applied by a fellow Micmac on Membertou and proclaiming "I hate cops", had already faded away. The last entry of the induction report read starkly, "Large scar inside left forearm". What Donald C. MacNeil had called a "superficial" wound had left its mark more than a year after it had been inflicted by Roy Ebsary's knife.

With these preliminary tasks complete, the young Indian went to the laundry-room, where he exchanged his street clothes for prison garb, before heading to his cell with his mattress slung over his back. His cell number was thirteen, the same numeral as his September birth-date. A good omen, perhaps.

As a lifer in a maximum-security institution, Junior Marshall had no automatic parole date, as inmates with lesser sentences did. But if he could convince authorities that he was neither dangerous nor an escape risk, maintain an offence-free record, and adhere to whatever long-term release plan institutional authorities prepared for him, he would be eligible for transfer to the medium-security prison at Springhill, Nova Scotia.

But there was another requirement for getting out of Dorchester that turned his life in prison into a double hell: the admission of guilt for whatever crime had landed him behind bars. Without that admission, the prison officials who regulated every phase of his life had absolute power to keep inmate 1997 in maximum security.

According to his first prison assessment, Junior Marshall was a co-operative inmate who grew defensive and hostile only when describing his offence. In the cumulative summary of his case written in July 1972, the induction training officer at Dorchester, Raymond Maillet, described him as "the typical Indian lad that seems to lose control of his senses while indulging in intoxicating liquors. Apparently he enjoys a good fight while intoxicated. He refused to admit that liquor is a problem or that it was fast becoming a problem."

Maillet further noted that the shy and nervous youth did not seem to have accepted the sentence of the court and suggested "that inmate Marshall be retained in our maxium-security institution for the time being, or at least until such a time as he is prepared to accept his lengthy sentence."

The induction officer also recorded a fact that many prison authorities would be writing about over the coming years: "The subject claims to be innocent of the the present charge."

From the beginning of what was to be a two-and-a-half-year stint in Dorchester before his transfer to another federal institution, Junior Marshall had more things to worry about than the plans of prison administrators for the convicted murderer who wouldn't admit his guilt.

One of them was James H——,* the six-foot-four-inch Black who provided the main nourishment for Junior Marshall's paranoia from the moment the two prisoners passed through induction into Dorchester together. After a violent spree in Halifax, Jimmy H—— ended up with four convictions against him and a lengthy prison term. He had received nine years for robbery with violence, fifteen years for attempted murder, eight years apiece on two charges of robbery with an offensive weapon, and four years for attempted

---

*The names of all inmates have been abbreviated to protect their identities. Their full names and their criminal records have been verified by the author.

robbery with an offensive weapon after a violent escape from custody.

The word on Jimmy H——, as relayed to Junior by fellow inmate Don L——, was that he was "one mean nigger", someone to keep away from. Unfortunately for Junior Marshall, that proved to be much harder than it was for anyone else: Jimmy already knew that the young Indian was in for murdering a Black, and, as the self-proclaimed head of the Black United Front in Dorchester, he intended to do something about it.

It began as a war of nerves. Other Blacks going through the induction process eyed Marshall wherever he went, then began dropping "kites", notes bearing the grim information that he would be killed when the group got into the general population. Junior Marshall lived uneasily under the state of fear that Jimmy H—— and his cohorts tried to impose on him. "I just stuck with my buddy, Don L——, he was a pretty hefty kid, too, right, so I stuck with him. Of all people, I didn't want to get close to that black guy."

When he found out that Jimmy was running a boxing exhibition as part of the prisoners' regular recreation activities, Junior went to the gymnasium and asked for a match. Jimmy, the referee, pitted the young Indian against a street-hardened Black who knew a little about boxing. It was the first time in his brief prison career that Marshall, a superb athlete, would show the devastation he was capable of inflicting in a fight. Lacking formal technique, but possessing the natural moves of a street fighter, he took his opponent out with "the left hook that shook B.C.", as spectators would later describe it.

After the bout, Jimmy invited "the Indian guys" to a party he was hosting on behalf of the Black United Front, everyone, that is, except Junior. When another Micmac asked him why Marshall had been left out, Jimmy said what he had already gotten across to Junior in other ways: "He did in one of the brothers on the outside. We don't accept him."

Shortly after his bout in the gymnasium, two prisoners began shadowing Marshall. At meals, in the gymnasium, at the movies, the two men, one black, the other white, were constantly behind him. Never speaking, they simply kept close and waited. Not knowing if they were trying to spook him or were looking for an opportunity to strike, Junior kept company with a contingent of prisoners from Cape Breton. But when he reported one day to the kitchen, where he worked as a dishwasher, his workmate was one of the men who'd been following him. Though nothing was said, Marshall sensed trouble. He began washing and rinsing dishes and food trays and putting them in the machine. His partner was removing uneaten food from the trays and at first passing them, then throwing them, towards Marshall.

"I'm not gonna do all these myself," Junior said.

"Why not," the other man answered, "you're doing a pretty good job."

"I'm not gonna do them," Junior repeated.

The reply was a tray thrown into the hot water that struck Junior on the wrist. He knew a fight was unavoidable.

"Watch where you're throwin' them things," he said.

Another tray splashed in the hot water, glancing off his arm.

"Hit me again and you've got trouble," he said.

"What are you going to do about it?" The challenge was finally declared.

"We got into it," Junior recalled, "and the floor was wet and we had on these big gum-rubbers. They were fuckin' slippery as hell, these big rubber mitts we had on because the water is really hot. I corked him in the fuckin' mouth anyway. He had me by the hair, and he tried to hit me with one of those big fuckin' soup ladles. But he couldn't reach it 'cause I had him by the throat and he had me by the hair. Every time he'd let go of my hair, I just hit him. Then he said, 'Let's break it up before the guard comes.' I told him, 'I'll meet you later somewhere.' "

That night, Marshall looked up his antagonist but the man no longer wanted to fight. It was becoming clear to Jimmy that if they were going to get this surprisingly tough inmate, harsher measures would be needed.

The showdown came one afternoon outside the cafeteria. Fifteen Blacks armed with pipes and chains they had removed from food carts waited for Marshall to get off work. But other prisoners from Cape Breton, principally Micmacs, "caught the play" and came to his assistance. "A friend of mine grabbed one black guy and this guy had a knife with him and my friend told him, 'You guys want to start something, you'll be the first ones down.' "

The confrontation moved to the gymnasium, where it finally

erupted, sparked by a number of grievances other prisoners had with the group around Jimmy H——. "A big fight started in the gymnasium, in the pool room, and the Blacks were trying to get out the door because there were too many on them, there was cue sticks going at them and they were getting stabbed and every-thing."

The authorities, who were calling ranges at the time, broke up the rumble and took the instigators to the segregation unit. Marshall, who had just witnessed his first prison fight with weapons, quickly learned how valuable allies were in his brutal new world. For years to come, he would make sure that someone was always watching his back, until the day he became so feared himself it would no longer be necessary.

As that first summer in Dorchester slipped away, Junior Marshall received some bad news. After initially reserving its decision, the Nova Scotia Supreme Court dismissed his appeal on September 8. Years later, Moe Rosenblum, who had presented the appeal, would leave no doubt about what, in his opinion, would have happened had he been aware of the 1971 reinvestigation of the Seale murder by the RCMP and Jimmy MacNeil's startling new information before he made his arguments in front of the Appeal Court. "If I'd known about what was discovered in the reinvestigation, that boy would have been out of Dorchester after those first six months."

A day before Marshall's nineteenth birthday, Sydney's chief of police, Gordon MacLeod, forwarded a report on Junior Marshall to the National Parole Service. It reduced the Marshall case to four neat paragraphs, offering John Pratico's evidence against Marshall without reference to his drunken condition on the night of the murder or his eleventh-hour attempt to change his story. It also stated that in witnessing the stabbing, Maynard Chant "knew both the deceased and the accused," even though he had in fact testified that he knew neither of the boys at the time he allegedly witnessed the stabbing.

The report made no reference to the 1971 RCMP reinvestigation or to Jimmy MacNeil's sensational claim. If the National Parole Board were looking to the Sydney police to get some idea of the type of personality they were dealing with, Chief MacLeod's last paragraph must have been a great help. "A comment from the judge to the jury was that the man who stabbed the late Sanford (Sandy) Seale intended to murder him because of the severe lacerations which were caused by the plunging of the weapon."

To fight the depression caused by his unsuccessful appeal, Junior Marshall applied himself with a vengeance to athletics. "I was hoping them guys would let me out after my appeal. That was the only thought that kept me going in the first few months at Dorchester. When they turned me down, it was just like getting sentenced all over again. I didn't know what the hell I was going to do. I guess I ended up taking it out in sports."

Over the next several months, he ran the track, and played baseball and floor hockey. When the colder weather came, he switched to ice hockey. One night he was checked into the boards and injured his wrist. The prison doctor told him at the time it was only a bad sprain. From that day forward the hand remained stubbornly crooked, began to wither, and caused him constant pain. To hold it in place, he bound it in two elastic bandages which he rarely took off. He would have to wait seven years for a correct diagnosis of the injury.

During his first two and a half years in Dorchester, the young Micmac was a model prisoner. The exceptions were trifling. After refusing to get a cup of coffee for a guard, he was charged with disobeying a direct order in his place of work, the kitchen. The refusal resulted in his pay category being downgraded. The second incident occurred in the prison laundry. While counting Marshall's belongings prior to accepting them for cleaning, the laundry operator noticed his towel was ripped. Holding it in the air, he informed the inmate he was going to be charged with destroying government property.

"That fuckin' thing was ripped already," Marshall protested.

"No, no, it's a fresh rip," the man insisted.

"So is your arse," Marshall replied, his anger flaring.

Later convicted of damaging government property, he was fined sixty cents. As irritating as the charges were, other inmates at Dorchester had more significant trouble, as he was soon to find out.

Freddie L——, an Indian from Alberta who had twenty-two convictions to his credit before he met Junior Marshall, was a man who came by his fear of knives honestly. During one of his many prison stints, the last one dating from 1970 when he received a ten-year sentence for robbery in North Vancouver, Freddie was invited into the washroom by a fellow prisoner to smoke a joint. As he took his first toke, the other man attempted to cut his throat. Freddie bore not only the outward reminder of his host's gruesome hospitality—an angry three-inch scar just below the Adam's apple–but a constant inner fear that made paranoia his chief instinct. "I never trusted nobody after that," he told Junior Marshall, who had asked how he'd gotten the scar on his throat.

One afternoon, Marshall and some other inmates were standing in the yard when an inmate from Newfoundland approached Freddie and suddenly put a knife to his throat. Word had it that the two had been feuding about drugs for the past week. "Next time you fuck with me, I'm going to kill you," the Newfoundlander bluntly told him. Speechless, Freddie turned white as the point of the blade pressed against his old scar. Having made his threat, the man left, unaware of the fatal mistake he had just made. The trembling Indian came over to Junior Marshall with a grim declaration:

"That bastard won't live another night in this prison."

"I thought he was just joking," Marshall later recalled. "I said to myself, 'He'll probably punch the guy in the fuckin' mouth and that'll be that.'"

But Freddie had more dire reprisals in mind. That same night there was a prisoners' rock concert organized by Jimmy H——. Word had been circulating all evening that someone was going to "get it", though nobody seemed to know just who. After the incident in the yard, Freddie had gone to the equipment room and spirited out a baseball bat. He then talked to some other prisoners, who agreed to help him with a simple and deadly plan. One of them would invite the Newfoundlander into the TV room when the band was playing at its loudest and get him to pour himself a cup of coffee. When his hands were full, another inmate would shove him through the doors of an adjoining room, where Freddie would be waiting in the dark with the baseball bat. The prisoners in the TV room would then block the doors, sealing off any attempt at escape by the doomed man.

Everything went according to plan. The last thing the victim must have heard was the pounding of the rock band until Freddie caved in his skull with a blow from the bat. When authorities found the body the next day, the prison was locked down and the search commenced for the killer. Mysteriously, Freddie was quickly apprehended and the rest of the prisoners were let out of their cells. Everyone knew it was "a rat job" and they waited to see who else would disappear from the population, the usual tip-off that deals had been made in return for information. "Everybody put two and two together when Jimmy and a few of his friends disappeared from Dorchester. We knew who was rattin' 'cause they were fuckin' poppin' out of the population like rabbits," Junior remembered.

Later that night, an older inmate explained to Junior the lesson of the previous day's grisly events. "You don't pull no fuckin' knife in this place and not use it – not in this place. Because sure as shit, you'll be gettin' that knife back some place you don't want it."

Towards the end of 1974, Junior Marshall had had enough of Dorchester Penitentiary. The death of the Newfoundlander, the first prison murder he had experienced, had frightened him. In addition to his own confrontation with Jimmy H——, he had also seen the results of a number of terrible beatings, generally administered with weight bars. He decided to tell his classification officer what all the authorities so desperately wanted to hear: that he'd killed Sandy Seale. Maybe then he would get his long-overdue transfer to the medium-security prison at Springhill.

"I remember the guy telling me I'd never get out of prison if I kept up my story about being innocent. So I gave 'em a bullshit story about it and the fuckers believed it," Junior later explained. "When I was trying to tell them the truth about Sandy's murder, they didn't believe it. But I had to get out of Dorchester. It was too fuckin' dangerous, too depressing."

The ploy worked. A transfer warrant was signed by prison authorities on October 31 and the twenty-year-old prisoner arrived at Springhill four days later.

16/The Secret

At the bottom of the sketch, a road forks sharply as it reaches the middle of the page. The left fork is called "Injustice", the one to the right "Justice". Just below the point where the two forks branch off from the main road, a small figure in pigtails stands in front of two red question marks. An orange cross, rimmed in blue, occupies the upper half of the page, casting a dark shadow over a tiny figure beneath it. Where its cross-pieces intersect, the initials "R.N.E." appear. Sticking in the right side of the horizontal cross-piece is a dagger spattered with blood. In the upper right-hand corner of the page, a purple building stands, its two windows covered by heavy black bars. The words STATE PEN are written on the roof. Behind the barred window on the side of the building a young man's face peers out, frowning deeply. A small corner of the sun shines faintly in the extreme upper left of the page. Beneath it, casting its reptilian gaze over the scene, is a disembodied orange and yellow eye. Written above it are the words PUBLIC EYE.

For three years, the teenage girl who made the sketch had been living with a terrible secret. Donna Elaine Ebsary, only daughter of Roy Newman Ebsary, had been home watching television with her mother on the night of May 28, 1971, when her father and Jimmy MacNeil walked through the door just after midnight. Jimmy seemed very excited and was congratulating Roy: "You did a good job," he said. Her father's gruff response, "Shut up, don't say anything," had aroused Donna's curiosity. Although her mother immediately sent her to bed, the thirteen-year-old had instead watched from the staircase while Roy and Jimmy went into the kitchen and then crept up behind them to see what they were doing. What she saw made her shiver: her father was standing over the sink washing blood from a knife.

All night she wondered what had happened. The next day on the radio she heard the news that Sandy Seale, a black teenager, had been stabbed near Wentworth Park after the dance at St. Joseph's Parish hall broke up. The scene in the kitchen began to take on a terrible significance, especially when the radio started broadcasting a description of the suspect police were looking for: an old man with grey hair wearing some kind of cape. At school that week, the other children teased her that her father, well known for his bizarre dress, was the man police were after. A few days later, after Donald Marshall, Jr., was arrested for the murder, Donna tried unsuccessfully to convince herself that her father wasn't the real culprit.

Shortly after the young Indian was convicted of the murder, detectives from the Sydney city police had come to the door and the whole family had been taken in for questioning–all except Donna, who remained in the car with the family dog. For a time, the situation had seemed very tense, but then the police went away and things returned to normal at the Ebsary home–with one major exception. Her father, the eccentric gay blade, bellicose raconteur, and heavy drinker, gave up liquor and took to his room to pursue a more sedentary occupation: writing. For seven years he never left the house and rarely ventured out of his room, which he converted to resemble a ship's cabin. For some reason, the extroverted Roy Ebsary had become a hermit.

Although the rest of the family studiously avoided talking about Jimmy MacNeil's allegations, Donna Ebsary continued to be plagued by the idea that an innocent man was in prison for something that her father might have done. Whenever she got the chance, she would comb the house looking for the knife she had seen him wash off in the sink, planning to turn it over to police if she could find it. She never did. Too afraid to go to police by herself and without any friends, the short, blocky girl, whose nickname at school was "Swamp Witch", kept her dread story to herself until the autumn of 1974.

When she went back to Sydney Academy that year, Donna attended a lecture on the martial arts given by a dark-haired young man who immediately captured her interest. Dave Ratchford had just set up a club called the Sydney School of Oriental Martial Arts, a free school where students could study subjects ranging from kung fu to Oriental dance. According to its founder, the club was designed to redress the bad image that "goofy TV shows and movies" had given to a serious métier.

After the lecture, Donna Ebsary remained behind, determined to find out whether the new club might be a place she could fit in. Impressed with what Ratchford had to say, she decided to join. At first she came out once or twice a week, but soon she became a fixture at the school – and an indispensable assistant to its owner. "My wife at the time took an interest in her, trying to help develop her hygienically. She wasn't very well kept, she smelled, no teeth. She was this wide...she was a mess. But yet the kid was very bright," Ratchford recalled.

So bright, in fact, that after a very short time sixteen-year-old Donna Ebsary began to run the club. She taught herself book-keeping and did the accounts, organized the club's activities, and even looked after the Ratchfords' two children. It was, in Ratchford's opinion, the young teenager's first positive social contact, and she clearly intended to make the most of it. "After a while, she became such an essential part of my life that I relied on her for everything," he recalled.

One night after class, Ratchford noticed Donna hanging back, apparently waiting for the others to go. She looked unusually tense, so he wasn't surprised when she asked him if they could talk about something in "complete privacy". Dave Ratchford had listened to many versions of the "teenage blues" from the young members of his club and wasn't particularly interested in what he thought was going to be a recitation of Donna Ebsary's emotional growing-pains.

After unsuccessfully trying to swear him to secrecy, Donna unfolded a tale that transfixed her reluctant confidant. When, shaking and half crying, she got to the part about having seen her father wash off a bloody knife in the sink, Ratchford was "stunned". Knowing Donna, he didn't doubt her truthfulness for a moment and was just as decisive about what had to be done. "I said, 'I'm morally and legally obligated, Donna, to tell somebody this.' I said, 'Do you realize there's a boy in jail serving time for something he didn't do?' I said, 'That's not right.' She was terrified. No way she wanted me to go to the police about this, no way."

Donna's reluctance was inspired by her father's reign of terror over the years of her childhood, the details of which became clearer as the young girl and Ratchford talked far into the night. The kung fu instructor was told horror stories of how Roy would fling a live cat into the stove or chop up the furniture with an axe in one of his rages. And the trembling teenager told him that her father talked incessantly about the killing he had done during the war.

But after a little convincing, Donna Ebsary relented and agreed to go to the authorities – no small act of courage, since she was still living at home. At ten o'clock the following morning she and Ratchford showed up at the Sydney city police station.

"I asked to see the detectives. They asked me what it was in regard to. I said I had some information regarding a murder. They led me down, I went into the office where Bill Urquhart, both Bill Urquhart and MacIntyre were there." Ratchford told the policemen that Donna claimed to have seen her father wash blood from the knife that might have killed Sandy Seale. Before he could further explain himself, he was informed that the case was closed and that the detectives were busy. "They just kind of gave us the bum's rush. I was stunned! I was stunned!" Ratchford recalled of the encounter.

No statement was taken from Donna Ebsary, and Sydney's Crown prosecutor was not advised of this new evidence which so dramatically backed up the account of the night of the murder given to police in 1971 by Jimmy MacNeil. (Years later, John MacIntyre would deny that Donna Ebsary and Dave Ratchford had come to see him about the Seale murder.)

Not willing to accept what he took to be an official brush-off, Dave Ratchford returned to the martial arts club and called a friend in the RCMP. When Constable Gary Green showed up a few minutes later, Donna once more recounted her story. "I said, 'Gary, you're a federal policeman, you should have some clout down there. Go down and see what you can do. Check it out or something,'" Dave Ratchford remembered telling his friend.

When Constable Green returned a short while later he had disappointing news. The new chief of detectives, William Urquhart, wouldn't let him have access to the files of the Seale murder and informed him that he had no jurisdiction in the matter. The case was closed, and there was nothing Green could do except pass Donna's information along to his superiors, which the young constable did without any result.

Despite her best efforts to free that sad face in the paper prison, Donna Ebsary was left standing at the forks, wondering how to get down the rocky road to justice.

17/Springhill

The next five years and three months of Junior Marshall's life were spent at the medium-security federal institution at Springhill, Nova Scotia. With its off-white stucco exterior, the then three-year-old institution looked more like a college campus than a prison, an impression that was reinforced by its much younger inmate population as compared with Dorchester's. As one correctional officer put it, "A guy could make a fortune with a Clearasil concession in this place."

Although the nature of an inmate's crime initially decided whether he went to maximum-security or medium-security, his personality, prison performance, and escape-risk assessment soon became more important to correctional authorities. Aggressively violent inmates who were viewed as high escape risks were sent to Dorchester, while a convicted murderer who obeyed the rules could end up in Springhill's more agreeable environment. Unlike the forbidding walls of Dorchester with their barbed wire, Springhill was enclosed by a chain-link fence, security was less obvious, and the regulations governing the daily lives of the S-4 institution's 450 inmates were more relaxed. An inmate's cell time, for example, was restricted to the hours he slept at night and the five brief intervals each day when the population was counted. No pass was required to move around the prison, and inmates took their meals communally in a cafeteria rather than alone in their cells.

The cells, though still the regulation sixty square feet, were brightly painted and more private than at Dorchester. They had solid rather than barred doors, with a small Plexiglas window at the top which inmates were forbidden to cover. Each cell had a bunk bolted to the floor, a desk, a chair, a shelf, hooks or closet space, a toilet, hot and cold running water, a light that was both occupant- and centrally controlled, and a large window blocked by three cement posts instead of bars. Outside the five-hour work day and the lockdowns during meal periods, an inmate was essentially free to run the track, work out in the gymnasium, play cards, or visit friends on other ranges, provided he obeyed the institution's internal rules. "At least at Springhill you could walk around, feel more comfortable. You didn't worry so much about getting beat up or stabbed. There was a little civilization there. But it was a false freedom," Junior recalled.

One of the main differences between maximum and medium security was the relationship between an inmate and his case-management team. At Springhill, three of the four members of the team worked directly out of the unit where the inmate was serving his sentence. The man responsible for the management of an inmate's file within the institution was called a Living Unit Development Officer, or LUDO. He was available to discuss an inmate's case on a daily basis, and his recommendations had a crucial impact on the fourth member of the team, the inmate's parole officer, who visited the prison twice a week. Without the LUDO's support, it was virtually impossible for an inmate to win parole, as Junior Marshall so fervently hoped to do as he began serving time at Springhill.

In the beginning, institutional personnel were as glad to have the new inmate as he was to be there. Marshall upgraded his education from grade six to grade ten, joined the executive of the Native Brotherhood, attended Alcoholics Anonymous classes, and proved himself to be one of the best athletes in the population. His work record, too, was exemplary.

In fact, Junior Marshall was working hard to show prison authorities that he was worthy of the day parole for which he would be eligible on June 4, 1978. If one reason for telling authorities he'd murdered Sandy Seale had been to get out of Dorchester, the other was to begin the process that would lead to the parole he so desperately craved. He knew that his refusal to admit guilt during the first four years of his sentence had been held against him by his classification officers. They never missed an opportunity to remind him that, unless he owned up to his crime, he would never get out of prison. "I was just trying to get the hell out of prison, you know. In there, whether you did or you didn't do it, it doesn't mean nothin' to them. And when you're doing life, there's no date when the doors automatically open, you're just doing life."

His admission of guilt, short-lived as it was, sat well with the Springhill staff. In a cumulative summary of his progress six months after entering the Nova Scotia prison, caseworkers expressed satisfaction with inmate 1997, as a typical report of this period showed: "At this time he has acknowledged guilt and is becoming more open and honest in the counselling situation, though he is still quite guarded and tries to tailor his answers to meet what he perceives the interviewer's expectations to be." According to Bernard Cormier, his initial LUDO, the twenty-year-old Indian was a "very good inmate" who seemed "in touch with reality". It was high commendation to receive in a prison system where it was estimated that twenty-five per cent of the inmate population could benefit from psychiatric help.

But as the months dragged on, Marshall was only "good" when he had to be. Shortly after his transfer to Springhill, he asked for a meeting with his classification officer and told him that he had not stabbed Sandy Seale and would be actively pursuing an appeal of his conviction. Asked why he'd changed his story, he told the truth: he had simply wanted to get out of Dorchester. With the renewal of his claim of innocence, never again to be repudiated during his eleven years in prison, Junior Marshall was back where he started from when he entered Dorchester, snagged in the ultimate Catch-22.

Determined not to admit guilt for something he hadn't done, he made a simple but monumental decision which he would later credit with helping him to survive inside: "I decided after a point that I would treat prison life as normal life. That way I thought I might have a chance to get through it." This attitude led inexorably to drug use – the prison population's major bulwark against the oceanic boredom of doing time. Passed along during the weekly visits prisoners received from family and friends, or smuggled back by inmates on day parole who had to return to the institution at night, the drugs available at Springhill were no different from the ones that could be bought on the street: marijuana, hashish, hash oil, mescaline, Valium, LSD, and even horse tranquillizer.

The favorite method of smuggling drugs into Springhill was "suitcasing", whereby an inmate on day parole would insert a lubricated cigar tube filled with drugs into his rectum. Since a doctor had to be present before guards could conduct a cavity search, inmates usually passed the routine search they were subjected to when they returned to the institution at night. Some methods were more direct. "You know, we've got no wall here and I've seen civilians just wander up to the chain-link fence and toss over a bag of dope. If the inmates get their hands on it, they throw it in the garbage and dig it out at a later time," a correctional officer at Springhill said.

Once inside, drugs were stashed in the users' cells, which the guards were reluctant to search on a regular basis unless they strongly suspected that an individual was dealing. But if an inmate was in business, he would often have another inmate "hold" his stash in return for free drugs. That way, if a disgruntled customer or a rival dealer ratted to authorities and there was a search, nothing would be found in the dealer's own cell or "drum".

Officially prohibited but tolerated in practice, soft drugs were viewed by many guards at Springhill as one of the ways of keeping the peace. "Home brew", alcohol fermented from fruit, orange juice, or even ketchup, was seen as a far greater threat to the peace and order of the institution and was scrupulously suppressed. The most violent incidents in prison were often traced to inmates "pilling up" and then drinking home brew. According to the inmates themselves, the next most dangerous situation was a "dry" period when, for a particular reason, such as a violent incident or a riot, there was a security crackdown and drugs were kept out of the institution.

Over the years, Junior Marshall would experiment with most of the drugs available inside, eventually becoming a heavy user of marijuana and, in the latter part of his life sentence, Valium. For the inmate who could no longer drink wine in St. Anthony Daniel Cemetery with his friends, drugs became a necessary substitute. "Dope in there became like alcohol – you needed it. You really got fuckin' depressed if you didn't get it," he later explained.

There were always enough faithful girlfriends who visited once a week to ensure that Springhill's drug supply never dried up. Junior's first prison girlfriend was an employee of the Native Brotherhood who asked to be put on his visiting list after a chance meeting in the visiting and correspondence room at Springhill. But Junior's relationship with this woman, who regularly brought him drugs smuggled into prison in her boot, ended suddenly because of an offhand remark by his younger brother Pius. Pius suggested during a visit to Springhill that Junior wasn't the only Marshall she was interested in. Junior immediately broke things off. In his quest for a new source of drugs, he would rapidly learn that Springhill wasn't as safe a place as it might have looked. Without money, a prisoner got only as much comfort as he was strong enough to take.

Grant L—— weighed four hundred pounds and devoured sandwiches by the plateful in his well-stocked cell. But the huge prisoner from the Annapolis Valley was not as soft as he looked. When aroused, Grant exhibited the nimbleness of a dancer and often surprised the unfortunate people who mistook him for easy prey. The rotund arsonist could deliver a kick to a height of six feet with deadly accuracy, a handy ability considering his business interests in Springhill: selling drugs and loan-sharking.

Like everyone else inside, Grant was watching the calendar for the day he would be paroled. To minimize the risks of jeopardizing that magical date, he resorted to the use of surrogates in the most dangerous aspects of his business enterprises. In his drug operation, that meant getting other inmates to smuggle in his inventory in exchange for getting "turned on" free of charge. The inmates Grant used knew that the only alternative was to pay four dollars for a marijuana cigarette that barely got a guy off the ground, let alone high. There was nothing, as Junior Marshall would soon learn, skinnier than a Springhill joint destined for the commercial market. But the surrogates were just as anxious about their own parole dates and would often sub-contract the potentially hazardous work of getting drugs through the visiting and correspondence room to the most desperate or hopeless inmates, only to cut them out with a mere pittance after the transaction was completed.

On the day that Murray F—— approached Junior Marshall to bring in two ounces of marijuana, he had a particularly good reason for not wanting to take the risk himself. He was getting out the next day and the 220-pound red-head didn't want to press his luck on behalf of Grant or anybody else. The proposition was both an enormous risk and an enormous temptation for Marshall. Murray, who neglected to say that the drugs weren't his, promised half an ounce of marijuana if Junior got the contraband past the guards. On the other hand, Junior knew that if he were caught with such a large quantity of drugs, it would be the first serious offence on his record. Since coming to Springhill, he had only two offence reports, both minor, for being caught in another living unit after hours. He had been barred from those units for thirty days after pleading guilty to the charges.

Junior Marshall's first effort as a smuggler was a success. After removing the drugs from a flower-pot in the visiting and corre-spondence room, where they'd been hidden by Murray's girlfriend, Junior stuffed the two bags of marijuana into his sneak-ers and cleared the routine security search. He then delivered the marijuana to Murray, who rolled him two joints and told him to "wait awhile" for his half-ounce. When he still hadn't heard from Murray after supper, Junior paid him a visit. He was told to come back at 9:30 that night. When he reappeared at the appointed time, Murray was too busy to talk to him. Junior got the message: the dope was in and the deal was off. Junior Marshall may have been a mule but he wasn't a horse's ass. For the first time since Dorchester, he prepared to let his fists do the talking, if that's what it would take to make Murray honor their deal. "I took him in my room and slammed him on the bed and told him, 'Where's my pay?' "

Only then did Murray, frightened by the sudden eruption from the normally quiet Indian, admit that the marijuana belonged to Grant L——. Marshall threw his welshing business partner out of his cell and decided to pay Grant a visit. When he arrived at his cell, the enormous inmate was having a late-night snack.

"You remember that two bags of dope that came in?" Marshall asked.

The big man looked at him with uncomprehending eyes, and continued working on his sandwich.

"The two bags of dope Murray brought you?" Junior prodded.

"What are you talking about, fool?" Grant replied haughtily, lowering his sandwich.

"You know fuckin' well what I'm talking about. I brought that dope in and I want my pay."

"What do you mean? I don't own no two fuckin' bags of dope."

"I know you own it because Murray told me. I brought that fuckin' weed in myself, he didn't bring nothin' in."

This came as news to Grant, who had already given Murray half an ounce of marijuana for delivering the drugs. The two joints Murray had given Junior had in fact come from the portion owed to him. It was a good lesson in business administration, prison style, but Junior wasn't ready to write it off to experience.

"You better pay up, Grant," he said softly, fully aware of his adversary's reputation for acrobatic attack.

"Get out, fool, get out of my house." Grant was now standing.

Before anything happened, the balance suddenly shifted in Junior's favor with the sudden appearance of Wayne M——, an older inmate Grant would never dream of tackling.

"What you tryin' to do, give the fuckin' kid a hard time?" Wayne said angrily. "He brought in the fuckin' dope, you fuckin' pay him, right now."

Twenty minutes later an emissary appeared at Junior's cell. "Here's something from Grant," he said tersely, dropping thirty joints on the bed.

Two weeks later, Junior Marshall exacted a further price for the attempt to play him for a fool, and exhibited a capacity for retribution, sometimes subtle, sometimes brutally direct, that would characterize his dealings with anyone who crossed him during his years in prison.

After finding out that Peter H—— was "holding" four bags of marijuana for Grant, he went to Peter's cell and removed a little of the drug from each bag. He then gave Peter, who was with him, a few joints and stowed away the third of an ounce he had skimmed, carefully replacing the bags in his friend's locker.

Whether Grant understood what had happened was debatable. A few nights later he called Junior Marshall into his cell and gave him a joint.

"You know, I think Peter took a little bit out of each bag he was keeping for me," Grant said quietly.

"Really?" Junior replied.

"Yeah, but I'm not going to say anything to him." The big man waited until Junior took a long toke before he continued the conversation.

"You didn't happen to see him smokin' anything, did you?"

"No, I never seen him smokin'. But I gave him some weed a little earlier," Junior said.

"Yeah," Grant replied dreamily, "he was high when I met him."

One of the frustrating routines Junior Marshall was subjected to at Springhill was the compulsory psychological testing. Like Sisyphus rolling his stone, inmate 1997 would answer the questions honestly, only to be asked them again at the next session. Junior recalled: "One question on the test said, 'Did you ever murder anybody?' and I always checked it 'No'. And every time my report came in, it read it wasn't valid because I wasn't truthful. They asked, 'Did you ever murder anybody?' or, 'Would you ever murder anybody?' or, 'Would you murder your mother?' I kept saying 'No', and in the end they had me doin' ink blots like retarded people do."

One day Junior received a message that his LUDO and the prison psychologist wanted to see him. He hadn't requested the meeting and wondered what it could be about. At the meeting, he was asked if he would like to go to a minimum-security institution or a farm-camp. He told them he would. The psychologist then said that he wouldn't be going anywhere unless he faced the fact that he had committed a murder. Marshall exploded. "I swung my parka at them bastards and I said, 'Fuck you guys, no more of this.' That's when I excluded myself a long time from everybody. I refused to talk to all kinds of people after that. I decided to just do my time."

Had he been aware of events back in Sydney towards the end of 1975, that might have been an easier thing to do. Donald C. MacNeil, the lawyer who had successfully prosecuted him in 1971, refused a court order to pay his wife $50,000 in alimony, and instead moved $65,000 in assets to the United States. In November, he was found guilty of criminal contempt and served a few days in the same Cape Breton jail where Marshall had begun his life sentence four years earlier. Three years later, at the age of fifty-four, the once formidable lawyer would be dead from chronic lung disease.

One night early in 1976, Junior Marshall had just finished dinner and was relaxing in his room when a guard came to his door and told him that his classification officer wanted to see him. Five minutes later he was told that his grandmother had died. They handed him an application for a temporary leave of absence (TLA) to attend the funeral and informed him that they would be conducting a routine community assessment prior to granting approval for his return to Sydney.

The next day Marshall was informed that he had failed his community assessment, that John MacIntyre, who was now Sydney's chief of police, didn't want the convict returning home out of fear for the lives of the witnesses who had testified against him at his 1971 trial. "When they told me that, I just shook my head. I said, 'Who's running this boat, you guys or MacIntyre?' "

In a towering rage, Marshall then asked to be put in solitary confinement. "I told them I just wanted to go to the hole for a coupla days to get everything off my mind. I told them I just wanted to spend time alone."

When they informed him that they couldn't place him in solitary without a reason, Junior Marshall grabbed his classification officer's desk and used it to pin him against the wall. "Now you got a fuckin' reason. You don't take me to the hole, I'm gonna smash this whole office up, including you. Now you take me there or somebody's gonna get fuckin' hurt around here," he said.

An hour later, Junior Marshall was in solitary confinement.

On May 12, 1977, inmate 1997 had an important meeting with his parole officer, Diahann McConkey. For the first time since prison authorities had received new instructions pertaining to temporary absences for lifers, Marshall was applying for leave from Springhill. The purpose of the TLA was to visit his new girlfriend, Shelly Sarson, whom he'd met while she was visiting her brother, inmate John Sarson. He also wanted to attend meetings at the Micmac Friendship Centre in Halifax. The 23-year-old inmate explained to his parole officer that he was afraid of becoming "institutionalized" and thought the contact with the outside world would do him good.

McConkey was of two minds as she interviewed Marshall. Although he talked openly with her about his performance as an inmate, his relationship with institutional staff, and his future plans, he would not discuss the appeal of his conviction beyond doggedly maintaining his innocence. She found him to be "somewhat ambivalent" about the three previous temporary leaves, all escorted, he'd been granted up to that point, two to play hockey at the Springhill arena and the third to attend an exhibition hockey game in Moncton. He said he didn't enjoy being paraded in public as a convict, being forced to follow his escort "like a sheep", knowing that a single deviation from the rules would land him back in prison with an offence report against his name. He told her he felt "a weird light-headedness" on those occasions he'd been away from Springhill and had even contemplated "taking off".

A large part of Junior's "ambivalence" about the TLA program had to do with something he preferred not to discuss with his female parole officer. He detested the indignity of the inevitable strip search he had to undergo on his return to prison. "When you came back, six of them strip you off. You got nothin' on and they check your underarms, between your toes, your mouth, ears, hair – everything. You had to stand naked while they went through your clothes. The little bit of life you got on the outside wasn't worth the fuckin' depression of comin' back. You felt like a goddam animal."

Diahann McConkey ended her report by dashing inmate 1997's hopes of receiving an unescorted leave from Springhill:

> Based on Marshall's institutional behaviour and progress, he would certainly appear to merit such consideration. However, Marshall's insistence that he is innocent, his feeling that he can't do much more time, and his ambivalence about being released on TLAs, might make him an escape risk. Thus, although the writer is recommending as a proposed action that Marshall be allowed to participate in a TLA programme, under escort, to the Micmac Friendship Centre, I would not, at this time, support a TLA program that would see Marshall receiving unescorted passes.

It was a watershed assessment. When Junior realized that the system wasn't going to reward him for the five and a half years of good time he'd served for a crime he hadn't even committed, he quickly lost respect for all of the rules – including the ones laid down by the most powerful of his fellow inmates. From this point on, two things would guide his destiny in prison: the determination that came from knowing he was innocent and the power in his fists.

In the coin of the realm at Springhill, Mike M—— was an estimable citizen. The short, stocky prisoner, who was a guest of Her Majesty as a result of his corporate enterprise in the drug trade, had adjusted his business operations with an entrepreneurial aplomb that would have quickened the pulse of any businessman. Shortly after his change of address, Mike M—— built a drug inventory at Springhill that contained everything from mescaline to horse tranquillizers and proceeded to compile a small fortune supplying his pool of customers.

In 1977 Mike M——, who also acted as Junior Marshall's barber, considered the idea of teaming up with the brash young Indian with the intimidating reputation. But when it came time for the laying on of hands, Mike M—— chose as his lieutenant the flashier Mike Mac——. Mike M—— did, however, continue to curry Junior's favor by the occasional gift of marijuana "to get the Indian guys high". It was a strategic altruism based on keeping one of Springhill's most dangerous prison factions on side. But Mike M——'s largesse did not strike Marshall as being in proportion to his resources, and he conceived the dangerous project of redistributing Mike M——'s wealth. He began with the personal drug supply of Mike M——'s right-hand man, Mike Mac——.

"I walked in on them one day and they were smokin' hash oil, so after they finished one off I was sittin' there waitin' to get high and Mac—— just put it back in his pocket." Junior noticed they had been treating themselves from a nearly full five-gram vial of hashish oil. Miffed by their greediness and knowing how swiftly Mac—— would rip off anyone who managed to obtain drugs better than his own, Junior Marshall decided to even the score. That night, with Mac—— at the movies, he and another Micmac, Joe D——, went to his cell – "a real no-no in there" – to search for the vial of hashish oil.

Before they could begin, disaster struck. In his effort to "tight squeeze" Mac——'s door without actually closing it, so that a person looking down the corridor wouldn't know there was anyone in his cell, Joe inadvertently locked them in. "Jesus Christ," he said, turning to Junior, unprepared for his companion's unruffled reply.

"I'm gonna look for that dope, and if I find it, I'm gonna put it in my pocket, and if that door open, anybody come down, I'm gonna punch 'em in the fuckin' mouth."

With those words, the two Indians ransacked Mac——'s room. But after turning it upside down, they still hadn't found what they were looking for. Exasperated, Junior leaned up against a small corner cupboard and his hand accidentally nudged the glass vial. "I got it, Joe," he announced triumphantly. "Now how the hell we gonna get out of here?"

Luckily for the trapped pair, another inmate happened by. Although he tried to avoid them, he couldn't help seeing the two heads poking out of Mac——'s cell.

"Hey, open the door," Junior said, hoping the guards hadn't locked the control box. If they had, the outside button prisoners used to open their cell doors wouldn't work. The two Indians held their breath as the other inmate pressed the button. The door opened. Their reluctant rescuer scurried away down the corridor, but Junior called him back. "Know why we were in there?" he asked.

"None of my business," the inmate answered.

"You know why we were in there?" he repeated.

"I don't know."

"We ripped someone off for some dope."

"It's none of my business," the man answered, wanting nothing so much as to get away.

"You want to get high?"

"Sure."

Marshall handed him twenty papers which he had expertly dabbed in the hashish oil. "I'm gonna tell you one fuckin' thing. Don't smoke them papers with anybody unless you know them good, and yous guys keep your fuckin' mouths shut."

That was the end of the matter until the next day when Mac—— showed up at Junior's cell.

"I heard you were in my cell with a white guy," he said.

"Are you sure it was a white guy, Mike? I was with Joe all night."

"That's the story I got," Mac—— said.

"Well, I wasn't with no white guy."

"Did you rip me off?"

"I might have and I might not have."

In the language of Springhill, the gauntlet had been dropped, but Mac—— didn't have any intention of picking it up, at least not personally. Instead, he went to Melvin R——, a black inmate who earned his drugs by enforcing other people's beefs. For the next week, Melvin began giving Junior the silent stare, the unmistakable portent of looming trouble. But Marshall stared right back until he finally approached the man he had often tussled with playing floor hockey.

"Melvin, what have you got going between you and me? You givin' me bad vibes every time we meet."

"It's not that, man. Mac—— come to see me and he offered me a lot of dope to lay a beatin' on you."

"You gonna try that, Melvin?" Junior asked.

"All I want, man, is to get high. I'm not gonna beat up nobody." And so the man who had blown off a grocery clerk's head during a robbery when he was seventeen years old called a truce between himself and Junior Marshall.

"He always wondered if he could take me," Marshall recalled. "As far as throwing hands go, I was a little faster than him, he was so muscle-bound. But it never come to a point where we found out."

Junior got his chance to make a move on Mike M—— himself when he heard that one of M——'s favorites, Peter A——, was about to get out. Reasoning that Peter might know where M—— kept his drugs, Junior paid him a visit the day before he was scheduled to leave. As it turned out, Peter not only knew where the drugs were stashed but told Junior that Mike M—— kept his money in the same place. For half of the cash, seven hundred and fifty dollars, he agreed to betray his friend. Junior met his terms and Peter told him that Mike kept his drugs inside one of his stereo speakers in his own cell. Before deciding what to do, Junior checked out Peter's story. "When I opened that speaker, there was more fuckin' dope in there than in the Springhill Hospital. He had hash, weed, Valium, acid, PCP's, horse tranquillizers, the fuckin' place was a gold mine."

The next morning Junior got up bright and early and instead of going to breakfast walked over to Peter's unit, where Mike M—— also lived. As agreed between them, Peter pressed the button on Mike's cell door after the drug boss had left for breakfast. Peter himself then went to breakfast to put in an appearance in front of Mike.

Junior, meanwhile, had arranged with an Indian friend who also

lived in M——'s unit to open the door leading to the fire escape on
the pretence that he wanted fresh air in the unit while he mopped it
out. Then, instead of entering by the front entrance, which would
have taken him past the guards' office, Junior went in by the side
door to escape detection. Once past the guards, he walked into the
cell Peter had opened for him and "raided the refrigerator".

By lunch-time, every Micmac in Springhill thought he was back
in Cape Breton – in the Highlands. Enraged, Mike M—— vowed to
kill the man who had plundered his cache. Junior Marshall wasn't
impressed. Taking one hundred Valium a week to keep his own
volcanic frustration in check, he walked the corridors of Springhill
untroubled by the threats of others, while inside him a bomb began
to tick.

On October 19, 1977, Diahann McConkey once more interviewed
inmate 1997 at his own request and wrote the following report:

> Much of the interview centred around a discussion of
> Marshall's continued declaration of innocence. He is main-
> taining the position that although he was present at the scene
> of the crime, an unknown third party committed the offence.
> Marshall cites the fact that he himself was also stabbed in the
> arm as verification for his position. He states that throughout
> his incarceration, he has been pressured to admit his guilt and,
> with one exception, has failed to do so as he himself knows he
> is innocent. The one exception came at a time when Marshall
> had been told that as long as he maintained his innocence, he
> would remain in Dorchester Penitentiary. According to
> Marshall, as he very much wanted to go to Springhill Institu-
> tion, he decided to play along and admit his guilt. As soon as
> he arrived at Springhill, however, Marshall returned to his
> former position of maintaining his innocence and has contin-
> ued to hold this position. Marshall expressed considerable
> frustration at the fact that he has been told by institutional staff
> that as long as he holds this position he is unlikely to get
> unescorted TLA's, day parole, or full parole. Despite this,
> Marshall states that he will continue to hold this position even
> if it means he spends the rest of his life in prison. He indicated
> that he wanted to talk to me in order to make his position clear.
>
> The writer pointed out to Marshall that it is extremely rare

for an innocent individual to be convicted of murder and that on the very rare occasion when this does happen, the individual involved makes a considerable ruckus in terms of filing appeal after appeal. Marshall stated that he would have appealed but that he could not afford the necessary lawyers to do so. The writer pointed out to him that, given the nature of the offence, he probably could get help for an appeal through legal aid or penitentiary legal services. According to Marshall, he had discussed this area with penitentiary legal services who told him he had no grounds for appeal. Marshall expressed the opinion that he is being prevented from appealing because should he subsequently win a new trial and be acquitted, as he is certain would be the case, then the penitentiary services would have to pay him a considerable amount of compensation for the six years he has been incarcerated.

Marshall voiced the opinion that the parole service is supposed to be on his side and expressed some anger at the fact that we were not fighting on his side to help him prove his innocence to institutional authorities. The writer pointed out that not only are we on the side of the inmate but that we are also on the side of the rest of society and that according to all the evidence I had seen, it certainly appeared as though Marshall was in fact guilty. The writer requested Marshall to consider the possibility that perhaps he did in fact commit the offence but is unable to remember doing so. Marshall, however, denies that this could be the case.

Subsequent to the interview with Marshall, the writer discussed this area with Gord Helm, LUDO. Although he is not Marshall's LUDO, Gord said that he had discussed the case with Raymond Lees [Marshall's LUDO], who had read the transcript of the trial and that, according to Mr. Lees, after reading the transcript, there was no doubt whatsoever in his mind that Marshall was in fact guilty.

In regards to Marshall's other area of concern, that being his eligibility for TLA's, the writer explained to him the procedures that must be followed in obtaining TLA's for individuals serving life sentences. Marshall indicated that he was not interested in TLA's simply for the purpose of getting out of the institution but only if they were part of a long range, gradual release program for him. The writer explained to Marshall that, as was the case when I interviewed him in May of this year, I would recommend him for escorted passes but would be unwilling to make a positive recommendation for unescorted passes. The writer informed Marshall that in view of his continued declaration of innocence, his statements that he feels he cannot do much more time, and his admission to the writer that he feels rather mixed up when out on temporary absence passes and has been tempted to take off, I considered that he would be an escape risk on an unescorted pass. Somewhat surprisingly, Marshall did not argue with the writer on this point but appeared to accept my position. The writer further informed Marshall that I would be willing to recommend him for escorted passes only if the institution were also willing to submit such a positive recommendation, as institutional staff know him better than I do. Thus, it was suggested to Marshall that he should again discuss this matter with his range officer and his LUDO and get their feelings on this matter.

On the whole, the writer feels that Marshall is very unsettled at the present time. Although maintaining his innocence, Marshall is doing so in a very calm and matter of fact manner. His lack of protestation in this regard leads the writer to suspect that perhaps Marshall is approaching the point where he will be eventually willing to admit and deal with his offence. Nevertheless, Marshall remains rather unsettled and somewhat hostile at the present time and, in this writer's opinion, at least, could well become a security risk. For this reason, I would not be willing to recommend him for any unescorted temporary absence passes at the present time. Marshall has been so informed by the writer.

Despite his parole officer's assessment, inmate 1997 doggedly applied for a temporary absence in the middle of December. His application would read in part: "I would like to spend Xmas on the outside and would also like to spend it with my girlfriend. My parents are planning to take a trip to Pictou for a day. I would like to get started on future things & giving me 3 days would help me also because my day parole date is soon and I feel it's the right time for me to get started, for to start a new life."

His request was denied. Christmas of 1977, like the six before it, was spent in the mirthless depths of a federal penitentiary.

Junior Marshall began the new year angry and depressed. Knowing that his continuing protestation of innocence had cost him the chance to go home for Christmas, he was beginning to feel that his situation was hopeless. He was further saddened by the changes he saw in his younger brothers and sisters when they came to visit, and the news that boyhood friends like Kevin Christmas had married and left the reserve. Everyone else was moving ahead and changing, while he stagnated in the iron backwater of a federal prison. "It come to the point where I didn't want visits any more. I couldn't walk out with them people, do the things they could do. When you're rotting away inside, the hardest thing is watching your visitors leave."

Junior was eligible for day parole on June 4, 1978, but the frustrated inmate, inured to rejection, wasn't holding his breath. He knew that when the parole board reviewed his application they would again try to persuade him to renounce his claim of being innocent. His only hope was that Penitentiary Legal Services would take up his cause and help him win a new trial. One of their staffers, Debbie Gass, was assigned to his case, and Junior told her what he'd been saying to institutional authorities for years: that he hadn't murdered anybody. She promised to read his transcript to see if it might suggest any grounds for an appeal. In the meantime, Marshall began what was to be his worst year in prison to date with a flurry of minor offences and then, on January 9, the first of two explosions.

The trouble began with a note from a friend at the prison farm-camp asking Junior if he'd received his "half" of some MDA, a powerful hallucinogenic, that had been sent in with another prisoner. He hadn't, so he promptly paid a visit to the inmate in question. Marshall didn't know the man, who was in for small-time drug trafficking. More importantly, the new inmate didn't know Marshall – or the code that applied when a greenhorn had a "beef" with a lifer.

"You know, I got this note from the farm-camp askin' if I got my half of the MDA," Marshall said.

"I don't owe you nothin'," the other man replied.

Marshall shoved the note under his nose.

"Read that. You got it, man, and you fuckin' cleaned up on it."

"Well, I brought it in, you know."

"That's not the point. Somebody sends a note to split, you split," Marshall said.

"Where the fuck do you think you're gettin' off with that shit?" the inmate said, getting to his feet.

Marshall hit him once. An hour later they still hadn't found his adversary's glasses.

The new inmate then made his second serious mistake when he reported the incident to authorities. Junior was immediately put into segregation in the Adjustment Centre, a quiet room for prisoners whose offence was not deemed serious enough for a trip to the hole. Shortly after he was locked up, two LUDO's appeared with the inmate Marshall had "tuned up".

"What's going on between you two?" one of them asked.

"Listen, the guy spilled the beans, let the rat do the talking," Marshall replied, glaring at the now frightened informer.

"You started punchin' me out," he protested.

"You know why too," Marshall said.

"Why?" the man asked.

"Between you and me, I know why I punched you out. Dem guys don't fuckin' know it and if you wanna tell 'em, go ahead. And another thing. You get the fuck out of my cell now while you're still standin', you rat-bastard."

No matter what happened in prison, Junior knew that the cardinal rule was never to forget what side of the bars you were on.

For the next four days, inmate 1997 remained alone in the Adjustment Centre, his only other punishment being that he was fed from the "food cart". That meant the meals usually came cold and the various portions were lumped together in an unrecognizable mash. "I used to feed it to the fuckin' rats that come up from under the building," Marshall recalled.

(One of the most satisfying work details Junior drew at Springhill would come on the day that he helped slaughter the hordes of rodents in the garbage shed by dousing the hills of decomposing food in which they lived with gasoline. It was one of the few advantages Dorchester had over Springhill. "There's no rats in Dorchester, I mean no four-legged ones," Marshall recalled.)

When he got out of segregation, he learned that the inmate who had informed on him had been sent to the farm-camp. A month later the man was paroled.

Three days after Marshall emerged from segregation, his parole officer was writing another report on inmate 1997, this time to give her reasons for turning him down for the Atlantic Challenge Winter Survival Program. In order to qualify for the six-day wilderness excursion, an inmate had to be eligible for day parole, a detail authorities had overlooked when they approached him about taking part. But the parole officer wasn't anxious to personally pass on the bad news, as she made clear in a report on January 16, 1978.

> It was the writer's feeling that, in view of the previous confron-tations between the writer and Marshall, the last thing Marshall needs now is for me to interview him again and tell him that I can't recommend him for something else. This has already occurred too many times.
>
> The writer discussed this area with Marshall's LUDO, Kim Thompson, who agreed with my feelings on the subject. Kim also noted that there was no way the Institution would recom-mend Marshall at this time for this project even were he eligible. In fact, the Institution recently denied Marshall's request for an escorted TA as it felt that, in light of his unstable-ness at the present time, he represents too high a security risk.
>
> It was ultimately agreed that the writer would not interview Marshall at this time and Institutional personnel will explain to Marshall that he is not eligible to participate in the Atlantic Challenge project.

Fresh from his four days of segregation, the subject of the memo was bitter at the lost privilege. Junior recalled: "All along they led me to believe I was gonna get it. Then when it come down to the crucial fuckin' question, it was the same as always – no."

Soon after he was turned down for the Atlantic Challenge, Marshall was caught off limits in another inmate's cell. He was found guilty of a violation of the regulations by a disciplinary court, barred from that unit for thirty days, and given a penalty of five nights' cell time. A few days later he was caught off limits in the same unit and this time was barred from visiting there for ninety days.

Marshall's rapidly deteriorating behavior in the institution did not go unnoticed by his parole officer. On February 28, a case conference was held at Springhill involving inmate 1997's range officer, Chuck Stonehouse, and his LUDO, Kim Thompson, as well as parole officer Diahann McConkey. The purpose of the meeting was to pin down the status of the case and arrive at a plan for the future management of Marshall's increasingly troublesome situation.

"It was decided," wrote McConkey, "that once all avenues of appeal are eliminated, the case will be discussed with the Parole Board in order to ascertain if they would, at some future date, be willing to consider a gradual release program possibly leading up to full parole for Marshall even though he persists in maintaining that he is innocent of the murder charge."

But before the parole board was approached, it was decided that a community assessment of Junior Marshall would be useful, "to shed some light on the subject". It was decided to contact Marshall's parents, the Chief of Membertou, the inmate's lawyer, the native court worker on his reserve, and Chief John MacIntyre of the Sydney city police. But before that could be done, more dramatic events intervened.

March 26, 1978, was an unusually bleak day for inmate 1997. Debbie Gass from Penitentiary Legal Services set up a meeting with Marshall to inform him that, in her opinion, his chances of getting an appeal of his conviction were slim. She then informed him that Penitentiary Legal Services had in any case lost its budget and would no longer be providing service to the institution. As a later report of this meeting would put it, his case had "now become a hopeless one".

That same night Marshall had to appear before a disciplinary court in his own living unit to answer a charge of being out of bounds in another unit from which he had previously been barred. The fuse that Debbie Gass had lit that morning was burning dangerously low when Marshall suddenly walked out of the court hearing, cursing the presiding authorities and challenging them to a fight. "It come to a point where I stood in front of the office and challenged them to come on out, and they wouldn't come out. I told them I was gonna kick their fuckin' heads off," Junior recalled.

After allowing him to rage for a few minutes, LUDO Raymond Lees advised the overwrought prisoner to go to the hospital and get something to calm himself down. Junior grudgingly complied. On his way over to the hospital, he fell in with inmate John S——. As they reached the walkway in front of the hospital, John R——, who had been complaining to various inmates that Junior had ripped him off in a drug deal, had the great misfortune of choosing that moment to appear on the scene.

"How you doing, Johnny?" John R—— asked, ignoring Junior, who gruffly interrupted.

"Listen, what are you doin' telling people I robbed you? I fuckin' know who robbed you and you know who robbed you too," Marshall said.

"I don't know," John R—— said.

John never saw the left hand that hit him so hard his tongue would still be hanging out when he was wheeled unconscious into the prison hospital. Shaking uncontrollably, Junior Marshall proceeded to the hospital himself to get the medication he now needed even more than before.

"What can I do for you?" the male nurse on duty asked him.

"Gimme a downer, gimme something to put me down," Marshall answered from between clenched teeth.

"You explain what's wrong with you first," the nurse said.

"Just gimme some fuckin' downers, man, I was sent here to get some, no questions asked! Gimme anything!"

At that moment, John R—— was wheeled into the hospital covered with blood. The nurse looked at Marshall's bloody left hand.

"Gimme something, will you!"

"Right away!" the nurse answered, handing the quivering prisoner two pills.

"I took two morphine pills, knock you right out, so I dropped them and I was walking out of the hospital when a whole bunch of guards arrived," Junior remembered.

Marshall was immediately taken to the hole. In making his report of the incident, guard C. E. MacKenzie recorded the inmate's words as he was locked in solitary confinement, where he would spend the next fifteen days. "Inmate Marshall said he wish he would have met five of those young cocksuckers."

Unknown to the guard, Junior was referring to the group of young men, including John R——, who looked to Dick H——, one of the biggest dealers in Springhill, for drugs and protection. Junior Marshall knew that Dick H—— would be looking him up when he finally got out of the hole.

Dissociation, or "the hole", was located off a long hallway with a few cells on either side. Each contained a toilet and a hardwood bed. At seven o'clock every morning, the mattress was removed, to be brought back again at seven at night. When it was taken away in the morning, a fluorescent light came on in the cell and stayed on until 10:30 p.m.

Because he found his cell suffocatingly hot, Junior used one of his woollen blankets to block off the heating duct, a measure that worked well enough until a guard noticed the blanket and took it away. There was nothing to do but read and smoke. His favorite books were Westerns, especially the ones where the long-suffering protagonist returned after years of hardship to mete out a fearful retribution to his enemies. When he grew tired of reading, he closed his eyes and saw the vision that often visited him in the dead hours of solitary confinement: *A lonely grove in the woods outside Sydney. The people whose lies had put him away tied to trees. A tall figure standing before them, a rifle in his hands...*

Towards the end of his solitary confinement, Junior received a visit from his range officer and his LUDO, who took him to the courtroom office in number six building for a 1½-hour meeting. The correctional officers found him calm and co-operative, "seemingly humbled by the days he had by this time spent in segregation," as they would later write.

The two men seized the opportunity to lay down the law to their contrite charge. He was to get good work reports, avoid any fights in athletic events, enrol in relaxation therapy, keep himself "offence free", keep out of other inmates' cells, and change "several basic components of his attitude". If he complied, a new TLA program would be developed which would possibly lead to his long-range release over a period of years, but only if the decision-making authorities agreed. The institutional officers stressed they could promise him nothing. In recording Marshall's receptiveness to these suggestions, LUDO Kim Thompson made a familiar observation:

He related the incident which had occurred to the realization of the dead end of his legal appeal. . .but also was unable to relate the relationship between the violent reaction in the walkway to the same type of situation that it is felt by the courts occurred in the park in Sydney. Some amount of time during the interview was spent reflecting to Junior the seriousness of this recent incident as it sheds light upon the crime itself.

Despite his feeling that Junior Marshall had learned something from his stint in the hole, Kim Thompson wasn't overly optimistic about the inmate's prospects for institutional success, as the last paragraph of his report made clear:

Obviously the case is becoming a difficult one. Appeal prospects have become exhausted. Tension and anxiety have mounted to a peak. Incidents have begun to occur and at the same time expectations are beginning to mount. . . .In the midst of the crossroads, is beginning to emerge a pattern of feeling and reaction in the subject that sheds greater light upon the crime and upon the need for future protective elements in planning. This one ain't no fun.

Had Junior Marshall ever seen the report, he no doubt would have agreed.

Moments after Junior's release from solitary confinement, Dick H—— crossed the yard and affably took him by the arm.

"C'mon, I want to talk to you," he said, leading Junior away from the other inmates to the side of one of the buildings. The tall, bald king of Springhill's drug trade was calm and friendly and Junior detected no hint of animosity. If Dick were going to pull anything, he wouldn't do it in broad daylight without any backup, although Junior noticed that John R——, the inmate he'd been sent to the hole for "levelling", was watching from across the yard. When they were well away from everyone, Dick leaned up against a wall and began to talk about Junior's time in the hole.

"So when did you get out, man?"

"Oh, about ten minutes ago," Junior answered.

"How'd they treat you in there?"

As Junior began to answer, Dick grabbed him by the throat and drove the back of his head into the brick wall. Stunned, Junior still managed to get free of the other man's grasp and hit him with a punch that shattered the big man's nose. Holding his face in both hands, Dick ran back to his unit with Junior in pursuit. When they reached number ten unit, four of Dick's black security squad jumped up and started toward the intruder. Junior ran away, but it wasn't a retreat. After his pursuers gave up the chase, he went to a cleaning closet and unscrewed two squeegees from the heavy industrial mops used to clean the corridors. Concealing them in his shirt, he returned to number ten unit, where Dick was still tending to his broken nose. Standing in the doorway, he brandished his weapons and issued a challenge. "Any of you fuckers wanna go, let's go. I'll beat the fuckin' coconut off the first one that tries," he said.

There were no takers.

By supper-time, news of Junior's solo confrontation with Dick H—— and his men was all over Springhill. Even the recipient of the smashing left hook was impressed. He neither reported the incident nor took further reprisals on behalf of John R——. Later that night he showed up at Marshall's cell with a gift of twenty Valium.

"I underestimated you, kid," he said.

On June 5, 1978, three months after institutional authorities requested a community assessment of Junior Marshall to assist them in working out a new TLA program, Kevin Lynk , a parole service officer, filed his report. It contained Officer Lynk's impressions of five interviews he conducted in Sydney with people who knew the inmate:

> Mrs. Donald Marshall was interviewed at her home at 38 Micmac Street on the Membertou Reserve in Sydney, Nova Scotia. Mrs. Marshall is extremely defensive of her family in general and in particular, our subject Donald. Mr. & Mrs. Marshall have 12 children, 8 of which are living at home at this time. The oldest, Pius, is 23 years old and is unemployed. David, 20, is in grade 12 at Sydney Academy, and Josephine, 19, is in the same grade. Terry, 16, quit school and is now unemployed. John, age 14, Laura, age 13, and Simon, age 11, are all in grade school. A grandchild, Steven, also resides in this home.
>
> This office has had a considerable amount of contact with

the Marshall family over the past few years, as Mr. Marshall is Honorary Chief of the Micmac Tribe in the province of Nova Scotia and is a well-respected individual. One of the Marshall's sons, David Peter, who was mentioned above, was recently an inmate at the Cape Breton County Correctional Centre and received parole to return to school. The involvement with the Marshall family through David left us with the impression that Mrs. Marshall is an over-protective mother to the point where she will not accept reality and maintains all of her children are innocent of any wrongdoing whatsoever. She becomes high-strung and emotional and will not accept the truth under any circumstances.

At the time of my interview, Mr. Marshall was not at home. . . .The Band Council elections had taken place just the day before, and there was a great deal of drinking and celebrating on the Reserve the night before. Our subject's brother, Pius, arrived home during my visit suffering from the after effects of the previous night's celebration and quickly helped himself to a couple of pints of beer in the refrigerator. He indicated, at this time, that he had been involved in a brawl the night before but was not sure who he was involved with. Even though Pius himself did not know much of the details about the night before, Mrs. Marshall immediately took his side without knowing any more detail than I did.

Needless to say, the Marshalls would be willing to accommodate our subject if he were released under any release program. Our subject seems to have both parents convinced that he is innocent. Although the father did not attempt to return my call, it seems as though he accompanies his wife on various visits to lawyers, police, etc., proclaiming subject's innocence, and if he does not believe he is innocent himself, he is completely dominated by his wife in this matter.

Chief Alex Christmas could not be reached on the day of my visit as he also was celebrating his re-election to the position of Chief of Membertou. He subsequently telephoned me. . . and indicated that there would be positive support and no negative reaction from anyone on the Reserve to Marshall's returning there. He could foresee no problems.

Mr. C. M. Rosenblum who represented Marshall during his

trial in 1971 was contacted. Mr. Rosenblum was quite cynical in discussing the case and indicated that the mother and father were still trying to appeal the case and that they had set up an appointment with him about two weeks ago and then did not show up. As far as an appeal goes, Mr. Rosenblum stated there were no grounds whatsoever for an appeal, and he had attempted an appeal to the Supreme Court of Nova Scotia, but this was turned down. In Mr. Rosenblum's opinion, the case was conclusively proven by the Crown and in this instance there were two eye-witnesses. He states that they may as well have had the incident on videotape. Mr. Rosenblum indicated that there was absolutely nothing that can be done, and he is, quite frankly, sick of hearing Donald Marshall's name mentioned. I see no benefit in continuing any contact with Mr. Rosenblum from our point of view.

Chief John MacIntyre was the investigating detective. He was contacted at his office at the Sydney City Police Department and recalled the incident quite clearly. There is no doubt in his mind whatsoever about the guilt of our subject. The case was proven conclusively in Court with two eyewitnesses and also conclusive evidence from the Identification Section of the Royal Canadian Mounted Police. According to Chief MacIntyre the cuts on our subject were self-inflicted and were not inflicted by either party at the scene of the murder. Chief MacIntyre would be opposed to Marshall coming to this area on a three-day Temporary Leave of Absence....

Mr. Bernie Francis who was a court worker at the time of the murder was contacted....He is convinced that Marshall is guilty of the offence.

According to Mr. Francis, who has known our subject from childhood, the mother is a key problem area in this instance. He remembers our subject as a rather bold kid who needed more attention than the others in the family. He recalls one instance when our subject was about 12 years old, he damaged a pop machine at the community centre on the Reserve in front of 12 adults. When Mrs. Marshall was advised of subject's actions, she denied that he did this as did our subject and incidents such as this continued and became more serious as time went on. Mr. Francis recalls Marshall as being an excel-

lent liar and is able to convince almost anyone of his innocence. He agrees that Marshall should not be released from
the Institution until he comes to grips with reality and admits
to the murder. He sees no point in his returning to the Reserve
proclaiming his innocence and making everyone believe that
he was an unfortunate victim of the white-man's law. . . .

Parole officer Lynk concluded his report with this appraisal:

While there appears to be support for Marshall in the community and little or no negative reaction to his case on the
Membertou Reserve, there still remains the problem of
Marshall himself denying his guilt and being supported in this
by an over-protective mother. Time does not appear to dimin-
ish their feelings in this regard, but I would suggest that it is
quite important for Marshall to open up and discuss the
offence before he is considered for Temporary Leaves of
Absence or Parole. I feel that as time nears his PER [Parole
Eligibility Review], he will feel some pressure and perhaps
begin to speak honestly and openly about the offence. Until
he does so, it will be difficult to supervise him on TLAS or
Parole as he will have the opinion, as will his mother, that he
had done no wrong. If and when Marshall comes to grips with
the offence in realistic terms, there would appear to be more
than adequate support for him in this community.

On June 14, 1978, Junior went before the parole board as part of his
application to take part in the Atlantic Challenge Program, a ten-
day wilderness expedition scheduled for later that summer. He
explained to board members that participation in the program
would give him some idea of whether he could "make it" on the
outside. He told them he was trying to help himself inside by
learning a trade and attending meetings of the Native Brotherhood.
When the inevitable question of his self-proclaimed innocence
was raised, Junior told the three board members that an unknown
old man had stabbed him and Sandy Seale that night on Crescent
Street by Wentworth Park.

When it came to a vote, two of the three board members were in
favor of granting Marshall day parole to participate in the camping
expedition. The third member, Cal Bungay, disagreed. Because of

the split on the parole board, the matter was forwarded to Ottawa
for more votes. While awaiting the final decision, inmate 1997 tried
to take care of another matter that had been bothering him for
years.

Ever since an injury he'd received playing hockey early in his
term at Dorchester, Junior Marshall's right hand had been next to
useless. Whenever he moved it, he felt shooting pains in his arm,
and if his work in vocational plumbing required putting any pressure on the wrist, he could hear bones grinding. After several visits
to the prison hospitals at both Dorchester and Springhill, he was
told that the bulge on his wrist was a cyst. The prison doctor at
Springhill suggested some painful therapy. Junior recalled: "He
wanted to hit it with a book, you know, smash it with a book and
break that cyst up. I told him, 'You're fuckin' crazy,' so then he tries
giving me a needle in the wrist and it just gets worse. Finally I told
him he didn't know what he was doing and he threw me out of his
office."

The pain and the ever-decreasing mobility of his injured hand
prompted inmate 1997 to make a formal grievance to Springhill's
warden: "I request to have my wrist examined by a chiropractor. It
has been bothering me for a few years and I've seen the Doctor
many times about it, and he finds nothing wrong with it. It inter-
feres with my work & also with sports, mentally and physically; I
would like to get it looked at by the right people. I have a fairly
sized lump on my wrist joint & I can't bend my wrist. I would like
an X-Ray done on it & if it needs an operation I wish to get one –
Marshall, 1997."

Thirteen days later, Warden Gibbs replied in writing to 1997's
complaint, informing him that the problem was well within the
competence of the institutional physician – provided the inmate
didn't refuse his treatment as he had in his last visit to the doctor.
The problem with his hand was a ganglion, which did not require
the attention of a specialist.

> If you have any further problem with your wrist, I suggest that
> you again see the institutional Physician as he is the only one
> who can refer you to a specialist if he sees fit. I also advise you
> to follow the prescribed medication if you are examined by
> the institutional Physician and he so orders.

Finally, for your information, chiropractors are not recognized as yet by the medical profession in Canada.

Nine months later, Junior's wrist injury would finally be diagnosed for what it was. His belated treatment would involve neither ganglions nor books.

After the incident with Dick H——, Junior served a stretch of relatively tranquil time, partly because his application for day parole to participate in the Atlantic Challenge was ultimately approved and partly because he was taking fifteen Valium a day.

On July 11, he was interviewed by his LUDO, range officer, and parole officer to discuss the results of his recent community assessment and to talk about his upcoming day parole. When asked what he thought the various people interviewed had said about him, he drew "a fairly accurate" picture of Officer Lynk's report. He also described himself and his friends back in 1971 as "a group of drop-outs who were going nowhere and were frustrated".

The authorities used the interview to try out a new approach with the inmate whose progress towards parole had been stymied for several years by his stubborn declaration of innocence. For the first time in their dealings with Marshall, they didn't insist that he admit his guilt as the starting point for his rehabilitation, as parole officer Diahann McConkey recorded in her report:

> Marshall was informed by the writer and by Institutional staff that, from our point of view, whether or not he actually committed the offence was no longer important. What was important, was the fact that the picture presented of him in his community assessment as well as his behaviour at the Institution earlier this spring, had led us to the conclusion that Marshall was the sort of individual who could have committed a murder.

If the difference between being a murderer and having a murderous streak was not exactly the kind of character restoration Junior Marshall had in mind when he protested his innocence, he didn't bother to argue with his interviewers. In fact, to their recorded surprise, he agreed with them. His new co-operation prompted some advice by McConkey about what he would have to do if he was ever to get out of prison:

> In view of the feelings of the writer and Institutional person-

nel that Marshall is still the same sort of individual who could
commit murder or another violent offence, considerable discussion centred on what Marshall would have to do in order to
change this situation. Marshall was informed that not only
would he have to change his behaviour, but that he would also
have to change his personality, his attitudes, and his responses
to situations and people. As an example, it was pointed out to
Marshall that not only would he have to not express the
bitterness and hatred that he has inside himself but that he
would also have to get rid of these feelings completely.

It was pointed out to Marshall that we realized that we were
asking a great deal of him and were requesting him to work on
a lot but that this was the only way for him to work himself out
on to TA's, day parole, and eventually on to parole. It was
stressed that none of these releases were foreseen as being in
the immediate future for him. . . .Marshall appeared, on the
whole, to be satisfied with the results of this most recent
interview.

In fact, Junior's apparent satisfaction masked something very
different from agreement with what his caseworkers had told him.
He had simply come to the conclusion that it wasn't worth arguing
with people who would always find another reason for keeping
him inside. If he was ever going to get out of Springhill for more
than a week's camping, he would have to do it himself.

It was a world Junior Marshall had almost forgotten: trees, lakes, an
enormous expanse of sky, and no bars.

On August 8, 1978, he and five other inmates left Springhill with
Lin Jensen, who was in charge of the Atlantic Challenge wilderness
excursion. The group travelled thirty miles into the woods, portag-
ing most of the way with two canoes. Junior's group built a raft and
ferried over to an island, where they set up camp and went fishing.
"I felt good, you know. You sleep under the stars and nobody
bothers you, there's not a care in the world. You get up in the
morning, jump in the lake, wash up, and come back for breakfast.
Me and the boys used to do it a lot back home."

Over the next ten days, the inmates performed a number of
survival tasks under Jensen's supervision. Junior did most of the
cooking and was put in charge of an orienteering group that

successfully found another inmate whose location was indicated
by the co-ordinates on a map. He also did some unplanned babysit-
ting. Lin Jensen had brought along his young nephew from Penn-
sylvania, and after finding out that Junior was an Indian, the boy
became his shadow. Years later, this boy's admiration was a good
memory for Junior. "First day out, I took this kid under my wing.
He was just a little kid, so I end up carrying his camping gear, my
camping gear, the canoe – he gets the paddles. I didn't mind
though. It made me feel normal having him around."

They had been a good group, and when Jensen hiked out to send
a message to their parole officer about the progress of the outing,
he returned that evening with a treat – seven pounds of fresh
hamburger. Junior promptly fried it up for their first solid meal in
days.

Before dawn on the day they were to leave, Junior got up and
walked to the lake. The morning sky glowed shell pink above the
far shore and wisps of mist hovered over the still waters. Alone in
the deep silence of the new day, he took off his clothes and bathed.

A few weeks after his return to Springhill, Junior was caught
smoking marijuana by a guard and his temporary absence program
was cancelled. After two months of good time, during which he
graduated from his vocational plumbing course with a B average,
his TA program was restored. On December 13, desperate to get out
of Springhill again, he applied for parole to take part in the Atlantic
Challenge winter survival program, also with Lin Jensen. But a
week later, Junior and four other native inmates were put on report
after a TA to Halifax. The occasion was a Christmas dinner laid on by
the Micmac Friendship Centre and the inmates were caught drinking.

As 1978 came to a close, Junior's range officer, Chuck Stonehouse, summed up the young inmate's situation in a routine report:
"Director cut off all TA's for Jr. Jr. seems to be going nowhere."

At six foot four and two hundred and twenty pounds, the last thing
John MacL— had to worry about was people picking on him.
Considered the best floor-hockey player in Springhill, he was also
touted as one of the few untouchables in the prison, an inmate who
finished every fight on his feet. One night during a floor-hockey

game, he sent a chill through the crowd by systematically demolishing a player who had checked him heavily to the floor.

But one of the people watching had a different reaction. Tired of listening to stories about John MacL——'s invincibility, Junior Marshall decided to let everyone know that he at least wasn't afraid of the big man. As John was coming off the floor after the game, Junior taunted him in front of the other inmates.

"Hey, you're good at hittin' little guys from behind, why don't you try me out?"

"You're fuck all, Marshall," the other inmate answered.

"That right? I'll meet you on the floor some night," Junior responded.

Three or four times after that Junior tried to goad him into fighting during floor-hockey games, but John MacL——, who had heard a little about Marshall, brushed him off. Leaving the floor after being thrown out of a game, Junior purposely back-handed the puck into MacL——'s face. A few punches were thrown, but before any serious damage could be done, the fight was broken up. But the incident had worn out John's patience. Before the next floor-hockey game, word went out that he was going to settle things with Marshall once and for all. On February 12, 1979, the packed bleachers in Springhill's gymnasium fell silent as he made his first rush down the portion of the floor Junior was defending. Drawing a bead as his target built up a full head of steam coming down the wing, Junior moved laterally toward him, hitting him with a solid check into the bleachers. But he was too low when he made contact and the big winger crawled over top of him.

MacL——'s second rush was a different story. Marshall lined him up perfectly and, shoulder to shoulder, drove the winger into the bleachers with a resounding crash. The spectators waited for the inevitable as the two players eyed each other for a split second before dropping their sticks. After sparring for a moment, Junior landed a crashing left hook on MacL——'s temple and the big man wobbled. But Junior, too, winced in pain as he felt his wrist snap. With his right hand already out of commission from his old injury, it was time to adopt less elegant tactics. Junior grabbed his opponent by the hair and began kicking him. When the fight was finally stopped, Junior Marshall had added another name to the list of inmates who would henceforth stay out of his way.

It was an expensive victory. He was suspended for the entire year from the prison floor-hockey league and his broken left hand cost him the day parole he had been granted to take part in the Atlantic Challenge winter survival excursion. After the fight, Junior was sent to the civilian hospital in Moncton, where Dr. D. I. MacLellan put a cast on his broken left hand. But Dr. MacLellan also X-rayed the right hand Junior had injured in Dorchester so many years before. The X-ray showed two broken bones in the right wrist. "He told me that my bones, them two bones that broke, he said there was no blood circulation going through them. He said they just died out on me."

After the cast on his left hand was removed, Junior returned to Moncton Hospital, where Dr. MacLellan rebroke the right wrist, removed the dead bones, and surgically implanted plastic replacements. His hand was in a cast for the next two months. After it was removed, he was scheduled to have four follow-up appointments with Dr. MacLellan to ensure that the old injury was healing properly. He would keep only three of them. By October 3, 1979, the date of his last appointment, he would be dealing with the fallout from his most serious prison offence to date.

Junior's fight in the floor-hockey game once again derailed his chances of getting temporary absences. In April he was denied leave to visit his brother before his pending marriage. When he next applied for day parole to take a job on a nearby golf course where his friend and fellow inmate Wayne M— worked, his parole officer, Diahann McConkey, and his range officer, Chuck Stonehouse, made negative recommendations to the parole board. McConkey referred to Junior's difficulty with "sustaining positive behavior", which she felt made him too high a risk for a regular day parole program. She offered a now familiar reason for her decision and Junior Marshall's deteriorating behavior: "The major problem in this case, and perhaps the one that is responsible for most of the above noted problems as well, remains the fact that Marshall has been convicted of murder and throughout the close to eight years of his incarceration has persistently denied the offence."

When Junior appeared at his parole hearing on April 19,1979, he was asked about his erratic behavior and his failure to follow through on any long-term release plans that had been developed for him. He attributed his shortcomings to being "very unhappy at

Springhill Institution", where "things sort of built up inside him and caused him to get into trouble."

The board informed inmate 1997 that they couldn't totally trust him on the type of day parole he was applying for, as he "might run away from the golf course and return to Cape Breton." In recording their decision, the board suggested that the way out of prison for the subject was to remain offence-free for six months, at the end of which time they would "look again" at a plan for temporary absences. Their report read, in part: "The subject appears to be pinning all his hopes of release on an appeal although the possibility of a successful appeal is extremely remote. We tried to convince him that earning parole is a far more likely way to get out: DECISION: Day Parole Denied."

If inmate 1997 didn't seem perturbed by the board's decision, it wasn't because he'd lost interest in regaining his liberty. Rather, he simply intended to grant himself a leave of absence from Springhill. After eight years in prison for a crime he hadn't committed, Junior Marshall had decided to escape.

The first time Junior heard of the Native Brotherhood Canoeing Expedition was in a conversation with fellow inmate Adrian P——. The two Micmacs were sitting in Adrian's cell when Junior raised the subject of his planned escape. "I'm thinkin' of takin' off, man, I can't stand this place no more," he said.

"You got nothin' to lose. You get old waitin' for them to let you out," his friend advised.

Adrian then told him about the next Atlantic Challenge, a special canoeing expedition for native inmates only. It was scheduled for later that summer, long after the cast was due to be removed from Junior's second broken wrist, so there would be no problem getting the required medical clearance. Sylvester Paul, a Micmac and ex-convict, was one of the two escorts, and he would put in a good word for Junior if he decided to apply.

That same day Junior filled out the necessary forms and came to a strategically important decision. Since he'd been denied so many TA's and day paroles over his protestations of innocence, he would henceforth keep silent on that score. He didn't want to give the authorities any excuse for denying him this most important outing.

He and Adrian then discussed all the things Junior would be

needing: the names of friendly inmates already on parole, maps, a ride out of Nova Scotia, and, of course, money. The last item was the least of Junior's worries. For months he had observed the ritual fleecing of greenhorns by some of the wealthier inmates around the card room's poker table. After figuring out how the regulars worked the table in pairs, Junior beat them at their own game, collecting eight hundred dollars during a single marathon session.

The change in inmate 1997's behavior did not go unnoticed. Both institutional personnel and his parole officer supported his application for the Atlantic Challenge canoeing trip. On August 8, Junior received approval from the National Parole Board. He hurried to Adrian's cell to break the good news.

On September 11, 1979, Junior received his day parole certificate, allowing him to be absent from Springhill Institution from September 15 to September 24. On September 15, he and five other native inmates drove through the gates of Springhill on the first day of their ten-day parole. Three were assigned to each escort and Junior was in a group that included Brian S— and Adrian P—, who both knew about his intended escape. While his friends joked back and forth in Micmac, Junior remained quiet, preoccupied with formulating his plans.

While they were making camp at their first stop outside Truro, Junior spotted some Micmacs from the nearby Shubenacadie Reserve. An impromptu party was organized and his new companions quickly returned with some vodka and marijuana, with which they discreetly feted their six unfortunate brethren. After a few hours passed, Junior told one of his hosts he was planning to escape, but needed a ride if he were to have any chance of getting away. The man promptly offered his services. Although he was willing to leave that very night, Junior turned him down. He knew an escape on the first day would mean the trip would be cancelled for the other inmates. It was agreed that the driver would pick him up on the night of September 24 at the Abenacki Motel, where the prison party was due to stop on their way back to Springhill.

For Junior, the days ahead ran together like the incoherent episodes of a dream. Although he fished and swam and joked with his companions, his secret purpose left him isolated from the others. Unlike his last excursion, there were no camp-fire chats about his case. He found it particularly hard to talk to Sylvester

Paul, knowing the trouble he would soon be bringing to the man who had sponsored him for the trip. On the fifth day out, his preoccupation led to carelessness. While he was scouting out the river for the main party, he lost his footing and fell down a fifty-foot cliff to the river below. For a terrible moment he thought his leg was broken, but later that night the pain subsided and he could walk fairly comfortably.

On the last morning, it rained. The clouds ran in soft furrows back to the horizon and Junior slipped outside in his bare feet to watch the dark curtain of rain advance slowly over the hills. But by midmorning the weather began to break. Sunlight slanted through the clouds in broad columns and where the storm lost its grip on the sky, patches of blue showed through the brightening thunder-heads. It felt good moving through the fresh-smelling woods. Raindrops clustered on the trees and bushes, and when the sun struck them properly, Junior watched them jewel into color. By noon it was a beautiful day.

Long after they had broken camp and were on the road, their escort announced a change in plans: they wouldn't be stopping at the Abenacki Motel after all, but driving straight through to Springhill. Adrian and Brian looked at Junior, unable to help. If he were to escape now, he would have to do it on his own. Two hours later, when the party stopped at a roadside canteen for coffee and to gas up the station wagon, he decided to make his break. With his keeper deep in conversation with the garage attendant, Junior Marshall slipped away from the canteen and struck off into the woods. For the first time in eight years, the falsely convicted murderer was once more at large.

Two days after his escape, Junior was arrested by four RCMP officers in his girlfriend's apartment in Pictou. He was conveyed from there to the Pictou County jail, en route to Springhill, where he was immediately placed in solitary confinement.

On October 18, 1979, Junior appeared before provincial court Judge David Cole to be sentenced for being unlawfully at large. His pre-sentence report described him as a good worker, who alternated between serving exemplary time and experiencing "setbacks". The report ended on a familiar note: "Marshall has really not accepted his guilt for his offence and claims now this recent incident was a means 'to get his day in court', and manage to get his story heard and case reviewed."

He was sentenced to four months consecutive to his life term and returned to Springhill. The next day he applied for legal aid. As he had in 1978, range officer Chuck Stonehouse offered a bleak picture of inmate 1997 as the seventies drew to a close: "Jr. has set himself back quite a bit. He seems very depressed lately. He is very quick tempered and easily explodes."

On February 9, word began to circulate that there was going to be a fight in the yard between Mike M—— and an inmate the drug dealer suspected of harassing his "kid". Junior and some other prisoners went out to watch. Mike M——'s target was Boots B——, a quiet lifer whose most visible passion was running. He was jogging when Mike appeared on the scene. As he rounded the track, Mike, who had been drinking home brew, sucker-punched Boots, touching off a brief scuffle.

"You want to fight, I'll fight after I run," Boots said, pushing his attacker away.

"I wanna fuckin' fight *now*," Mike roared.

"After I run, we'll fight," Boots repeated, and jogged off.

Mike pulled a knife, as did Rick C——, the inmate the two were fighting over. As the two went after Boots, Junior instinctively grabbed Mike. Judging from Mike's eyes, Junior guessed he'd been dropping pills with the home brew, and he decided to disarm him. He took the knife and tossed it down a man-hole, "cooling out" the incident.

The next morning word filtered back to the authorities that Junior had been involved in a knife fight the previous night. He was called into the office and questioned. Junior explained what had happened, but they demanded the name of the man he'd disarmed. Junior flung the invitation to rat back in their faces. "I told them they were just trying to peg me as a fuckin' rat so they could talk about me in the general population. It was one of their favorite tricks for getting rid of a guy who wouldn't kiss their ass. So I said, 'No fuckin' way, I'm not telling you nothin'.' "

The next day, February 11, he and six other inmates were transferred out of Springhill to the maximum-security institution at Dorchester. Officials at Dorchester were perplexed by the arrival of the new prisoners and set about reviewing the circumstances surrounding their transfer. In Junior's case, it didn't seem warranted by the facts, and on April 22 he was returned to Springhill with a recommendation for a progress review in three months. It was to be more of a visit than a stay.

For five months after his return to Springhill, inmate 1997 was a model prisoner. But on his way back from dinner on the night of August 25, Junior walked into number 11 unit just in time to hear Eddie P—— tell four other inmates that they would "pay" for what they'd done. Eddie had just been released from the hole after taking an overdose of pills, and Junior, who had already witnessed one prison suicide and didn't care to see another, was trying to get the troubled inmate back on his feet.

Eddie explained that, while waiting for dinner call that night, inmate David F—— had poured a cup of coffee on the floor, prompting an argument with the caretaker, who had just finished cleaning it. Eddie told the caretaker that he was wasting his breath, since there were "too many goofs around" who didn't care what they lived in, including their own filth.

Word got back to David F—— that Eddie had called him a goof and the angry inmate immediately made plans for revenge. His reaction wasn't quite as trivial as the event that had triggered it. During a closed inmates' court, Eddie had recently identified David F—— and Aubrey S—— as the culprits behind a rash of cell thefts. The coffee incident was the last straw for David F——, who arranged for another inmate to invite Eddie into the shower, where he was waiting for him. When Eddie, who as a fighter "couldn't lick a stamp", arrived, he was punched and kicked but managed to escape before David F—— could do real damage. On his way out of the shower, he noticed Aubrey S—— and another inmate he thought was Rick C—— watching for guards at the top of the stairs. After cleaning himself up, Eddie visited David F——'s unit to deliver the threat that Junior had overheard.

Junior asked who else had been involved and Eddie named Aubrey S—— and Rick C——. Junior decided to do some visiting. Before he went looking for the first man on his list, David F——, David found him.

"If I punch out Eddie, are you gonna back him up?" David asked bluntly.

"Why the fuck you want to go after him again? You already punched him out," Junior replied.

"I just want to know if you're gonna back him up."

"You're fuckin' right I am."

"Because I got some back-up of my own."

"You better have, fucker, 'cause you're gonna need it," Junior warned him.

After David F—— left, Junior went looking for Rick C——, whom he found in Mike M——'s cell. Junior and Rick exchanged sharp words before Mike intervened to ask when the incident had taken place. When Junior told him lunch-time, Mike said Rick had been with him over lunch. Assuming that Eddie had been wrong about Rick, Junior then went looking for Aubrey S——.

For a variety of reasons, Aubrey was not one of Junior's favorite people. Junior suspected him of being the "king rat" who had put a number of drug dealers in Springhill in the hole in order to allow his own pill business to flourish. His suspicion wasn't allayed when he found Aubrey in one of the range offices playing cribbage with a guard. He called him out and the two inmates went down to the cleaning room.

"Why did you help set up Eddie?" Junior asked.

"I don't know what you're talking about," Aubrey replied and started to walk away.

Junior grabbed him by the shirt and punched him twice in the face. Dazed, Aubrey ran into the dead-lock box in his frenzy to escape, cracking his cheekbone. Marshall later learned that he had gone to the hospital, but not before telling Roger M——, a lifer Aubrey was supplying with Valium, about the incident. Roger M—— and David F—— promptly called on Junior, who was drinking tea in Mike M——'s cell.

"Who punched out Aubrey?" Roger demanded.

"I did, you fuckin' yoyo-head. And I know why you're backing him, too. He supplies your dope. Now don't fuck around or somebody gonna get hurt," Junior told them.

"You keep your fuckin' hands off Aubrey or you deal with us," Roger told him.

"Really? You guys wanna fuck around, come on upstairs. First guy that comes in there, I'll tear his fuckin' head off."

Junior picked up his tea and left. Unsure of what he'd started,

Roger asked Mike M—— what he should do. "Don't fuck with him, Roger. If he flips, you're gonna wish you were back in Archambault. Straighten it out, man," Mike advised.

When Roger appeared at his cell door, Junior was already holding the two-foot length of hardwood that he used to prop up his window.

"I just wanted to get the story straight, man, that's all," Roger said.

"Roger, it doesn't fuckin' concern you, it's none of your fuckin' business. Dave F—— tells me he's got all kinds of back-up, and if you're one of them, you better get more. Now get the fuck out my house."

The tension between Junior and Aubrey continued to build into September. Aubrey aggravated matters when he passed over Junior while handing out Valium to a group of prisoners in the card room one day. Noticing the young Indian's chagrin, he promised to give Junior some next time.

That weekend Chrissy B—— visited Junior's cell to share a joint, but it was clear he had already left the planet by other transport. Quizzed by Junior, Chrissy told him he'd received a few Valium from Aubrey.

Junior went looking for Aubrey to remind him of his promise. He found him in the card room playing poker. After the game, he followed Aubrey to his cell, where another inmate lay passed out on the bed with fifteen Valium in his stomach–an overindulgence that would earn him a trip to the hole.

"You got any Valium or what?" Junior asked.

"Jesus, you know I never had any since last week," Aubrey replied.

"You fuckin' liar. Chrissy just came by my cell and he told me you gave him some. You better find some more, you fuckin' weasel," Junior told him, promising to come back later.

Later that day Aubrey had an outside visitor. While he was in the visiting and correspondence room, staff picked up a kite dropped by Aubrey claiming that Junior Marshall had threatened to kill him if he didn't give him drugs. The note was immediately handed over to Security and Aubrey was taken into protective custody.

By Sunday night, everyone knew that Aubrey was in protective custody. Junior was told by a group of inmates that Aubrey had boasted to them of a plan to have Marshall "piped" for the beating he had given him over the Eddie P—— incident. In a later report of the incident handed over to prison authorities, Aubrey was quoted as saying, " I'll get even with that bastard one way or the other."

At 10:30 Monday morning, Junior was summoned from the welding shop to number three building, where two security officers and both his LUDO's were waiting for him. He was asked what was going on between him and Aubrey. Junior explained that he'd beaten Aubrey after he'd helped to set up Eddie P—— in the shower.

The authorities then raised the question of the threat on Aubrey's life and accused Junior of threatening four other inmates since his return from Dorchester. The young Indian was told that two-thirds of the inmates in Springhill were "scared to death" of him. Although he denied having threatened to kill Aubrey or anyone else, his entreaties fell on deaf ears. He was once more taken to the hole with the threat of a transfer to Dorchester hanging over his head.

Faced with that depressing prospect, Junior made a desperate appeal to the Regional Classification Board in a letter written from the hole on October 7, 1980:

> I've been back 5 months now & I have did three quarters of this 5 months in my cell: Reason: I knew I had to stay away from the people in here. Another reason for doing cell time, welding, and run the track was I have been working 9 and a half years to get an appeal on my Murder charge and three quarters of the work has been layed out concerning this matter. I have 7 months left before my parole hearing & I took my welding course because of that. I have put in to go home for 3 days to see what kind of settlement we can come up with concerning the other 25% left to be done on my appeal: And that's trying to get the money for my lawyer. I feel I'm well supported concerning this matter. So I'm asking you people on the board to reconsider me to stay in Springhill & not to be transferred back up to Dorchester. Reason: I feel that Aubrey S—— was out for Revenge to get even with me. And by doing so He went to Security & told them that I was going to do him in: after he faced the fact that he failed to stand by his committment, that by saying he didn't have the nerve to Pipe me: So

instead he went to Security & *reversed* the story; That it was
me that was going to do the Piping, stabbing, or whatever he
had planned. After Aubrey S—— was locked up in P.C. It was
then I was told; I was supposed to be piped. It wasn't Aubrey
S——'s life on the line; It was mine & I never even knew about
it. But I'm suffering; because of the consequences.

Thank You
for taking time to
Read my letter.
Yours Sincerely, Junior Marshall

NOTE: if reconsidered, I will try harder to stay by myself and
stay away from trouble in the Units. Thats my committment & I
feel I could stand by it if I'm giving *one* more chance.

Junior sank back into the oblivion of the hole, awaiting the
board's decision. "I don't know if it was forty or forty-two days in
that fuckin' place. The maximum time in the hole is s'pose to be
thirty days but they'd take me to the adjustment centre for one day,
then throw me back in the hole. I despised them after that."

Cut off from visits, news, and the Valium to which he was
addicted, Junior endured the most hellish period of his long
incarceration. He wrote of his frustration to his old friend Roy
Gould: "I never threatened anybody in here. . . .Since I come back
from Dorchester, I spent a lot of time in my cell and running the
track all summer. . . .It still doesn't work no matter how goodie-
goodie a guy is in here. . . .I've been railroaded again. . . .But I can't
do fuck all about it."

Even the guards responded to his obvious misery by giving him
the job of mopping out the hole and bringing food to the other
prisoners in solitary confinement, an assignment that added to the
half-hour per day he was allowed out of his cell. However, one of
the security officers found out about the arrangement and
promptly cancelled it.

For more than a month, authorities at Springhill pondered what to
do about inmate 1997. There was less debate on the subject of his
application for day parole to visit Cape Breton for three days,
thanks mainly to the Sydney city police, who made a negative
contribution to Junior's community assessment. As parole officer
Robert MacDougall wrote in his report of September 24:

Inspector William Urquhart of the Sydney Police Department was contacted in order to elicit his reaction to the subject's request for a 3 day temporary absence to return to the Membertou Reserve with hopes of gaining support for his appeal. As expected, the police reaction in this case is quite negative, as they are very concerned about the risk the subject presents should he return to the area. Inspector Urquhart feels that the subject is a high risk for re-offending and should not be given that opportunity to do so. As earlier stated, the reaction of the Sydney police to the subject's return to the Membertou Reserve is negative.

Junior's application for a leave of absence was denied.

On October 30, 1980, he was released from the hole to make his final plea to authorities to remain at Springhill. They were not persuaded. On Halloween night, Junior Marshall was returned to maximum security at Dorchester Penitentiary, where he would serve out the rest of his life sentence.

18/The Name

"Trick or treat?" Junior quipped to the guard as he passed through the forbidding doors of Dorchester Penitentiary. The guard, remembering Marshall as a model prisoner from his early Dorchester days, informed the new arrival that a guard had been killed a few days before and that the prison was still in an uproar. "You picked a fine time to come back to us, Junior. I don't think we even got a room for you."

"Why don't you just send me home then, just send me the fuck home, okay?" he joked.

But the joking abruptly stopped when he got inside. The guard's death and the chaos it ushered in were all Junior heard about for the next two weeks. He was told that the three inmates hadn't, in fact, murdered their hostage and set his body ablaze, as was first reported, but that he was killed accidentally when another guard blindly fired his shotgun through a plywood partition after hearing his colleague call out for help. Fires had already been burning in that corridor and the man's corpse had simply fallen into the flames.

Prisoners who had been in the hole at the time told stories of how the three inmates who had taken hostages to force their transfer to another institution were savagely beaten after their capture. "The boys that were in the hole seen it and they told us about it when they come out. They said, 'You wouldn't fuckin' believe it, the beatin' them guys got. They had one guy, he was knocked out fifteen minutes ago and they were still beatin' him. And we started hollerin' about it, 'Leave the fuckin' man alone!'"

Inmates in the general population where Junior was housed (he would later request a move to the lifers' wing because of the incessant noise) told stories of what happened after the ensuing riot and lockdown were over. "They told me the guards opened their doors, search them, and tear their fuckin' room apart, you know. You're walking out the door, somebody grabs you by the hair and just sprays fuckin' mace in your face."

Apocryphal or not, the stories were circulated as gospel, ushering in a period of high tension between inmates and grieving guards. Six weeks after his transfer from Springhill, Junior incurred his only "serious" offence report in Dorchester. A jar of honey he was eating as part of his jogging program was found in his cell and seized by guards as "contraband". Inmate 1997 said that he hadn't realized honey was contraband and was let off with a warning. He later learned the guards were concerned that the honey would end up as an ingredient in someone's home brew.

The next few months passed serenely. Junior incurred no further offence reports and kept to himself, as the sparse records of this period of his incarceration showed: "Should learn to overcome tendency to isolation by personal effort and with the advice of others. . . .Is a loner. Needs to learn to look for help, in religion or through others." But the reports were not entirely free of a theme that had dogged him throughout his prison years: "Becomes easily upset. Intolerant of authority; embittered and resentful. Needs to accept sentence."

On April 6, his new parole officer, Maud Hody, wrote the first report of Junior's progress since his latest return to Dorchester:

> . . .Mr. Marshall is now eligible for full parole. . . .However there are very serious reservations with respect to him, since he appears. to resort to violence whenever he is seriously upset, and makes a nuisance of himself in the institution. Finally, after years of toleration, Springhill gave up.
>
> Perhaps Mr. Marshall will be able to reach some form of understanding of himself, both as a human being and as an Indian, during the time that it seems likely he will be required to be at Dorchester. Until he learns self-control and learns to understand himself, there is very little hope of his succeeding in any form of release. . . ."

Brian G—— had the distinction of being the only inmate Junior

Marshall ever feared. Imprisoned for life for murdering a man he found with his wife, Brian G—— was a burly loner who could "go off-side" with the slightest provocation. When that happened, it was best to be somewhere else, as the inmate server in the kitchen found out when he didn't give the explosive lifer enough food.

"Put more on that," Brian snapped, holding out his tray.

"I can't," the French-Canadian inmate answered. He enjoyed a measure of security, since he served from behind a door leading to the kitchen.

"You little Frenchy cocksucker, you feed me right now!" Brian shouted, almost tearing the protective door off its hinges.

"Fuck off!" the other inmate said.

"You open that fuckin' door, you little asshole. I'm sick of you dishing out everything in the kitchen to your fuckin' buddies."

As the other inmates in the supper line, including Junior, withdrew from Brian, the guards moved in and subdued him before the incident became serious.

That night during recreation in the gymnasium, a gang of French-Canadian prisoners went after Brian, who grabbed a three-foot weight-bar and jumped up on the stage at one end of the room. A handful of other inmates quickly blocked off the doors so that no one could get out, including Junior, who had been playing floor hockey with friends. "The first fuckin' frog that gets up on this stage, I'll have his fuckin' head," Brian roared, banging the weight-bar off the stage as he spoke. The stand-off went on until 4:30 a.m., when Brian asked the inmates barricading the doors to allow the other prisoners, who weren't involved in the incident, to go home. When the doors were opened, a contingent of guards moved in and took Brian to the hole.

Uncomfortable in the explosive atmosphere of Dorchester, and tired of trying to raise the money for lawyers who didn't seem to be doing anything for him, Junior decided to drop the appeal that Truro lawyer Melinda MacLean had been working on for more than a year. The catalyst for this decision had come in March, when, because of his appeal, Marshall had told authorities that he wasn't interested in being considered for full parole. He was swiftly informed that his new parole eligibility date would be June 4, 1982 –a year later than his original date. The prospect of doing addi-

tional time was more than he could bear, as a letter he wrote to Roy
Gould made clear.

April 19 -81

Hi Chief

Just a line to let you know I have received your letter & it was
nice hearing from you. Theres not much happening around
here, No stabbings anyway. A guy got it about 3 weeks ago but
he's alright now.

I'm doing pretty good! Right now, I'm working on getting to
the Farm Camp. If I get there, then I'll have a chance to get
home for the summer games. There's nothing more I want &
that's to get home for the games.

Did you get my papers from Melinda? I have to go for my
parole Roy. I gotta get out of prison! & I think it's high time
people start helping me out. I can't do it alone. You guys are
gonna have to start helping me.

I hate repeating myself & getting a little tired of the whole
subject.

If I put in for a pass to go home would you guys support me?

Jesus, I cry a lot, huh? No Roy, I'm serious, a joke is a joke but
they are going too far out of reach. They know I never killed
that guy. But still I'm paying the fuckin' price. Now my parole
has been set back for a year because I never admit to the
charge & when that is up they'll do the same thing. There's no
end to it & these fuckers expect me to put up with it. I already
did put up with it Roy. I did 10 years & it wasn't easy. So I'm
asking you people to start helping me out. I don't think it's fair
for what they did to me & there was nothing done about it.
Well enough of that. But I hope you understand. Let me know
when you'll be up O.K.? I'll give you a call maybe next week.

Did you put me on the Membertou's ball team roster? I
might be home you know.

I hear the ole man is trying to get a new truck. If he does, I
hope he takes care of it. Boy he's bad for cars. Well, I better let
you go so take care & see you soon.

Buddie Jr.

P.S.
Send some pictures!
Don't be so tight!

After putting in more than six months of offence-free time, Junior approached his new classification officer, Margaret MacWilliam, for a transfer back to Springhill. He told her he wanted the transfer in order to get his plumbing ticket and possibly win day parole to the Carlton Centre in Halifax, a halfway house for convicts en route between prison and the street.

The request led to a major case conference on June 23, 1981, at Springhill attended by six institutional personnel who had previously dealt with Marshall and his two new caseworkers, Margaret MacWilliam and Maud Hody. Junior's former caseworkers at Springhill made it "abundantly clear" that they didn't want the troublesome inmate back at the institution. "In particular," wrote Maud Hody, "they suggested that he should wait longer before seeking release, spending more time in Dorchester and demonstrating his ability to remain free of drug use....Most particularly, the staff at Springhill suggested that Mr. Marshall must deal with his 'murderous' side including the details of the very unpleasant murder, and his attacks on other people, including other inmates and – nearly – a staff member at Springhill. He must admit to the crime (if he did it) and deal with the factors that lead to his violence...."

When he got the results of the case meeting, inmate 1997 calmly responded by trying to conform to what his former caseworkers at Springhill said he would have to do if he was ever to get back to that institution or win his parole. He continued to run the track and avoid drugs, and he even requested regular sessions with a psychologist. It was no more than an elaborate sham, but Junior had come to the conclusion it was the only way he would ever be let out of prison. "It was the same game I played at Dorchester to get out of the fuckin' place and get to Springhill. They wanted to hear I did it, so I told them. When I got what I wanted, I took it back. Them guys would never listen to the truth."

But suddenly, with the ball in mid-court between the desperate prisoner and the bureaucracy that held him in its paper spider-web, the universe was turned upside down. By an incredible coincidence, he learned the name of the man who had murdered Sandy Seale.

The visit Junior Marshall would never forget began routinely enough on the afternoon of August 26, 1981. His girlfriend Shelly Sarson, who had hitchhiked the roads of Nova Scotia and New Brunswick winter and summer to visit him since their chance meeting in 1976, appeared at Dorchester with her brother Mitchell. The conversation was going along aimlessly enough until Mitchell suddenly asked Junior a question.

"Do you know a guy named Roy Ebsary?"

"I don't know him," Junior replied.

"He knows you pretty good," Sarson said.

"Yeah? I can't place the name."

"Well, he told me he killed a black guy and stabbed an Indian in the park in 1971."

A rush more powerful than any induced by the drugs he'd taken over the last ten years surged over the 28-year-old Indian. "An old man?" he asked, half afraid of Sarson's reply.

"Yeah, an old guy," Sarson said, adding that he'd lived in Ebsary's house on Falmouth Street while attending school in Sydney.

"Glasses, white hair?"

"Yeah, and he's fuckin' crazy, too," Mitchell volunteered.

"You gonna back me up on that?" Junior asked.

"I got to think about," the young man said.

"You think about it *good*," Junior told him.

The moment his visitors had gone, Junior rushed to a telephone and called Roy Gould, who had worked quietly behind the scenes trying to get Junior's case reopened by writing letters to any bureaucrat or politician in a position to help.

"Roy, you're not going to believe this!" Junior said.

"What?"

"I found the fuckin' guy who killed Seale."

"Who?"

"Roy Gould!" Junior said in his excitement.

"Fuck you!"

"I mean Roy *Ebsary*!"

Half an hour later, Dan Paul, a member of the Union of Nova Scotia Indians, showed up at the Sydney city police station and passed on the news to Inspector William Urquhart, who was now hearing Ebsary's name in connection with the Seale slaying for the third time. Ten years earlier, the McNeil brothers had told Urquhart that Roy Ebsary was Sandy Seale's real killer. Three years after that, he was given the same name by Dave Ratchford, who told police Donna Ebsary had seen her father washing blood from a knife on the night of the murder. Urquhart, then in charge of the detective squad, hadn't even taken a statement outlining that remarkable allegation. This time he did make out a report of his meeting with Dan Paul and passed it on to his superiors:

> Turned over to me, Insp. W. A. Urquhart, Sydney Police Officer By Dan Paul, Aug. 26th–1981. Time, 4:30 P.M. I notified C.P. [Crown Prosecutor] Brian Williston as Dan Paul told me that Roy Ebsary is the one that stabbed Sandy Seale in the Park. This information came from Junior Marshall, I told Paul that was not enough information. He is going to try and get the name of the person who gave the name of Ebsary to Jr. Marshall.
>
> Insp. W. A. Urquhart
>
> 27th Aug. Time, 11:20 A.M.
> The above information given to Deputy-Chief M. J. MacDonald, above date and time.
>
> Insp. W. A. Urquhart

A flurry of activity followed Mitchell Sarson's sensational revelation. The Union of Nova Scotia Indians contacted Steve Aronson, a Halifax lawyer who had recently negotiated the first native land claim in Nova Scotia, and asked him to take on Junior's still very sketchy case. In early September, Roy Gould, Dan Paul, and the young lawyer visited Junior in Dorchester, where the inmate signed papers empowering Aronson to act on his behalf.

The man who had given up in despair of getting an appeal suddenly had new hope, much to the dismay of correctional workers, who thought they had convinced him that earning parole was the surest way out of Dorchester. Oblivious to the negative reaction his renewed efforts to prove his innocence were having on institutional authorities, Junior applied for an unescorted TA to go home for Christmas. In his application for day parole, he said that he wanted to see his parents and meet with the Union of Nova Scotia Indians about his appeal. Another community assessment was requested and parole officer Archie Walsh talked to Junior's parents, Chief Alex Christmas of Membertou, and Sydney Police Chief John MacIntyre. Chief MacIntyre was once again opposed to

Junior's return to Membertou, as the parole officer noted in his report: "Preliminary investigation reveals strong reaction from Chief of Police Sydney to a proposed U.T.A. [unescorted temporary absence]. . . .Although the subject has confirmed accommodation on the Membertou Reserve in Sydney, I feel Chief MacIntyre's concern about the safety of other citizens should be considered. . . ."

The parole board heeded Walsh's advice and denied Junior permission to go home for Christmas. "We do not think that Christmas time, on his home Reserve, where he might run into witnesses at his trial, is a good time for subject's first release in about two years. Although he is willing to take antabuse, there is likely to be a great deal of drinking and hostilities could surface."

On the 9th of December, Junior was informed by letter of the board's decision. But it didn't have nearly the same impact on him as another piece of information that came to him courtesy of inmate librarian Al M——. Al, who liked Junior, used to save him copies of the *Cape Breton Post* so he could keep up with the news out of Sydney. In early December, Junior was transfixed by a story about a stabbing that had taken place on Falmouth Street in Sydney, the street where Roy Ebsary now lived, according to Mitchell Sarson.

Junior spent the longest week of his life waiting for the next edition of the newspaper to see if there would be more information about the stabbing. Sure enough, there was a story reporting that Roy Ebsary had been charged with stabbing Wilfred "Goodie" Mugridge in the chest on December 5. Junior called his lawyer and passed on the information.

In the cold, bright days of January, as inmate 1997 entered his eleventh year behind bars, he decided to write a letter to the man whose crime he had paid for with his youth.

D. Marshall Jr.
Drawer A&B
Dorchester, N.B.

Mr. Roy N. Absary
68 Falmouth St.
Sydney, N.S.

Dear Sir.

My name is Donald Marshall Jr. And I'm serving a life

sentance For the Murder of the late Sandy Seale. It was brought to my attention that you know the circumstances surrounding this important matter. I have maintained my innocences for 11 years and unfortunately could not get a retrial.

I know the facts. And that is why I am asking you to come out with what information you may have. Mr. Absary, I've been locked up for 11 years. I am still a young man so believe me when I tell you that I went through hell dealing with this difficult case.

I suffered long enough my friend for somebody's mistake and knowing I'm an innocent man, I'm asking you to be sincere and to help me concerning this very important matter. I will pray that you'll be honest about it and ask God to give me the strength to forgive you and to forgive the people that were involved with my Trial.

> Thank you for your time
> Sincerely Yours.
> Donald Marshall Jr.

Copies of the letter were sent to the Sydney police, the Union of Nova Scotia Indians, and Marshall's lawyer, Steve Aronson. By this time, Aronson had already interviewed Mitchell Sarson, who repeated his story that Ebsary had in fact confessed to him that he had stabbed Sandy Seale. Armed with Sarson's new evidence, the recent stabbing charge against Roy Ebsary, and his client's protestations of innocence, Aronson wrote to Chief John MacIntyre of the Sydney city police requesting that he look into the matter. The letter prompted a meeting involving Chief MacIntyre, the Crown prosecutor for Cape Breton County, Frank Edwards, and Donald Scott, the Officer/Commanding of the Sydney subdivision of the RCMP. Chief John MacIntyre asked that the RCMP look into the matter, just as he had ten years earlier.

19/Vindication

Harry Wheaton looked like an airline captain on the New York-to-Paris run. Tall, blue-eyed, and disarmingly urbane, the plainclothes co-ordinator of the RCMP in Sydney had, in fact, always wanted to be a pilot. As a seventeen-year-old growing up in Salisbury, New Brunswick, a farming community fifteen miles outside Moncton, he learned to fly small aircraft but didn't have the money to pursue his commerical pilot's licence. Notwithstanding his mother's hope that he would become a priest, he turned instead to the RCMP, joining the force in 1962. Not long after his 10½-month boot-camp in Regina, the smooth-talking rookie with the infectious smile began to make his mark, just as his father, a road-master with the CNR, said he would if he put his head down and worked hard.

During his first real posting in the small community of Sheet Harbour, Nova Scotia, the young constable rescued a man who had passed out in the bottom of a well, overcome by fumes from a gas pump he was operating. Wheaton climbed into the well and carried the victim up on his back, landing in hospital in the bed next to the man whose life he'd saved. His actions won him a Commissioner's commendation for bravery and the admiration of the community, including that of Karen Henley, the young Sheet Harbour woman he would soon marry.

Wheaton went on to show that he had more to offer as a policeman than physical courage. His facility with the more sophisticated sections of the Criminal Code earned him undercover assignments investigating organized crime in Toronto and Montreal, as well as stints looking into white-collar crime in the Maritimes. In 1973 he took over Sydney's drug section and earned the nickname "Dirty Harry" for his tough street investigations. After fifteen years with the RCMP, he became one of the youngest operational men to be promoted to the rank of sergeant.

Early in his career, one of his superiors, Keith Hall, gave the ambitious constable some advice he never forgot: "He told me I would have my good times and bad times, I would be promoted and I would be passed over, but one thing the force would always need was someone to do the police work. If I made myself the person that they needed to do the police work, I'd get ahead in the Mounted Police."

There didn't seem to be much need for police work when his commanding officer, Don Scott, called Wheaton into his office on February 3, 1982, and assigned him to the Donald Marshall case. After explaining the details of the meeting he'd just had with Sydney Police Chief John MacIntyre and Crown prosecutor Frank Edwards, Scott gave Wheaton the job of interviewing Mitchell Sarson, the Pictou youth to whom Roy Ebsary had allegedly confessed that he'd stabbed Sandy Seale.

After they finished talking, Scott handed Wheaton the slim file Chief MacIntyre had given him earlier in the day. Wheaton left the meeting with the impression that it was not an especially important assignment—the work, perhaps, of a single good day. After all, as every policeman knew, the prisons were filled with self-styled "innocent" men.

That impression didn't change after he read the June 4, 1971, statements of John Pratico and Maynard Chant. It looked like a "good case" to Wheaton, particularly since he knew so many of the players from his earlier Sydney days, including Justice Louis Dubinsky, Crown prosecutor Donald MacNeil, and Chief John MacIntyre.

After reading the file, Wheaton visited Chief MacIntyre for a further briefing on the case. The chief went over the same ground covered in the file, but mentioned to Wheaton that Marshall had escaped from custody in 1979. "The way he [MacIntyre] described it to me, he escaped by paddling down the rivers, which didn't make sense really," Wheaton recalled in 1984. "And he ended up being captured in Pictou. And Sarson was from Pictou, so he figured there was some nefarious sort of collusion between the two that way, and that's how this Sarson may come out. That's what he had in his mind, so that was also in my mind, of course."

But despite his now reinforced sense that the file was an open-and-shut affair, Wheaton was bothered by the fact that Roy Ebsary *had* been charged with knifing a Sydney man just before Christmas. Vaguely recalling Ebsary's name from his days as an undercover drug investigator in Sydney, Wheaton decided to check with "Woody" Woodburn, the Sydney police officer whose investigation led to Ebsary's being charged with the 1981 stabbing of Goodie Mugridge. Woodburn told him that Ebsary was an eccentric homosexual who had "a thing" about knives. Despite the fact that he looked like "a little old man", the seventy-year-old Newfoundlander was, according to Woodburn, "a real sneaky old son of a bitch".

To illustrate his point, Woodburn told Wheaton that after stabbing Mugridge just below the heart with a kitchen knife, Ebsary had been questioned by police but refused to give a statement. He then went directly to the Sydney City Hospital, where he crept into the intensive-care unit, lifted the oxygen tent covering his friend, and whispered that Mugridge's own brother had stabbed him. He hoped the injured man would repeat this story to police, since both he and Mugridge had been drinking heavily at the time of the incident. But a nurse overheard Ebsary and called police, who subsequently charged him with the stabbing.

His interest piqued, Wheaton made inquiries on Falmouth Street, where Ebsary had lived ever since 1979, when Mary, his common-law wife, had thrown him out of the house for carrying on with a young man. Neighbors told the RCMP investigator that Ebsary was a "weird old man who ran around wearing a cape and medals". And they reported another eccentricity that Wheaton found extremely interesting: Roy Ebsary carried a knife concealed in a walking stick, a knife he liked to brandish when drinking.

Later that week, Wheaton ran a check on Ebsary's criminal history and found that in 1970 – less than a year before Seale was stabbed to death – he'd been charged with possession of an offensive weapon: a knife. The information meant nothing in itself, but it gave the investigator a "feeling". He still had no reason to attach much importance to the assignment, yet when it came time to interview Mitchell Sarson, he found himself choosing a partner who reflected his own vague sense that the investigation might not be so straightforward after all.

Corporal Jim Carroll, like Harry Wheaton, had joined the RCMP in 1962, receiving his basic training in Ottawa. Born just outside of Truro, Nova Scotia, the heavy-set policeman was known as a systematic plodder who showed infinite patience in pursuing his investigations. His forte was arson investigations, the slowest and most methodical of police work. "Jim would put on an old pair of cover-alls and rubber boots and go into the ashes and sift through them until he found the char marks and go into the basement and find the burn patterns and check the charred remains of electrical boxes until he found out what had gone on. No matter how long it took, Jim would just keep sifting through until he had the answer," Wheaton said of his partner.

Over the next difficult weeks, Jim Carroll's painstaking approach would be the perfect foil for Wheaton's more intuitive style, an important consideration in the unlikely event that the Marshall investigation turned out to be something other than the routine investigation it seemed.

After reading the transcript of the original trial and the statements of Pratico and Chant, Carroll shared Wheaton's opinion that the case looked to be in order. The Crown had produced two eyewitnesses and Marshall himself had been a fairly uncooperative witness, judging from the number of times he had to be asked to repeat his answers. In fact, Carroll felt more than a little uneasy about the assignment. It was unusual for the RCMP to review another police department's file; he had never done it in his twenty years on the force.

The RCMP officers might have had an easier time determining if further investigation was necessary had they known about the statement Jimmy MacNeil gave to then Sgt./Det. MacIntyre on November 15, 1971, in which he too identified Roy Ebsary as Sandy Seale's killer. But that statement and others, including the first statements of Chant and Pratico, were not in the file Chief MacIntyre gave to the RCMP. "I saw no Jimmy MacNeil statements. All I saw was the eyewitnesses' statements and some other peripheral statements, like from police officers who were first on the scene," Harry Wheaton later recalled.

On February 9, Wheaton and Carroll drove from Sydney to Pictou, to interview Mitchell Sarson. Before interviewing him, the investigators went to the local RCMP detachment to get an assessment of the man whose statement to Steve Aronson had brought about the reinvestigation. Their fellow officers described Sarson as a harmless young man who had been busted for minor drug offences in Pictou but who otherwise worked with his mother cleaning out the local tavern after hours.

Sarson lived with his family in a storey-and-a-half frame house around the corner from the tavern where he worked. The tall, anemic youth said he met Junior Marshall at Dorchester, where he'd been visiting his brother, John Sarson. His sister Shelly had also met Junior there and became his girlfriend. In 1979, Marshall had "buggered off" on his way back to prison from an inmate canoe trip and came to live with Shelly for a few days before he was recaptured. Wheaton recorded the discrepancy with Chief MacIntyre's story of Marshall paddling his way to freedom, and possibly vengeance, down the rivers of Pictou County, and made a note to ask his colleagues back at the local detachment for details of the 1979 escape.

Sarson then told the officers about his connection with Roy Ebsary. In the winter of 1979 the young man wanted to take a drywall course at the Adult Vocational School in Sydney, but needed a place to stay. Another Pictou resident arranged to have him live with Roy Ebsary, whom he knew from the war. "Mary worked at night and Roy and I used to talk a lot," Sarson told the officers. "One night right out of the blue he told me he stabbed a colored fellow in the park. I asked him what happened and he said he was walking through the park and got held up by a nigger and an Indian. The nigger said he wanted all his money. Ebsary said, 'All my money?' The nigger said, 'Yes,' so he hauled his knife out and stabbed the nigger once. He showed me how he pulled it out with his left hand and jabbed him once. He mentioned that he gouged the right arm between the wrist and elbow on the inner arm of the Indian. I am kind of fogged up on which arm he said. The words used were, 'Gimme all you got,' so Roy said, 'You want all I got?' The nigger said, 'Yes,' so then he stabbed him."

Sarson, who considered Ebsary to be "the biggest bullshitter" he'd ever met, thought no more about the story until he mentioned it to Junior Marshall more than a year and a half later at Dorchester. To his great surprise, the inmate was transfixed and asked Sarson to repeat the story to his lawyer, Steve Aronson. "I was surprised to hear Ebsary had stabbed a guy in Sydney recently," Sarson said in his statement. "Ebsary is queer and weird; that's why I got out of Sydney and came back to Pictou. Ebsary told me he was alone when it happened. Junior never admitted to me that he was trying to roll Ebsary. He did tell me that he was with the nigger that night."

After the interview, Harry Wheaton was careful not to express an opinion about what the two policemen had just been told. As the senior investigator, he didn't want to color his partner's opinion before he had heard it, a rule of thumb that had stood him in good stead through twenty-five murder cases in which he'd been involved. In fact, Carroll's opinion was the same as his own: Sarson had been telling the truth. Whether Roy Ebsary had been telling the truth to Sarson was a different matter.

Back at the Pictou detachment, Wheaton asked about Marshall's 1979 escape and recapture. He was told it had been a non-violent, routine affair. Wheaton was mildly "turned off" by what he took to be MacIntyre's "coloring of the thing".

That night, Wheaton and Carroll stayed at the Heather Motel in New Glasgow. When they finally turned in after a long talk about the day's events, Harry Wheaton looked out the window at the deserted Trans-Canada Highway that snakes through the small Nova Scotia town on its way east to Cape Breton.

"I began to worry after I finished with Sarson and I said to myself, hey, I've got to be really thorough on this and really careful and really get into it because there's more here than meets the eye."

Once back in Sydney, Wheaton reread Junior Marshall's 1971 statement to the Sydney police and was struck by the similar language that he and Sarson ascribed to Seale's alleged attacker that night on Crescent Street. He found Marshall's physical description of Seale's assailant even more striking. The short old man with white hair could indeed have been Roy Ebsary. Still far from convinced he was on to something, Wheaton decided to get a first-hand look at the character he'd heard so much about. When he finally found him walking down the road by Wentworth Park, he was startled by what he saw. Ebsary was wearing a long blue coat over his shoulders that to a Catholic like Wheaton quickly conjured up a priest's soutane. He decided to find out more about Roy and looked up the old man's estranged wife. Although Mary Ebsary was too nervous to give him a statement during that first visit, she confirmed Sarson's story that he'd lived at the Ebsary home while he attended the Adult Vocational School in Sydney.

The next day Wheaton returned to the small house on Mechanic Street to interview Greg Ebsary. Greg, now a taxi-driver, told the Mountie that his father had literally remained in the house for seven years after the murder. For at least two of those years, Roy had sequestered himself in his room, which he decorated like a ship's cabin. He read voraciously and would often act out the lines of the various people in the books. At night he used to slip out to the backyard to walk his dog, an animal with which he practised bestiality, according to what one of Roy's neighbors told the RCMP. In 1979, Mitchell Sarson arrived on the scene and Greg said that his father had changed. "Greg had no hesitation in telling me that the pair of them were a pair of queers and that the old man used to dress Sarson up with an ascot and whatnot and call him his 'pretty boy' and all this sort of stuff," Wheaton recalled.

After reporting his growing reservations about the file to his superior, Don Scott, Wheaton decided that he and Jim Carroll should pay a visit to one of the eyewitnesses who had given evidence at Marshall's 1971 trial. They settled on Maynard Chant. On February 16, 1982, a bitter day with the wind keening in off the North Atlantic, the two investigators parked in the lot outside Louisbourg's fish-plant, where Maynard worked. They walked from one end of the plant to the other before they found him at a cutting table filleting fish. Chant's supervisor told the Mounties that if they took Maynard out of the assembly line, it would "foul up" the process: if they wanted to talk to him, they'd better make it fast. Wheaton introduced himself to Chant and told him what he was investigating. The burly young man with the ruddy complexion turned completely white. "I've got something I want to talk to you about," he said, agreeing to meet them that night at his parents' house.

While they waited for the meeting, Wheaton and Carroll debated what Chant would say. Carroll was fairly certain that the young man would simply repeat his testimony of eleven years earlier. Wheaton wasn't so sure. Unknown to the two detectives, "the Lord had started working all up inside" the young man as soon as Wheaton had stated his business in the fish-plant. Ever since he'd become a born-again Christian in 1979, Maynard Chant had been waiting for this day. In more ways than one, it had been a long time coming.

Shortly after Junior Marshall began his life sentence at Dorchester Penitentiary, Maynard Chant had entered an underworld of a different sort.

Bored by life in Louisbourg and craving precisely the kind of excitement that was stifled by his family's strict Christian regimen, young Maynard had travelled to Montreal, where he plunged into the city's booming drug subculture. He soon found out that if you were willing to do a little selling, you could get all the drugs you wanted without paying a penny.

Maynard did such a good job as a street pusher that he was approached to take a shipment of drugs back to Cape Breton. His first job as a courier, a career that would last five hectic years, was to transport ten pounds of marijuana and a pound of mescaline to Louisbourg and get it out on the streets. To the teenager who in his own words was enamored of "the quick buck" and who would "slit your throat for a quarter", it was a satisfying lifestyle: easy money and all the drugs he wanted against what his contacts assured him were the minimal risks of getting caught.

Maynard's favorite method of transporting drugs was hitchhiking. Under normal circumstances, cars moving from one province to another were never checked, and if the driver was stopped by police, Maynard merely got out with his knapsack and went on his way. It was much safer than moving drugs through airports, especially as Maynard's involvement in the business deepened and his shipments increased in value. "It was a contract thing. They'd give me five or six thousand dollars and my objective was to double their money," Maynard recalled. "I was dealing through the second-class mafia. It was definitely connected. I was ready to sign contracts for a two-year agreement for carrying, you know, to carry drugs from such and such a place to another."

After a few years in the business, Maynard had established a reputation as a competent and trustworthy courier. His contacts in

Montreal offered to make him the principal courier for Cape Breton Island and more than once invited him to smuggle drugs from Europe into North America. Both propositions appealed to the young man's greed, but a nagging fear kept him from accepting the promotions.

Over the years, Maynard was increasingly haunted by thoughts of Junior Marshall. Despite the fact that Junior was locked up for life in a maximum-security prison, he regularly scaled the walls of Dorchester and slipped into the troubled dreams of the drug courier from Louisbourg. Occasionally Maynard would be walking in the woods when the young Indian would suddenly appear on the path in front of him with a hunting knife, beckoning to him with his free hand. Other times, Marshall's face would emerge out of the crowd in a smoke-filled bar, his eyes aglow with a malevolent yellow light, like a cat before it strikes its doomed prey. Worst of all were the times when Maynard dreamed of opening his bedroom door to find his grim nemesis standing before him, just as the two had once unexpectedly met in the Sydney county jail. The daytime corollary to Maynard's recurring nightmare was the possibility of being sent to the same prison as the man he had convicted with his lies, a fear that kept him from moving too far up the corporate drug ladder. "Whenever they'd offer me bigger deals, I'd say to myself, 'Man, you do time and you're in trouble.' So I'd say no, I'd pass this one, thanks. So even though your thirst for money is there, before I got involved too heavy, I kept on thinkin', 'Listen, Marshall's behind bars and you're in a big debt to this fella because you really don't know the truth, and if you go behind bars you might as well forget it.' "

Despite Maynard's prudent refusal to move into the world of big-time drugs, trouble eventually caught up with him. His one and only arrest for drug trafficking – selling two grams of hashish to a friend – ended in an eight-hundred-dollar fine. "The police just happened to check our car. Everything was filled with smoke and I said, 'Don't open up the window, man.' I said, 'Give me a chance to eat some of what I got,' but the guy did it, so I got busted. . . .It was so stupid."

From that point on, it became necessary for Maynard to find other people to "middle" his deals, an arrangement that further minimized the chances of getting caught but greatly increased the risk of being "ripped off". Maynard soon learned that his contacts were less than forgiving with those who were either greedy or stupid enough to "blow a deal". Two men who had "middled" a couple of transactions for him were brutally murdered in Montreal over a sour deal, one stabbed seventeen times in the chest and the other nearly decapitated with a crowbar. In 1979, the day finally came when Maynard himself faced a visit from Montreal.

"I got ripped off – eight or nine ounces of black African worth maybe twenty-five hundred dollars – and they definitely had to come down and the fellow said, 'The best I can do for you is give you three days because these guys are, they don't fool around, you know, you may lose an arm or a leg or something. I don't say they're goin' to kill you but these guys are heavy.' "

For years Maynard had been two people, "the great big gangster" while on the road, and "the Christian boy who respected his parents" when in Louisbourg. His "split personality" had bothered him before but not to the point where he ever allowed the two worlds to mix – at least not until now. Paranoid from heavy drug use and afraid for his life, he walked into the family living room one night and began to tell his father "what his young fellow was up to".

Walter Chant was dumbfounded by the details of Maynard's life as a drug dealer, including how he had hidden "pounds and pounds and pounds" of drugs in his father's caskets at the funeral home. As the 22-year-old illuminated the dark corners of his hitherto secret life, Mr. Chant at first wept and then suggested to Maynard that he retreat to a Christian camp he used to attend as a boy, where he could "think this out". "By this time I was really desperate," Maynard recalled. "When somebody is threatening to do something to your body, you're desperate and you just want to get away from it, eh? Makes no difference whether you've got the money or not. That's just the way these people are. You know, they don't care. They want to do something to your body. They're really crazy."

Panic-stricken, Maynard got his brother Sheldon, a driver for Curry's Ambulance Service, to take him to Camp Evangeline outside of Debert, Nova Scotia. He was agonizing over what to do next when one of his cousins asked him to go to church. Sitting in the Pentecostal Assembly, the troubled young man felt "more of an

atheist" than in the days when he'd skipped out of church early to
follow more lively pursuits. But he also knew there was nothing he
could do to avert the terrible punishment that awaited him when
his visitors from Montreal arrived. Maynard Chant had finally
become a lost soul.

"I didn't know what to do, so after the call came forward for
somebody to go up for help, for salvation, I said, 'Definitely that's
me.' I got out and I started to make the walk. It was the longest
walk I ever made in my life. That's when the change came. That's
when it came. You wouldn't believe it. My mother always said to
me, 'Maynard, you don't toy with God. You'll come to the point
where God's going to reject you when you need help.'"

For a terrible moment, down on his knees in front of a congregation of three hundred, the young man thought that moment had
arrived. He was praying for help but nothing was happening. As he
turned to look at the congregation, he was shocked to see his
mother standing behind him.

"I said, 'Listen, Ma, it's no use,' because by that time I was really
in a deep depression because I was seeking for help and I wasn't
getting it. She just looked at me and I knelt back down and I didn't
know what was goin' on. They had ministers praying behind me,
silently praying behind, just battling the forces of evil, I guess. And
just right there, then and there, it seemed like somebody took
about one hundred and fifty pounds off my shoulders, you know. A
lot of people say this God thing and this Christian thing is not real.
Well, you can't tell me it because I've experienced a lot of things
and the most real experience that I've had was that day Christ saved
me."

When Maynard returned to Louisbourg, his "miracle" continued. The visitors from Montreal had come and gone, leaving their
respects for Maynard with the middleman he suspected of ripping
him off in the drug deal. Although he owed more than sixteen
thousand dollars in drug debts, his phone suddenly stopped ring-
ing. It was as if the Lord had taken care of not only Maynard's soul
but his creditors as well.

But there was one matter he had to deal with himself: his false
testimony about Junior Marshall. Two weeks after his conversion,
he confessed his lie to his pastor and brother-in-law, the Reverend
William Legge, and later to his mother. "I told him first and he said,

'Listen, man, just keep it under your hat for a while, keep prayin'
about it, and I'll pray with you, and you know, in time, the Lord will
work things out.'"

Two and a half years later, the answer to William Legge's prayers
walked into the Chant home in the persons of Harry Wheaton and
Jim Carroll of the RCMP. With a wake in progress, the two policemen were shown to a small room off the front parlor by Maynard
and his pregnant wife. Maynard knew that he was risking making a
"real ass" of himself by telling the truth, that it would bring him
"nothin' but destruction". Even at this late date, a voice inside him
told him to "keep this together, a little secret here and you can
hold onto it for the rest of your life." But Maynard Chant had spent
his season in Hell and had no intentions of returning. Holding his
wife's hand, he unravelled the story of his old lie, just as he
believed the Lord wanted him to. The truth came out like water
cascading over a cliff.

Both Wheaton and Carroll listened in shocked silence as Maynard explained how he had never witnessed the murder, how he
hadn't even been in Wentworth Park at the time Sandy Seale was
stabbed. He told them that anything he knew about what happened
came from Junior Marshall after their chance meeting on Bentinck
Street moments after the stabbing, just as the teenage Indian had
testified in court. With his chin on his chest, Chant said he had tried
to tell police that he hadn't seen anything that night but the Sydney
detectives investigating the murder had threatened him with the
testimony of another witness. As Jim Carroll would later record in
Chant's written statement, Chant felt he had no choice but to tell
the Sydney detectives what they wanted to hear: "The policeman
was very aggressive, making statements that I had lied because a
witness had told them he had seen me there in the park that night.
He told me he knew I was on probation and that I could get from
two to five years for perjury. I didn't even know what perjury was."

Maynard called his mother into the room and Beudah Chant
confirmed her son's story about his treatment by the Sydney
detectives. She later gave a statement to Jim Carroll telling how
upset Maynard had been at the time, how the police had helped
him with his false story: "I remember one of the two policemen
telling Maynard at some stage that he couldn't say he saw a knife,
only what looked like a knife. About two years ago, Maynard told

me he had given false evidence at the trial, that he had not seen anything of the murder. He said he tried to tell the truth but they had him so scared he couldn't say anything different. They wouldn't listen to him." Mrs. Chant also mentioned that Maynard had admitted his lie to his father, Walter Chant, and the family's spiritual mentor, the Reverend William Legge.

Jim Carroll, who tried to disguise his shock at that revelation, asked Maynard if his parents had been present during the interviews with the Sydney detectives. The veteran policeman was surprised to learn that the fourteen-year-old had been unaccompanied when questioned by Sgt./Det. MacIntyre (MacIntyre would later deny this) and alone again when taken to court. "If we had been doing it, our force, we have certain guidelines – have a parent or guardian or social worker there to keep you on the straight and narrow, to make sure the juvenile is not being mistreated mentally or physically, or whatever, but also for a more important reason: that is, to make any statement or any confession, verbal or otherwise, more admissible in court," he later observed.

Carroll's surprise at the interrogation techniques of the Sydney detectives increased when he discovered that two other juveniles, John Pratico and Patricia Harriss, had also given statements to police without their parents being present.

Maynard Chant talked on. For more than a decade the truth had been bottled up inside him and the two policemen couldn't write fast enough to keep up with the story the young man was finally getting off his chest. Harry Wheaton, who had heard many stories, true and false, over the years, watched Chant move from remorse to euphoria as he spoke. The body language was revealing and Maynard's words had the ring of truth. There was no doubt in Wheaton's mind that he and his partner now had "a tiger by the tail", as Maynard's later statement to Jim Carroll would make all too clear:

> The Crown Prosecutor, I believe his first name was Donny, come to my home and drove me to his office which at that time was in the new courthouse on the ground floor. John Pratico and two plainclothes policemen were with us in the same room. The Prosecutor kept repeating our stories until they were fresh in our minds; we went into court, I believe it was the same day after the meeting in the office. John and I

repeated the same story in court. A couple of times before the jury trial, two detectives come to my home and drove me to Wentworth Park; they wanted me to show them where Pratico had been hiding on that night and where I had been standing on the tracks. They marked the spots in chalk; they were suggesting different spots and I agreed with them; basically I felt they were trying to help me rather than pressure me.

By the time Harry Wheaton closed his notebook at 6:16 p.m., the happiest man in the room was Maynard Chant. He knew he could be sent to prison for the perjured evidence he had given, but he had already cleared his conscience in a higher court. "I felt really good, yeah, I felt really good. I really felt like from that point on my life began to unwind the way God *really* wanted me to live," Chant later said of the interview with the RCMP.

The two Mounties got in their car and began the drive back to Sydney. Wheaton asked Jim Carroll what he thought of the story they had just been told. Had Maynard Chant been lying in 1971 or was he lying now? Snow as fine as sand was blowing across the highway in shimmering rivulets and Carroll watched it in the lights of the police car for a long time before answering. "It sounds like the truth to me," he said. Like his partner, he had no illusions about the seriousness of these new events.

Wheaton, too, believed Chant. The rest of the trip passed in a silence as deep as the winter night that enveloped them. Harry Wheaton knew that he would now have to scrutinize the entire case the Sydney police had built against Junior Marshall and eventually confront Chief John MacIntyre with his findings. It was a task no policeman would relish.

Jim Carroll, meanwhile, was contemplating a very different matter. The quiet policeman, who was not usually surprised by the misery human beings could inflict on each other, was stunned by the fact that so many people had known about Maynard's false testimony, yet no one had tried to do anything for the man who was languishing in prison for a crime he might not have committed.

Two days after interviewing Maynard Chant, Wheaton and Carroll pulled up in front of Dorchester Penitentiary to talk to the man at the centre of the strangest case either one of them had ever had – Junior Marshall.

For Carroll, who oddly enough had never visited the prison in his lengthy Maritime service with the RCMP, it was a forbidding introduction. As he and Wheaton walked through Dorchester's lobby towards the security gate, they were met by a guard leading eight teenage prisoners to a waiting van. All eight were wearing leg irons joined by a short chain which forced them to shuffle behind their keeper, lending an odd air of infirmity to the young prisoners. They were also handcuffed through a loop in their belts, preventing them from lifting up or even straightening their arms. To Carroll, they looked no older than fourteen and fifteen. A guard explained that the teenagers were being transferred to Springhill after an "incident" in the prison. "They were scared. Their faces were the color of snow, they had just been exposed to a very violent happening the night before. They were apparently in their cells but they could see in the corridor what was going on. There were about fifty or sixty people going to take on three or four and wipe them out," Carroll said.

After being scanned with a metal detector and physically searched, the two Mounties were admitted into the prison, where they were met by a correctional worker, Dale Cross, who briefed them on Marshall and let them peruse his prison records. Cross said that the young Micmac had been a good prisoner and observed that if Marshall had admitted to murdering Seale, he would probably already be out of prison. Wheaton and Carroll exchanged a silent glance as they followed Cross to the small interrogation room.

The room was six feet by six feet and contained a small table and some chairs. When the tall, athletic prisoner finally arrived, dressed in his prison denims and a baseball cap, Harry Wheaton was surprised. There were no signs of having done "hard time" on the handsome Indian, who gently refused their invitation to sit down. "I didn't expect to see you guys here," Marshall said softly. After nearly eleven years of trying to get someone to listen to him, he couldn't quite believe the RCMP were actually investigating his case.

Wheaton did all the talking, while Carroll stood by to take a statement if that became necessary. Wheaton had decided to play it tough with the 29-year-old inmate. He offered no information on the investigation to date, no signs of sympathy, just a blunt appeal

for his story. To set the right tone, Wheaton asked him if the
baseball cap he had just taken off belonged to him.

"Yeah," Marshall answered casually.

"Then why has it got somebody else's name on the sweatband?"
the Mountie asked. It was Wheaton's way of serving notice that he
wasn't there to be "storied" by the young prisoner. He asked
Marshall what he had to say.

"Where do you want me to start?" Marshall said in a low voice.

"You've had eleven years to think about it, my friend. Where do
you want to start?" Wheaton answered.

Haltingly at first, then with increasing confidence, Junior told
his story. He took the Mounties back to his return to Sydney from
Bedford on the afternoon of May 28, 1971, and led them up to the
bloody encounter with Roy Ebsary on Crescent Street shortly
before midnight. For the first time, Junior Marshall admitted that
he and Sandy "had been after money that night" when they'd run
into Ebsary and MacNeil.

"Was there any conversation between the old man and Seale
before the stabbing?" Wheaton asked.

"Yeah, Sandy said, 'Dig, man, dig.' He was standing in front of
the guy with his hands in his coat pockets. Then the old guy said, 'I
got something for you,' and stabbed him," Junior said.

Wheaton was once more struck by the similarity between the
words Mitchell Sarson and now Marshall attributed to Ebsary
before the attack. He was also impressed with the matter-of-fact
way Marshall related his story. There was no attempt to play on the
Mountie's sympathies, and, with one exception, the interview
passed with no sign of emotion from Marshall. Wheaton was
beginning to believe he was talking to an innocent man. As
Marshall talked about his life in prison, Wheaton detected a mas-
ochistic note in the young man's voice, as though he were punishing himself for what had happened on that spring night so long
ago. "At one point, tears came to his eyes. I think it was when he
mentioned the trouble this thing had meant to his family," Wheaton remembered.

As Jim Carroll began to take down Marshall's statement, shouts
suddenly filled the corridor and cell doors began to clang in the
main section of the prison. An excited guard appeared and
informed the RCMP officers that a riot was in progress and that they

would have to leave at once. It was suggested that Junior Marshall be put into protective custody, but the veteran of more than a decade behind bars quickly quashed that idea. "I told 'em, 'Put me back in the population, I don't care if a riot is goin' on.' They put you in PC, first thing you know you're pegged as a rat and you get it."

As Wheaton and Carroll were leaving, Marshall called out to them, "Hey, you guys comin' back?"

"Count on it," Harry Wheaton answered before inmate 1997 was led out of sight back to the cell blocks. Without knowing it, Junior Marshall was twenty days away from walking out the door he had entered nearly eleven years before.

But not as a free man.

The next day Harry Wheaton briefed his commanding officer on the results of the reinvestigation to date, including the interview with Marshall. Don Scott was aghast. It was agreed that before sharing the information with Chief MacIntyre, they should interview John Pratico. Wheaton and Carroll couldn't locate the young man but they eventually found his mother, Margaret Pratico, who lived in a rooming house just around the corner from Roy Ebsary.

As an interviewee, Margaret Pratico was something of a challenge. On the doorstep, she said she would neither give Wheaton a statement nor tell him where her son was living. But gradually the reassuring policeman calmed her down and the conversation moved to an old sofa in her front room. There, Margaret told the Mountie that on the morning after the stabbing, John awakened just as a radio report of the incident was ending. "John hollered to her from the bedroom and wanted to know who it was that was stabbed in the park and wanted to know the details of it. So to me, if he was an eyewitness, what the hell is he doing the next morning asking what the details of the murder are?" Wheaton remembered.

When Wheaton asked where he could find John, Margaret told him that he was living in New Waterford. Ironically, his landlady was Sandy Seale's grandmother. Margaret then told him another detail that he found even more interesting. Between Marshall's preliminary hearing and his Supreme Court trial, John Pratico had suffered a mental breakdown and had been hospitalized. Wheaton and Carroll proceeded to the Cape Breton Hospital, where the director of medical records, Ann McLeod, informed the Mounties that Pratico had been a psychiatric patient there since 1970. She also confirmed his trip to the Nova Scotia Hospital in Halifax between Junior Marshall's preliminary hearing and his trial.

On the 19th of February, Harry Wheaton interviewed the man who had been John Pratico's psychiatrist since August of 1970. Dr. M. A. Mian told the policeman that at the time of the trial in 1971, his patient suffered from a schizophrenic illness which led him to fantasize and distort reality to put himself in the limelight. Dr. Mian explained that Pratico still received psychiatric treatment. After taking a statement from Dr. Mian, in which the doctor said that his patient was in 1971, and continued to be, "a very unreliable witness", Wheaton and Carroll set out to find John Pratico. Realizing that patience would be required, they agreed that Jim Carroll interview the second man whose testimony had sent Junior Marshall to prison.

Carroll began by making inquiries at the Cape Breton Hospital as to Pratico's possible whereabouts. He was told that the young man attended a weekly treatment centre in New Waterford, where caseworkers from the hospital offered counselling and other services on an outpatient basis. Ironically, the caseworker who dealt with John Pratico turned out to be Jim Carroll's next-door neighbor. Neighbor or not, Andy Arsenault was suspicious that the Mountie would try to put something over on his young charge to the point where he even tried to get Pratico a lawyer to protect his rights. When a meeting was finally arranged at the treatment centre, it was agreed that Arsenault would speak to Pratico first, and only after that would an interview with Jim Carroll be permitted.

"Arsenault had to talk to him before I did, but Pratico was actually in the waiting room where I was, walking around in circles and smoking hard," Carroll recalled. "We struck up a conversation and by the time he'd chatted with Arsenault, he already felt comfortable enough with me that Arsenault ended up leaving us in the room together. As far as I could make out, he was just a young man who lost out on a lot of the breaks of life. He didn't have any education, not a great family life."

Carroll explained to Pratico that he was investigating the old Sandy Seale murder case and asked him if he would look at the statement he'd given to Sydney detectives in 1971 prior to taking the stand at Junior Marshall's trial. Pratico hung his head to one side and stared blankly at the page he'd been handed. A long moment passed before Jim Carroll realized that the young man who had scratched out a living as a dishwasher, cleaner, and babysitter, and who was now on welfare like his mother, was having trouble reading. Retrieving the statement as if his subject had merely forgotten his glasses, Carroll read it aloud and asked Pratico if it were true. No, the dark-haired young man told him, it wasn't.

For years John Pratico had wanted to tell the truth but he didn't think anyone would listen. He later explained his predicament: "I used to say, 'My God, there should be something I could do.' But then the justice system, you can't beat the justice system, eh? I could go over there and be called a liar, you know what I mean? 'That fella is, he's nuts,' or whatever. You know, a loon type."

Like Maynard Chant before him, John Pratico volunteered that he'd never seen Junior Marshall stab Sandy Seale, that he'd lied on the stand. In fact, he hadn't even been in Wentworth Park when the murder took place on nearby Crescent Street. He told the Mountie that the Sydney detectives had pressured him into giving false testimony, as Jim Carroll carefully recorded in his statement:

> MacIntyre asked me what happened in the park that night; I said I didn't know, I had heard of the stabbing at this time but not who did it or who had died. MacIntyre said I did know and if I didn't tell I would be put in gaol. MacDonald wasn't saying anything. I was scared; he said he knew what happened, for me to tell them. They told me about Marshall and Seale, that Marshall stabbed Seale, they put words in my mouth, so I just agreed with what they were saying. I told them I saw Marshall stab Seale from the bushes where I was drinking; they took a statement from me and I signed it. I guess I knew Marshall would be in trouble for what I said but I was being badgered by the police and scared what they would do to me, my nerves were really bad then.

When he finished talking, John Pratico "felt like a million dollars". The quiet policeman who listened to him for over an hour had done him more good than all the psychiatric drugs he'd taken during the long years Junior Marshall had spent in prison because of his lie, or so it seemed on that cold February afternoon. "That's off my mind. It played on my mind. That's caused half my trouble, I mean my mind, I have to take the medication, but that got a load off my mind. I opened up to Carroll because he seemed so kind, so considerate, he wasn't pushy. He wasn't pushy at all," Pratico said of the interview.

A few months later when he had to vacate his apartment, the young man called Jim Carroll. Would the Mountie help him move? Although it was not Carroll's idea of how to spend his time off (he would prefer to sit back and listen to the Scottish Highland music he passionately loved), he agreed, thinking that his day would be taken up lugging the usual furniture. But when he arrived at Pratico's apartment, there was only the tenant himself and two cardboard boxes of clothes on the way to another rooming house. John was all smiles.

Convinced now that Junior Marshall hadn't murdered Sandy Seale, Wheaton and Carroll decided it was time to bring in the man they thought probably had: 71-year-old Captain Roy Newman Ebsary. The self-styled reverend, war hero, and littérateur had to be interviewed early in the day, since he was usually well into his cups by lunch-time, holding court in his Falmouth Street flat with a collection of winos who watched in awe as Roy re-enacted the significant battles of the Second World War.

On February 22 they picked him up and brought him to RCMP headquarters in Sydney. He was badly hung over, leaned on his cane, and complained during the interview of various aches and pains. The Mounties had agreed beforehand that Wheaton would do the talking, and if need be "play the heavy" with their strange guest. Every time he tried to draw Ebsary out on the Seale murder, the old man began quoting Scripture. He launched into a dissertation on the Creation, and Wheaton humored him for a time by throwing in the odd biblical allusion of his own.

Jim Carroll tried to remain impassive but he couldn't help smiling when Ebsary scaled some of the loftier peaks of the theological sublime. Suddenly Wheaton asked the old man point-blank what he knew about the rolling attempt and the stabbing back in 1971. Ebsary denied all knowledge of the event. Wheaton exploded, according to a strategy he and his partner had worked out before the interview and based in part on what Greg Ebsary had told Wheaton about Roy. "All right, Jim, get this disgusting faggot out of my sight, get him out of here!" he roared.

Ebsary shook with rage and Wheaton thought for a moment the cane would be coming his way. But the old man's tremor subsided and Carroll eventually drove him home. As he let him out of the car, the Mountie had a final word for his eccentric passenger. "You know, if you have anything to discuss, don't hesitate to call. I think you hold the key to this whole situation and we're sort of anxious to get it cleared up." There weren't many people who could make a request for a murder confession sound inviting, but the slow-talking Jim Carroll was one of them. The old man nodded, made a genteel gesture with his cane, and disappeared inside.

At 4:30 that afternoon, the investigators got an unexpected break. A call was put through from detachment to Harry Wheaton's office and the two excited Mounties immediately huddled around the receiver. It was Roy Ebsary.

"All our talking today was not in vain," the old man said.

"What do you mean by that?" Wheaton asked.

"Well, you know, I am a British officer and a gentleman."

"Yes."

"You called me a homosexual," the voice at the other end of the line said accusingly.

"Yes," Wheaton answered sternly.

"All our talking today was not in vain, you know."

"Why is that?"

"Well, I did it," Ebsary said.

"Are you admitting to stabbing Seale?" Wheaton asked, his heart skipping a beat.

"Yes."

"Would you like to speak to me?"

"No," Ebsary answered, "the other fellow."

"Okay, I'll send Jim down."

Notebook in hand, Jim Carroll was on his way out the door before the phone hit the cradle. But when he arrived at Ebsary's Falmouth Street flat, the old man and a companion were already fighting the Battle of the Bulge in a living room strewn with dog droppings and empty wine bottles. The policeman tried to get Ebsary into another room where the two could speak in private, but Ebsary kept shouting commands to the drunk in the kitchen while the ubiquitous dog scaled the furniture and howled at a light fixture.

Carroll knew that a statement taken under these conditions would be worth next to nothing as evidence, but he decided to ask Ebsary to put something in writing just to see what he would say. It turned out to be a brilliant stroke. The old man's head momentarily cleared and he quickly declined to give a statement. But if he could meet Junior Marshall's parents, assess their character, he might change his mind. Could Jim arrange that?

The Mountie promised to set the meeting up for the next day, provided that Ebsary promised to stay sober. The old man agreed and Carroll returned to headquarters, where he told a delighted Harry Wheaton what had happened. If Ebsary confessed to anything in the presence of the Marshalls, they could give evidence in any subsequent court action. Carroll immediately got on the phone and called Membertou.

If the voice on the telephone had asked Caroline Marshall to cut off her right hand, she would have gladly done it, had she believed that would help get her son out of prison. For more than a decade, she and her husband had tried everything to have Junior's case reopened, including a desperate but futile appeal to Chief John MacIntyre to review the case. The Marshalls readily agreed to the meeting with Ebsary. Donald Marshall, Sr., had met Carroll during the investigation of a murder on Membertou and trusted him. So the next morning, the Grand Chief of the Micmac Nation and his wife showed up at RCMP headquarters and were taken to a large conference room. They were advised to pay special attention to anything the old man might say of an incriminating nature. They were also told that Ebsary could react violently but that they would be fully protected.

When Jim Carroll went to pick up Ebsary, he discovered, much to his discouragement, that Roy had been drinking again. Carroll reminded him of the meeting with the Marshalls, who were already waiting for him, and the old man hurriedly got ready. But he got very upset in the police car when he discovered that the meeting was going to take place at RCMP headquarters rather than at the Marshalls' home. When he calmed down, Ebsary said that he could clear Junior Marshall of the murder, but first he had to meet the boy's parents. Carroll decided to take a statement to see how far Ebsary was prepared to go.

"What can you tell me about the Seale murder?"

"As far as I was concerned it was an ordinary night. We were robbed and had to defend ourselves," Ebsary said.

As ludicrous as the assertion appeared, it was true. Ebsary had routinely been rolled in Wentworth Park, as had several other "stemmers" who drank there. It was a common occurrence well known to the Sydney city police.

"How did you defend yourself?"

"We were held up by two muggers, who demanded all our money or whatever the hell we had in our pockets. I shelled out everything I had in my pockets, I shelled out everything I had in my pockets, but the other fellow was fighting with Marshall, do you see the point? Marshall was giving him a hard time, he had a reputation for that, all Sydney knows that. MacNeil told me before this happened Marshall had robbed him before, beaten him up on Hardwood Hill. You arrange for an interview with Mrs. Marshall and I'll tell her the truth, I was a witness to the stabbing," Ebsary said.

"Are you going to implicate yourself?" Carroll asked.

"If necessary, yes," Ebsary answered.

"Do you know what that means?"

"Yes, it means that I'm willing to go all out to prove Marshall did not stab Seale."

"Are you prepared to say or admit you know who did stab Seale?" Carroll asked.

"Yes, I'll tell his mother."

"Are you saying you are responsible?"

"No, I'm not saying I'm responsible; I'll convince her her son didn't. Before I could make a statement like that I should see a lawyer," Ebsary told him.

For what it was worth, he signed the statement at 12:16 p.m.

At RCMP headquarters, Carroll introduced Ebsary to the Marshalls and explained that Roy claimed to have a way of clearing Junior of the murder. He then left the conference room and let the three of them chat.

"What beautiful hair you have, what beautiful hands, madame," Ebsary said to Caroline Marshall.

"Thank you," the nervous woman replied.

Ebsary walked over, took her hand and kissed it. Donald Marshall, Sr., took a step closer to his wife and looked down at the small man in front of him.

"Was it you who stabbed Sandy Seale?" he asked.

"Can I come over to your house?" Ebsary responded dreamily.

"Some time maybe, when all this is over," Caroline Marshall answered.

"I'd like to come home with you," Ebsary said, his blue eyes, watery and enlarged behind thick glasses, staring at her as though Donald Marshall, Sr., were not in the room.

"Maybe one day," Mr. Marshall said.

"I know your son is innocent," Ebsary said.

"What do you mean?" Mrs. Marshall asked.

"I can get him out of jail, you know," the old man continued.

But beyond that tantalizing assertion, he offered no more information. Jim Carroll returned to see how things were progressing. Catching his eye, Donald Marshall, Sr., shook his head. Carroll, who had been hoping Ebsary might expand on the cryptic words of his statement, was to be disappointed. Ebsary later promised him he would clear the matter up after his March court appearance on the charge of stabbing Goodie Mugridge in the chest with a kitchen knife. Until then, his secrets would remain his own.

Knowing from Marshall's lawyer, Steve Aronson, that the inmate had written a letter to Ebsary asking what he knew about the murder, Carroll asked if Roy had answered him. The old man said he had tried a few times to phone Junior at Dorchester but had been unable to get through. Carroll suggested he write. Ebsary said he would think about it. The next day he answered Junior's letter.

Ebsary's letter, dated February 24, 1982, arrived at Dorchester Penitentiary typed on a piece of paper bearing the Ebsary family crest, a two-headed falcon raising its wings for flight. Inmate 1997 could scarcely believe his eyes as he read it.

Dear Don,

I've tried to reach you by phone but no luck...I'm collaborating with the RCMP to get you out of that mess...I can't do much until after the 5th of March...Yesterday at my request I met your Dad and Mom...I've been beaten up/ can't walk, can't see too well.

Having failed to reach you by phone, the RCMP suggest I

drop you a line...your letter was stolen as well as a sum of money while I was unconcious...Police investigation, etc. etc...no favorable results...I'm not running kid...I'm in your corner...I'll do all I can to get you free...I promised your mom and Dad that, yesterday...I can't see too well, but I trust you get the message.

I'm in your corner...Anyhow...I'm sorry kid things turned out the way they did...But it is written..."The truth shall set you free."

You see, old boy, I only re-acted as I was trained...There's a lot to be taken into consideration...I'm a loner...The months you've spent in Solitude, I too have spent in solitude...I listen to no one...I have no friends...every moment you have spent alone I too have been alone...Alone we get to know ourselves.

Anyway, hope for the best...

> Sincerely,
> Capt. R. N. Ebsary...DCM. CMG.

Junior Marshall felt dizzy as he finished the letter and quickly read it over again, one, two, three times. He then rushed off and had copies made, sending them to his lawyer, the RCMP, and the parole board.

For the first time since he'd gone to jail as a seventeen-year-old, he had the feeling that things were finally beginning to go his way.

On February 27, a meeting was held in RCMP headquarters between Don Scott, Harry Wheaton, and Sydney police chief John MacIntyre. Wheaton produced the recanting statements of both Pratico and Chant and they were given to Chief MacIntyre to read. Scott then advised the chief in general terms where the investigation stood. Wheaton recalled that MacIntyre "became very bombastic, started throwing papers around. He still had a file with him. He threw [down] the Patricia Harriss statement, [said] 'How can that be?' and pounded the desk."

Chief MacIntyre insisted that his two eyewitnesses from 1971 couldn't have been lying because their stories had been corroborated by a third witness, Patricia Harriss. He claimed that she too had placed Marshall and Seale alone on Crescent Street on the night of the murder. Wheaton had already read Harriss's testimony but didn't remember her saying that. He made a note to reread the transcript and also to find the young woman to see if she would support what the chief was saying. Before the meeting ended, Wheaton asked Chief MacIntyre if he had any other material relevant to the case. "He said no, he had none," Wheaton remembered.

The investigator informed the chief that he now intended to interview all of the witnesses at Marshall's 1971 trial. "So anyway, after we finished there, he went off with the O/C by himself sort of thing. And Don told me after he was trying to convince him this was all a bunch of hokum and the matter should be concluded. And Don told him point-blank we couldn't conclude it, and we both made it quite clear to him we were going to have to pursue it."

When Harry Wheaton checked the trial transcript, he found that his recollection had been correct: Patricia Harriss had not testified that she'd seen Marshall and Seale together that night on Crescent Street. After some inquiries around town, he learned that the young woman, a hairdresser, had recently returned to Sydney from Toronto. He contacted Harriss and a meeting was arranged for March 1 at RCMP headquarters. Wheaton, Carroll, and Frank Edwards, the Crown prosecutor, were present at the meeting. As with Pratico and Chant, the Mounties showed Harriss her 1971 statement and asked if it was true. To their amazement, the attractive brunette was as eager to set the record straight as Maynard Chant and John Pratico had been. She flatly denied that the statement she'd given to John MacIntyre at 1:20 a.m. on the morning of June 18 was free, voluntary, or true.

Harriss, who was fourteen in 1971, said she was interrogated by then Detective William Urquhart, who took a statement from her at 8 p.m. that evening. In it, she said she'd seen Junior Marshall on Crescent Street with two men, one of whom had grey hair and wore a long blue coat. Then Sgt./Det. MacIntyre arrived to take over the questioning. After interrogating Miss Harriss for several hours, he took a second statement, which she now claimed was false.

Patricia Harriss's statement to Harry Wheaton painted a now familiar picture of the methods of the Sydney detectives who had done the original investigation. In it she said:

> I remember meeting Junior Marshall and there were other people on the street in this area. Who they were I don't know. I

recall in my first statement to the police there were two
people. The police took at least three statements from me. I
don't recall exactly how many times I was taken to the police
station. I found them needlessly harping at me, going over and
over, telling me what they thought I should see. They took
statements from me and changed them. This took hours and
hours and my parents were not allowed in. They came to the
police station and they let me out once to see them but that
was it.

I don't feel their actions were proper. I recall them banging
their fist on the desk. I definitely did not see Sandy Seale in the
park that night. I don't recall if I said that in court or not. The
police had me so scared throughout this affair that I felt
pressured and agreed with things I shouldn't have agreed.
Now that I am a mature adult I feel this was most improper and
I have thought of this through the years, often questioned this
whole thing in general. . . .

After Patricia Harriss left, the two RCMP members exchanged
quizzical looks and not just because they now had all the key
witnesses at Marshall's original trial charging that the Sydney
detectives had coerced them into signing false statements. Harriss
had referred to an earlier statement she'd given to Urquhart in
which she claimed to have seen at least two people on Crescent
Street where she'd met Junior Marshall on the night of the murder.
Why, if John MacIntyre had provided them with all the information
he had in his file, hadn't they seen that statement?

On March 2, Wheaton and Carroll returned to Dorchester to
complete their interview with Junior Marshall. This time they met
him in a second-floor room that inmates used as a disciplinary
court. Once again Wheaton played it tough, warning Marshall, "If
you do want to get out of here and you are telling the truth that you
didn't kill that man, you'd better tell me everything, because if you
lie to me, I'm going to know it and you may as well forget it. There's
only one guy who can get you out of here, me."

After twenty years in the RCMP, Wheaton had learned that the
majority of inmates would try to lie, cheat, or childishly connive
around the facts, to work up "a hook", a legal angle to demonstrate
that they were technically innocent of whatever crime had landed

them in prison. "Now, in this instance, based on what I knew about Pratico and Chant, the thing smelled, and the guy was clean, he was innocent. So therefore I didn't want him to screw up, I wanted him to tell the truth. 'Don't play the con with me!' And I was very hard, because I felt that maybe that was the only thing that he would understand. I honestly feel he did understand me and understood me very well."

Marshall told the Mounties that back in 1971 he was "a bad young guy" who drank a lot and "generally hung around". He said he was frequently questioned by John MacIntyre for a string of minor offences, including knocking over gravestones and igniting dynamite caps on the railway tracks in Wentworth Park. "MacIntyre didn't like me, as I wouldn't talk or confess to these crimes," he said.

When it came to an account of the events of the night of May 28, Junior admitted that he had asked Sandy if he wanted to "roll someone" to make some money. They spotted Ebsary and MacNeil and struck up a conversation. "We talked about everything, women, booze, about them being priests, and hinted around about money," Junior said. When Ebsary and MacNeil started to walk away, Junior called them back. "I don't remember exactly what was said, but I definitely remember Ebsary saying, 'I got something for you,' and then stabbing Sandy. I let go of the guy I had and Ebsary came at me. He swung the knife at me and I held the knife off with my left hand. The knife sort of caught in my jacket and I pulled free and ran and felt blood running from the cut. I can't describe the knife and Sandy fell and stayed there."

He told the Mounties he ran away from the scene and met Maynard Chant on Bentinck Street walking towards the park. The two boys returned to the scene of the stabbing and Marshall went to a house and asked the occupant to call an ambulance.

"I knew Sandy but not real well and it's too bad he died but I didn't kill him, Ebsary did. I am willing to take a polygraph test to prove I am innocent. I did not stab Sandy. I gave police a statement when it happened and a week later I was picked up by MacIntyre. He didn't question me very much; he said he had two witnesses to say I did it and locked me up."

All his professional life, Harry Wheaton had been an implacable advocate of capital punishment. Looking at the young Micmac who had spent a life sentence in prison for a crime he hadn't committed, the horror of what might have been shook him to his roots. Never again would he be certain enough of the system to endorse the dread exchange of a life for a life in the name of justice.

Harry Wheaton and Mary Ebsary had established an afternoon ritual long before the investigator ever asked her for a formal statement about the events of May 28, 1971. Throughout the investigation, Wheaton would turn up at the small house on Mechanic Street around five o'clock and take tea with Mary before she went to work as the nightshift laundress at the Wandlyn Motel. As the evidence against her estranged husband accumulated, Wheaton knew that at some point his investigative objective would change. Instead of establishing Junior Marshall's innocence, he would be charged with proving Ebsary's guilt. He suspected that Mary and Greg Ebsary would eventually become instrumental in building the case against Roy, if only because they knew his habits so well. Hence, the long, informal chats with Mary, sometimes alone, sometimes with Greg, sitting at the kitchen table.

What started as deep background for a police investigation quickly turned into friendship. Wheaton found it difficult not to respect Mary Ebsary. For most of her life she had supported the family and somehow managed to keep a roof over their heads, despite her husband's antics. She was fiercely protective of her children, and in a curious way of Roy too. Although she had thrown him out of the house in 1979 after twenty-nine tempestuous years of common-law marriage, she was very reluctant to speak against him. "I do think in the first years of their marriage there was love there, and I still think that ultimately, because she'd say things about, you know, 'When you clean him up and he washes his hair, he has beautiful hair,' " Wheaton would later recall.

Greg Ebsary was less concerned with defending the man he believed had ruined his childhood. The butt for years of school-yard jibes about his father's eccentric behavior, and disgusted by Roy's indiscriminate homosexuality, the taxi-driver readily told Wheaton about the old man's dark side. As Greg spoke of the reign of terror Roy imposed on his family when drinking, Mary Ebsary came out of her shell and admitted that for years she too had been afraid of Roy.

On the afternoon of March 4, in a desultory aside, Mary mentioned Roy's fascination with knives. She said he had a grinding wheel in the basement where he used to make stilettos out of old steak knives by sharpening them on both sides and then fitting them with home-made handles. Alarm bells went off in Wheaton's head. As casually as he could, he asked if any of those knives might be around, knowing that the murder weapon in the Seale slaying had never been found.

Greg Ebsary nodded, explaining to Wheaton that when the family moved from Rear Argyle Street, where they had lived at the time of the murder, to Mechanic Street, he packed Roy's knives and hid some of them in the basement of the new house. He asked Greg if he could see the knives. The young man led him down a steep flight of cellar stairs to a hoary basement, guiding him through the clutter to an old workbench set off in the corner. "I put them here," Greg said, reaching for an old peach basket that was resting on a beam above the workbench. Wheaton gingerly accepted the basket from the young man and looked at the collection of knives inside. Hoping against hope that he had finally found "good corroborative physical evidence", Wheaton went back upstairs and flashed one of his best smiles at Mary, who was still sitting at the kitchen table.

"Ho! Look what we have here, Mary!" he said. "Now, Greg, I don't want you to interfere. Mary, you tell me, if one of these knives was used to stab Seale, which one would it be?"

Mary scanned the ten knives on the kitchen table and without hesitation picked out two that were nearly identical. Their blades were sharpened on both sides, tapering to a razor-sharp point. Both had handles fashioned from a short length of green rubber hosing fixed in place with friction tape. Mary studied them for a moment. "If it was any one, I'd say it was that one," she said, pointing to the knife with a piece of tin foil wrapped around the handle. Wheaton asked why. She explained that Roy used to carry a knife like that in his belt or coat and that his clothing would often be slashed from moving the weapon in and out of his pockets.

Wheaton marked the weapon Mary selected as knife #8 and asked the Ebsarys to give him a statement. Starting with Mary, they both described Roy's peculiar behavior after being questioned by the Sydney police in connection with the Seale murder following

Jimmy MacNeil's 1971 claim that the courts had convicted the wrong man.

> After the murder and him taking the polygraph, Roy became a recluse. He went to his bedroom and literally stayed there. He would not leave the house and did not associate with anyone other than the immediate family. He quit going to the tavern and stopped drinking and became a hermit. When Mitchell Sarson came to live at our house, Roy completely changed. He started drinking again and running around with Sarson. Roy was not as violent during this period as he was eleven years ago. In 1971, he was extremely violent in his tantrums, he would break up the house. Today we have turned over a number of knives Roy would have had at the time of the murder.

On a later occasion, Wheaton asked Mary what she remembered about the night Sandy Seale was stabbed. She stated:

> On the night of the Seale murder, I was at our home, at that time 126 Rear Argyle Street, Sydney. I was watching TV in the living-room and I recall Roy and Jimmie MacNeil coming home. Jimmie stopped in the doorway of the living room and said something like "You saved my life" to Roy. Roy said, "Shut up." I recall Roy telling Jimmie to cut across the field going home, not through the Park. He said something about "they won't catch you."
>
> I didn't pay much attention to Roy, as he was always bringing someone home with him. Roy drank heavily and was violent, so I never said anything to him. He always carried a knife and when he got angry that was his favorite weapon.

Wheaton asked if the Sydney police were aware of Roy's violent side.

> I recall I called the Sydney Police on numerous occasions when Roy was in one of his destructive, violent rages and nothing was done. The Sydney Police were well aware of Roy, as I turned him in in 1970 for carrying a knife as he was going to stab the chef at the Isle Royal Hotel. His exact words referring to Toni, the chef, were, "When he opens the door, I'll gut him."

Mary Ebsary claimed to have been questioned by John MacIntyre for two hours, much longer than the twenty-two minutes shown on her 1971 statement. She also said that the person whose signature appeared as a witness to her statement, Detective William Urquhart, had left the room five minutes into her interview with John MacIntyre. But she told Wheaton she couldn't recall what else she'd said to the chief of detectives on the night of November 15 during their lengthy interview.

Greg Ebsary had a better recollection of his 1971 interview with John MacIntyre:

> I was at the Sydney City Police that night for approximately three hours. I talked with John MacIntyre a great deal more than what is in the statement. One thing being, what happened that night in the Park. He accused me of this, and I denied it, as I had not. I was truthful and honest and told him of my father's violence, carrying knives, and manner of dress. I do remember that I was very frightened, and it seemed to me that he was trying to intimidate me.

If Greg Ebsary were telling the truth, Wheaton wondered how Chief MacIntyre could have failed to connect Ebsary with the murder, given the other evidence he had about the eccentric appearance of the man Marshall claimed had attacked him and Seale, and the weapon the man had used: a knife.

But for now he had other things to think about. Back at the Sydney headquarters of the RCMP, Wheaton called the crime laboratory in Halifax and asked for Richard McAlpine, a specialist in blood detection. McAlpine wasn't overly optimistic when he heard what the staff-sergeant wanted. "Don't expect miracles after eleven years, Harry," he said.

Wheaton forwarded the knives to Halifax by registered mail and then began to worry about the peach basket in which they'd been stored. What if fibres from the potential murder weapon had fallen into the basket during the Ebsarys' move from Rear Argyle to Mechanic Street? Returning to Mary's, the investigator retrieved the basket. He also asked if she remembered how Roy had been dressed on the night of the murder.

Mary said he'd been wearing a navy blue topcoat, a white shirt, and two wrap-around gold belts, items she believed he still had.

Wheaton asked Constable Doug Hyde to seize various items of clothing from Ebsary's Falmouth Street flat, and Mary Ebsary identified the garments in question. Wheaton then sent the peach basket and the clothing to the crime lab. Richard McAlpine promised to get back to him as soon as possible.

McAlpine's speed merely hastened Wheaton's discouragement. He was unable to detect blood on any of the items and suggested that Wheaton call fibres expert Adolphus Evers, a civilian member of the RCMP crime laboratory in Sackville, New Brunswick. Wheaton half-heartedly placed the call but was soon on the edge of his seat again.

Not only had Evers given fibres evidence at Marshall's 1971 trial, he had kept a swatch of material from the yellow jacket Junior had been wearing on the night of the murder and a microscopic slide of fibres from Sandy Seale's jacket. Evers had been in court on the day Junior Marshall was convicted, and as he watched the teenager break down and cry, he just didn't feel right about the verdict. He decided to preserve his evidence, just in case. Eleven years later, his premonition was vindicated. Wheaton told him he would have the potential exhibits sent to Sackville immediately and Evers promised to phone the investigator the moment his tests were complete.

Once more, Harry Wheaton's fondest investigative hopes were put on hold.

While his partner was waiting for the results of the lab analysis, Jim Carroll was doing a little waiting of his own.

On March 9, Roy Ebsary went on trial for stabbing Goodie Mugridge in the chest after a wine and Kentucky Fried Chicken party at his Falmouth Street flat. The stabbing took place on December 5, 1981, and it was through newspaper accounts of the incident that Junior Marshall was able to get Roy's address and subsequently mail him the letter.

The only real witness at Ebsary's trial was the victim himself, Goodie Mugridge, an itinerant handyman, who gave the court a chilling account of the unprovoked knife attack that nearly ended his life. He testified:

"I got up from the end of the table, I had a heavier coat than this here on, to button my coat up. When I got up to get ready for the taxi he jumps up with a cane and he got me here in the side. Then he pulled a knife."

"He jabbed you with a cane?" Crown prosecutor Frank Edwards asked.

"Yes, in the side here."

"And you are indicating your lower right chest area, he hit you with a cane?"

"Yes, on the right-hand side."

"Did the cane break the skin?"

"The cane didn't break the skin but it gave me an awful blow and then he pulled a knife and got me in the side here," Mugridge said.

"Now you are indicating your right chest area again?"

"Yes, he got me in the side with the knife and the puncture cut my lung, pierced through the skin, cut my lung and then he got me in the heart there."

"He stabbed you again?" Edwards asked.

"He stabbed me twice. I was trying to get out the first time he stabbed me, I was trying to get out through the door because I was bleeding quite heavy and the blood was coming out through my mouth, through my nose, so I was trying to get out and then he got me again with the knife there. I finally got out, I went over about three or four steps there and I got out on the sidewalk and everything started turning dark."

When asked where the knife had come from, Mugridge gave an answer that carried Jim Carroll's mind back to 1971 and Sandy Seale's murder. "Well, it came so fast, he must have had it on him, I don't know where he hauled it from, it came so fast."

The accused never took the stand. The trial lasted less than a day and when it was over, Judge Charles O'Connell of the provincial magistrates' court found Roy Ebsary guilty of causing bodily harm to Wilfred "Goodie" Mugridge by stabbing him in the chest with a knife, contrary to section 245(2) of the Criminal Code of Canada.

It was the verdict Jim Carroll believed could crack the Marshall case. Roy Ebsary had often told him that what he would do for Junior Marshall depended on what happened to him on March 9. Carroll assumed that if Ebsary were convicted and faced a prison term anyway, he would, at his age, make a clean breast of the Seale stabbing at the same time. But before he got a chance to see if that theory was correct, Crown prosecutor Frank Edwards asked for a pre-sentence report and a psychiatric assessment. Judge O'Connell agreed.

Roy Ebsary was examined by doctors from two mental institutions, and at a subsequent trial to determine his fitness to stand trial for the Mugridge stabbing was found to be unfit by reason of insanity. The fact that he already had stood trial and been convicted didn't seem to trouble anyone. His previous not-guilty plea was set aside, his conviction was erased, and the seventy-year-old self-styled captain was sent to a mental institution on a lieutenant-governor's warrant. Whether or not he would ever get out again depended entirely on whether the "organic brain damage" forensic psychiatrists deemed he was suffering from proved reversible.

With that twist in the legal road, Jim Carroll reluctantly gave up hope of getting Roy to confess to the murder of Sandy Seale. But within a matter of months, Ebsary emerged from hospital a supposedly cured man. In fact, he had simply "dried out".

His second trial for the stabbing of Goodie Mugridge ended in acquittal, and the big policeman with the patience of Job found himself back on the strange old man's trail.

On March 12, 1982, a ten-page report signed by Harry Wheaton was forwarded to Don Scott, the Officer/Commanding of the RCMP Criminal Investigation Branch in Halifax, and from there to the provincial Attorney General's Office. It contained a synopsis of the interviews with key witnesses at Marshall's 1971 trial as well as a verbatim record of the phone conversation in which Roy Ebsary admitted to Harry Wheaton that he'd stabbed Sandy Seale. Wheaton's own assessment of the case was an exercise in professional understatement. "At this juncture, on balance, and keeping in mind the mental capabilities of the majority of the persons involved, I have very grave doubts as to Marshall's guilt."

Scott was less circumspect. Referring to Chief MacIntyre's disagreement with the findings of the investigation, Scott recorded his efforts to check out the Sydney policeman's concerns.

> Chief MacIntyre brought up several points that we both thought should be clarified to determine the accuracy of this investigation. As a result of this meeting, I requested all witnesses to be interviewed and, in particular, the Harriss girl to determine the accuracy of her statement that only Marshall

and Seale were present [on Crescent Street], as this seemed
critical in Chief MacIntyre's mind, that this proved Marshall
was lying.

You will note that Harriss' statement is quite revealing and
as a result of her remarks it would appear to strengthen
Marshall's claim that there were these other men present and
his recollection of what happened that night is accurate.

It would appear from this investigation that our two eyewitnesses to the murder lied on the stand, and that the other
main witness, Harriss, lied as well, under pressure from the
Sydney City Police. We also have statements from Marshall
and MacNeil, stating that Ebsary is the person responsible for
Seale's murder, as well as a verbal admission to our investigators that he was responsible.

After reviewing this case, I feel that Marshall is innocent of
the offence and that we presently have enough evidence to
support a prima facie case against Ebsary for the murder of
Seale.

As the RCMP investigation embraced more and more people who
had testified at Junior Marshall's 1971 trial, word spread that the
case had been reopened and that a new suspect in the murder had
been found by police. The steel town was galvanized with excitement when Ian MacNeil of the *Cape Breton Post* , the brother of the
Crown attorney who had prosecuted the young Indian so many
years ago, broke the story that Junior Marshall was about to get out
of prison:

Against a background of intrigue, falsehoods and born-again
Christians, a Sydney man is expected to be pardoned from
Dorchester Penitentiary within several days after serving 11
years of a life sentence for a murder that police now suspect
was committed by somebody else....The *Post* has learned
that if justice department authorities are convinced there is
solid evidence of wrongdoing in the case and Marshall is
released, a Sydney man will be taken into custody within a
matter of hours.

If that news was greeted with euphoria on Membertou, it had a
very different impact in the suburban Westmount house where

Sandy Seale had once lived. Angry and confused, Oscar Seale called RCMP headquarters and asked for a meeting with the officers who were reinvestigating the case. Wheaton and Carroll agreed to visit the Seale home, but it was a mission neither policeman looked forward to.

In 1971, Sandy Seale had been snatched from his parents, the innocent victim of an apparently senseless act of adolescent rage. Six months after the shock of his death, they had endured the agony of a trial where two eyewitnesses described how their son's life had been snuffed out at the end of a knife wielded by Junior Marshall. With the young Indian's conviction, the slow accommodations of grief were eased by the sense that the murderer had been justly punished and was serving a life sentence in a federal penitentiary.

But now they were hearing that Marshall hadn't killed their son after all, and that Sandy had died in the course of an abortive mugging. Having taken their son's life, fate appeared to be coming back for his reputation, and Oscar Seale wasn't about to take that sitting down, as Harry Wheaton soon found out. "He blamed us for opening the whole mess up which had been settled and how his wife hadn't slept for so long and how this was wrong morally. The guilty man was in jail and we were taking him out of jail and this was wrong," Harry Wheaton remembered of their conversation.

As much as the two RCMP members wanted to explain to Oscar Seale that both Pratico and Chant had repudiated the testimony that had convicted Junior Marshall, they could not. It was still a confidential police file and nothing could be divulged until the Attorney General made a decision on the matter. "I levelled with him as far as I could and told him there were good sound reasons for what was being done," Wheaton said.

Oscar Seale was not reassured. For half an hour he paced up and down his living room, under the dazzling smile of his dead son, whose portrait looked down from the mantelpiece, telling the Mounties that the case had been solved, that John MacIntyre was an excellent policeman, that the guilty man was already behind bars. As he paced and talked, Oscar Seale grew increasingly agitated. "I thought he was going to hit me," Harry Wheaton recalled. "He'd walk over to me and he was like this, you know, slapping his fist into his hand, and you could see that the man had been an athlete."

Although he couldn't brief him now, Wheaton thought Oscar's anger would subside when the truth was revealed. The investigator was wrong. Nothing he would ever learn about the case would lead him to reassess the circumstances of his boy's death. In the impregnable keep of Oscar Seale's heart, Sandy's memory was beyond the reach of police investigations, media reports, or courtroom verdicts. A year and a half later, he would sit in open court shaking his head as he listened to a taped interview in which Roy Ebsary described stabbing his son.

"I would put up, or pay you as a reporter or anybody else to go and seek in this and pay for every nickel it cost you, if you want, to get all of the trial evidence, every bit of material and search it, and I'm sure you'll find out that Ebsary did not kill my son," he later told a journalist.

On a wild March afternoon, with the wind whistling up the Sydney River, Harry Wheaton got the long-awaited call from Adolphus Evers. "Harry, I have some news for you," he said. "Be good to me, Dolph," Wheaton replied hopefully.

The precise voice at the other end of the line began to review his analysis of the knives Wheaton had sent him. As Evers talked on, the investigator grew more and more excited. The forensic analyst had found one light-brown wool fibre on knife #8 – the one Mary Ebsary had chosen as Roy's favorite – that was consistent with the sample fibres he'd retained from the jacket Sandy Seale had been wearing on the night of the murder. Evers also removed three synthetic fibres from the same knife that were consistent with the synthetic fibres in the sample cut from the jacket Junior Marshall had been wearing on May 28, 1971. As Evers apprised him of the probabilities involved, Harry Wheaton realized with a shock that he had found the weapon that had killed Sandy Seale eleven years before. "Dolph, if you were here, I'd kiss you," Wheaton exclaimed.

Evers said he would mail the lab report to Sydney right away. Wheaton immediately called on Jim Carroll and broke the news. The investigators then telephoned Crown prosecutor Frank Edwards, who in turn informed the Attorney General's Office of the new evidence. It was a dramatic turn of events. To this point, the case against Roy Ebsary had been largely circumstantial: now the RCMP had physical evidence connecting the old man to the stabbings. Any lingering doubts the investigators may have had about Junior Marshall's innocence were laid to rest. Whether the Attorney General would agree remained to be seen.

Although inmate 1997 had been eligible for full day parole on June 4, 1981, his refusal to admit guilt, coupled with his insistence on pursuing his appeal, had left him languishing behind bars into 1982. After eleven years in prison, he had never received a single unescorted temporary absence – except for the one he granted himself in 1979 when he escaped custody. Doggedly, he kept trying. On January 31, just days before the RCMP began their reinvestigation, he had applied for day parole to the Carlton Centre in Halifax. His file was forwarded to the centre's selection committee for a community assessment. Junior's case-management team at Dorchester proposed to grant him a three-day parole to the halfway house, to be followed by regular day parole if his behavior proved satisfactory. But before the selection committee could complete the community assessment, a letter from Stephen Aronson landed on the desk of the Carlton Centre's superintendent, Jack Stewart.

The letter, which informed Stewart that a new RCMP report on Marshall's offence was now in the hands of the Attorney General, prompted a confidential information report (CIR) from the Carlton Centre to officials at Dorchester and the National Parole Board in Moncton. The gears of the bureaucracy would never mesh so quickly for Junior Marshall as they did in the wake of Jack Stewart's startling letter.

> This CIR is being submitted because certain information came to light during the course of the community investigation which should be thoroughly considered in Mr. Marshall's day parole hearings.
>
> This information was relayed by telephone and this CIR will act as written documentation.
>
> On March 14, this office was contacted by Mr. Stephen Aronson, an attorney acting for Mr. Marshall, who informed us that he had been working on a new investigation by the RCMP into Mr. Marshall's offence, and that certain information had come to light. Mr. Aronson was interviewed that day at the

Carlton Centre and at the request of this writer, delivered by hand, the following day, a letter which is enclosed. . . .

Mr. Gordon Gale of the Attorney-General's office, Halifax, was contacted on the 23rd of March 1982 to determine what, if anything, in the report he could share with this office. Mr. Gale cooperated with this writer and while I could not receive a copy of the police investigation, he did say that he had "good reason to believe that Mr. Marshall did not kill Mr. Seale." As the conversation progressed, Mr. Gale informed me that their department was reviewing the case carefully and that they were examining Section 617 of the Criminal Code of Canada to determine what their best course of action would be. According to Mr. Gale, all evidence they have at this time points to a Mr. R. Ebsary, a resident of Sydney, as the individual that they would possibly be charging once the conviction of Mr. Marshall had been dealt with. When asked how sure they were of Mr. Ebsary's actions on the night of the offence, Mr. Gale informed me that Mrs. Ebsary had turned over a knife or knives to the RCMP in Sydney and that fibre analysis had been undertaken. The result of the analysis showed that fibres were still on the knife and that under analysis the fibres matched perfectly with clothes worn by the victim, Mr. Seale, and by Donald Marshall on the night of the offence. His assessment of this evidence was that it supported Mr. Marshall's version of the offence, and pointed very strongly to Mr. Ebsary.

Mr. Aronson and Mr. Marshall's family are understandably very anxious to get him out of prison and have the conviction overturned, preferably by the Royal Prerogative of Mercy. In addition, the press in Cape Breton are aware that an investigation by the RCMP was conducted into the Marshall case, and are pressing very hard for more information. Emotions in this case and the fact that Mr. Marshall [Sr.] is the Grand Chief of the Micmac Nation provide all the ingredients for a media circus. If Mr. Marshall is granted a day parole to the Carlton Centre, our main goal will be to buffer him as much as possible and attempt to establish a support system outside the Centre in the event that action is forthcoming to overturn his conviction.

The new information created a rush to endorse Junior Marshall's application for parole, beginning with his case-management team at Dorchester, who approved his request the very day Jack Stewart contacted them. His parole officer, Maud Hody, noted:

> His penitentiary career has not been without incident, but all incidents in the past seem to have been related to his hopes for an appeal of his conviction, hopes which were consistently dashed during the period between 1972 and the present. He has been considered a likeable and earnest inmate who has not succeeded in overcoming his desire to prove himself innocent, and, in the process, irritating many case workers who wished to persuade him to forget his obviously hopeless appeal and to devote his energies instead to the immediate task of getting himself out.
>
> Therefore, because he has been accepted by the Carlton Centre and because he is considered at least an average day parole prospect, I am recommending that he be granted day parole to the Carlton Centre.
>
> With respect to Mr. Marshall's case, recent and persuasive evidence has been unearthed that he is, in fact, as innocent as he has claimed to be, without exception since 1971....It now appears that the previously unknown assailant has identified himself and has supplied the investigating police with evidence of his own guilt. This evidence is now in the hands of the Attorney-General of Nova Scotia, who plans to take action on it.
>
> Although these recent events are materially affecting the speed of case preparation, the recommendation for day parole is based on the grounds cited above. Mr. Marshall is considered a relatively good day parole candidate and the Carlton Centre is prepared to accept him. Therefore, the case management team recommends that he be granted day parole.

This agreeable portrait of Junior Marshall was written by the same parole officer who eleven months earlier had referred to his "very serious" personality problems which left him with "very little hope" of succeeding in any form of release.

Maud Hody wasn't alone in paying tribute to the amazing rehabilitation of inmate 1997. The next day the National Parole Board approved his application without even receiving his community assessment from the Carlton Centre. The parole board's decision came the night after Harry How, Nova Scotia's attorney general, said on television that new evidence in the Marshall case "cast considerable doubt" on the previous conviction.

Junior Marshall, it seemed, wasn't the only person who was girding for the media blitz that the unprecedented case would inevitably inspire.

When Junior's caseworker, Margaret MacWilliam, informed him that his day parole had been granted and that he would be going to the Carlton Centre within a matter of days, she volunteered that he must be "happy" about the turn of events.

For once, inmate 1997 could afford to speak his mind. "I told her, I said, 'I'm glad nobody broke me in this fuckin' prison.' And I said, 'Next guy that comes up to you guys, and if he's sincere enough to tell you that he didn't do it, I think you guys should look into what the fuck is goin' on, not sit there and try to brainwash the poor bastard.'"

But his case had been a difficult one, MacWilliam offered. "You're fuckin' right it was," Junior replied.

When she asked him how he was going to begin his new life outside the prison, inmate 1997 didn't have to think about his reply. "I said, 'The first thing I'm going to do when I get out, I'm getting a nice bottle of rum and a good piece of tail.'"

On the morning of March 29, 1982, Junior Marshall cleaned out his cell for the last time. "I watched all the lifers coming down to breakfast. They were happy for me. It was like a little bit of everyone was getting out. I'd been in there so long it seemed like I was leaving home," he said.

Before the morning was out, he had given away most of his possessions and said his goodbyes to a few special friends. Checking his pocket from time to time to make sure he still had his parole card, he awaited the arrival of his parents. They were two hours late.

Caroline Marshall had woven and sold baskets at Whycocomagh in order to buy Junior a new blue suit for coming out of prison. When she saw him in it, standing tall and handsome beside his suitcase, the world blurred through her tears. The family shared an embrace, then walked out of Dorchester for the last time. As their car snaked down Dorchester's long laneway to the road below, Junior Marshall never looked back.

20/Surfacing

Junior Marshall's new life began under siege. Drawn by the story of a man who had served eleven years in prison for a crime he might not have committed, the curious media quickly made the 29-year-old Micmac the most sought-after interview in the country. But, emotionally dehydrated from his long years in prison, and facing an unprecedented legal predicament, Junior wasn't ready to meet the press. It would be two and a half months before he gave his first public interview to the Atlantic bureau chief of the *Globe and Mail*.

Frustrations in the media contingent were running high. Anxious to be sympathetic but unable to get an interview because of legal sensitivities that would become apparent only later, one Toronto reporter tried to snap Marshall's picture through the windows of the Carlton Centre. The normally tranquil house was quickly rechristened "The Alamo" by other inmates who were caught in the media stake-out. Since no one knew what Junior looked like, everyone who left the halfway house during those first days was assailed by a pack of reporters.

One national television crew demanded entry to interview the celebrity inmate, arguing that staff at the centre had no right to exclude them from a public building. Jack Stewart, the street-wise superintendent of the halfway house, agreed. But when he informed them that he also had the right to order a body search of anyone who entered the institution, a right he fully intended to exercise if the TV crew pressed their demand, their enthusiasm waned.

Over the next several months, Stewart became one of the most important people in Junior Marshall's life. He was available to his special charge twenty-four hours a day, fended off unwelcome intruders at the centre, and played the role of lay psychologist, adviser, and friend to the beleaguered young man. Later, when the restrictions of day parole threatened to overwhelm the new inmate, Jack Stewart intervened to humanize the institutional directives that continued to rule Junior Marshall's life.

Where Stewart's protection stopped, Charlie Gould's began. The native community, including Junior's parents, assigned Gould the job of looking after the parolee as he began to navigate the open waters of "freedom". The huge Micmac social worker was the perfect guardian angel. In his fifties, Gould hovered around Junior like a vigilant bear, warding off the legion of people eager to find out more about his case. Gould was studiously diplomatic but he always managed to put his massive body between Junior and any would-be intruder. "Not today, boys," he would say to reporters with a smile, "the kid's been through a lot and he can't talk about it yet." The words may have dripped with goodwill but Charlie Gould had a way of making clear that what he said wasn't up for debate.

As assiduous as the Carlton Centre was in screening calls for their star boarder, Shelly Sarson could always get through. After their lengthy jail-house romance, she had expected that she and Junior would be together, as they had been during the tempestuous days following his 1979 escape. It wasn't to be. After several phone calls studded with silences he could no longer fill, Junior knew he would have to set her straight. He drove to Pictou and told Shelly it was over.

Junior's initial experiments with freedom leaned heavily on diversions he had once used to dull the pain of doing time. He joined a Halifax softball team and continued the training schedule he'd followed in Dorchester. He jogged every day through the winding lanes of Point Pleasant Park and occasionally slipped out of the city to go trout fishing with Micmac friends from Cape Breton who came to visit. It was understood that Junior was too unsettled to return to Membertou, and in particular to Sydney, which held too many ghosts for the young man.

As the weeks went by without word of how the authorities planned to deal with his case, Junior began to chafe under his regimented existence at the centre. The most insignificant details of his daily life were becoming insufferable. When he wanted to cash his cheque from the Department of Indian and Northern Affairs, he had to show his parole card to the tellers. It was a lot of shame for an innocent man to absorb for sixty-two dollars a week. He disliked being known as an ex-convict, resented living with other inmates at the centre, and felt degraded by having to report his every move to institutional staff. He knew from his lawyer that the RCMP had a confession from Roy Ebsary, so why didn't the system that had already robbed him of so much just let him get on with his life?

Sensing how close Junior was to the edge, Jack Stewart tried to ease the terms of his parole. Stewart secured a string of weekend passes for him to participate in various sporting events and an entire week away from the centre to attend a Micmac gathering in Margaree, Cape Breton. It was an unheard-of privilege for a paroled lifer just six weeks out of prison. But, try as he might, Jack Stewart knew that the best he could give to his increasingly frustrated charge was an ersatz freedom. It wasn't enough.

On July 4, Junior failed to return to the centre as required under the terms of a special pass he'd been granted to take part in a Micmac baseball tournament. Nor did he call with a reason for his delay. Had he been an ordinary day parolee, the incident could easily have landed him back in Dorchester. When he showed up a day later, his case-management officer, his counsellor, and Jack Stewart were waiting for him.

"It is understandable," wrote counsellor Gerry Smith after their interview with Junior, "under the prevailing circumstances of this unique case that subject is undergoing severe 'bumps' and at various stages he simply 'shuts down' and begins to cope. His coping mechanisms appear to be that of mentally acting in a manner which allows subject to live free, as if there are no prisons to be responsible to: this is not viewed as being too dangerous and subject is constantly being made aware of and reminded of his commitments to day parole."

Junior was not punished for his truancy but was told that he would be if he broke the rules again. He promised to keep within the regulations but seethed inside at the continuing interference in his life. As he would later tell the *Globe and Mail,* "I don't want their money. All I want is what belongs to me, my freedom."

In darker moments, instincts acquired in the iron cocoon swiftly rose to the surface. One night in a Halifax bar, a prostitute asked Junior to buy her a drink; he obliged. When she asked for another, he told her he had no more money. She started to complain but he quickly cut her off. If he'd wanted to buy her another drink, he would have asked her. The girl walked off in a huff. On the way out of the bar, an enormous Indian woman sitting with two Blacks shouted to him from a corner table. As he approached the table, Junior thought he recognized the woman, who was glaring at him with flat, unfriendly eyes over a half-dozen empty beer glasses.

"Don't I know you from Shubenacadie?" he asked in his deceptively soft voice.

"Don't give me that Indian-brotherhood bullshit. What are you doin', wasting my girl's time?" she said accusingly.

The old rage flared up. Ever since he'd gotten out of prison, he'd been amazed at how many "phonies pressed their luck" in the outside world. Few of them, he thought, would last five minutes inside.

"Listen, bitch, that whore came on to me, I didn't come to her. If you want trouble, let's go right now, I'll beat the fuckin' coconuts off both your friends here." Nobody picked up the gauntlet.

It was around this time, with Junior in a psychological foot-race between the man he had been in prison and the man he must become if he was going to survive on the outside, that he met Karen Brown. When they were first introduced at Kevin Christmas's house in Halifax, she had been no more to him than an attractive blonde who was "too classy-looking" to even think about. He spent an uncomfortable evening playing cards with her before she and two friends left for a rock concert. She offered Junior her ticket but he declined.

They met a few times after that and eventually began going out. Karen worked full-time at a bank and part-time as a cocktail waitress in a Halifax club. Junior got into the habit of seeing her home. She wasn't like the other girls he had met since coming out of prison. With Karen, ordinary things made for a good time. They played cards (he was an expert cribbage player), cooked, and took marathon walks around the city. Karen persuaded him to go to a bingo game one night and Junior won a thousand dollars. From then on, bingo became a weekly affair. As they got to know each other better, he was surprised to learn that she was the daughter of former Nova Scotia cabinet minister Garnet Brown. He wondered what this daughter of the establishment could possibly see in him.

Money soon became a problem. His only source of income, a small weekly cheque from Indian Affairs, wasn't enough to take Karen out to dinner, let alone live outside the Carlton Centre. The one job offer that had come his way, to be a prison liaison officer at Dorchester Penitentiary, wasn't exactly what he had in mind. "Them people must have thought I was brain-damaged to go makin' me an offer like that. I just got out of the fuckin' place and they expect me to jump right back again. And another thing, prison never worked for me, so how could I tell other guys it could work for them?"

By early July, Junior was granted "a five and two day parole", which meant that he slept two nights a week in the Carlton Centre and five nights in a room he rented for himself near by. In agreeing to this arrangement, Mary Casey of the National Parole Board wrote a confidential note on the bottom of her approving memo: "I do have some concern that our 'generosity' in granting day parole may have relieved the urgency with which the criminal justice system might otherwise have handled this case. In spite of that, however, I think he has earned an expansion of his day parole and we should not deny it except for reasons related to risk."

Mary Casey wasn't the only person who thought that the justice system was dragging its heels. With more time to himself, Junior's obsession with his case bordered on the unbearable. As the silence from authorities became deafening, he began to drink heavily. Sitting by himself in a bar one night, he caught his own reflection in a mirror – a careworn young man riding an express train to oblivion. "I said to myself, 'This is no fuckin' life for me. I'm a Reserve boy and I'm goin' back on the fuckin' Reserve."

He returned to his dingy room and packed. He kept thinking about Karen. With his suitcase in hand, he walked to the Middle Deck, the bar where she worked, and watched her through the window. Hours passed. Inside, the bouncer had been watching Junior for almost as long as Junior had been watching Karen. He finally spoke to her. "There's a guy out there three or four hours now, watching you," he said.

Karen looked out the window. "Jesus, that's..." she said, her voice trailing off as she hurried outside.

"What are you doing?" she asked him.

"Nothin'," he answered softly, "just thinkin'."

"Are you all right or what?" she said, noticing his suitcase and wondering if he had lost his room.

"I don't know," he answered.

"You got a place to stay?"

"Not really. But I tell you, either I'm goin' back home to Cape Breton or I'm gonna stick with you."

Without understanding why, Karen instinctively knew that Junior had reached a crisis. For the first time since they'd met, he was reaching out to her for something and she had no intention of turning him down. She handed him her keys. "Get in the car and you wait for me," she said. Ten minutes later she returned, and they drove back to her apartment.

Although Junior Marshall had found a home, his relationship with Karen would be tested to the limits by the events of the next two years.

21/ Judgement Day

On June 16, 1982, federal justice minister Jean Chrétien formally referred Junior Marshall's case to the Nova Scotia Court of Appeal, saying that it wasn't "the first error the judicial system in Canada has been confronted with". The hearing was to be conducted under section 617 of the Criminal Code, which deals with applications seeking the Mercy of the Crown by convicted persons. Officials in the justice department told reporters that the rarely invoked procedure was only used in cases where there were "compelling indications of a miscarriage of justice".

But the 2½-month wait between Marshall's release and Chrétien's decision was more than some people could bear. On June 14, someone in Sydney wrote the following letter to the federal minister advising him of Junior Marshall's innocence and naming Sandy Seale's real killer.

Dear Mr. Chretien,

I am writing to give you some information about the Junior Marshall case. I am afraid to reveal my identity because there could be serious repercussions against me for speaking out.

The real murderer of Sandy Seale is Roy Ebsary....Roy Ebsary's daughter Donna told the police that she had seen her father and another man wiping a knife the night Sandy Seale was murdered and she knew her father had killed the youth. You may be wondering when Donna Ebsary told the police this, it was in 1974. That is correct, the police have known that Junior Marshall was innocent for 8 years. Donna told the present police Chief, John MacIntyre, about her father and he said he wasn't interested, and that they had their man behind bars. John MacIntyre was not Chief of police when this crime was committed but he worked on the case and was considered a "Hero" for solving the crime so quickly.

John Pratico, one of the witnesses in the Marshall case, suffered from mental illness. He had been in Dartmouth mental hospital shortly before he gave his testimony at the trial. His Psychiatrist and his mother both stated that he was not fit to give evidence but they took his evidence anyway. Pratico was intoxicated when he claimed to have seen the crime committed.

Chant, another witness, has since confessed that he lied at the Marshall trial because John MacIntyre told him he was going to be sent to Dorchester if he didn't help get the conviction.

It all boils down to an innocent man spending 11 years in prison for a crime he did not commit. There is no way that the State can ever make restitution for the crime against Junior Marshall, and in some ways we are all guilty for turning our backs on him. . . .

The scary part of this story is that two teenage friends, one black and the other Indian, walked home one night from a dance and all at once many lives would never be the same again. Another point for reflection is that it could happen to anyone if the police needed a conviction badly enough.

I hope some of the information will be of assistance to you when you make your decision. I hope you will give Donald Marshall Junior a new trial so that he can prove his innocence. All of the information I gave you can be documented. Junior Marshall deserves the chance to live the rest of his life free and innocent in the eyes of all.

> A deeply concerned
> Citizen

Shortly after receiving the letter, Douglas Rutherford of the federal justice department sent a copy under a confidential covering note to Gordon Gale in the Nova Scotia Attorney General's Office.

Dear Gordon,

Enclosed is a photocopy of a letter that arrived here last week in a plain envelope postmarked Sydney, Nova Scotia.

I thought you should see it and be aware of its contents in view of the proceedings now pending in the Nova Scotia Supreme Court (Appeal Division).

Yours sincerely,
Douglas J. A. Rutherford
Assistant Deputy Attorney General

By the time Jean Chrétien received the anonymous letter, the decision on how the matter would be handled had already been made, although there were some last-minute hitches. Under section 617 of the Criminal Code of Canada, the minister had three options. He could (a) direct a new trial or hearing, (b) refer the matter to the court of appeal as if it were an appeal by the convicted person, or (c) merely ask the court of appeal for advice on the case before deciding what ought to be done.

In his conversations with federal justice officials, Junior's lawyer, Stephen Aronson, was told that Chrétien was in favor of the last option, which would have left the final determination of the case to Ottawa. But members of the Nova Scotia bench demurred. They argued that if they were going to hear an appeal of the original conviction, they also wanted the power to make a ruling in the case. Reluctantly, Ottawa agreed. This decision would leave Junior Marshall's life on hold for nine more agonizing months. It would also cost him seventy thousand dollars in legal bills to prove what the Attorney General of Nova Scotia and the Minister of Justice of Canada already knew: that the evidence no longer supported his conviction for the murder of Sandy Seale.

Although Aronson had originally hoped that Chrétien would simply give Junior a full pardon (never had a convicted murderer had his conviction overturned under section 617 of the Code, though several, including Steven Truscott, had tried), he had prepared for the worst. That would prove to be a sound modus operandi for the young lawyer throughout the difficult months ahead.

Enjoying excellent rapport with the RCMP, Aronson kept abreast of what Harry Wheaton and Jim Carroll had uncovered and carried out a parallel investigation of his own. By the time the matter went to court in December, he had compiled nineteen affidavits, including recanting statements from the three teenage witnesses whose testimony led to Junior's conviction in 1971. In addition to admitting to perjury, all three claimed that the police had pressured them into giving the false statements on which their testimony was based. Chief John MacIntyre and Inspector William Urquhart of the Sydney police filed affidavits of their own denying the allegations.

On July 29, Aronson made application to the Appeal Division to set a date for a hearing to determine the admissibility of fresh evidence pursuant to section 610 (1) (d) of the Criminal Code. It wasn't as straightforward as it might have seemed. The fact that Chant and Pratico were now recanting their 1971 testimony did not in itself guarantee that the court would admit their affidavits as "fresh evidence". (The usual criterion for admitting fresh evidence is that at the time of the original trial, the information was not available, and that had it been, it would have raised a reasonable doubt in the minds of the jury concerning an accused person's guilt.)

On October 5, a panel of five judges reserved judgment on whether they would allow the affidavits as fresh evidence, but agreed to hear oral evidence from seven of the people who had signed them. As critical as he was to a full airing of the facts under review, John Pratico wasn't one of the seven. Crown prosecutor Frank Edwards was ostensibly opposed to hearing any evidence from Pratico because of the young man's long history of psychiatric treatment. But the lawyer was prepared to admit that Pratico had not witnessed the murder, as he now claimed in his affidavit.

It was a strangely contradictory position, shared in part by Junior's own lawyer. If Pratico were credible enough to be believed when he claimed not to have witnessed the murder in 1971, why wasn't he credible enough to say so on the stand in 1982? Whatever the answer to that question, one incontrovertible fact flowed from John Pratico's exclusion from the upcoming hearing: the claim by both 1971 eyewitnesses to the murder that the police had coerced them into lying by playing one off against the other could not be explored at the hearing if only Maynard Chant testified. As anxious as the Crown prosecutor was to establish that

Junior Marshall had been convicted on perjured evidence, he wasn't at all interested in answering an equally important question: why had the two teenagers lied in the first place?

That was a consideration that led directly to the issue of compensation for Junior Marshall, a subject no one in either Ottawa or Halifax was eager to address. By the time the two-day December hearing was through, it would appear to some observers that Frank Edwards wasn't so much acting for the Crown against Junior Marshall as defending the system against the charge that a miscarriage of justice had sent the falsely convicted teenager to Dorchester for an undeserved life sentence.

In the months leading up to the December hearing, Stephen Aronson's fledgling law practice was totally taken up with the Marshall case. Knowing that his client had no money, Aronson had taken the case on for twenty-five per cent of whatever compensation Junior might eventually receive for his false imprisonment, although it was far from clear that he would ever get anything.

In the meantime, the slight, soft-spoken lawyer with limpid blue eyes personally defrayed the costs of carrying the case, including frequent trips to Ottawa for conferences with justice department officials, junkets to Sydney to round up witnesses, and endless long-distance telephone calls with police, prison officials, other lawyers, and the media. For the 34-year-old former legal aid lawyer, his commitment to Marshall's case was simply a matter of principle. He knew and respected the Micmacs from previous cases and was determined that his client was not going to get anything less than the best he could offer—whether he could pay for it or not.

The December hearing wasn't the only legal iron in the fire. On July 27, Aronson had formally requested that his client be released from the Carlton Centre until his guilt or innocence was determined by the court. The request was granted two days later. Six weeks after that, Aronson commenced a legal action against the City of Sydney and the original investigating officers in the Seale murder case for malicious prosecution, false arrest, and imprisonment. At this point, a civil action was not Aronson's preferred way of winning his client compensation, but in the event that a settlement with the federal and provincial governments couldn't be reached, he wanted to leave Junior's legal options open. And then there was the major job of researching the compensation issue, a virgin area in Canadian jurisprudence. Junior Marshall's legal struggle was turning into a war with many fronts and not enough soldiers.

As his personal financial situation weakened, Aronson's commitment to the young Micmac remained steadfast. Lawyer and client became close personal friends and, next to Karen Brown, the soft-spoken Aronson was undoubtedly the most important person in Junior Marshall's life. Until his client was cleared, Aronson would stick by his side – all the way to financial ruin.

On December 1, 1982, Junior Marshall was late for the most important court date of his life. Stephen Áronson explained to the five judges hearing the case that his client was taking a driver's test that morning. When he arrived ten minutes later, Junior looked tense, "like a man to about to jump out of his skin", one reporter remarked.

Junior was the first to take the stand. Aronson's direct examination of his client built swiftly to the salient point under consideration: had he stabbed Sandy Seale? Junior testified that he had not.

But Frank Edwards, a balding Cape Bretoner who "came up hard" and earned his law degree at night while working as a teacher, made very clear in his cross-examination that he was interested in a very different matter: the alleged robbery attempt of Ebsary and Jimmy MacNeil by Marshall and Seale. Although Junior admitted that he was out to get money any way he could that night, he denied that a robbery attempt had ever taken place. "I didn't do anything to get the money off them. The intentions of getting money was there. The attempt – any other thing else that will indicate that I tried to rob these people, I didn't. There was no indication from me or Sandy," Marshall testified.

He told the court that he and Sandy had talked to the two other men and that when they walked away, he had called them back. He testified he then grabbed Jimmy MacNeil when the young man stumbled off the curb. It was at that point that Roy Ebsary stabbed Sandy. The Crown prosecutor offered a different account of events.

"Right. So I suggest to you, Mr. Marshall, that you grabbed James MacNeil because you were the bigger and Seale was going to confront Ebsary because he was the smaller in order to get money from them. Isn't that right?"

"No, that's not right. Regardless—it didn't matter who I grabbed if I did grab anybody. The point I'm doing...getting at is them people walked away. Why did they walk back, you know."

"But the point is, Mr. Marshall, that when they did come back—"

"Why did they come back?"

"You're staying with your testimony that you intended to get money from them no matter what you had to do. Isn't that right?"

"Off them. Off them or out of a store or anything else. My intentions was to get money regardless if I stole it off somebody, bummed it off somebody, or took it out of a store or someone's house," Marshall said, realizing with a sickening feeling in the pit of his stomach that he was on trial again.

The Crown prosecutor then brought out that, according to Marshall's 1971 court testimony, Ebsary had invited the two boys back to his house for a drink just before the stabbing, indicating where he lived with a wave of his arm. Junior acknowledged his former evidence, not anticipating the incredible suggestion Frank Edwards was about to make.

"The point is, Mr. Marshall, isn't it true that if you had made some efforts you could have discovered who those two fellows were? It's likely you would have discovered who they were?"

"On my own, I probably would have," the witness answered, still not understanding what Edwards was driving at.

"But you really weren't interested in finding out who they were at the time, were you?"

"I was scared to death. It's not—I'm not a policeman. It's not my job to investigate. I told them who they were. I wasn't sure where they lived. It wasn't up to me to go look for them."

"Isn't it true, Mr. Marshall, that the reason you didn't go look for them or have anybody go look for them was because you were scared of being charged with robbery?"

"Robbery? No, I wasn't. I did go look for them," Junior said truthfully.

Ignoring his reply, Edwards pushed on.

"You never believed you were going to be convicted of the murder, did you?"

"No," Junior replied.

"So, believing that, you felt that there'd be no problem keeping a secret about the robbery or the attempted robbery. Isn't that correct?"

"It didn't—it's not important because there was no attempt made..." the beleaguered witness replied.

Not only was Junior being cross-examined about a criminal matter he had never been charged with, he was also being blamed for not apprehending the man who had killed Sandy Seale in 1971. The Micmac who had come to court for some belated justice and was instead faced with more accusations withdrew from the Crown prosecutor's line of questioning in quiet outrage.

"Now, had you ever rolled anyone prior to that night?" Edwards asked. It was a question that had nothing to do with the events of May 28, 1971, and Aronson objected. The court allowed the question but Junior Marshall did not.

"I can't answer that," he said.

"You realize that you're in court and you're under oath, don't you?"

"Yes, but I'm not dealing with if I robbed anybody before," he answered.

"And you realize that unless one of their Lordships say that you do not have to answer the question that you have to answer the questions put to you. Do you realize that?"

"Yes I do."

"Yes. Then I will ask you once again. Prior to that night of May 28, 1971, had you ever rolled anyone before?"

"I give you an answer. It's nobody's business."

Frank Edwards then asked the court's leave to confront the witness with the March 2, 1982, statement to the RCMP taken in Dorchester Penitentiary in which Marshall said that he'd rolled people before the night of the Seale murder. Although the statement was not in evidence before the court and the defence was disputing that it had been free and voluntary, the Crown prosecutor was permitted to question the witness about it, over the strenuous objections of Stephen Aronson.

Confronted with the statement, Junior maintained his story: he had been out to get money that night but no robbery attempt ever took place. "As far as I'm concerned, I never grabbed the guy. I never put my—his arm around his back. I did not jump from behind. And I'm not dealing with a robbery here. I'm dealing with a murder here and I'm being—I'm dealing with two things at once. I can't answer your questions."

After Junior left the stand, the hearing proceeded to deal with the fresh evidence Aronson hoped would lead to his client's acquittal. Jimmy MacNeil testified that Roy Ebsary stabbed Sandy Seale after the two unarmed youths had allegedly accosted them for money on the night of May 28. Maynard Chant and Patricia Harriss both admitted they had lied on the stand after being pressured by two Sydney detectives into giving false statements that incriminated Junior Marshall. Donna Ebsary, Roy's daughter, told the court that she had watched her father wash blood from a knife in the kitchen sink just after the stabbing on Crescent Street. Her brother, Greg, attested to his father's extreme violence and obsession with knives. Finally, Adolphus Evers of the RCMP crime laboratory in Sackville testified that he'd found fibres on one of Roy's old knives consistent with fibres from the coats Marshall and Seale were wearing on the night of the murder. The odds of those same fibres being present on the knife on a chance basis were "very, very remote", the forensic specialist said.

After the seventh witness had given his evidence, the two-day hearing was adjourned for the preparation of transcripts and the final summations of both lawyers. Technically, the court had three options: it could order a new trial, acquit Marshall, or uphold his original conviction. But when both solicitors came in with recommendations that the conviction be quashed because there was no more evidence against Marshall, the judges had very little choice in the matter.

In his factum, argued before the court two months after the hearing, Stephen Aronson asked the court to quash his client's murder conviction on the basis of the fresh evidence he'd presented, arguing that a "miscarriage of justice" in the most serious sense of those words had taken place.

Crown prosecutor Frank Edwards also recommended Marshall's acquittal, but he offered a very different analysis of the whole affair.

> Here, if the Court does ultimately decide to acquit the Appellant, it is no overstatement to say that the credibility of our criminal justice system may be called into question by a significant portion of the community. It seems reasonable to assume that the public will suspect that there is something

wrong with the system if a man can be convicted of a murder he did not commit. A minimum level of public confidence in the criminal justice system must be maintained or it simply will not work.

For the above reasons, it is respectfully submitted that the Court should make clear that what happened in this case was not the fault of the criminal justice system or anyone in it, including the police, the lawyers, the members of the jury, or the Court itself.

To function, our system depends on getting the truth and that is exactly what it did not get in 1971. The Appellant may argue that he told the truth, but the fact remains that, not only did he put himself in a position which precipitated the stabbing, but he failed to disclose to anyone what he and Seale had actually been up to. Instead, he told police and his lawyers about an attack by two priests from Manitoba who did not like "niggers or Indians". It is not difficult to speculate upon how believable either the police or the Defence Counsel found that story.

It is submitted that had the Appellant been forthright, the odds are that both the police investigation and/or his defence would have taken different directions. The likelihood is that he would never have been charged, let alone convicted.

When the stories told by Chant and Harriss were added to the Appellant's lack of candour, the flow of subsequent events was as inevitable as it is now understandable....

It was the thinnest of legal wallpaper to cover over some very disturbing cracks. Frank Edwards knew that there were three affidavits filed with the court swearing that two Sydney detectives had pressured Chant, Pratico, and Harriss–all juveniles at the time –into signing false statements that led directly to Junior Marshall's conviction on perjured evidence. Yet without a mention of the self-admitted perjurers, or any investigation of the very serious implications of their affidavits, he wanted the appeal court to exonerate the police of any responsibility in the matter.

Edwards also knew that Sydney police chief John MacIntyre had filed an affidavit with the court saying that in 1971 he had turned over "all statements" taken in the course of the investigation of the Seale murder to the man who originally prosecuted Marshall,

Donald C. MacNeil, who would normally have, according to the ethics of his profession, surrendered them to Marshall's lawyers. Yet Moe Rosenblum and Simon Khattar never saw the first statements John Pratico and Maynard Chant gave to the Sydney police in 1971, statements that flatly contradicted their false and, as far as Marshall was concerned, damning statements to police a week later. In affidavits of their own, both lawyers said that had they known about the first statements back in 1971, their client would never have been convicted. Chant's and Pratico's credibility would have disappeared down the chasm that separated the first and second versions of what they claimed to have seen. But despite the fact that Donald C. MacNeil had not extended the courtesy of full disclosure of the Crown's case to Rosenblum and Khattar – an omission that had dire consequences for the accused, according to his lawyers – Frank Edwards wanted the appeal court to declare blameless any of the lawyers at Marshall's original trial.

Most remarkable of all, Frank Edwards knew that within ten days of Marshall's false conviction for the murder of Sandy Seale, the Sydney police, the RCMP, and, a few weeks later, the Nova Scotia Attorney General's Office were all aware of the alleged robbery attempt from the November 15 statements of Jimmy MacNeil and Roy Ebsary. Yet the Crown prosecutor declared that the course of justice likely would have been different if Junior Marshall had disclosed to authorities what "he and Seale had actually been up to" that night. Justice had apparently been perverted by a seventeen-year-old Indian who misled authorities by pleading not guilty when charged with a murder someone else had committed instead of confessing to another offence with which he had never been confronted. It was a stunning reversal of a fundamental principle of the law: from the moment a person is accused of a crime and enters a plea, he is clothed in the presumption of innocence until the Crown proves otherwise. And if the Crown should falsely convict a person it has accused, it is the Crown, and not the victim of the mistake, who must answer.

Three months after the Marshall case was heard, the Appeal Division of the Nova Scotia Supreme Court endorsed the Crown prosecutor's blind defence of the system. In rendering their judgment of acquittal, the five judges denied that there had been any miscarriage of justice and blamed the young Indian for the course of events in 1971. Their judgment read in part:

Donald Marshall Jr. was convicted of murder and served a lengthy period of incarceration. That conviction is now to be set aside. Any miscarriage of justice is, however, more apparent than real.

In attempting to defend himself against the charge of murder Mr. Marshall admittedly committed perjury for which he could still be charged.

By lying, he helped secure his own conviction. He misled his lawyers and presented to the jury a version of the facts he now says is false, a version that was so far-fetched as to be incapable of belief.

By planning a robbery with the aid of Mr. Seale he triggered a series of events which unfortunately ended in the death of Mr. Seale.

By hiding facts from his lawyers and the police Mr. Marshall effectively prevented development of the only defence available to him, namely, that during a robbery Seale was stabbed by one of the intended victims. He now says that he knew approximately where the man lived who stabbed Seale and had a pretty good description of him. With this information the truth of the matter might well have been uncovered by the police.

Even at the time of taking the fresh evidence, although he had little more to lose and much to gain if he could obtain his acquittal, Mr. Marshall was far from being straightforward on the stand. He continued to be evasive about the robbery and assault and even refused to answer questions until the Court ordered him to do so. There can be no doubt but that Donald Marshall's untruthfulness through this whole affair contributed in large measure to his conviction.

The judges, like Frank Edwards before them, apparently believed that it is not enough for an innocent man to plead not guilty to the crime he is charged with. He should also, in the course of proving his innocence, confess to other offences with which he was never charged and which had absolutely no bearing on his guilt or innocence in the charge he did honestly answer. After that, he must assist the police and the court in the investigation and trial of his alleged offence. And if the criminal justice system, without all that assistance from the accused, makes a mistake, the victim of that mistake must shoulder the blame.

As an analysis of why an innocent man had been sent to prison for life, the judgment was pitifully grandiose and self-serving. Knowing only a fraction of the story, the judges had exonerated a system that the two-day hearing had not even remotely scrutinized. For ignoring the obvious – that Junior Marshall had been convicted in 1971 by perjured evidence which those who gave it now laid squarely at the feet of the Sydney police – and accusing the Appellant of another crime without the trouble of laying a charge, allowing a plea, or permitting a defence, the judgment was quickly assailed in the press as a political rather than a judicial document, a mere whitewash.

In the legal community of Halifax another question was being asked: why had the man who had been attorney general in 1971, Mr. Justice Leonard Pace, sat as a judge in Marshall's 1982 hearing when his old department had already had dealings in the matter? Eleven years before, the Attorney General's Office had received a copy of the first RCMP reinvestigation of the Seale murder which included Jimmy MacNeil's claim that Roy Ebsary, not Junior Marshall, stabbed Sandy Seale. Inexplicably, the Attorney General's Office never passed that new information along to the lawyer who was preparing Marshall's appeal, an appeal that was denied in 1972 and that Moe Rosenblum believed he could have won had he known about Jimmy MacNeil's new information.

Leonard Pace declared that he had "no personal recollection" of the case. The Attorney General's Office would later say that their original file on the Marshall case, including the report of the 1971 RCMP reinvestigation, had been destroyed under the Public Records Disposal Act and was therefore unavailable for perusal by the acquitted man's lawyer.

Later, during an interview concerning the Marshall case, Crown prosecutor Edwards commented on the propriety of Mr. Justice Pace's taking part in the appeal hearing. "Why don't you ask me why I didn't object to the former attorney general sitting on the bench during the Marshall hearing? The answer is that back in 1971 I was a teacher in an outport community in Newfoundland. I simply didn't know that he was attorney general of Nova Scotia at that time."

Junior Marshall was walking down the hall of the Victoria General Hospital in Halifax on the way to visit his father when his mother came running toward him, tears streaming down her cheeks. Unaware that, moments before, Karen Brown had called the hospital room with news of his acquittal, the young man thought his father, who had just had a kidney transplant, had died.

"It's over, Junior: they're not blaming you any more," Caroline Marshall told him, putting a decade of sorrow and lost love into her embrace.

"What?" he asked.

"The court said you're innocent today!"

"Really! I told them guys I'd beat them and I did beat them!" he exclaimed.

With his arm around his mother, he walked to the room where Donald Marshall, Sr., was hooked up to a dialysis machine. His father's smile told him that the Grand Chief of the Micmac Nation had no more false shame to bear. The two men embraced. Although he never said it to Junior, the ailing man's joy was tempered with the sadness that a large part of his son's life had been lost regardless of what the judges had decided.

Meanwhile, Stephen Aronson's Dartmouth law office was overflowing with reporters who had come to attend the celebration press conference. By the time Junior arrived, it was clear he had been doing a little celebrating of his own. He told the press, "A long time ago, I said I was going to beat the system, and I beat the system. As long as you're right, you can prove to people you're right. I proved my point."

When asked where he wanted to go now, Junior grinned. "To heaven."

Led by CBC television reporter Michael Vaughan, the assembled press gave three cheers for the man whose story they had been following for more than a year.

But celebration wasn't the only item on the agenda. Stephen Aronson expressed the hope that Sandy Seale's real killer would be brought to justice and then called for a public inquiry into the circumstances of Junior's false conviction. "There remains a dark cloud hanging heavily over the original police investigation in 1971 by the Sydney city police department and many questions remain unanswered," he said.

These words were his last as Junior Marshall's lawyer. Unable to carry the staggering $79,000 legal bill that Junior could not afford to pay, and disgusted with a justice system that had cast new aspersions against his client in the very act of acquitting him of murder, Stephen Aronson was quitting the law.

Later, when the federal and provincial governments were both denying any obligation to compensate Marshall, Aronson left no doubt about where he stood in the shabby debate. "I do think it's the province's responsibility, not the federal government's, because the province administers justice. And if there's anything that bugs me about the Marshall case, it's been the total irresponsibility of the province."

22/The Reverend Captain

On May 12, 1983, two days after Junior Marshall was acquitted of killing Sandy Seale, Roy Ebsary was charged with second-degree murder for the same offence. The provincial court judge who had found Ebsary guilty of the Goodie Mugridge stabbing read the charge to Roy as he lay in a bed in the Sydney City Hospital, the same hospital where Sandy Seale had died in 1971. The 71-year-old "Reverend Captain" was in a head-to-waist body cast recovering from a broken neck sustained in a fall at his boarding house.

The charge resulted from the RCMP reinvestigation of the Seale murder which had continued, on and off, for more than seven months after Junior Marshall's release from Dorchester Penitentiary. Hampered in the beginning by what they took to be lack of co-operation from John MacIntyre, the investigators' work became easier after April 20, 1982, when the attorney general of Nova Scotia, Harry How, ordered the Sydney police chief to turn over all materials in his possession on the Sandy Seale murder case to the RCMP, under the terms of the Police Act. At last the Mounties had all of the statements taken during the original investigation of the crime, leaving them free to pursue new witnesses.

One of the most important people Harry Wheaton and Jim Carroll interviewed after Marshall's release from prison was Roy's daughter, Donna, who managed a furniture business near Newton, Massachusetts, in the United States. Donna told the Mounties that on the night of the murder she had seen her father leaning over the sink washing off a knife which he later took upstairs. As a school-girl, she had often tried to find it.

"At school everyone talked about the murder, and I know they were looking for an old man with a goatee, white hair, and a cape. Outwardly, to other kids, I pretended it was not my father, but inwardly I knew it was."

The young woman said she tried to tell what she knew to the Sydney police in 1974 but they wouldn't listen. She then told a few friends that " Father did it" but still couldn't get anything done for the innocent man languishing in jail. "I felt totally frustrated to think Marshall was in jail and my father had committed this crime, and there was nothing I could do about it. . . . Around 1975, Uncle Bob Ebsary was over from Newfoundland. Father and Uncle Bob were drinking and I heard Father tell Bob about the attempted robbery. He said, 'They asked for my money, and I said, I'll give you what I have.' Father then made an underhanded stabbing motion as if he had a knife in his hand. . . ."

The two Mounties travelled to St. John's, Newfoundland, to find Roy Ebsary's relative, hoping to add a third witness to their list of people to whom the old man had confessed stabbing Seale. The most difficult part of their task was finding him; as it turned out, Robert Ebsary had changed his name to Robert McLean. But, once located, the man readily gave a statement that corroborated Donna Ebsary's story.

"I think around 1975 I visited Roy Ebsary, a relative of mine in Sydney, Nova Scotia. During the visit we were having a few nips. I asked him if he would relate a few of his stories on tape. I recall him telling me about an attempted robbery in a park and he stabbed a fellow. He said it was two people who tried to rob him, he didn't say if it was a Black. . . . After I read the recent pieces in the paper I wondered if that was the story Roy told me. It seemed very real to Roy as he related it to me and demonstrated it to me. We were up in his room when he told me about it. The next day I looked for the tape we made of our conversation and Roy had destroyed it. He said he couldn't have that around. . . ."

The Mounties also visited Edward O'Toole in St. John's. O'Toole was married to Roy Ebsary's niece, and the investigators had been told that for several years O'Toole had kept in touch with Ebsary.

Wondering if he too had been told about the stabbing, they decided to interview him. Although he knew nothing about the event that the Mounties were interested in, O'Toole did have a vivid recollection of how his relationship with his distant relative had ended.

"I have never met Roy Ebsary, but when we first moved into our home on Pennywell Road we had a card from him congratulating us on our new home. This was sometime around 1975. We thought it was a nice gesture on his part, so my wife asked me to write him back. We continued to communicate by letter, tape, and telephone until about two years ago. At that time I received a letter from him with a picture of a penis attached. I was shocked at this and I realized he was probably a homosexual. . . ."

Two bulls, one old, one young, were standing on a hill watching a herd of cows grazing in the field below.

"Let's run down and fuck one," the young bull said to the old bull.

"Let's walk down and fuck them all," the old bull replied.

It was a joke Harry Wheaton liked to tell and Jim Carroll liked to hear, less for its ribald humor than for the approach to police work it contained. In the end, patience and persistence yielded greater rewards than explosions of energy or ego. Despite his bitter disappointment that Roy Ebsary hadn't given him a confession after the Mugridge trial, Jim Carroll stayed on the trail and gradually built up a relationship of sorts with the man he believed had stabbed Sandy Seale. "Throughout, I was keeping contact with him and occasionally he would be robbed or beaten down at the park and he would call up, usually intoxicated or whatever, and telling a tale of woe that somebody had thumped him and he was unconscious, didn't know who it was or what was taken," Carroll remembered.

The reward for Carroll's forbearance was continuing intelligence on Roy's state of mind, information that he was eager to have in the slim hope that at some point, under the right circumstances, the old man would be ripe for a confession. The investigator watched Ebsary closely as he entertained "quite a colorful guest list" of ex-inmates of the Correctional Centre whom he'd met while in jail on the Mugridge stabbing charge. Carroll soon picked up on the fact that Ebsary appeared to have an especially close relationship with a young man who regularly visited his flat on Falmouth Street. The old man even bought a car for his young companion, which he quickly proceeded to smash up while driving Roy around Sydney.

Eventually the man left Sydney and got into trouble with the law in St. Peter's, Cape Breton. In tears, Roy called Carroll, asking that the young gentleman be "returned to his nest". When Carroll inquired into the matter, he learned that the man had been sent to a mental hospital in Dartmouth for thirty days' observation. Though distraught at this news, Roy Ebsary was grateful for the policeman's help. He agreed to talk to Carroll about the Seale murder.

The investigator knew that Roy kept a daily typewritten log, as if he were a ship's captain. "He'd have a sheet of paper in the typewriter and he'd get up and type in the time, 600 hours. On deck, weather cloudy, cool, raining, temperature, that sort of thing. He had comments about different terms, nautical terms that he would use a lot. The mail, he had a term for the mail – dispatch I guess he called it. 'Received your last dispatch, yesterday's date', referring to a letter from Australia or California or something."

Since Roy kept such detailed descriptions of daily occurrences, Carroll wondered if he had kept similarly explicit accounts of things that had happened many years ago. But when he asked if the old man had such records for 1971, Roy told him they were probably in Newfoundland, though just where he did not know. Carroll then asked if he would mind "just typing out" what was on his mind about the Seale murder.

Once more Ebsary put him off. His glasses were broken and he couldn't hold them on his nose. Just when Carroll began to despair that Ebsary would confess, Roy made a suggestion of his own: what about a tape recorder? Carroll promised to return with a tape recorder and a clean tape so that Roy could "get straight" what he had to say about the events of 1971. The Mountie rushed home and picked up his son's tape machine and returned to Ebsary's flat. Although he had originally planned to give the tape recorder to Roy and then leave him alone to dictate his thoughts, he changed his mind when he found a wino on the premises when he got back. "I could just visualize my young fella's tape recorder ending up in the pawn shop for a quart of wine. So I decided to get rid of the drunk and take my chances, so I broke out a loan and the fellow caught a taxi and left. So we sat down at Ebsary's kitchen table and put the tape recorder between us and inserted a new cassette."

Carroll took the tape recorder and read in the time and date, 11:50 a.m. on the 29th day of October, 1982. Before he began taking Roy's statement, he got the very important matter of the standard police warning out of the way, recording it along with Ebsary's statement.

"Now, Captain, before we go any further, I have to give something that is called a Police Warning, it is as follows..."

"Right, go ahead," Roy said.

"You need not say anything, you have nothing to hope from any promise or favor and nothing to fear from any threat whether or not you say anything. Anything you say may be used as evidence. Do you understand that?" the policeman asked.

"Yes."

"Now, also, with the Bill of Rights you realize that you are entitled to counsel and it's...the wording of that is, you have the right to retain and instruct counsel without delay. Now..."

"Right," Ebsary said.

"Do you understand that?"

"Yes."

"Do you wish to have your lawyer?"

"I–do you know what I call my lawyer? A dimwit," Ebsary answered.

Jim Carroll drew a big breath and told Ebsary that he would prefer not to ask questions, to have Roy simply talk about the events of eleven years ago. The old man seemed happy to oblige and launched into the following statement:

"I remember the night vividly, it was a kind of misty night, a fine rain was falling so I had to take off my glasses; well, I can't see very well, anyway, well, with the glasses off I couldn't see at all. So I went over to visit Mr. O'Neil [MacNeil]. Now, not the young O'Neil [Jimmy MacNeil], [but] his father, and we sat and we consumed...it was a few days before my birthday, so the wife bought me a couple bottles of wine, so naturally I put the two bottles of wine in my pocket and went over to visit Mr. O'Neil [MacNeil]. His son wasn't home, so, okay we consumed one bottle of wine, Mr. O'Neil

[MacNeil] and I. Then the son came home and we consumed the second one. Now then, when I was about to leave to go home the boy said he wants to go down to the State Tavern to meet someone, I don't know who, but he didn't have any success because, ah, so we decided to go home and we walked, let me see, we, we must have came up George and I've gone through the park several times with the police, but Went...Wentworth Park that time, Cres... Crescent Street at that time was one of the darkest areas in the city, it was, there was no lights there. Right? So, when the police asked me down there who attacked me, I wasn't able to even tell them the color. I said two men attacked me.

"Okay, he turns around and he says to me, 'Give me everything you've got in your pocket,' and I gave him everything I had in my pocket, but when I put my hand in my pocket, I discovered I had a penknife. Now, it was only a penknife, it was no knife that you took from my home and it was a penknife, and that penknife was give to me by young Jacques Brittain, a young Frenchman that the authorities here had placed in my care, and I was training him to be a cook, and he wanted, he said he wanted to live somewhere where there was a family, so I took him home with me. Okay? But he gave me this penknife. The blade was about three inches long, three inches long. So, when this bastard said to me, 'Give me everything you got in your pocket,' I said, 'Listen, you fucker, you're going to get everything I got in my pocket.' So I gave him everything I had in my pocket, everything, my watch, my ring, but the fuckin' knife was in my fuckin' pocket and I opened it in my pocket and I said, 'Brother, you asked for everything, you're going to get everything,' and I gave him everything. Now, the blade was that small that that boy that night ran, he ran.

"In the meantime, Marshall was strangling the other boy across the road, that young O'Neil [MacNeil], because Marshall was a thug and so was Seale. So thugs become heroes and honest men become what? Honest men become what? You don't know? I do," the old man said. "Okay, how am I doing?"

"Just fine," Carroll answered.

"Have I got all my marbles?"

"I'm not going to shut the tape off, Captain, I'm just going to let it roll. Is there anything further you want to add there as to what happened from that point on?"

"Now listen, young Seale ran that night, ran. He ran. Now listen, [it] was only about fifty feet from South Bentinck to Crescent Street, fifty feet, but he ran the whole length of that bloody street, so I didn't think the boy was hurt. I didn't think the boy was hurt, but the next morning, young O'Neil [MacNeil] came to my house and he said, 'Ebsary, do you know a young fellow was killed in the park last night?' 'Well,' I said, 'he must have had bad luck, he must have had bad luck, he took us for all we had but he must have bumped into somebody who gave him the works.' Now, I didn't believe I did it. I couldn't convince myself that I did it. Do you understand that?"

"Yes."

"You do? Honest to God?"

"There is one thing that you mentioned in your remarks there, you say that the young fellow was Seale, [that he] asked you, did you mention Seale's name, or did you say the young fellow?"

"The young fellow," Ebsary replied, admitting that he did not know either Seale or Marshall on the night of the incident.

"You say he asked you for everything you had in your pockets."

"Right."

"And you say you gave it to him; now. . ."

"Right, right."

". . .what did you mean by giving it to him?"

Although Carroll knew he had Ebsary on tape claiming he "gave everything" to Seale that night, he still lacked a verbatim admission to the stabbing–something he desperately needed if the evidence were ever to stand up in any subsequent court action. But Roy was as evasive as ever.

"He said, 'I want everything you got in your pocket.' Now, I've been mugged before, coming through the park, umpteen times, but I never complained to police, what the hell was the use, but when he said, 'Give me everything you got in your pocket,' when my hand felt the knife and it was only a penknife, it wasn't one of the knives you took from my home."

Before his subject could get off on a tangent, Carroll put his question again.

"What actually happened to the knife? What did you do with the knife?"

"I know where the knife is," Ebsary answered.

"No, I mean on that particular night, what did you actually do with the knife when he asked you what you had in your pockets? You opened the knife blade, you say?"

"Right."

"What...actually, what motion did you make then?"

"I stuck the knife in the ground," was Ebsary's quixotic reply.

"Not in Mr. Seale?" Carroll's hopes for a confession were fading fast.

"No, I stuck the knife in the ground. Now, the people who say they saw me wash blood off that knife were telling bloody lies, because you stick a knife in the sod and there's no blood on the goddamned knife, is there? Is there?" Ebsary asked.

Again Carroll felt tantalizingly close to a confession. Roy seemed to be saying that he'd stuck the knife in the ground to clean blood from the blade before leaving the murder scene.

"So, you're not saying you defended yourself or stabbed Mr. Seale?" he asked.

"Yes, I did defend myself. Sure I defended myself. What the hell else was I supposed to do?" Ebsary said, suddenly flaring up.

"Well, I'm not here to criticize your right to defend yourself, Captain, but in fact when you took the knife out of your pocket, what did you do with it before you stuck it in the ground?"

"I made a swipe at Seale," the old man said.

Jim Carroll worked hard to control his excitement.

"What particular part of his anatomy did you swipe at?" he asked, the words hanging there for a moment before Ebsary answered.

"I don't know, I don't know, I told you I was after consuming two bottles of wine. I just made a blind swipe, but he ran."

"Would you say the upper part of his body from the head down to the waist, or from the waist down, or..."

"Probably got it, probably I got him in the guts, probably I got him in the guts," Ebsary said.

"Was it just one blow?"

"One blow," the old man agreed.

Ebsary said he then ran over to assist MacNeil, who he claimed was being "strangled" by Junior Marshall, contrary to MacNeil's own description of what had happened to him. "...So you know what I did? I had, I still had the knife in my hand, so I ran across the road and I stuck Marshall in the arm."

At long last, Jim Carroll had what he'd been after. "At any time later on did you realize that this could have been the person that you fought with in the park, I don't mean a lengthy fight, but a robbery or whatever?"

"I told you, to me it was only an incident," Ebsary said.

"You had been mugged there before you say?"

"Yes, darned right I've been mugged there before."

"And have you had to defend yourself before?"

"Right."

"Or did you just give in?"

"Gave in, I got beat up."

"Okay, so..."

Before Jim Carroll could ask his next question, Roy volunteered a devastating piece of information.

"But I swore by my Christ, I swore by my Christ, that the next man that struck me would die in his tracks."

It was as clear an indication of intent to kill as a policeman was ever likely to get, and it was vitally important because intent is a crucial element in proving a charge of second-degree murder, the offence Junior Marshall had been charged with in 1971 and the charge Carroll believed Ebsary himself might one day face. Roy now began to open up with more details, "almost as if the tape recorder was a radio microphone and he was speaking to the world," Jim Carroll remembered.

"I just have one final question I'm going to ask you and that is, why have you decided to tell me today what we have just discussed now? Is there a reason? Do you feel obligated or..."

"Yes, yes, I do feel obligated."

"Explain that to me, this will be the final remarks," Carroll said.

"Yes, I've served time in the slammer too, and I only spent a few months there, nine months, but I realized what young Marshall must have gone through, eleven years..."

The old man's voice trailed off and he began to cry.

As Roy Ebsary's trial approached, the two investigators were satisfied that they had built an impressive case: two corroborating eyewitnesses to the murder, a free and voluntary taped confession by the accused to the RCMP, three verbal confessions by the accused to three different people, a letter from Ebsary strongly suggesting that he had stabbed Sandy Seale, strong circumstantial evidence from three members of the accused's family, and compelling physical evidence from a forensic specialist linking one of Ebsary's knives to the clothing of the victims of his knife attack. Having gathered much stronger evidence against Roy Ebsary than the Sydney police had ever presented against Junior Marshall in 1971, Wheaton and Carroll were confident the Crown would get a conviction. But having the evidence and presenting it were two different matters, as the two investigators would soon find out.

At the accused's preliminary trial on August 5, 1983, provincial court judge Charles O'Connell was so unimpressed with what he saw from Crown prosecutor Frank Edwards that he ruled that there was insufficient evidence to warrant a murder indictment in Ebsary's case and reduced the charge. "There is no evidence of intent, which is an ingredient in a murder offence, but there is evidence of a killing," Judge O'Connell said in committing Ebsary to stand trial for manslaughter. The judge made his decision without ever hearing the taped confession Jim Carroll had obtained after so many months of patient police work. According to the investigator, the prosecutor's office had decided that the confession was "just the ramblings of somebody that's maybe half-drunk", and not "awfully important". Interestingly, when Junior Marshall had faced a charge for the same crime, the presiding judge at his trial, Louis Dubinsky, without benefit of a confession of intent from the accused, had advised the jury that "the nature and extent of the wounds inflicted on the late Mr. Seale are such that whoever caused these wounds intended to kill him. . . ."

On September 13, 1983, Junior Marshall's thirtieth birthday, Roy Ebsary's trial for the manslaughter death of Sandy Seale ended in a hung jury. They apparently couldn't decide if the 72-year-old accused had acted in self-defence when he stabbed Sandy Seale on Crescent Street that spring night back in 1971.

Some observers believed that the jury's failure to reach a verdict had a lot to do with the case presented by the Crown. Felix Cacchione, Junior Marshall's new lawyer, was outraged at Frank Edwards's performance. The *Micmac News* editorialized that the Crown had to "lay all its cards on the table", if justice was to be done.

The critics could point to some interesting facts. Only six of a possible fourteen witnesses were called by the Crown, and no exhibits were tendered, including Ebsary's taped confession and the fibres evidence Harry Wheaton had so brilliantly recovered eleven years after the crime. Chief John MacIntyre didn't take the stand, although he could have told the court that Roy Ebsary had given him a statement in 1971 claiming he had not stabbed Sandy Seale – a very different claim than he was making in his plea of self-defence. Finally, none of the three people Ebsary gave verbal confessions to – Robert McLean, Mitchell Sarson, or Harry Wheaton – were called to testify against the accused.

Mr. Justice Lorne Clarke reluctantly ordered Ebsary to face a second trial on a charge of manslaughter when the criminal term of the Supreme Court opened in Sydney in six weeks' time. Watching Roy Ebsary walk out of the courtroom under his own recognizance was more than Noel Doucette, president of the Union of Nova Scotia Indians, could abide. "It's a sad irony," he told a reporter. "Twelve years ago Donald Marshall came into this same courtroom in shackles. It took a white jury only forty-five minutes to convict him. Then you see Ebsary, a white man, just walk in and out of here as if he had done nothing at all. It's justice for the white man, and for the Indian it's the law."

Ebsary's next trial was a very different affair. The taped confession that the prosecutor's office thought wasn't "awfully important" at the time of the accused's first trial was introduced with devastating effect. The jury of seven men and five women found Ebsary guilty as charged after a three-and-a-half-hour deliberation. On November 24, 1983, Mr. Justice R. McLeod Rogers sentenced Ebsary to five years in prison, observing that the old man had exhibited no remorse for a killing that had been executed in a "very rational and cold-blooded manner", and for which another man had wrongfully spent eleven years in prison. In his charge to the jury, Mr. Justice Rogers referred to Jim Carroll's taped interview with Ebsary as a "damaging document". The RCMP, who had been unhappy with the Crown prosecutor's handling of the first Ebsary trial, offered a different review of the second proceedings. "It should be noted Prosecutor Edwards presented this case in a most professional manner," Jim Carroll wrote in a report of the trial.

The manslaughter conviction was appealed. Ten months later

the Appeals Division of the Nova Scotia Supreme Court ruled that Mr. Justice Rogers had erred in his instructions to the jury. A new trial was ordered.

At Roy Ebsary's third manslaughter trial, Crown prosecutor Frank Edwards introduced into evidence both the taped confession obtained by Jim Carroll and the fibres evidence discovered by Harry Wheaton. On January 17, 1985, the jury of seven women and five men found Ebsary guilty as charged.

On the front page of the *Micmac News,* Roy Gould recorded the euphoric, if bitter, reaction of the Marshall family. "We knew that someday, someone else would be convicted. . . . They should lock him up, just like they did to my son. I'm very happy with this decision," the Grand Chief of the Micmac Nation said, a sentiment echoed by Junior's mother. "They think it's a joke what my son has gone through. . . taking eleven years of his life. The truth came out, and that's all I'm concerned about."

Two weeks later, Mr. Justice Merlin Nunn sentenced Roy Ebsary to three years in prison, observing that he hoped the passing of sentence was "the final chapter" in the now fourteen-year-old case.

It was not. Roy Ebsary's lawyers launched an appeal seeking a fourth trial. Nearly six months later, the Nova Scotia Supreme Court upheld Ebsary's manslaughter conviction but reduced this sentence to one year in county jail. The decision has been appealed to the Supreme Court of Canada.

23/Squeeze Play

Coincident with the trials and tribulations of Roy Ebsary, Junior Marshall's compensation case was entering the gears of the system under the direction of Felix Cacchione. It was Cacchione's first case in private practice after an 8½-year stint as a legal-aid lawyer.

The 33-year-old former Montrealer accepted the file knowing that it had driven Junior's previous lawyer, Stephen Aronson, out of the profession. Cacchione had gone through Dalhousie Law School with Aronson, and his friend's decision to close his practice over the celebrated case made him all the more determined to see it through, even though he was well aware that compassion for his client was not proving to be the guiding principle of the provincial government. But Cacchione, who grew up in Montreal's tough East End, wasn't afraid of a fight, especially when he thought the odds were stacked against his client. From his experience with other native files, the dapper Italian-Canadian knew exactly what Junior was up against. "Here's this kid who's really got shafted, and I had the same feelings that I'd had when I represented other native people, and that was that not only are they behind the eight ball because of their legal predicament, but they're behind the eight ball because of their native status."

Days after Junior's acquittal and the laying of the second-degree-murder charge against Roy Ebsary in May 1983, Cacchione wrote Nova Scotia attorney general Harry How asking for a meeting. He wanted to discuss the two outstanding issues that flowed from the recent appeal court ruling: a public inquiry into the circumstances of his client's wrongful conviction in 1971, and compensation. It would be four months before Harry How answered any of Cacchione's letters and two more before the government agreed to discuss the issues face to face.

The November 1983 meeting was called by Ronald Giffin, who became attorney general after Harry How was appointed to the bench as one of the key elements of a provincial cabinet shuffle by Nova Scotia premier John Buchanan. Giffin set stringent conditions on the meeting: it was to be totally secret and there were to be no reporters waiting outside the door to ask questions when it was over.

The minister showed up with his deputy, Gordon Coles, and Cacchione brought along his law partner, Michael Lambert. The level of trust between the two sides was not high and would all but disappear over the coming months. Cacchione bluntly stated his client's desire for a full public inquiry into the circumstances of his false conviction. "We just said that the primary concern was an inquiry. That it should address the issue of his conviction, the police investigation, and compensation be viewed in light of that. It was our feeling that you couldn't assess the damages in a vacuum. If you didn't look at all the circumstances, in effect that's what you'd be doing. The one comment that Giffin made was that he didn't want the public inquiry to be used as a discovery process against the police officers in terms of us using the inquiry, gaining information from that, to bolster a civil action against the police."

Gordon Coles said he would look into Mr. Cacchione's concerns. Unknown to the young lawyer, the Attorney General's Department had already begun documenting possible abuses by the Sydney police in the Marshall affair many months before—within days, in fact, of Junior's acquittal. On May 13, 1983, a letter was sent from the Attorney General's Department to the Commanding Officer of "H" Division of the RCMP. It contained a number of startling points, including the possibility of new charges against Junior Marshall.

Re: Donald Marshall, Jr.

As you are aware the Appeal Division has allowed Mr. Marshall's appeal and directed that a verdict of acquittal be entered. In view of this, we have instructed the Prosecutor, Frank Edwards, to proceed with the laying of a charge of second degree murder against Roy Newman Ebsary. The police function in the charge against Mr. Ebsary will be the responsibility of your force as the Attorney General's directive turning the case over to your force remains in effect.

We have requested that Mr. Edwards review the evidence and advise us as to what evidence exists in regard to charges against Mr. Marshall and any others involved in this case.

There remains the question as to whether there should be any inquiry into the handling of the original investigation and the prosecution of it. Accordingly, I request that you have your files reviewed to determine whether there are, in your opinion, any instances of improper police practices or procedures in regard to the investigation by the Sydney Police Department. In doing this I would ask that you point out what they are and what would have been a proper police practice or procedure. The purpose of this is to use it as background material to enable us to advise the Attorney General and come to a conclusion as to whether or not the matter warrants any type of inquiry into the actions of the Sydney Police Department in regard to the case or in regard to the actions of the prosecutor.

> Gordon S. Gale
> Director/Criminal

The irony was staggering. The Attorney General's Department was clearly grappling with the issue of possible misconduct by the Sydney police and the Crown prosecutor in the Marshall case three days after five judges of the Nova Scotia Supreme Court grandiloquently pronounced there had been no miscarriage of justice in the original handling of the case!

In fact, the RCMP had approached Crown prosecutor Frank Edwards in May 1982 about interviewing Chief John MacIntyre and Inspector William Urquhart over the allegations that witnesses at Marshall's 1971 trial had been "induced to fabricate evidence" by the two policemen. The investigators were called off. "Mr. Edwards has advised me that he further discussed the matter with Mr. Gordon Gale of the Attorney General's Department, and it was felt that these interviews should be held in abeyance for the present. This file will be held open pending further instructions as well as new areas of investigation which may come to light," Harry

Wheaton wrote in a report to his commanding officer, Donald Scott.

But now that the main items on the legal agenda had been cleared away with Marshall's acquittal and Ebsary's murder charge, it was up to the Attorney General's Department to direct the RCMP to pursue possible wrongdoing by the Sydney police. In seeking an opinion about whether there were any grounds for an inquiry into the original handling of the Marshall case, Gordon Gale specifically requested that the RCMP review its files rather than investigate. Since Mr. Gale had already instructed Frank Edwards to tell the RCMP not to interview the two Sydney detectives in 1982, his meaning was clear: MacIntyre and Urquhart were not to be interviewed as part of the RCMP's look at the quality of the original police investigation of the Sandy Seale murder case. It was a nuance that Superintendent Douglas Christen, the officer in charge of the Criminal Investigation Branch, didn't miss when he passed along Gale's request to the Sydney Sub-Division of the RCMP. Christen wrote: "It may certainly be difficult to define what is improper police procedure; therefore, the reviewer may wish to comment on the manner in which a certain procedure was done, as compared to the manner or investigative procedure he personally would have followed. We do not expect any investigation to be undertaken, but restrict our examination to all material on hand."

The letter, dated May 19, 1983, was forwarded together with the correspondence from the Attorney General's Department to the non-commissioned officer in charge of Internal Investigation, Staff Sergeant Harry Wheaton. Just over a week later, the investigator whose work, along with Jim Carroll's, had won Junior Marshall's freedom and built a solid case against Roy Ebsary reported back to the Officer in Command of the Criminal Investigation Branch.

Stonewalling by the Attorney General's Department wasn't the only problem Felix Cacchione had to worry about as he tried to carry out Junior Marshall's instructions to seek an inquiry into his false conviction. Throughout the summer and autumn of 1983 the lawyer had observed a steady disintegration of his client's mental state. Each time Roy Ebsary went to court, Junior Marshall also had to appear. Although Junior was ostensibly called as a witness, Cacchione became convinced that the Crown was in fact putting

him on trial for the alleged attempted robbery that led to Sandy
Seale's death.

"I could see cracks in the foundation after I went back to Sydney
with Junior for Ebsary's second trial, where, when Junior finished
testifying, he just came off the stand and was in a rage because in
fact what they had done is make him the accused in the matter.
They were there to blacken him and to make sure that any avenues
of sympathy would be cut out," Cacchione remembered.

With his client's psychological and financial resources all but
depleted, Cacchione renewed his efforts to work out a negotiated
settlement with the Attorney General's Department on the compensation issue. On January 21, 1984, he dropped the lawsuit
initiated by Stephen Aronson against the City of Sydney, Chief John
MacIntyre, and Inspector William Urquhart, having been told by
the Attorney General that the action was an impediment to any
inquiry. He was then told that as long as Roy Ebsary was still before
the courts, there would be no decision on either compensation or
an inquiry into Marshall's original conviction.

The obvious stalling by the provincial government sparked a
scathing outcry in the press, which had now been following the
Marshall story for two years. As the *Globe and Mail* editorialized on
February 16, 1984:

> The Nova Scotia government has said it is reviewing Donald
> Marshall's claim for compensation. It now has one less reason
> to dawdle. Mr. Marshall has decided not to pursue a lawsuit
> against the City of Sydney, Nova Scotia, its police chief and a
> retired police inspector. . . .
>
> Federal Justice Minister Mark MacGuigan says Ottawa won't
> pay a cent, because Mr. Marshall was prosecuted under provin-
> cial jurisdiction. Nova Scotia premier John Buchanan said last
> month that any decision on compensation would have to wait
> until the end of Mr. Marshall's civil suit against Sydney and the
> appeal of Mr. Ebsary's conviction.
>
> But the Ebsary appeal has no bearing on the treatment Nova
> Scotia should give Mr. Marshall. Now that the Sydney case has
> been dropped, Mr. Buchanan's Government has no excuse not
> to compensate Mr. Marshall for his legal costs and, beyond
> that, for the effects of a prosecution which fingered the wrong
> man and rounded up the evidence to convict him. The man

has been left waiting too long for justice.

The mounting indignation across the country extended far beyond the editorial pages of newspapers, as hundreds of individual citizens wrote to the government to register their shock at how the province of Nova Scotia was treating a man who had been wrongfully imprisoned for his entire adult life. Felix Cacchione was buoyed by the tide of media and public support Junior was receiving, but he held out no great hopes for a dramatic policy reversal by the government. Concluding that he would probably have to go to court to win compensation, Cacchione began building his case. He commissioned an actuary's report that estimated Junior's lost income for the years he'd spent in prison at $330,000. Although there were no Canadian precedents for the kind of wrongful imprisonment Junior had suffered, Cacchione compiled a list of similar cases from around the world, noting the settlements involved. The most applicable one was the case of New Zealander Arthur Alan Thomas, who had been falsely imprisoned for twelve years for the so-called "Crewe Murders", a double homicide in Auckland. After his innocence was established, Thomas was awarded $1.2 million New Zealand and his father also received "hurt money" from the government.

Doubting that the government would ever order a public inquiry, which he believed would prove the Sydney police had played a part in his client's wrongful conviction, Cacchione applied to the Attorney General's Department to see their current file on Marshall. Permission was denied by Deputy Attorney General Gordon Coles under the provincial Freedom of Information Act.

Although Felix Cacchione didn't know it, he was now in a position very similar to the one Moe Rosenblum had been in immediately after Marshall's conviction in 1971. At that time, Rosenblum had been preparing the appeal, completely ignorant of the fact that Jimmy MacNeil had come forward ten days after the trial to say that Roy Ebsary had actually committed the crime. That information and more was contained in the 1971 RCMP reinvestigation of the case, which the Attorney General's Department had in its possession but failed to share with the defence counsel.

The decision by Gordon Coles not to yield the Attorney General's file on Junior Marshall to his current lawyer likewise deprived Cacchione of information that had a direct bearing on his client's ability to wage his compensation case. On May 30, 1983, Harry Wheaton had submitted his review of the original Sydney police investigation into the murder of Sandy Seale. He first addressed the question of the three witnesses who claimed they were pressured into making false statements by the Sydney police.

> Maynard Chant was picked up by the two police officers [Detectives MacIntyre and MacDonald] and driven to the Sydney City Police offices and a statement was obtained between 5:15 p.m. and 5:35 p.m. and he was released. While there is no doubt in my mind that Mrs. Chant would readily give the police permission to interview her son, it would not be our policy, nor good police practise, to interview a juvenile alone who was a possible key witness to this crime.
>
> Detective MacDonald in his statement advises the Chief spoke to him briefly outside the police car, nothing was said between Catalone and Sydney and then he was interviewed by the Chief alone without Detective MacDonald present. Chant, for his part, says he feared the police officer.

Wheaton then turned his attention to the second statement Maynard Chant had given police incriminating Marshall in the murder of Sandy Seale.

> Chief MacIntyre claimed that besides himself five people were present during the taking of the statement – Det. Urquhart, Chief Wayne McGee, Chant's probation officer Lawrence Burke, Chant's mother, and Chant himself. But while that's how the three policemen present remembered the event, the other participants disagreed.
>
> Probation Officer Burke, for his part, recalls the incident and states he was not present during the interview but had conversation relative to it. Judge Edwards, who was sitting in the same building, recalled the incident the same as Mr. Burke. Mrs. Chant recalls being picked up by Chief McGee and being taken to the Town Hall. At the Town Hall she recalls talking with all the aforementioned and telling her son to tell the truth. He was then taken into a room and interviewed by the Chief and Detective Urquhart. Maynard Chant remembers the interview the same as his mother. In the room he recalls

being told by Chief MacIntyre that he saw Donald Marshall stab Sandy Seale. Chief MacIntyre told him that he was seen in the park by another person and had to see the murder. He further advises that he threatened him with revocation of his probation for theft of milk bottle money. Faced with this situation and being entirely alone, as his mother had told him to co-operate fully with the police, he answered the questions with the answers as given to him by Chief MacIntyre....I would submit for your consideration that it is highly suspect that all these persons were present. Once again, the presence of the parent or guardian would be required by our policy and the procedures used appear very questionable. In regards to his giving false evidence on the stand, Chant advised that he could not bring himself to do so at the Supreme Court trial. A check of the transcripts found this to be true and Chant was declared a hostile witness. He ultimately agreed with the evidence as given in the Preliminary. I feel the Chief and the Crown Prosecutor had to know the credibility of this witness was shaky in the extreme during the trial in 1971 in view of the three conflicting statements and his manner of giving evidence. Chant for his part feels that he was set up and orchestrated into being an eyewitness by Chief MacIntyre. He has told me he knows he did wrong and is willing to accept any punishment that is meted out in this regard.

Wheaton then moved on to the second eyewitness whose perjured testimony sent Junior Marshall to prison for life, John Pratico. He began with a recitation of an interview with Pratico's mother, Margaret.

She advised he has been receiving mental help since childhood and asked us not to speak to him as his personality can swing from the calm to rage very easily. To the best of Mrs. Pratico's knowledge, John was handled almost exclusively by Chief John MacIntyre and she stated that he was extremely upset after the Preliminary Hearing and had to be taken to the N.S. Hospital, Dartmouth, N.S. When asked if he told lies, she advised he lives in a sort of fantasy world....In conclusion and addressing the question of proper police practises, I do not think it proper to have used a mentally unbalanced witness

who had to be taken to a mental institution between Preliminary and Supreme and who at Supreme Court approached the
Defence and told them he was lying.

Finally, Wheaton considered the treatment the Sydney police
had given their third key witness, Patricia Harriss.

In reviewing the Sydney City Police file after the order had
been made by the Attorney General that they turn over all
documentation, I found a partially completed statement dated
17th June, 1971–8:15 p.m. In this statement she states that
Marshall was with two other men, one of whom was short with
a long coat and gray or white hair. This statement was stopped
shortly thereafter. It might be pointed out that this would
conflict with the final draft of the Pratico and Chant statements
which place Marshall and Seale alone on Crescent Street.

The next statement appears at 1:20 a.m. on the morning of
the 18th of June and only Marshall and Seale are on Crescent
Street. No mention is made of the man who would fit Ebsary's
description. Miss Harriss, in her 1982 statement, advises that in
fact the police took three statements from her. She states that
between the taking of the first statement until she told them
what they wanted to hear, a period of a minimum of five hours,
they scared the devil out of her. Her mother waited outside the
room and at one point when she began crying, they let her
speak to her and gave her coffee. She describes the interrogation as the police going over and over what they thought she
should see, banging the table with their fist. She recalls feeling
she was obliged to give evidence as per the last statement or
she would be in trouble. Again, in regards to proper police
practice, I feel the police felt they had a rather mature fifteen
year old on their hands; however, be that as it may, if Miss
Harriss' story is accepted and there is documentation in the
form of two statements as well as my interview with her
mother, then this is certainly not proper police practice and
using her as a witness is unethical.

Summing up, Wheaton suggested there was a great deal of
pressure on John MacIntyre to solve the crime, pressure from his
Chief of the day, the black community, and the public in general.

Faced with the foregoing and the witnesses at hand, Chief

MacIntyre chose to believe the statements he wanted to believe and told the witnesses they were telling the truth and they agreed with him....This case was investigated solely by Chief MacIntyre with some help from Detective Urquhart and basically solved in one day, the 4th of June, 1971, when statements were taken from Pratico and Chant and the charge then laid and warrant issued. I found Chief MacIntyre to be adamant that Marshall is and was guilty and still refuses to look on the matter in balance. I would submit for your consideration that if a police officer in his drive to solve a crime refuses to look at all sides of an investigation and consider all ramifications, then he ultimately fails in his duty.

Harry Wheaton's report, prepared at the behest of the Attorney General's Department to shed light on the issue of police influence on the course of justice in 1971, was never made public. The compensation negotiations between the government of Nova Scotia and Felix Cacchione would be completed without Marshall's lawyer ever seeing the document that had such a crucial bearing on his client's interests.

In the early months of 1984 public pressure to compensate Junior Marshall grew by leaps and bounds; the Nova Scotia government's compassion did not. Attorney General Ronald Giffin instructed his beleaguered staff not to accept calls on the controversial case. But it was too late for official silence. Junior Marshall had become a national symbol of failed justice that was beginning to besmirch the images of two governments. In Ottawa, the Conservative Opposition hammered the Liberals for their backroom haggling with Nova Scotia over who should pay Junior Marshall's compensation. "I have no hesitation at all [in saying] that if this Donald Marshall had been white with a family behind him, I don't know if the miscarriage of justice would have happened, but if it had happened, it would have been resolved before now," Tory member of Parliament Pat Nowlan told the Canadian Press in February.

When Solicitor General Robert Kaplan tried to tell an outraged House of Commons that compensation couldn't be paid because an important aspect of the case was still before the Nova Scotia courts (Roy Ebsary's pending appeal), he was shouted down by Newfoundland MP John Crosbie, who roared back what was on everyone's mind. "He has been in jail for eleven years. Never mind the court."

In Nova Scotia, Premier Buchanan's Tories were facing more disturbing charges. On February 24, a shrill editorial in the *Halifax Daily News* openly accused the government of a cover-up.

> It's time the spotlight was turned up brighter on the Nova Scotia officials who are covering up in the Marshall case.
>
> Why has Marshall's lawyer Felix Cacchione twice been denied access to Marshall's file?
>
> Why is the provincial government putting up a phony excuse about not compensating Marshall yet because it would affect the Roy Ebsary appeal of his murder conviction?
>
> What the hell has that got to do with it?
>
> More important, why doesn't the government have the guts to admit there was a miscarriage of justice, deliberate or not?
>
> The handling of the Marshall case has been clumsy at best, not to mention racist and deceptive. It has a bad odor and the longer the delay in giving this man his due compensation the worse it will get. . . .

As the country grew weary of waiting for its politicians to make amends, hundreds of letters to Junior began arriving at Felix Cacchione's law office. People like Ed Mallon of Deep River, Ontario, simply wanted to reach out to a fellow human being whose suffering had touched them deeply.

> Dear Donald:
>
> You don't need to answer this letter. I'd prefer it if you didn't bother. I just want to say how glad I am that your innocence has been established, and that you're a free man today. Millions of Canadians like myself will be following your future career and wishing you well. . .I hope you get *big* compensation for those lost years. Enclosed are a few dollars to help with your legal expenses.
>
> All the best to you and your dear parents.
>
> Ed Mallon

The most organized impatience with the way Nova Scotia was handling the Marshall case came on February 14, when a fifty-year-old United Church minister, Robert Hussey, established a trust fund for Junior Marshall. Reverend Hussey knew better than most what the young Micmac had been through: three of his twenty-five years as a minister had been spent as chaplain in a Quebec prison. In the first week of his campaign, Reverend Hussey and his four associates – Ian Soutar, an investment analyst, Clifford Powell, retired president of Schweppes-Cadbury Ltd., Brian Powell, a teacher, and lawyer Derek Hanson – raised three thousand dollars. Eighty per cent of the money was donated in Quebec, some of it by welfare recipients and pensioners. Before he was finished, Reverend Hussey would raise more than forty-five thousand dollars for Junior Marshall.

Inspired by Reverend Hussey's example, the Committee of Concerned Nova Scotians for Justice sprang up in Halifax. The group wanted John Buchanan to hold a public inquiry into the circumstances surrounding Junior Marshall's wrongful imprisonment, as they constantly reminded the Nova Scotia premier in a series of open letters published in local newspapers. One of the letters ended: "...Why do we need such an inquiry? Because by knowing at last what really happened to Donald Marshall and why, we can try to stop it from ever happening again."

Prisoners' Rights Groups, the Federation of Labour, the Union of Nova Scotia Indians, the Moderator of the United Church, the Dalhousie Law Students Society and a string of federal members of Parliament and senators joined in the demand that Junior Marshall be dealt with swiftly and fairly.

The Nova Scotia government was slipping dangerously out of touch with the mood of the country. On February 28, 1984, the first working day of the Nova Scotia legislature's winter session, the political Opposition lambasted the Buchanan government over its handling of the Marshall case. All three Opposition parties demanded that the Attorney General launch an inquiry into the affair and compensate Marshall for his wrongful imprisonment. Although Ronald Giffin stubbornly held to the position that he would not consider compensation or an appeal until Roy Ebsary's case passed through the courts, it was clear the government's resolve was weakening.

The last straw came on March 2, when federal Justice minister Mark MacGuigan said that the Government of Nova Scotia was pettifogging in its stated reasons for withholding compensation.

Speaking to law students at Dalhousie University, Mr. MacGuigan said it plainly: "Compensation doesn't need to await the completion of the Ebsary appeal." MacGuigan would later explain to a reporter that he at one point threatened Nova Scotia with a unilateral federal inquiry into the *cause célèbre* if the province didn't take strong remedial action–even though his own advisers doubted the constitutionality of such an inquiry. He also said that Nova Scotia had privately proposed a joint federal-provincial inquiry into the circumstances surrounding Junior Marshall's wrongful conviction–providing that Ottawa agreed to pay the young Micmac's compensation. But senior officials in the federal Department of Justice feared setting a precedent that might force Ottawa to pick up the tab for mistakes made by the provinces in the administration of criminal justice, and the offer was declined.

On March 5, 1984, the Nova Scotia government finally bowed to public pressure and appointed a one-man commission to look into the compensation issue. But before the first cheer for this apparent change of heart was raised, the shabbiness of the announcement became obvious. Prince Edward Island Supreme Court Justice Alex Campbell would be considering the question of compensation and legal costs *without* reference to the events surrounding Junior Marshall's wrongful conviction in 1971. In addition, the government would not be bound by Mr. Justice Campbell's findings, nor would they necessarily be made public.

In other words, either Junior Marshall made a backroom deal with the Attorney General's Department or compensation would be determined by an inquiry which had no powers to delve into the central question at issue: how had the travesty of justice ever occurred in the first place? The squeeze play was on.

If there was any doubt about that, Felix Cacchione's two subsequent meetings with representatives of the Attorney General's Department over the compensation issue removed it. "These meetings were just incredible, they really were, you know. It was, 'Listen, we're going to have the inquiry and no matter how long it takes, who knows what the result's going to be. You may get an award of $5 million, but we don't have to accept it. Nor do we have to make it public. Or you may get an award of $100,000 with him bearing his costs.' So at that point it was fairly obvious to us that there was no way around it; we either had to settle for the best possible figure for Junior or just go with it [the inquiry], and Junior was in no shape to do that," Cacchione recalled.

On April 3, 1984, Mr. Justice Campbell persuaded the Buchanan government to make an interim payment of $25,000 to Marshall while he studied the compensation issue. By a unanimous resolution of the provincial legislature, the federal government was asked not to tax the payment; Ottawa agreed.

But neither Reverend Hussey's group nor the Halifax-based Nova Scotians for Justice would disband. Dr. John Godfrey of the Committee of Concerned Nova Scotians for Justice still wanted an inquiry, and, as Reverend Hussey put it, "We're not convinced the Nova Scotia government desires to grant any compensation."

The negotiations between Felix Cacchione and the Attorney General began with an offer of $100,000, out of which Junior was required to pay his own legal costs. Considering that the benefactor of such an arrangement already owed $80,000 in legal fees to Stephen Aronson and had not yet had a bill from Cacchione, who had worked on the case for over a year, the offer was not overly generous. Disgusted by the arrogance of the power arrayed against him, Cacchione demanded $550,000.

By August 1984, the final amount was arrived at over the telephone. The Attorney General's last offer was $270,000, with Junior Marshall bearing his own legal costs. He grimaced when the figure was presented to him in Felix Cacchione's law office; it was, after all, a blunt valuation of eleven years of his life. And there were strings attached. Before he received a penny of the ex gratia award (a payment made without any admission of wrongdoing), Marshall had to sign a release waiving any rights he might have to sue the Attorney General's Department. Even though he had been subsisting on part-time jobs and wanted desperately to put some money in his parents' hands, he couldn't bring himself to agree with the deal.

Days passed and Felix Cacchione patiently waited for his client to make up his mind. Finally, the pressure from the Attorney General's Department became too great and he had to have an answer. He contacted Junior and the two met in Cacchione's law office. " 'Yeah,' he says, 'I'll go,' "Cacchione recalled of the conversation. " 'I want to give some money to my folks because they spent a lot of money visiting me in the joint.' "

Cacchione handed him the releases. Junior took them and left with a blank expression on his face.

Two weeks later, Cacchione was still waiting to hear from his client. At 10:30 p.m. on September 12, the day before Junior's birthday, Cacchione called him at the small apartment he shared with Karen Brown. Sensing that there was something wrong, he drove over.

"I saw a man who was broken, a man who was crying, a man who had nothing left inside but rage. I talked to him about the releases that night and he said, 'No, I don't give a shit, I don't want to sign them.' I said, 'That's fine, we'll go with the inquiry, I'll just tell them tomorrow but I'll check with you before I make the call.'"

When Cacchione called the next day, Junior said he wanted to talk about it again. The two men met in Point Pleasant Park and Junior told him the reason he'd been so upset the night before. He was driving back from Bridgewater when he heard on the radio that Roy Ebsary had been granted a new trial by the Appeal Division of the Nova Scotia Supreme Court. He knew he would have to testify yet again. When he got back to Halifax, he went to a bar, where his girlfriend later found him having a drink with another woman. There had been a scene. But the broken man of the previous night seemed better now.

"He appeared rational, talked to me, understood what I was saying, and it was just put to him, 'Listen, Junior, if you want to take it, sign the papers; if you don't want to take it, just tell me, and I'm off, and I'll tell them we'll go ahead with the commission.' He said no and signed the document."

When Felix Cacchione came home from work that night around 5:30 p.m. he lay down for a much-needed rest. He'd been up all the previous night with his client and the emotional strain of the case was beginning to take its toll. He still couldn't believe what a judge, whose assistance he'd sought on a matter to do with the case, had told him. "Felix, don't get your balls caught in a vice over an Indian."

He had just drifted off to sleep when the doorbell rang. It was Karen Brown. Junior had been drinking and he'd just been arrested for assaulting a police officer. Karen hadn't come home for his birthday and Junior had gone looking for her. The couple had been having an argument on the street by her parked car when three policemen showed up. One of the officers put his hand on Junior's shoulder and told him he would have to come to the station for being drunk in a public place. Junior hit him, knocking him over the hood of the car, before he was subdued by the other two officers.

Cacchione called Jack Stewart and the two rushed to the jail to bail out his client. "He was crying, he was just a basket case," the lawyer recalled. The policeman, John Keylor, was very understanding when he was advised of Junior's situation. If Junior would sign a release saying he wouldn't prosecute the police officer for wrongful incarceration, Keylor wouldn't press charges on the assault. Junior quickly agreed.

After his release from jail, Junior went to the Carlton Centre. On the night he should have been celebrating the end of a nightmare from which he'd been trying to awaken for thirteen years, he was back with the only people who seemed to understand what he'd been through. He watched a Canada-Russia hockey game with Jack Stewart and Felix Cacchione and then went to bed.

Cacchione got home at 3:30 that morning but couldn't sleep. He wandered down to the Halifax Commons, where some of the faithful were already camped, eagerly awaiting the Papal Mass that would be celebrated later that day. How lovely it would be, the young lawyer thought, to feel what they're feeling. But he had been inhabiting a very different universe for the past several months and their joy seemed foreign to him. He walked back to his office and at five o'clock in the morning dictated Constable Keylor's release.

Epilogue

The clearest entry on the otherwise untidy balance sheet of the Donald Marshall affair was the cold arithmetic of restitution. All told, he received $315,000 for his eleven years in prison – $270,000 from the government of Nova Scotia and another $45,000 from the trust fund established for him by the Reverend Robert Hussey. After paying his lawyers (both reduced their bills because of the modest size of his final award), he was left with $215,000 to start life afresh.

Slow to accept this stark assessment of his worth or the fact that there would now be no inquiry, Marshall let six weeks go by before he picked up his cheque from Felix Cacchione. The young lawyer was just as uneasy about the settlement, though for different reasons. "This thing was going on in the back of my mind, have I sold him down the river, you know, did I just sort of dispose of this?" Cacchione agonized. "It really left me with a very empty feeling, but I know that Junior couldn't have done any better because of the forces that were at play."

Marshall's settlement was also a far cry from what one very prominent Canadian had earlier said he would like to see done in the unprecedented case. "If I were prime minister, I would give Donny Marshall a cheque for $1,000,000 and I wouldn't care if he spent it all suing the system, because we owe it to him. When you see the young man, you tell him that and give him my best wishes."

These sentiments once belonged to Brian Mulroney. He passed them along to the author during an informal chat in his room at the Heather Motel outside Stellarton during the Nova Scotia by-election that sent the Conservative leader to Parliament as the member for Central Nova in the summer of 1984. Later that same year, after Mr. Mulroney was elected prime minister, his government's contribution to Donald Marshall's cause was something less than the campaigning politician had envisaged.

The federal government declined to pay Marshall's legal bills, which had been run up in the costly struggle to prove his own innocence. Instead, federal justice minister John Crosbie reimbursed Nova Scotia for half of the $270,000 ex gratia payment made to Marshall. To Felix Cacchione, it was a pitiful contribution, both to his long-suffering client and to Canadian jurisprudence. "Here we had a chance in this country to make some new law with respect to the rights of the accused and people who are wrongfully imprisoned and what do we get? A cost-sharing agreement between two levels of government after the system has ruined a major part of someone's life. I was disgusted."

Former Sydney chief of police John MacIntyre returned to selling cars after he retired from the police force in 1984. He sued the Canadian Broadcasting Corporation for a November 27, 1983, radio broadcast which he felt unfairly linked him to the chain of events that ended in the innocent teenager's being sent to prison for life, but on the day the trial was set to begin MacIntyre withdrew his action before a single witness gave evidence. Once more the public was cheated of an opportunity to know the facts of the Donald Marshall case, renewing demand for a full public inquiry.

But many of the people who had lived through the event were already well beyond the salves and solace such an official investigation might have provided. The two families who had lost the most over the years remained pitifully divided, prisoners of a grief so fiercely partisan that it left them paralysed before each other's suffering. Passionately wed to a version of events that made his long-dead son a hero, Oscar Seale rejected the verdicts of two juries that convicted Roy Ebsary of Sandy's murder. The inescapable corollary to that position was open scorn for the justice system that had put Donald Marshall back on the street.

Faced with this unrelenting belief in Junior's guilt, the Marshalls defiantly reminded their community of what his long years of imprisonment had meant. "They will never know what it's like to lose a son the way we did. I felt their eyes on the other members of my family for eleven years. But we believed in Junior then, and now the rest of the world knows he never killed anyone. Now we can walk with our heads up, no matter what Oscar Seale thinks," Donald Marshall, Sr., triumphantly declared.

As for Maynard Chant and John Pratico, the self-admitted perjurors won less than universal applause for their courageous, if tragically belated, attempt to set the record straight in the Seale murder case. Pratico attributed part of his ongoing mental problems to the guilt he carried for so many years for helping to convict an innocent man with lies he swears he was pressured into telling. "It has played on my mind. That's caused half my trouble," he would later say.

Maynard Chant stood toe to toe with different demons. "You know, like, I suffered. You know, I've had people come up to me right out of the blue and say, 'Who do you think you are, doing a thing like that to this young man?' I would say, 'I could try to tell you about it, if you want, if you want to listen.'" Many people did not.

Jimmy MacNeil, who in 1971 and again in 1982 told authorities that Roy Ebsary, not Junior Marshall, stabbed Sandy Seale, still lives in the small white house in Whitney Pier, seeking that full-time job he has never found. He wanly commented on the case in which he figured so prominently, "Just by being around this thing, people think I'm some kind of freak, for cripes' sake. I didn't do nothin' that night. All I ever did was try to tell the truth. It has stained my life."

For the two men whose daily routine is spun from those events, sometimes tawdry, sometimes remarkable, that draw people into the slowly grinding gears of the justice system, the Marshall investigation stood apart. It was a case that transcended police work to rest on a higher plane; it had, in a way, become a parable of crime and punishment. Harry Wheaton, who returned to senior uniformed duty with the RCMP after the celebrated investigation, retained uncomfortable memories of the cavalier response of the Nova Scotia justice system: "The Attorney General of Nova Scotia came to our annual officers' mess dinner and said that he didn't understand why the press was making all the fuss over the Marshall case. I had to be restrained from leaving the room in the middle of his speech. The man simply didn't realize the suffering and heartache involved in this thing, nor the immense social issues that are still at play. I just couldn't stomach the trivializing of a case that changed so many people's lives and my whole outlook as a policeman."

His partner, the slow-talking Jim Carroll, was promoted to sergeant shortly after the Marshall investigation. He still found himself reflecting on the case years after the young Micmac's acquittal. "There was a weakness in the system there somewhere along the line. This should never have happened. . . . I would like to think that what happened in '71 wouldn't happen now or couldn't happen. But overall, my outlook on life and human nature doesn't change that much. Nothing amazes me any more."

In the last, desperate days of spring 1982, inmate 1997 dreamed of how freedom would feel. He savored the prospect of bringing his case before a society which had been deaf to his protestations of innocence for more than a decade but which at last seemed ready to listen. In that imagined new existence, as vivid as the prison movies that once were Junior's only links to the life he had lost, Sandy Seale's real killer would bear the blame for his crime. Society would apologize to the Micmac inmate for the theft of his youth, and his rehabilitation would race, frame by brilliant frame, toward a happy ending: reunion with the people who had stuck by him for so many years and the exhilaration of starting over.

It was not to be. When the court finally set him free, it was not because he was pronounced innocent of murder, as he had once been found guilty: rather, it was because the evidence no longer supported his conviction – a pinched legalism that exorcised no ghosts. Far from getting an apology, Marshall found himself being blamed for the course that justice had taken in 1971. Roy Ebsary, the man who admitted to having stabbed Sandy Seale, was still walking the streets of Sydney in 1986 while the Nova Scotia Supreme Court Appeal Division dallied over whether he should be granted a fourth trial. For Marshall, one courtroom seemed to lead inexorably to another, if not as the accused, then as a witness under fire for an offence with which he had never been charged.

In the years following his acquittal, the events of 1971 cast a long shadow over the life of Junior Marshall. His love affair with Karen Brown fell victim to profound cultural differences and the intolerable pressures of endless court appearances. Life on Membertou became impossible; he found it difficult even to visit. Prior to his acquittal, there were endless questions about his ordeal from his former friends. Their empathy was swamped by a curiosity that was oblivious to Marshall's slow-healing wounds. After his compensation settlement, Junior would be inundated by offers to invest in a variety of business ventures whose essential rationale seemed to be the size of his new bank account. Although he shunned the business proposals, he often gave money to those who needed it, including a mortally sick Indian child who needed money to go to Lourdes in search of a miracle.

Uneasy on the reserve and out of place off it, Junior stayed on in Halifax, becoming a celebrated habitué of two or three bars. Fearing that he was losing himself in this alien environment, he at first agreed to check in to a detoxification centre on the advice of friends like Felix Cacchione and Jack Stewart, but quickly changed his mind. Instead, he bought a house outside the city but rarely stayed there. Finally, without ever moving in, he instructed Felix Cacchione to rent it. He had been seeing a psychologist, but his sense of well-being vanished the moment the sessions were over. The people he felt most comfortable with were former inmates of Dorchester or Springhill who knew enough about life inside to sense what the long-time inmate might be going through.

Institutional personnel who were following his case discerned a pattern they feared would lead straight back to prison. They were not surprised when Marshall was arrested for assaulting a police officer, or when he later lost his licence for impaired driving. As one officer of the court put it, "The system that screwed up, and now appears to have died of fatigue in the Seale murder case, has treated Marshall like a convicted killer for his entire adult life. Is it really so strange that the guy is having such trouble getting it together on the outside?"

A soft wind off the river carried the murmuring of voices from below. The failing sun flushed Wentworth Park in a sudden pumpkin-hued light—a dazzling protest against the gathering autumn dusk. From where Junior Marshall and I were sitting on a leaf-strewn, grassy knoll overlooking the band shell, we could see a dozen or so boys from Membertou, loosely grouped at the bottom of the path leading into the park from George Street. They were passing a bottle around and every so often two or three of them broke away from the group to grapple or shadow-box, their sham ferocity betrayed by the youthful laughter that quickly followed.

More than once while I was working on this book, I had asked Junior to come to the park and walk me through the events of 1971; he would not. But this night, with his court case concluded and my own work long since done, he suddenly asked me to stop the car on Crescent Street so he could show me "where it happened". I wondered if I was about to learn what nobody had ever really found out – how this quiet man had come to terms with the past.

In that soft voice, barely above a whisper, that I had grown to know so well, he explained where he had met Sandy on that spring night so long ago. He pointed out the foot-bridge where they had talked and then the spot where the two boys had spoken with Roy Ebsary and Jimmy MacNeil before the stabbings. Afterwards, he gazed for a long time at the Indian boys below us, then turned to me and said, "You know, when Sandy died, a big part of me went with him."

I waited in the gloom but there were no more words. There was a moment when the silence of the northern night, tinted with winter-breath and the death of leaves, closed over him and bore him away – the park, the past, and the falling dusk blending to one fine centre in him. Then, with a shout from below, the moment was gone and the tall figure, now lost in shadow, got up, cupped his hands, and lit a cigarette.

"C'mon, let's get out of here," he said, "I'm cold as hell."